TEACHER PREP

MERRILL
PRENTICE HALL

Teacher Preparation Classroom

Your Class. Their Careers. Our Future. Will your students be prepared?

We invite you to explore our new, innovative and engaging website and all that it has to offer you, your course, and tomorrow's educators! Preview this site today at www.prenhall.com/teacherprep/demo. Just click on "go" on the login page to begin your exploration.

Organized around the major courses pre-service teachers take, the Teacher Preparation site provides media, student/teacher artifacts, strategies, research articles, and other resources to equip your students with the quality tools needed to excel in their courses and prepare them for their first classroom.

This ultimate on-line education resource will provide you and your students access to:

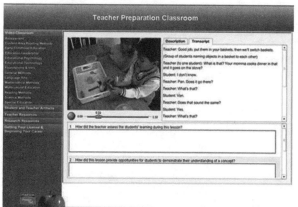

Online Video Library. More than 250 video clips—each tied to a course topic and framed by learning goals and Praxis-type questions—capture real teachers and students working in real classrooms.

Student and Teacher Artifacts. More than 200 student and teacher classroom artifacts—each tied to a course topic and framed by learning goals and application questions—provide a wealth of materials and experiences to help your students observe children's developmental learning.

Lesson Plan Builder. Step-by-step guidelines and lesson plan examples support students as they learn to build high-quality lesson plans.

Articles and Readings. Over 500 articles from ASCD's renowned journal *Educational Leadership*. The site also includes Research Navigator, a searchable database of additional educational journals.

Strategies and Lessons. Over 500 research-supported instructional strategies appropriate for a wide range of grade levels and content areas.

Licensure and Career Tools. Resources devoted to helping you pass your licensure exam; learn standards, law, and public policies; plan a teaching portfolio; and succeed in your first year of teaching.

How to ORDER Teacher Prep for you and your students:

- For students to receive a Teacher Prep Access Code with this text, please provide your bookstore with ISBN 0-13-235071-8 when you place your textboo[...] der the text with this ISBN to be eligible for this offer:

Upon ordering Teacher Prep for their students, instructors will [...]
Prep Access Code. To recieve your access code, please email M[...]
and provide the following information:

- Name and Affiliation
- Author/Title/Edition of Merrill text

Assessing Learners Online

ALBERT OOSTERHOF
Florida State University

RITA-MARIE CONRAD
Florida State University

DONALD P. ELY
Syracuse University

PEARSON

Merrill
Prentice Hall

Upper Saddle River, New Jersey
Columbus, Ohio

Library of Congress Cataloging-in-Publication Data

Oosterhof, Albert.
    Assessing learners online/Albert Oosterhof, Rita-Marie Conrad, and Donald P. Ely.
        p. cm.
    ISBN 0-13-091122-4
1. Computer-assisted instruction—Evaluation. 2. Educational tests and measurements—Data processing. 3. Distance education—Evaluation. I. Conrad, Rita-Marie. II. Ely, Donald P. III. Title.
LB1028.3.O554 2008
371.33′4—dc22   2006035994

Vice President and Executive Publisher: Jeffery W. Johnston
Publisher: Kevin M. Davis
Editorial Assistant: Sarah N. Kenoyer
Production Editor: Mary Harlan
Production Coordinator: Andrew Jones, Carlisle Publishing Services
Design Coordinator: Diane C. Lorenzo
Text Design: Carlisle Publishing Services
Cover Design: Jason Moore
Cover Image: SuperStock
Production Manager: Laura Messerly
Director of Marketing: David Gesell
Marketing Manager: Autumn Purdy
Marketing Coordinator: Brian Mounts

This book was set in Garamond by Carlisle Publishing Services. It was printed and bound by R.R. Donnelley & Sons Company. The cover was printed by R.R. Donnelley & Sons Company.

Pearson Education Ltd.
Pearson Education Singapore Pte. Ltd.
Pearson Education Canada, Ltd.
Pearson Education–Japan

Pearson Education Australia Pty. Limited
Pearson Education North Asia Ltd.
Pearson Educación de Mexico, S.A. de C.V.
Pearson Education Malaysia Pte. Ltd.

10 9 8 7 6 5 4 3 2 1
ISBN-13: 978-0-13-091122-3
ISBN-10:   0-13-091122-4

PREFACE

This book is concerned with assessing learners within an online environment, and is written for instructional designers and educators involved with online training and education. The book can serve as a text in college courses concerned with the design and delivery of distance or other forms of online instruction, it can be used as an extended reference for participants attending workshops on online assessments, and it can serve as a personal reference for instructors of online courses that assess students online.

The practice of assessing learners is certainly not new, probably being older than history itself. The assessment of online learners, however, is clearly a recent phenomenon. Online assessment and, more broadly, the entire online learning environment provide expanded opportunities to actively and creatively engage the learner. At the same time, proven strategies for designing and implementing instruction and assessment remain critical components for effective learning, even as instructional and assessment paradigms change substantially to capitalize on potentials realized by going online.

In light of this, the approach we have taken in this book is to work from established fundamentals of assessment, applying these principles to the online environment. For instance, rather than beginning with how one can create and administer assessments online, we first look at what psychologists have found out about how one can assess a learner's knowledge. From that perspective, we discuss how these strategies apply to online settings. We similarly emphasize basic issues such as establishing evidence of validity for our assessments and taking steps to ensure that our evaluations of student knowledge will generalize beyond the performance sampled by our assessments. The context of our discussion is always that of the online environment.

We have organized this book into five parts, using the first part to establish a framework for assessing students. The first chapter in Part One provides a historical perspective for online assessment. We believe this is important when discussing rapidly developing phenomena such as assessing online learners. Here we look at the 150-year evolution of distance education, through which many parameters that distinguish online assessment from the more familiar classroom assessments were established. Remaining chapters in Part One are concerned with measuring knowledge, establishing evidence of validity, and generalizing observed performance to unobserved performance.

Part Two is concerned with establishing an assessment plan within online settings. This includes determining what to assess, which in turn is influenced by whether training or education is involved. The former requires more detailed assessments, whereas the latter samples content more broadly and places more emphasis on problem-solving skills. Establishing an assessment plan also includes deciding how assessments will be used—formatively, where assessments help guide what the learner does next, or summatively, where assessments certify what has been learned such as for assigning grades.

Parts Three, Four, and Five then apply this foundation to three basic formats of online assessment: written tests, performance assessments, and collaborative work. The online context strongly influences the discussion. For instance, one type of written test uses multiple-choice items. When online, these items are not limited to the traditional form of selecting an answer among written statements. Rather, it can involve a variety of media, allowing one to do such things as select the location within a photograph that illustrates a particular concept or select the audio excerpt that represents a particular style of music. Being online allows one to provide learners with immediate feedback at the conclusion or even during the assessment.

Discussion of these three basic formats of online assessment also includes practical suggestions for making the assessment process more efficient. Online environments tend to involve a considerable amount of one-on-one interaction between the student and instructor. Ironically, the software systems that have been designed for online learning often result in the instructor spending considerable time simply receiving work produced by students and returning formative feedback to the student. We look at specific techniques that reduce this overhead, allowing the instructor to commit substantially more time to that which computers presently do not do well—evaluating what students have done and generating detailed feedback that will guide their subsequent learning.

This book is designed to engage the reader. For example, numerous queries labeled "Apply What You Are Learning" invite the reader to immediately apply recently learned concepts to realistic situations. Subsequent text often builds on these queries. This book also engages readers by drawing upon the considerable experience each of us has had with assessments as students, instructors, or instructional designers. The introduction to each chapter uses familiar situations to establish relevance for issues to be addressed. Most chapters conclude with a section titled "Enhance Your Understanding" that presents activities to connect the issues and ideas addressed in the chapter to real-world needs in online learning.

This book is designed to be used as a learning tool. Material included here originally served for several semesters as the major written reference for a course concerned with assessing online learners. The majority of students participating in the course were enrolled in a master's program in distance and distributed education. Approximately half of these graduate students were themselves distance learners; however, everyone enrolled in the course participated online and was assessed online. Numerous revisions were made based upon input from these learners.

The careful design of assessments is particularly important in an online environment, in part because instructors have limited and in some cases no opportunity to interact face-to-face with learners. Many of the informal indicators available in classroom settings as to what students are learning are largely absent when the student is remote from the instructor. When written tests and other assessments are administered online, problems are more difficult to detect and are not as readily corrected during the assessment as when students and the instructor are at a common location. With online assessments, it is particularly important to get everything right and fully functional before the assessment begins.

When learners are at a distance, the careful design of assessments is particularly important, because society somewhat unfairly imposes higher expectations on the assessment of online learners. The effectiveness of traditional instruction is often assumed, but institutions delivering online instruction to distance learners are expected to demonstrate that learners have reached defensible levels of achievement. Assessments play a critical role in this determination.

We are deeply indebted to colleagues and especially our graduate students whose shared experiences and feedback have contributed significantly to the writing of this book. You will find their ideas and insights incorporated throughout this edition. We are grateful for the thoughtful and very useful comments and suggestions provided by the following reviewers: Xiauxing Han, University of Wisconsin, Green Bay; Jim Jeffery, Andrews University; Linda Lohr, The University of Northern Colorado; S. Kim MacGregor, Louisiana State University; Sara McNeil, University of Houston; M. G. Moore, Pennsylvania State University; Christine H. Olgren, University of Wisconsin, Madison; and David VanEsselstyn, C. W. Post, Long Island University.

BRIEF CONTENTS

CONTENTS

Note: Every effort has been made to provide accurate and current Internet information in this book. However, the Internet and information posted on it are constantly changing, so it is inevitable that some of the Internet addresses listed in this textbook will change.

PART I

Establishing a Framework for Assessing Students

Online assessment provides expanded opportunities to actively and creatively engage learners. As is true with all elements of the online learning environment, using proven strategies for designing and implementing assessment remain critical components for effective assessment and instruction. Although these strategies apply to traditional as well as online settings, the fundamentals of designing effective instruction and assessments include some special qualities when applied to online learning. Part One of this book is concerned with applying proven strategies to establish a framework for assessing students online.

Our discussion begins with a historical overview of technological developments related to distance education. This overview helps identify some of the special considerations associated with online assessment. For instance, in face-to-face settings, casually observing learners helps verify whether the assessments are valid. These casual observations are reduced or absent when assessments are online. Similarly, instructors can often resolve unanticipated problems by being physi-cally present when a test is administered. When assessments are online, the ability to resolve these problems is diminished.

Chapters 2 through 4 then describe techniques that help resolve the issues introduced through our historical overview. Chapter 2 identifies strategies for measuring knowledge. Because a person's knowledge is internal to the mind and invisible, we need to establish observable activities that indirectly indicate what learners know or are thinking. Different types of performance are better at assessing the various types of knowledge. Online assessments are more amendable to some of these types of performance than others.

Chapter 3 is concerned with validity. Establishing validity is equally relevant to online and traditional assessments, although the emphasis in these two settings is different, substantially in some respects. Chapter 4 is about generalizing observed performance to unobserved performance. Any assessment is based only on a sample of what might be observed. An important question is whether different conclusions about what learners know will be made if a computer samples one set of test items rather than another, or if we ask students to complete one particular task rather than another task that might have been used. Our discussion identifies ways to help ensure our observations will generalize beyond those sampled by our assessment.

Collectively, the first four chapters establish a framework for assessing students. This framework is then used in subsequent sections where we describe how to establish an assessment plan, how to produce and administer written and performance assessments, and how to assess online interaction and collaboration.

1

Historical Perspective

This book is about assessing learners online, an event that involves students from a wide variety of learning contexts, ranging from large lecture-oriented classes to courses taught with learners at a distance. Assessments within each context are moving from almost exclusively offline to increasingly online.

Online assessment is a very contemporary phenomenon that uses the most current electronic technologies. It involves instructors and instructional designers who are innovative and who wish to go beyond conventional approaches to instruction and learning. And it allows students to use electronic devices with capabilities well beyond what their parents or even their older siblings used in their education.

Because the technologies associated with online assessment have evolved so quickly, it may appear that new assessment fundamentals are being devised or are rapidly transforming. However, most of the fundamentals that have historically defined quality assessments are still highly relevant. Foundational issues such as evidence of validity and generalizability of performance remain critical considerations when developing and using both online and offline assessments. Concern with the mechanics of test items remains an important factor even though computers are allowing for significant changes in the physical appearance of assessments and how assessments are administered. Significant changes are likewise occurring with respect to how results are conveyed to students. The appropriateness and usefulness of the feedback that students receive still relies on fundamentals though, such as how carefully student

work is scored and the level of confidence that is reasonable to associate with judgments of each student's performance. This book provides a detailed look at a number of changes to assessment that are resulting from technological advances associated with online assessment, but within the context of fundamental assessment issues. To do otherwise would distort and trivialize the discussion of online assessment.

Online assessment often occurs within the context of online learning, which to a large degree evolves from distance education. Our discussion of online assessment begins with a historical perspective of distance education, particularly the role of technological developments. This historical perspective is useful for three reasons.

First, many of the factors that take on particular significance when assessments move online have parallels within distance education. For instance, with both online assessment and distance education, students usually are physically separate from the instructor. Learning and assessment activities must function effectively with less frequent instructor interaction. From a development perspective, this requires more careful design work up front than is required when the instructor and student are face to face.

A second advantage is that many of the benefits (and challenges) that technological developments have brought to distance education can be used to help describe parallel advances and limitations within online assessment. The evolution of computers and the Internet provides obvious examples; however, earlier developments with various media have resulted in similar changes within distance education and assessment. Technological developments have blurred distinctions between distance and face-to-face learning, and even between learning and the assessment of what has been learned. Online assessments can play an important role in this integration.

A third advantage of a historical perspective is the opportunity it provides to introduce several foundational assessment issues. Online assessments have potential benefits that were impossible to realize even a few years ago. However, many of these benefits cannot be realized if fundamental assessment issues are ignored. A historical perspective of distance education is a particularly effective context in which to introduce these foundational issues and to help illustrate the benefits and liabilities that accrue as they are taken into account, or ignored.

The term *distance education* has been with us for more than a century, although the concept existed well before that.[1] The current surge of interest in distance education and particularly online learning[2] has been brought about by contemporary technology that facilitates communication between the instructor and the learner. Since its beginning, distance education has been considered to be a one-to-one relationship between an instructor and a learner who are generally not in the same place at the same time. Technological developments have made it feasible to expand this relationship to include group interactions.

The present chapter provides an introduction to the role that assessment has played during the evolution of distance education and identifies foundational assessment issues that are implicit to that history. The next three chapters then use this perspective as they address four topics that become our framework for discussing the online assessment of learners:

- How one measures knowledge
- How one establishes evidence that an assessment of that knowledge is valid
- How far one can generalize student performance beyond the sample of tasks that is included within the assessment
- How one assigns assessment's formative and summative roles

Sherron and Boettcher (1997), building on work by Bates (1995), divide the evolution of distance learning technologies into four generations. The first (1850s to 1960) generally involved a single technology: print, radio beginning in the 1930s, or television beginning in the 1950s. The second generation (1960 to 1985) used multiple technologies simultaneously, but not computers. The third generation (1985 to 1995) again used multiple technologies, but added computers and computer networking to the mix. The fourth generation (beginning in 1995) added high bandwidth to computer networking. Sherron and Boettcher point out that, as in other areas of society, a new educational technology does not necessarily replace an old one. Over time, the technology that is emphasized changes and technological advances combine with contemporary societal needs to significantly influence the interaction between technology and education-related activities.

Our historical perspective is organized into these same four generations, but the focus is on assessment issues that are implicit in the history of distance education. Table 1.1 provides a summary of this discussion. As noted earlier, foundational issues in assessment remain relevant and critical as assessment practices take advantage of technologies associated with online learning.

---

[1]Holmberg (1986) in a more detailed historical discussion traces formal distance education back to the mid 19th century, and much earlier if one includes nonorganized forms.

[2]In a survey funded by the Alfred P. Sloan Foundation of over 1000 colleges and universities, Allen and Seaman (2005) found that in fall 2004, more than 2.3 million students were enrolled in at least one online course. This was up from just under 2 million in fall 2003 and 1.6 million in fall 2002. With online assessment becoming an increasingly available option for classes taught face to face, the number of learners participating in some form of online assessment would exceed these values.

Table 1.1
Four generations of distance education and the assessment issues that were introduced

Time Period	Generation	Instructional Development and Delivery	Assessment Issues Introduced
1850s to 1960	Correspondence study, open universities, and broadcasting	Focus is on the delivery of instruction using a particular medium (print, radio, or television); less emphasis on the design of instruction The learner works in isolation	Does learning achieved at a distance equal learning achieved face-to-face? With learners at a distance, how does one achieve formative assessments? With learners at a distance, how does one go beyond measuring declarative knowledge?
1960 to 1985	Multiple technologies without the computer	Availability of multiple technologies in the home becomes commonplace, except the computer Multiple technologies used together to deliver instruction	How can one validate the assessments? Emerging technologies such as facsimile and telephone provide some criterion-related evidence of validity, but less so than what is obtained with learners face-to-face; construct and content-related approaches therefore play a particularly important role in validating assessments
1985 to 1995	Multiple technologies with the computer and computer networking	Availability of personal computers and the Internet greatly expedite communication and similarly affect options for designing instruction; learners no longer need to work in isolation Access to library and other resources becomes available to distance learners; learning activities become more proactive	With computers and the Internet allowing tests to be administered individually as students become ready, how can one ensure each student's test is equally difficult when different sample of items are used with each administration? Would decisions about a student's level of mastery be the same if a different sample of items were included in a test?
Beginning around 1995	Multiple technologies with the computer, computer networking, and high bandwidth	Learners are more sophisticated with electronic media Increased Internet bandwidth allows higher fidelity and use of video Video conferencing further blurs distinction between distance and face-to-face learning	How does one assess higher-level skills? Is the use of advanced media synonymous with assessing higher-level skills?

CORRESPONDENCE STUDY, OPEN UNIVERSITIES, AND BROADCASTING

Distance education[3] probably predates history. Holmberg (1986) traces the beginning of formal distance education to correspondence studies started in 1856 in Berlin. There Frenchman Charles Toussaint and the German Gustav Langenscheidt established a school for teaching language by correspondence. "Correspondence" may not be the best descriptor for this early effort given that students were certainly not encouraged to submit questions. "It would hardly be necessary since everything is fully explained in the course" noted the syllabus (Holmberg, 1986, p. 7). In contrast, Anna Eliot Ticker in 1873 established the Boston-based Society to Encourage Study at Home, which emphasized exchanging monthly letters between the teacher and the student to personalize instruction and to guide readings (Mathieson, 1971).

Verduin and Clark (1991) identify Isaac Pitman as the first distance educator. In Bath, England, in 1840, he started teaching shorthand by correspondence. Students would copy Bible passages in shorthand and mail them to Pitman for grading. As with modern-day distance education, this allowed adults to learn new skills without having to give up their employment. Pitman's venture grew, and within a few years he had hired a staff to handle grading of students' work.

In 1874, the Chautauqua Institution was founded in New York state by Lewis Miller, an inventor and manufacturer, and John Heyl Vincent, then a Methodist minister. The institution initially trained Sunday school teachers, following up a summer session with learning through correspondence. The curriculum expanded. William Rainey Harper, a professor of Hebrew, became familiar with learning through correspondence

while serving as a faculty member at the Chautauqua Institute. When he later became president of the University of Chicago, Harper established an extension division to deliver university courses by mail. In 1892, this became the first distance education program to be established at a university.

Eventually, correspondence study broadened to include the "open university," which offered its curriculum exclusively at a distance. The first open university was established in Britain in the 1960s. The idea began in 1926 when J. C. Stobarf, who was employed by the recently established BBC, proposed establishing a "teleuniversity" that would combine broadcast lectures with correspondence texts and visits to conventional universities. His idea was rejected, as were similar proposals by others. In the early 1960s, the BBC and the Ministry of Education were discussing plans for a "College of the Air." While head of the Labour Party, Harold Wilson had advocated the production of television and other educational materials by a consortium of institutions that would broaden access to a university education. When he was elected Prime Minister in 1964, he appointed Jennie Lee as Minister for the Arts and asked her to take over the University of the Air project. The British Open University was established as a result of her efforts.

A number of open universities were established in the 1970s. Moore and Kearsley (1996) associate the name "open" with universities that generally adhere to seven principles (pp. 42–43):

- Any person can enroll, regardless of previous education
- Students can begin a course at any time
- Course study is done at home or anywhere the student chooses
- Course materials are developed by a team of experts
- Tutoring is provided by other specialists
- The enterprise is national in scope
- The enterprise enrolls large numbers and enjoys economics of scale

---

[3]Actually, the term *distance education* was not popularized until quite recently. Rumble (1986) identifies the 1892 catalog of the University of Wisconsin as the first to use the term, however distance education was not used as a descriptor by ERIC until 1983 (Verduin & Clark, 1991).

In addition to Britain, open universities have been established in a number of countries including Canada, China, Costa Rica, Germany, India, Indonesia, Israel, Japan, Jordan, Korea, the Netherlands, New Zealand, Pakistan, Portugal, South Africa, Spain, Taiwan, Thailand, Turkey, United States, and Venezuela. In many cases, they now use multiple media, including computers and broadband networks; thus, the open university concept extends into the second, third, and fourth generations of distance education.

The application of radio and, later, television technologies to distance education was initially separate from correspondence study and open universities. Verduin and Clark (1991) point out that educational radio was at first considered to be unrelated to correspondence study. During distance education's first generation, focus tended to be on the medium used to deliver instruction rather than on the idea of providing educational opportunity to learners at a distance. Consequently, developments in the theory, philosophy, and technique were typically not shared across the various forms.

Over a period of approximately 25 years, beginning in 1918, the United States government granted more than 200 radio broadcast licenses to educational institutions, mostly universities, to provide instructional radio. This technology, however, failed to gain a large audience. According to Nasseh (available online), by 1940 only one college-level course was offered for credit through instructional radio. Radio broadcast supporting K–12 instruction continued for some time; however, by 1980 instructional radio had all but been eliminated and had been replaced by educational television.

One early and particularly innovative application of television for distance education was the Midwest Program on Airborne Television Instruction (MPATI). Headquartered at Purdue University in the early 1960s, lessons by master teachers were videotaped and then broadcast from a DC-6 aircraft flying a figure-eight pattern for six hours at 23,000 feet. Schools in six midwestern states could receive the UHF broadcasts, although problems such as winter storms, electronic equipment that relied on vacuum tubes, and the newness of videotape technology affected its reliability. Finding pilots willing to fly a figure-eight pattern for six hours was also a challenge. MPATI was of course a precursor to satellite broadcasts.

Harvard's Project Physics illustrates one of the earlier attempts to work around a significant limitation of television (and radio) broadcast—that of inflexibility in scheduling instruction. Project Physics involved videotaping whole courses, which, like the print medium within correspondence courses, allowed flexibility as to when and where learners could use the material.

Simonson, Smaldino, Albright, and Zvacek (2003), in their discussion of its history, define distance education as "institution-based, formal education where the learning group is separated geographically, and where interactive telecommunications systems are used to connect learners, resources, and instructors." The major characteristics of the field are woven into this definition: (1) separation of instructor and learner; (2) use of resources and media that permit communication between and among each participant; and (3) the institution-based setting in which the process takes place. Although interactive telecommunication systems were represented in other forms during the earliest stages of distance education, this definition applies quite well to that early history.

What Sherron and Boettcher (1997) describe as the first generation of distance education spans a time period (from the 1850s to 1960 or roughly 100 years) longer than the other three generations combined. This period is associated with several assessment issues, all of which remain relevant to this day. One of the dominant issues relates to the quality of learning achieved when learners are at a distance. This is clearly an *assessment* issue because quality of learning ultimately has to involve some measure of student achievement. The quality of learning question is often raised within the context of a particular delivery medium, such as the effectiveness of educational radio or television. A comparison often is involved; for instance, does correspondence through the mail (or education delivered by computer) afford the same learning that can be achieved face to face within a classroom? Clark (1983) challenged whether evaluation of media effectiveness is even relevant:

> [T]he best current evidence is that media are *mere vehicles* that deliver instruction but do not influence student achievement any more than the truck that delivers our groceries causes changes in nutrition . . . only the content of the vehicle can influence achievement. (p. 445)

One may or may not agree with Clark's thesis but either way *achievement* of learners is highly relevant to the evaluation of education in any form. The effectiveness and ultimately the credibility of instruction and of instructional delivery is fundamentally a question of what students learn, regardless of how conventional or innovative the instruction may be. Assessment of what students know is critical to all forms of education. Online learning without detailed attention to the quality of assessment is unwise and probably absurd.

Another assessment issue that is particularly relevant to distance education's first generation is the distinction between **formative** and **summative assessments** popularized by Bloom, Hastings, and Madaus (1971). Building on work by Michael Scriven and others in program evaluation, they establish the importance of formatively evaluating student learning. Formative assessments are those that occur *during* learning. They provide the basis for determining what to do next instructionally in light of what students know now. Formative assessment is what a mentor does continuously when working with an apprentice. It is what a good teacher does regularly when given the opportunity to work face-to-face with a student. In contrast, summative assessments occur at the end of instructional units. A summative assessment certifies what students have learned. Summative assessments can serve as a basis for modifying "next year's" instruction, but unlike formative assessments, do not provide the timely information needed to improve the effectiveness of a present learner's achievement. Formative assessments

must precede the conclusion of instruction. And to be useful, teachers must be able to quickly receive results from a formative assessment and immediately provide students with feedback from those results. When face-to-face instruction involves a fairly small number of students, formative assessments can easily occur continuously through informal but deliberate interactions. Even within large-lecture settings, facial expressions and occasional questioning allow for ongoing formative assessments.

Formative assessments typically do not take the form of a paper-and-pencil test, or its online equivalent. Nevertheless, within optimal learning environments, formative assessments occur frequently and greatly outnumber summative assessments. Formative assessments were largely absent, however, when the teacher and learner corresponded through monthly letters delivered through the mail. With online learning, formative assessments can be facilitated through e-mail, through small-group interactions, or in other ways. Particularly with broadband Internet access, formative assessments can occur through real-time dialog among learners and the instructor. Within distance education, formative assessments do not always occur naturally. This is one of the assessment concerns addressed in this book.

A third assessment-related issue pertains to the types of capabilities measured by our assessments. In this book, considerable emphasis is placed on the types of tasks students need to perform to evaluate the different capabilities that must be learned. For instance, we recognize that being able to perform a particular procedure in a science lab involves a different capability than being able to verbally describe or talk about that procedure. Cognitive psychologists refer to this difference as *procedural* versus *declarative* knowledge. What is often surprising is how dominant both procedural and declarative knowledge are in almost every academic skill one learns. For instance, knowledge of a concept, such as that of corrosion, depends heavily upon a learner being able to correctly determine whether or not previously unused examples demonstrate corrosion (procedural knowledge) *in addition to* being able to verbally describe what corrosion is (declarative knowledge).

Especially during the early part of the first generation, and arguably to this day, declarative knowledge dominates assessments, even to the exclusion of procedural knowledge. "Tell me what you know" is the classic strategy for assessing declarative knowledge. One rather interesting illustration of assessing declarative knowledge is seen in an exam given in 1860 to individuals applying for teaching positions in San Francisco. One portion of the exam asks candidates to name all the rivers, bodies of water, cities, and countries in the world, as well as the boundaries to each state within the United States—all in 1 hour.

Declarative knowledge turns out to be essential in education and goes well beyond knowledge of facts. But in distance education, including online assessments, it is still easy to largely ignore procedural knowledge and other types of capabilities that should be learned and certainly assessed. As noted already, our discussion of online assessment will give considerable emphasis to assessing the various types of capabilities that must be learned.

MULTIPLE TECHNOLOGIES WITHOUT THE COMPUTER

The second generation of distance education, from roughly 1960 to 1985, involved the simultaneous use of multiple technologies but without the computer. Many of the same technologies employed in the latter part of the first generation, such as print and television, continued to be used along with audio and video cassettes. The electronic media however had now become more commonplace both in the home and at school, first with television in the 1960s and later with audio and videocassette technology around 1980.

Many characteristics of the student environment that were prevalent in the first generation also continued. The student was still primarily isolated. Communication was typically one way, but now included fax and telephone in addition to postal mail. Materials were prepackaged and designed for independent learning. Development of instruction involved an instructional design team and included significant up-front investment to compensate for lack of immediate student-instructor interaction. The University of Mid-America— established in 1974 but no longer in operation— coordinated the creation of numerous courses within this mode for use by universities in seven midwestern states that were members of its consortium.

In our discussion of online assessment, **validity** of assessment obviously must represent one of our central themes. Validity involves the process of gathering evidence related to the appropriateness of what is being assessed. As is true with almost any evidence-gathering effort, including scientific inquiry and detective work, collecting validity evidence involves various methods. One type of evidence that has been particularly problematic throughout all generations of distance education is *criterion-related* evidence. Criterion-related validity evidence involves using other observations of examinee performance to collaborate what was observed in the assessment. In face-to-face settings, collaboration occurs frequently and naturally through an instructor's informal and other two-way interactions with learners. With distance education, though, the learner is isolated from the instructor, so criterion-related validity evidence is much more difficult to obtain. However, beginning with the second generation, some options that allowed for more immediate interaction with the learner began to emerge, such as the fax and the telephone. With the relatively recent availability of e-mail and particularly online conferencing, opportunities to collaborate what was observed through assessments increased. However, collaboration is still more problematic than when learners and instructor are face to face. The implication is that other types of validity evidence, specifically those we will later identify as construct-related and content-related, must play a more significant role in online assessment than in classroom assessments. Much as distance education depends on instructional system design to compensate for lack of direct student-instructor interaction, online assessments require significant up-front efforts during the development and production of assessments to insure their validity.

MULTIPLE TECHNOLOGIES WITH THE COMPUTER AND COMPUTER NETWORKING

With personal computers becoming so commonplace—including those many of us now carry in our pockets such as PDAs and smart phones—it is easy to forget how recently the notion of using computers for distance education and online assessment was considered radical. Although the 1950s predate many (but not all) of us, it was during this period that a study by the highly respected Rand Corporation concluded that the future availability of computers would ultimately be limited to only the world's dozen or so largest corporations, due to their considerable cost. It was in the 1970s that Steve Jobs and Steve Wozniak designed and built the first commercially successful microcomputers, the Apple I and II.[4]

The years that Sherron and Boettcher (1997) refer to as the third generation, 1985 to 1995, adds computers and computer networking to the multiple technologies being used with distance education. During this period, computers and networking significantly expanded available media, providing now-familiar options to distance education. These included electronic mail, chat sessions, bulletin boards, audio conferencing, various computer programs and resources

prepackaged on floppy disks and CDs, and of course the Internet.

The addition of computer technology changed the characteristics of distance education in ways never anticipated. Using mail to send work to an instructor and receive feedback took several days each way; e-mail delivered the same material almost instantly. Instead of working alone, discussion boards and live chat allowed distance learners to interact and work in groups, sharing products and ideas. Instead of depending largely on resources that could be delivered to learners' remote locations, websites of every description allowed access to library references, newspapers, technical reports, and exhibits more efficiently than had been the case in conventional classes just a few years prior. Technological developments during this period allowed students studying at a distance to increasingly be seen as active learners and contributors rather than relatively inactive beings to which knowledge was to be dispensed.

Educational research during the late 1970s and early 1980s provided the foundation for computer applications for distance learning and online learning in general. What was commonly referred to as computer-managed instruction (CMI) played a particularly significant role with respect to online assessment. CMI systems varied widely in their capability, some involving little more than a computer-based gradebook that helped the instructor keep records. The more sophisticated systems provided students with test items displayed on terminals connected to a central computer. Test items were typically selected randomly from a previously developed item pool. Often these items were stratified by instructional objectives or at least broad content areas. The central computer would retain test records for the instructor and might also provide immediate feedback to each student at the completion of a test. Feedback might be nothing more than a total score on the test. In some cases diagnostic feedback was provided indicating which instructional objectives had been mastered. An opportunity was then given to later take a retest that covered content not passed on the initial examination.

---

[4]The Apple II became the first computer widely distributed in schools. When purchased, the video screen or monitor was optional; often one simply plugged the computer into an available black & white television. Later, of course, it was common to package a high-resolution monitor with the computer. Interestingly, the trend is now somewhat reversed, with it common to purchase a flat-screen television for use with a previously purchased desktop or laptop computer.

These more sophisticated CMI systems are similar in a basic sense to current online assessment options available through commercial systems such as Blackboard and QuestionMark. The cost per student of hardware associated with these earlier CMI systems was very high, and test content was limited to basic text material without the multimedia capabilities available with modern systems.

Problems with interchangeability of test items are a significant concern with both the earlier CMI systems and modern online assessment systems. For instance, if different items are sampled from the item pool on a retest to reassess a student's proficiency, would differences in the difficulty of test items influence mastery decisions made about the student? Or if different samples of items are administered to students completing an online test, would these differences in item difficulty contribute to inconsistency by creating an easier test for one student than another? Even if item difficulty could be fully controlled (which it cannot), we establish later in the book that significant inconsistencies remain in the test because different test items measure knowledge in different ways.

Even if the same test items are administered to all students completing a test, this inconsistency is present relative to test items that could have been used to assess the same knowledge. This is one aspect of an important issue discussed in detail in later chapters: that of **generalizability.** The tests that are used to assess learner's knowledge always involve samples of task. With samples, there is a high likelihood that significant **sampling error** is involved unless deliberate steps are taken to control this error. When sampling error is not controlled, judgments made about what students have learned are usually wrong because sampled observations do not generalize.

As noted earlier, many of these fundamental educational measurement issues are not unique to online assessments. Inconsistencies inherent in assessments easily render online or more traditional assessments useless. Procedures used to control these inconsistencies are similar regardless of how tests are administered. However, with online assessments, the issue of inconsistencies may be more problematic. In part, this is because we still tend to associate accuracy with judgments that are assisted by a computer. Supposedly, computers don't make mistakes.

In face-to-face situations, the instructor more easily validates conclusions made through assessments by informally observing what students do. This is less of an option when assessments are online. As addressed in later chapters, additional steps must be taken when using online assessments to establish legitimate confidence in the generalizability of students' observed performance.

ADDITION OF HIGH-BANDWIDTH COMPUTER TECHNOLOGIES

The period that Sherron and Boettcher (1997) identify as the fourth generation of distance learning technologies began in 1995, just prior to the publication of their paper. The prominent medium added during this generation is high-bandwidth computer technology. This allows for two-way interactive real-time audiovisual capabilities and other applications that are data intensive. Extended face-to-face meetings between individuals and among groups is now feasible, almost regardless of where learners and instructors are located. A number of resources that previously could not be accessed quickly, such as full 30-frame-per-second digital video transmissions, are now available on demand.

During this period, it also became reasonable to expect learners to have access to and to demonstrate expertise in using sophisticated computer hardware and software, and high-speed access to the Internet. Now the learner's expertise often exceeds that of the instructor.

Certainly the availability, sophistication, and user-friendliness of computer software associated with distance education and online assessment has increased dramatically during this fourth generation. With equal certainty, as addressed later in this book, important needs remain with respect to characteristics of present software.

As the technical sophistication of learners, instructors, and computers have increased, the distinctions between learning at a distance and physically working face to face with other students and the instructor have diminished. Increasingly, traditionally taught classes are administering assessments online. Online assessments administered outside the classroom frees up class time, which in turn can be used for further instruction and other activities. With the wireless "wiring" of schools, universities, and other institutions, it is also reasonable to administer online assessments within classrooms to take advantage of a computer's multimedia and to automate test scoring, record keeping, and feedback to students. A number of years ago, Bloom, Hastings, and Madaus (1971) pointed out the improvements in learning that can result when the distinctions between instruction and assessment are blurred. Quite possibly, similar advantages can be realized as the distinctions between distance and face-to-face learning diminish, and as online assessment becomes a common denominator of distance and local education.

Earlier in this chapter, we quoted Clark's (1983) distinction between media and instructional content: "[M]edia are *mere vehicles* that deliver instruction but do not influence student achievement any more than the truck that delivers our groceries causes changes in nutrition . . . only the content of the vehicle can influence achievement (p. 445)." Clark's observation applies to online assessments. Computer technologies provide some powerful and exciting ways to deliver assessments, but these technologies are not synonymous with the content of these assessments. This book is about online assessments, which by definition are delivered by computer and network technologies. The central focus of this book is on assessment, albeit assessment delivered through a special medium. Our discussion is driven by the fundamentals of assessment, including its formative and summative roles, the influence that the nature of knowledge has on how one assesses knowledge, and issues of validity and generalizability. Our discussion takes advantage of capabilities associated with online assessment.

SUMMARY

Using the framework of four generations of distance education technologies presented by Sherron and Boettcher (1997), this chapter introduced several fundamentals that must be addressed in our discussion of online assessment. The first of the four generations spans a century and includes correspondence study, the introduction of open universities, and radio and television broadcasting. From its very beginning, the adequacy of what students are learning has been a dominant concern within distance education. Adequacy of learning is relevant regardless of the instructional environment, although the nontraditional nature of distance education tends to focus attention on establishing credibility and therefore the importance of assessing student knowledge.

Assessments must reflect the complexity of knowledge. This chapter introduced the distinction between declarative and procedural knowledge. Later chapters elaborate further on the types of knowledge involved and on the types of performance that provide good indicators when assessing the various types of knowledge.

Assessments are used formatively and summatively. Formative assessments occur *during* learning and are used to redirect instructional activities. Summative assessments occur near the conclusion of a unit of instruction and are used to certify student achievement. In face-to-face situations, formative assessments dominate. In addition to redirecting instruction, formative assessments help validate the assessment process and establish its generalizability. Within distance learning settings and online assessments, formative assessments are more difficult to employ. In later chapters, we address implications this has to establishing validity and generalizability.

The second generation in distance education technologies spans the years 1960 to 1985. This period introduced the simultaneous use of multiple technologies, but without the computer. During this period, electronic media became more commonplace in the home and school, however the distance education student still was primarily isolated and communication was typically one-way. An important assessment consideration is that when interactive two-way communication between student and instructor is restricted, criterion-related validity evidence—which relies heavily on continuous informal assessments—has to play a much less dominant role. Much more than with classroom assessments, the validity of assessments used with distance education must depend on formal procedures that are implemented during the development of an assessment. With later technological advances now associated with online assessments, options for student-instructor interactions have increased. This has improved opportunities for validating assessments; however, assessments administered online still are at a disadvantage with respect to establishing evidence of validity.

The third generation again involved multiple technologies, but with the addition of computers and computer networking. With the added technology, interactive capabilities that are now commonplace became possible, such as e-mail, chat sessions, and conferencing. The first examples of online assessment occurred during this time in the form of computer managed instruction (CMI). Depending on the capabilities of the software, CMI allowed learners to complete tests on demand and provided automated record keeping and feedback to students. However, generalizability of the assessments is a significant concern in this setting. For instance, will students perform the same on a test if a different sample of items is used in the assessment? The issue of generalizability is relevant to all assessments, online or otherwise, although automation associated with online assessments tends to camouflage the issue.

The fourth generation of distance education technologies brings us to the present availability of high bandwidths, which in turn allows for data-intensive applications such as audiovisual conferencing. The present period is also associated with dramatic increases in the sophistication and availability of computer hardware and software as well as students' adeptness with its use. The lines between face-to-face and distance learning have

increasingly blurred and the use of online assessment has become more widespread.

Modern technology provides powerful ways to deliver assessment but does not change the fundamentals that are essential to effective assessment. These fundamentals include distinctions between an assessment's formative and summative roles, implications that different types of knowledge such as declarative and procedural affect how one assesses learning outcomes, and issues of validity and generalizability.

The remaining chapters in Part One discuss these fundamentals and address their special relationship to online assessment. Chapter 2 describes strategies for measuring knowledge. It is recognized that a person's knowledge is internal to the mind and is invisible. A major task in assessment, therefore, is deciding what visible activities or *performance* should be used to indicate the presence of students' invisible knowledge or *capabilities*. Different types of performance are better at assessing the various types of knowledge. For instance, a test should ask learners to do different things if declarative rather than procedural knowledge is being evaluated. Chapter 3 then describes how to establish the validity of an assessment. In the assessment of learning outcomes, no other issue is as important as the assessment's validity. Chapters 2 and 3 are closely linked because establishing the validity of an assessment requires identifying the content and type of knowledge to be assessed. Chapter 4 addresses the issue of generalizability. Unfortunately, all assessments include only a relatively small sample of performances that could have been observed. Whenever sampling is involved, an important consideration is whether conclusions drawn from the observed sample are similar to those that would have been made had we been able to more thoroughly observe each student's performance.

Part Two of this book then describes how to establish an overall assessment plan. We discuss considerations and strategies to determine what to assess and how your assessments will be interpreted and used. Parts Three and Four describe how to develop various kinds of measures. In

Part 3, we focus on written assessments, including the familiar short-answer, essay, and multiple-choice formats. Part Four discusses performance assessments, which are a type of assessment particularly adaptable to distance education and online environments. Part Five addresses issues and describes options for assessing online interaction and collaboration.

TERMS INTRODUCED IN THIS CHAPTER

Summative assessments: occur at the end of instruction. Unit tests and projects are often given at or near the end of a unit of instruction to help establish how well the learner has achieved the knowledge and skills associated with that unit. The purpose of summative assessments is to certify achievement, and often provide a basis for assigning course grades.

Formative assessments: occur throughout and during the unit of instruction. Their purpose is to redirect instruction or learning to help ensure high achievement at the end of instruction. Formative assessments often are informal in nature, such as a teacher watching students' facial expressions or probing students' knowledge with casual questions. Formative assessments can involve exercises embedded within instructional materials, such as the "Apply what you are learning" exercises throughout this book.

Validity: is the degree to which a test measures what it is supposed to measure or is expected to measure. Alternately, the degree to which a test is interpreted or used in a manner consistent with interpretations and uses that the test can reasonably support. Validity is established through evidence. A later chapter discusses common types of validity evidence, including construct, content, and criterion-related evidence.

Sampling error: occurs when a sample is used, for instance the people who complete an opinion survey. Sampling error is the difference between responses provided by the sample and responses that would have been obtained had everyone in the sampled population participated in the survey. Sampling is also involved in assessments. For instance, when a test is used to assess knowledge of a particular content area, only a sample of possible test items can be included in the test. Sampling error would be the difference between the students' scores (e.g., percentage scores) on the sample of items included in the test and the scores these students would have obtained had they answered all possible test items associated with this content domain.

Generalizability: in educational measurement, is an approach used to evaluate sampling error. Within educational tests, sampling errors exist in various forms. For instance, in a sampling of items, sampling error exists because only a sample of items can be included in a test. An important question is how well students' performances on the test would generalize to their performance had they responded to all possible items associated with the content being assessed. Another form of sampling error is between scorers, such as between readers scoring responses to an essay item. Only a sample of possible readers (maybe just one reader) scores the essay responses. An important question is how well students' scores assigned by the sample of readers would generalize to their scores had all possible readers scored their essay responses. Other forms of sampling error, and therefore questions of generalizability, are also relevant to educational measurements.

2

Measuring Knowledge

This chapter is concerned with making learning visible. If you cannot see, hear, or use other senses to detect what another person has learned, you cannot know whether learning has taken place. A student's learning cannot be assessed unless there is *observable* evidence of that learning.

Making learning visible is difficult in any instructional setting. It is particularly difficult when learners are at a distance or when assessment occurs away from the instructor, such as when delivered online. However, even when an instructor is face to face with students, most of a learner's knowledge and mental actions are invisible to others. Because we cannot see a person's thoughts, we depend on indicators that suggest the nature of a student's knowledge. To illustrate, consider the following:

How could you indicate to others that you know the universe is very large and that it contains a very large number of objects?

How could you indicate that you know the concept of a computer virus?

In both cases, you might provide evidence of your knowledge through verbal statements or other actions, such as the following:

Regarding the magnitude of the universe, you might say that the universe is large because it contains Earth, other planets, and the Sun. The Sun is one of billions of stars in our galaxy, which are light-years away from each other. Our galaxy, although very large, is but one of billions of galaxies in the universe.

Regarding the concept of a computer virus, you might state that a computer virus is a computer

program, often mischievous or destructive, that is transferred unwittingly between computers through various means such as e-mail attachments and file transfers.

To provide evidence of knowledge, one must do things that others can see. Likewise, to assess a student's knowledge, an instructor must ask students to do something visible that indicates presence of that knowledge. A description of what students will be asked to do is called a **performance objective.** A performance objective describes an observable event that will indicate that a student has acquired the targeted knowledge.

Because selecting a performance that provides a valid indication of what students know is so critical, this book emphasizes the selection and use of performance objectives. Many instructors are not comfortable with developing or using objectives. This book takes a moderate approach and does not, for example, encourage you to write out performance objectives or distribute them to students, or discourage you from doing so. Nevertheless, we cannot escape the fact that a visible student behavior must be used to indicate status of the student's invisible knowledge. Our assessments are clearly limited by our ability to select appropriate behaviors for measuring student knowledge. In this chapter and later, we use performance objectives to help select behaviors to be included in our assessments. You ultimately may or may not use performance objectives. However, the process of selecting performances must be systematic and very deliberate.

We are going to categorize knowledge into several types of capabilities and then identify the performances that are particularly effective in measuring each. You already are aware of our need to do this. For instance, you recognize that asking elementary school students to solve multiplication problems such as 7×8 is useful for measuring knowledge of multiplication tables, but does not indicate whether the student comprehends the concept of multiplication. Likewise you recognize that describing what a computer virus is involves different skills than implementing procedures that prevent viruses from being transferred to another machine. Assessing different types of capabilities requires using different types of performance.

Realizing the distinction between a learner's capabilities and performance is critical to the assessment of knowledge, as is recognizing the different capabilities that make up knowledge and the different performances that are effective for assessing them. These are critical considerations in both online and face-to-face settings. However, *when assessments are online, and particularly when both instruction and assessment are at a distance, the instructor must choose performances to be observed carefully in order to get each assessment right the first time.* When assessments are online, there are far fewer opportunities to confirm evaluations through the frequent and subtle interactions that occur in face-to-face settings.

This chapter helps you achieve five skills:

- Recognize categories of learning outcomes
- Identify characteristics of performance that correspond to learning outcomes
- Select your own performance objectives
- Communicate performance objectives to students
- Distinguish between performance objectives and instructional goals

CATEGORIES OF LEARNING OUTCOMES

The following simple exercise helps demonstrate that different types of learning are involved. Two people or two groups of people are needed.

Ask the first person to watch you, and tell the second person seated nearby to look away. Hold up three fingers, and ask the first person to state how many fingers are shown. The first person will likely say "three." Ask the person who is looking away to state how many fingers are being shown. The second person will also say "three." The demonstration can continue using different numbers of fingers.

From outward appearances, the performance of both persons in this demonstration is the same. However, you recognize that very different capabilities are involved. The first person is illustrating the capability of counting. The second person is illustrating the ability to recall information. Although the first and second person might each have both capabilities, this often would not be the case for students who are learning the concept of counting. In a general sense, this is problematic because unless an assessment involves a student performance that uniquely establishes the *type* of capability the student has learned, the instructor will easily conclude that the student has acquired the targeted knowledge when in fact the student's performance is relying on a totally different skill. An instructor must carefully structure observations so that the learner's performance clearly assesses the type of capability being measured.

You can improve the chances of measuring the appropriate capability by knowing the types of capabilities involved. Cognitive psychologists identify three types of capability: **declarative knowledge, procedural knowledge,** and **problem solving** (see Figure 2.1). *Declarative knowledge* is knowing that something is the case. It is information that can be conveyed in words; that is, knowledge that can be declared. *Procedural knowledge* is knowing how to do something. Procedural knowledge involves making discriminations, understanding concepts, and applying rules that govern relationships. *Problem solving* builds on declarative and procedural knowledge. Problem solving may involve domain-specific strategies, suggesting that different strategies are employed when solving problems in different content

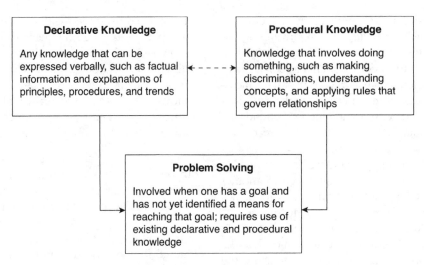

Figure 2.1
Types of capabilities

areas, such as math and writing. Because the various capabilities are assessed differently, each with different types of performance, it is important to look at the differences among declarative knowledge, procedural knowledge, and problem solving.

Declarative Knowledge

Declarative knowledge refers to information one can state verbally, including the recall of specific facts. However, declarative knowledge goes way beyond information that a student might memorize. It involves principles, trends, criteria, and ways of organizing events. Declarative knowledge includes recalling the definitions of words; recalling physical and chemical characteristics of elements and compounds; recalling that the trend each year is for an increase in the number of cars on the highway; recalling that books can be categorized as fiction or nonfiction and giving examples of each; recalling that Ohm's law pertains to the relationship among electrical resistance, voltage, and amperage; and recalling the similarities and differences between causes of the American Revolutionary War and the American

Civil War. Most anything that can be stated, such as in response to a question on an essay exam, involves declarative knowledge.

A very broad range of questions can be used to assess declarative knowledge. For example:

Tell me what is meant by relative humidity.

What is the difference between air and oxygen?

Why do interest rates affect the stock market?

Contrast the geography of northern and southern Africa.

Why do heavy objects like ships float in water?

Each of these examples measures declarative knowledge. None measures procedural knowledge, which we will learn requires the use of very different types of questions.

The importance of declarative knowledge is often downplayed, even to the extent of discouraging the teaching and assessment of this type of knowledge. This happens in part because declarative knowledge is often thought of as involving the memorization of facts. Although knowledge of facts (memorized or otherwise) is part of declarative knowledge, so is knowledge of trends, abstractions, criteria, and ways of organizing events.

Procedural Knowledge

Procedural knowledge is knowledge of how to do things. Examples of procedural knowledge include demonstrating conversions between Fahrenheit and Celsius scales; correctly classifying whales, sharks, porpoises, salmon, and other sea animals as fish or mammal; and identifying which astronomical objects in a photograph are galaxies. Other examples include classifying illustrations of investments as stocks or bonds, and generating rules that predict whether an object will float or sink in water.

Although the same content is often involved in both declarative and procedural knowledge, these two capabilities are distinct. For example, being able to describe the differences between stocks and bonds (declarative knowledge) is different from being able to classify previously unseen illustrations as stocks or bonds (procedural knowledge). Unfortunately, it is common to assume that a learner has achieved both types of knowledge after examining only one of these two capabilities.

2.1 Apply What You Are Learning

In each of the following pairs, one is an example of declarative knowledge and the other involves procedural knowledge. Indicate which (A or B) is an example of procedural knowledge.

1. A. Describing differences between cumulus and cirrus clouds
   B. Classifying clouds in photographs as cumulus or cirrus
2. A. Looking at class rosters, determining which class has the largest enrollment
   B. Recalling, the next day, which class has the largest enrollment
3. A. Knowing that a touchdown in U.S. football is worth 6 points
   B. Watching an example of a scoring play, distinguishing between a touchdown and a safety
4. A. Describing the difference between declarative and procedural knowledge
   B. Classifying descriptions as examples of declarative or procedural knowledge

Answers can be found at the end of the chapter.

Bloom (1956) and Gagné (1985) proposed categories of knowledge that have become widely used. At the basic level, both of their classifications correspond to the declarative and procedural categories currently used by psychologists. As shown in Table 2.1, Bloom refers to declarative knowledge simply as knowledge, whereas Gagné calls it verbal information. Bloom and Gagné both refer to procedural knowledge as intellectual skills, but they divide intellectual skills into very different subcategories. Terms used by Bloom are comprehension, application, analysis, synthesis, and evaluation. Gagné uses the terms discriminations, concrete concepts, defined concepts, rules, and higher-order rules. Their subcategories are not equivalent.

Bloom devised his categories through a series of informal conferences that he led from 1949 to 1953, during which a large number of performance objectives, primarily from college-level courses, were reviewed. Development of his taxonomy was governed by educational, logical, and psychological considerations, in that order of importance, with emphasis placed on developing categories that matched "the distinctions instructors make in planning curricula or in choosing learning situations" (Bloom, 1956, p. 6). Bloom's taxonomy remains widely used, although his subcategories of intellectual skills depart substantially from what is now known about procedural knowledge (Confrey, 1990; Gierl, 1997; Snow, 1989; Tittle, Hecht, & Moore, 1993).

Our discussion of procedural knowledge involves an adaptation of capabilities identified by Gagné. Table 2.2 lists the category names we will use, along with descriptions of how each type of capability can be assessed. Declarative knowledge is referred to as information. Procedural knowledge is divided into subcategories that we will call discrimination, concepts, and rules. What Gagné refers to as complex skills fits better into our third category, which cognitive psychologists call problem solving.

Discriminations. Discriminations are the most basic procedural skills. They involve reacting to

Table 2.1
Categories proposed by Bloom and Gagné

	Bloom's Taxonomy	Gagné's Capabilities
Declarative knowledge	*Knowledge:* Information, such as specific facts, principles, trends, criteria, and ways of organizing events	*Verbal Information:* Same as what Bloom calls Knowledge
Procedural knowledge	*Intellectual Skills*	*Intellectual Skills*
	Comprehension: Use of information without necessarily applying this information to new situations and without fully understanding the implications of this knowledge	*Discriminations:* Reacting to stimuli such as visual images and determining whether they are the same or different
	Application: Use of an abstract concept in a specific but previously unused situation	*Concrete Concepts:* Identifying physical objects or images that have a specified characteristic
		Defined Concepts: Understanding an abstract classification
	Analysis: Breaking a concept or communication into its component parts	*Rules:* Applying principles that regulate the relationship among classes of objects or events
	Synthesis: Putting elements together into a cohesive whole	*Higher-Order Rules:* Combining a series of rules into a single, more complex rule or into the solution of a problem
	Evaluation: Making a judgment about the value of products or processes for a given purpose	

Note: In addition to the categories shown in the table, Gagné adds *cognitive strategies, motor skills,* and *attitudes.* Bloom lists motor skills and attitudes as separate domains that he refers to as the psychomotor and affective domains. Other individuals have proposed taxonomies for these two domains.

Table 2.2
Techniques for assessing various capabilities

Capability	Assessment Technique
Declarative knowledge	
Information	Ask learners to state what they know
Procedural knowledge	
Discrimination	Ask learners to identify the object that is different in some way
Concept	Ask learners to classify diverse and previously unused illustrations as examples versus nonexamples of the concept
Rule	Provide learners with a relevant but previously unused example and ask them to apply the rule
Problem solving	Ask learners to generate solutions to a relevant and previously unused problem

stimuli, such as visual images, and determining whether they are the same or different. Examples include determining whether two pencils are the same or whether two sounds are the same. The learner is not told what characteristic is being compared, nor is the learner asked to give a name to what is being observed or to describe in what ways (if any) the stimuli are different. Instead, discriminations are concerned with whether learners are sensitive to relevant differences.

Students, other than young children, learn most relevant discriminations on their own. However, when someone is having trouble learning a skill involving procedural knowledge, the problem may be that he or she is missing an important discrimination. For example, a learner having problems with the concepts of simile versus metaphor may not see the critical difference between these two figures of speech. A learner who exclaims, "Now I see what you are talking about," may be conveying the importance of a missing discrimination. Normally, discrimination skills are not formally assessed in online settings. Problems associated with discriminations are more likely to be handled through e-mail in response to questions raised by the learner.

Concepts. Concepts involve a characteristic that can be used to classify physical objects or abstractions. To assess concrete concepts, have learners identify in some way the objects or images that have the specified characteristic. Examples include identifying which objects are refracting versus reflecting telescopes, or selecting photographs of galaxies from among photographs that contain other astronomical objects such as nebulae and globular star clusters. With online assessments, multiple-choice items often can assess knowledge of concepts, with each option involving a verbal description, photograph, or sound that characterizes examples and nonexamples of the concept. A series of true-false items can also be used, in which learners are asked to indicate whether or not each example is an illustration of the concept.

When assessing a concept, the examples to be classified should be provided by the instructor

rather than the learner. The examples should involve previously unused illustrations. For instance, one would assess learners' knowledge of the concept of refracting telescopes with previously unused pictures of telescopes. Some, but not all, of the telescopes would be refractors. If learners provide the examples, or if previous illustrations are reused, it is possible that knowledge of information is being assessed rather than knowledge of the concept. Therefore, asking students to provide examples of simile versus metaphor might be testing information (declarative knowledge) rather than knowledge of the concepts.

Because a concept involves a class of things, it should be assessed under a variety of conditions. For instance, if the concept of rectangle is being taught, the learner should be asked to identify rectangles that have light lines and heavy lines, those with lengths close to and much longer than the widths, and those displayed at different angles. Similarly, the concept of refracting telescope would be assessed using illustrations of both refractors and reflectors that are physically large and small.

To demonstrate mastery of a concept, a learner must perceive all qualities relevant to the concept and disregard all qualities irrelevant to the concept. For this reason, multiple-choice and true-false items tend to be more effective than essay at assessing concepts, because numerous examples and nonexamples can be incorporated into a single test. This is not a putdown of the essay format, which is very effective at assessing a learner's ability to communicate ideas in writing.

Abstract concepts involve understanding a classification of nontangible objects, events, or relations. Unlike concrete concepts, abstract concepts involve things that cannot be touched or directly sensed. Examples include the concepts of sailing, the game of basketball, or a mystery novel. Another example is the meaning of a tax shelter. Abstract concepts typically incorporate concrete concepts. For instance, sailing involves boats, wind, water, sails, and many other concrete items that can be touched or otherwise sensed. However, the concept of sailing also involves abstractions such as right-of-way rules and the boat's center of gravity.

Because abstractions cannot be touched or pointed at, learners are asked to distinguish between various examples and nonexamples of the concept. Of course this can be accomplished through written tests when these illustrations are presented as verbal descriptions. Online tests may have a special advantage because of their ability to quickly access sound files or video clips that illustrate the abstract concept, even as students respond to test items individually and at their own pace. For instance, knowledge of Renaissance music can be assessed efficiently online by having learners listen and respond to several segments of music that are and are not representative of that period.

Rules. Rules involve the application of principles that regulate the relationship among classes of objects or events. For example, a rule pertains to using the indefinite article *a* or *an* in sentences. Another example is applying Boyle's law, which establishes that the volume of a confined gas, when multiplied by its pressure, results in a constant numerical value. This rule is used, for instance, to calculate what the pressure of air in a pump would become if its volume were decreased by 90%.

To assess a rule, learners should be asked to apply the rule. Rules regarding the use of the indefinite article *a* or *an* in sentences can be assessed by asking learners to supply the indefinite article in sample sentences. Boyle's law can be assessed by having learners solve problems in which air pressure and volume must be computed for varying conditions.

As with concepts, the instructor *and not the learner* should provide the situations to which the rule is to be applied. Directions to the learner might even suggest which rule is to be applied, as in the problem "Convert 75° Fahrenheit to Celsius." The examples should involve previously unused applications of the rule. Creating unused applications often is very simple, such as using a

different Fahrenheit temperature for calculating the Celsius equivalent, or using unknown words when measuring learners' knowledge of spelling rules for words that contain *ie*.

Being able to state a rule, which is declarative knowledge or information, is different from using the rule. Stating, "The product of the volume of a confined gas and its pressure is a constant," is not equivalent to applying Boyle's law, nor is being able to state Boyle's law a prerequisite to understanding this rule. Information often facilitates learning concepts and rules but is not a prerequisite to and certainly is not equivalent to a working knowledge of concepts and rules.

Problem Solving

Cognitive psychologists indicate that a problem to be solved exists when one has a goal and has not yet identified a means for reaching that goal (Gagné[1], Yekovich, & Yekovich, 1993). An example of problem solving would be the process a learner must go through when required to write an expository paper or prepare a persuasive speech. Another example would be the process required by a learner to identify the best trajectory to send a space probe traveling from Earth to a landing on Mars.

By "problem solving," we are not referring to one's ability to solve a math problem such as multiplying pairs of two-digit numbers. That skill involves procedural knowledge, specifically a rule. Once that rule is learned, the student can apply the procedure to multiply other pairs of numbers. With experience, implementation of the rule is likely to become automated.

A student's ability to solve a problem is assessed in a manner somewhat similar to that used for assessing rules. Both involve presenting a specific situation in which students can apply their skill. However, in assessing problem solving, students are

---

[1]Ellen D. Gagné, with Carol Walker Yekovich and Frank R. Yekonic, authored the 2nd edition of *The Cognitive Psychology of School Learning* in 1997. Her father, Robert M. Gagné, authored *Conditions of Learning*, the most recent edition being published in 1993.

not told which relationships are involved; instead, they are asked to generate a solution from the knowledge they have or, more simply, to solve the problem. Learners have to transfer their knowledge of information, concepts, and rules to the problem situation, and they must establish when it is appropriate to use this knowledge. Learners must often automate rules in order to make their application effective. Some rules become strategies, which are used consciously to establish possible solutions to the problem. Often, any one of several responses represents a legitimate solution to the problem. Therefore, written tests involving multiple-choice or even essay items do not provide effective measures of problem solving. Performance assessments, in which students are observed, often individually and under controlled conditions are a better alternative.

Later in the book, when we discuss the development and use of performance assessments, we step outside what we will characterize as a narrow conceptualization of a "test." Certainly written tests, such as multiple-choice and essay, whether online or face to face, are acceptable examples of a test. But so is any activity through which the instructor is trying to establish what learners can do. This includes many assignments or projects. It may include activities that learners work on collaboratively, even if the collaboration is online. Distance learners often have an advantage here because learners participating at a distance are frequently also involved professionally in situations where the problem being solved is very realistic.

It is important to recognize the distinction between rules and problem solving. Many rules can be complicated, but being complicated, in itself, does not make the activity an instance of problem solving. For example, determining where in the local night sky the International Space Station will disappear as a result of entering Earth's shadow is quite complex. However, if the rules associated with this calculation are known and are being used, this represents the application of rules. If established rules are successfully being applied, they can be used over and over again in varying circumstances to determine when the space station will disappear within Earth's shadow. Because the same procedure can be reapplied each time, solving this complicated problem involves a rule (or rules). This is not what we are referring to as problem solving. On the other hand, problem solving is involved if, in the absence of these rules, learners are asked to discover variables that are relevant to determining when the space station will and will not be visible to a person on Earth. The kinds of variables learners would have to address include locating the space station within its orbit, establishing whether or not it was daytime or nighttime at a particular point on Earth, and establishing where the space station's orbit intercepted Earth's shadow. This is problem solving because, once the problem is presented, there is no set of rules that, if applied, would solve the problem. A goal has been identified but a means for reaching that goal, in the learners' mind, has yet to be established. Learners must use previously learned information, concepts, and rules in various ways to solve the problem. Different learners likely will solve the problem using different sets of information, concepts, and rules. They might create rules and concepts that are new, at least to them.

2.2   Apply What You Are Learning

Listed here are some educational goals. Which type of capability (information, concept, rule, or problem solving) does each goal involve?

1. Listing the names of planets in our solar system.
2. Contrasting the physical makeup of Earth and Jupiter.
3. Using a learned procedure to calculate the amount of time required for a planet to orbit a star in a circular orbit, given the mass of the star and planet and the distance between them.
4. Identifying by name planets shown in previously unseen photographs.
5. Classifying previously unused examples of physical objects as being in gas, liquid, or solid form.
6. In baseball, determining which pitch to throw next.
7. Describing the difference between applying a rule and problem solving.

Answers can be found at the end of the chapter.

Again, written tests can measure knowledge of information as well as most concepts and rules. Alternate means such as performance assessments are required to measure problem solving. In each case, the distinction between capability and performance must be maintained. For any capability that is assessed, a performance must be selected that will provide an indication of the learner's capability that is meaningful.

PERFORMANCE OBJECTIVES

In this section, we show how to create performance objectives to establish what an assessment will ask learners to do. Oosterhof (2003) proposes including up to four components in a performance objective:

- The name of the *type of capability* being assessed
- The *behavior* the learner will be asked to perform to indicate whether the capability has been learned
- The *situation* in which the assessment will occur
- Any *special conditions* that must exist for a learner's performance to be judged satisfactory

As we discuss these components, it is useful to keep in mind the purpose of performance objectives. Performance objectives describe an observable event that indicates that a student has acquired the targeted knowledge. The performance is an indication of knowledge; it typically is not the knowledge. The performance objective prescribes the observable events that provide a reasonable basis for concluding that knowledge has been achieved.

Goals rather than performance objectives are normally used when the capability involves problem solving. The complexity of what a learner might do within the process of solving a problem generally is beyond what can be specified within a well-constructed performance objective. Distinctions between goals and performance objectives are discussed later in this chapter.

Type of Capability

For each objective, it is useful to indicate the type of capability[2] being assessed. Again, because performance objectives only describe a visible manifestation of knowledge, it is always possible that the performance being observed is the result of a capability other than the one being assessed. Stating the type of capability involved alerts us to the type of performance we should use to help ensure that the targeted knowledge is being assessed.

To specify type of capability, we simply identify it by name: information, discrimination, concept, or rule.

Behavior

A learning outcome can be measured only if it can be observed. To create an observable event, a learner must exhibit a behavior. The central role of a performance objective is to identify a behavior that indicates that the targeted learning has occurred.

To be most useful, the behavior should be specified in a manner that can be observed directly; that is, no inferences should be required to determine whether the behavior has occurred. *The performance objective must specify exactly what you will see.*

---

[2]Different authors (e.g., Mager, 1984; Gagné, R. M., Briggs, L. J., & Wager, W. W. (1988). *Principles of Instructional Design* (3rd ed.). New York: Holt, Rinehart, and Winston.) divide performance objectives into somewhat different components. Virtually all authors agree that the purpose of an objective is to specify an observable performance that will be used to indicate that the targeted learning has been achieved. Consequently, most measurement books agree that a statement of that performance or behavior is a basic component of any objective. However, the type of capability involved strongly influences the type of behavior that should be used to indicate achievement of the targeted learning. Therefore, this book proposes that a performance objective should begin with a statement of the type of capability involved. With the type of capability in mind, focus is then placed on selecting a behavior that is appropriate for measuring that capability.

2.3   Apply What You Are Learning

Listed here are pairs of events. Within each pair, one can be observed directly; the other cannot. The event that can be observed directly is the better candidate for a performance objective. For each pair, select the one that can be directly observed.

1. A. Knows names of the chemical elements.
   B. Orally states names of all the chemical elements.
2. A. Describes how to locate a book in the library using the library website.
   B. Given a book's title and access to the library website, states the book's call number.
3. A. States the name of the historical period during which a painting was created.
   B. Is able to associate paintings correctly with historical periods.
4. A. When given necessary information, knows how to compute the monthly payment on a loan.
   B. When given necessary information, states the monthly payment on a loan.

Answers can be found at the end of the chapter.

Notice that in the first pair, one cannot directly observe "Knows names of the chemical elements." In the second pair, "describes how to locate a book" requires an inference to determine whether a description has occurred; the event "describes" is not directly observable.

By attaching the name of the capability to the statement of behavior, we create a performance objective. Here are some examples:

Information: Orally states the names of the chemical elements.

Rule: Given a book's title and access to the library website, states the book's call number.

Concept: States the name of the historical period during which the painting was created.

Rule: When given necessary information, states the monthly payment on a loan.

Whether or not you create performance objectives when developing a test, it is important to think in terms of specific behaviors that will be observed

through the test. Using descriptions of knowledge that require inference such as "the learner *understands*" or "the learner *recognizes*" does not provide sufficient guidance for constructing test items. More specifically, descriptions that require inference prevent you from verifying that the performance you will observe through the test matches the capability you are trying to assess.

Table 2.2 lists the type of behavior appropriate for assessing each type of capability. Notice that the behavior in each of the objectives stated previously closely corresponds to those listed in the table. For instance, the first objective involves *information* and the behavior involves learners stating what they know: "Orally states names of all the chemical elements." The second objective involves a *rule*, and the behavior ("States the book's call number") requires a learner to apply the rule; that is, to implement the process for obtaining a book's call number from the library's website.

2.4   Apply What You Are Learning

Listed here are three pairs of performance objectives. Within each pair, one behavior corresponds to the type of capability involved, whereas the other does not. Using Table 2.2 as a reference, identify which behavior correctly corresponds to the type of capability.

1. A. *Rule:* States the formula for converting inches to centimeters.
   B. *Rule:* Given the length of an object in inches, states the equivalent length in centimeters.
2. A. *Information:* States whether the value of stocks in the last month have increased or decreased.
   B. *Information:* Given the value of a stock last month and this month, states the percent and direction of its change.
3. A. *Concept:* States the difference between isosceles and equilateral triangles.
   B. *Concept:* Given a set of triangles, marks the equilateral triangles.

Answers can be found at the end of the chapter.

Situation

Often the context in which the learner exhibits behavior is relevant. May a dictionary be used when translating sentences from another language? May a calculator be used when solving math problems? What software will the learner be allowed to use when building a website? Most characteristics of a situation are not specified, either because they are obvious (such as the language in which the speech is to be given) or because they are judged not to be critical to defining the skill (such as the topic of the material being translated to another language).

Judgments have to be made about which, if any, situations will be specified as part of the performance objective. In some of the preceding objectives, the *situation* was already included (shown here in italics):

> **Rule:** *Given a book's title and access to the library website*, state the book's call number.

In the following objectives, adding the *situation* helps clarify each objective:

> **Information:** *When given a periodic table*, orally states the names of the chemical elements.

> **Concept:** *When shown an unknown painting that is clearly characteristic of the period*, states the name of the historical period during which the painting was created.

Special Conditions

Sometimes it is appropriate to place conditions on the action by, for example, indicating how quickly the learner must point to the appropriate letter in a word, or establishing a standard, such as the need to make a correct identification 80%, or possibly 100%, of the time.

Special conditions are sometimes confused with situations. A situation specifies the context in which the behavior will occur. Special conditions, in contrast, specify conditions that must be present in the learner's behavior in order to conclude that the targeted knowledge has been learned. As in any situation, judgment must be used about which, if any, special conditions are

to be specified. Here is an example of a special condition in a performance objective:

> **Information:** When given a periodic table, orally states the names of the chemical elements *in the order of their atomic weights*.

Special conditions are not always specified in a performance objective. Therefore, a performance objective does not necessarily include a performance standard or passing score. Not all authors agree with this point of view. For example, Mager (1984) proposes that a performance standard should always be included within the objective to define a successful performance. Later in the book, we will show that establishing a passing score on a test is not always possible or necessary. Even when passing scores are used, it may be appropriate to establish the passing score after the test has been administered and the performance of learners evaluated. In some situations, then, it would be inappropriate to specify a performance standard in the objective.

2.5   Apply What You Are Learning

Each of the three performance objectives listed here has been partitioned with brackets, and the partitions are numbered. Within these objectives, indicate whether each partition

    A. identifies the *type of capability*
    B. states the *behavior* to be observed
    C. specifies the *situation*
    D. specifies a *special condition*

[Information][1]: [Within five seconds,][2] [point to the picture of the musical instrument being played].[3]

[Rule][4]: [Given sentences spoken in English,][5] [orally state equivalent sentences in German].[6]

[Concept][7]: [Given two sounds whose pitches are discrepant in frequency by 1%,][8] [orally state whether the first or second sound has the higher frequency].[9]

Answers can be found at the end of the chapter.

SELECTION OF PERFORMANCE OBJECTIVES

Ultimately, the instructor selects or creates performance objectives for her or his own course. However, the following four guidelines may facilitate selection of a useful set of objectives:

1. Describe the results of learning rather than strategies for facilitating learning.
2. Use behaviors that are relevant indicators for the type of capability that is to be learned.
3. Obtain indicators of all critical aspects of the knowledge being assessed.
4. Obtain indicators for an appropriate sample of all knowledge that is to be learned.

Describe the Results of Learning

Performance objectives specify what the learner will be able to do if he or she has learned the targeted knowledge. According to Linn and Gronlund (1995), to name consequences of learning that are observable, performance objectives should *not* be specified in terms of the following characteristics:

- Instructor performance, such as saying, "Learners will be taught to solve quadratic equations."
- Course content, such as indicating, "The learner will know the difference between criterion- and norm-referenced tests."

To avoid these problems, always ask *what you will be able to see the learner do* after the knowledge being taught has been learned.

Use Relevant Behavior as Indicators

Performance objectives do not describe knowledge. They describe indicators of knowledge. Considerable care must be taken to make sure the behavior specified in the objective is relevant to the knowledge that is being assessed.

Again, this is the reason we recommend stating the type of the capability as part of the performance objective. Although it does not assure that relevant behaviors will be used to indicate learning, naming the type of capability can help make you aware of the types of behavior that are appropriate.

Assess All Critical Aspects of the Knowledge

Because only indicators of knowledge are being described, it is probable that one performance objective by itself does not address all critical aspects of a particular knowledge. Attending to all critical aspects of the knowledge—more than anything else discussed in this chapter—requires the abilities of a highly intelligent and perceptive instructor. The instructor must have mastery of what is being taught so that critical aspects of a concept or rule are evident. The instructor must be perceptive about how these critical aspects can be seen in the behavior of another person.

Assess an Appropriate Sample of All Knowledge

It is likely that the instructor will not be able to assess all knowledge that is to be learned within the course of a school year. When this is true, the instructor must select an appropriate sample of knowledge that is representative of overall content and does not exclude important skills.

CONVEYING PERFORMANCE OBJECTIVES TO LEARNERS

It may be obvious that expected performance should be communicated to learners. Knowing what is expected can help motivate learners and also help them determine when a skill has been achieved. When learners are at a distance, the instructor has far fewer opportunities to casually monitor what learners are doing and to correct misunderstandings about expectations.

Conveying performance objectives does not necessarily imply that learners should be given a list of objectives; a learner who lacks the skill that is about to be taught may be unable to comprehend the meaning of the stated objective. For some time, research has revealed no improvement in learning when learners are provided objectives before instruction (see for example Duchastel & Merrill, 1973; Melton, 1978).

Instructors can use explanations and illustrations to convey performance objectives to learners. Because the performance used to assess knowledge varies with the type of capability, the method used should take into account the category of performance that is to be taught. Table 2.3 lists the categories we discussed earlier and proposes a technique for conveying each type of capability to learners. For example, an instructor who wants learners to recognize musical instruments from their sound (information) might tell learners that they will be expected to state the name of an instrument being heard in a recording. An instructor who is about to teach learners how to use a formula to compute the standard deviation of a set of numbers (rule) might convey what is to be learned by giving an example of the computation or by providing an overview of the process. Conveying expected performance to learners involves first recognizing the type of capability involved and then using what you probably would describe as common sense to communicate that expectation to learners.

GOALS VERSUS PERFORMANCE OBJECTIVES

Napoleon Hill, an American author and philosopher who gained popularity in the early 20th century, said, "A goal is a dream with a deadline." This definition may have at least some relevance to education. Within an instructional context, **goals** are broader than performance objectives. As we have noted, a performance objective details the specific behavior that indicates that the learner has obtained the capability being assessed. For instance,

> *Rule:* Given sentences written in English, writes equivalent sentences in German.

The assessment of a well-written performance objective requires no inference. The behavior to be observed is a set of sentences written in German. One does not need to infer whether a learner can write equivalent sentences in German. One can observe this behavior directly.

> Goals are stated more generally than objectives. For example,
>
> Translates written English to German.

A goal is often the equivalent of several objectives. With written tests, it is usually better to work from performance objectives. With performance assessments, it is quite natural to use an instructional goal rather than performance objectives, since the skills being assessed are often highly complex in terms of the number of behaviors involved. The use of goals rather than equivalent sets of objectives allows brevity. Often with problem-solving skills, performance objectives, more than instructional goals, camouflage potential problems with generalizability. We address this issue in Chapter 4 and also in our later discussion of performance assessments.

Table 2.3
Techniques for conveying performance objectives to learners

Type of Capability	Instructional Technique
Information	Describe the kinds of information within a topic that learners will be expected to recall
Concept	Describe or list the names of concepts for which learners will be asked to classify examples
Rule	Provide an example of what the learner will be able to do when the rule is applied

Inferences are required to assess whether a learner has achieved a goal. This allows flexibility in terms of the specific criteria that will be used to judge a learner's performance. This flexibility can be damaging, though, because it increases measurement error resulting from subjectivity in scoring. For this reason, when we discuss performance assessments, we must give careful attention to how one scores a learner's work.

SUMMARY

That which one learns can be classified as declarative knowledge, procedural knowledge, and problem-solving skills. In this book we refer to declarative knowledge as information and divide procedural knowledge into four subcategories: discriminations, concepts, rules, and complex skills. An instructor cannot see what a learner knows or is thinking, even if the instructor and learner are face to face. Instead, one depends on a learner's performance to provide an *indication* of those capabilities. Being aware of the type of capability involved is important, because different kinds of learner performance are used to assess the different kinds of capabilities.

Performance objectives specify the behaviors that indicate that targeted knowledge has been learned. Performance objectives include up to four components: type of capability, behavior, situation, and special conditions. Naming the type of capability helps us select appropriate indicators of knowledge. The behavior is central to the objective and specifies what will be seen when learning has occurred. The situation describes the context in which the learner will be asked to indicate achievement. The special conditions, if necessary, specify conditions that must be met for the learner's performance to be judged successful.

When learners are at a distance, it is more difficult to communicate expectations. Performance objectives can be conveyed to learners without actually being stated. Where capabilities involve problem solving, performance assessments are used instead of written tests, and goals are substituted for objectives. Goals are stated more generally, and assessing whether a learner has achieved a goal requires inference. The flexibility inherent in goals increases subjectivity when scoring learner work.

ANSWERS: APPLY WHAT YOU ARE LEARNING

2.1 1. B; 2. A; 3. B; 4. B.

2.2 1. information; 2. information;

3. rule; 4. concept; 5. concept;

6. problem solving; 7. information.

2.3 1. B; 2. B; 3. A; 4. B

2.4 1. B (Option A requires learners to recall information and state what is known, whereas option B requires learners to apply an established rule for converting inches to centimeters); 2. A (Option B requires application of a rule for computing the percent and direction of change, whereas option A involves recalling information to state what is known); 3. B. (Option A involves recalling information to state the difference between isosceles and equilateral triangles, whereas option B requires learners to classify triangles as equilateral or not equatorial.)

2.5 1. A: 2. D; 3. B; 4. A;

5. C; 6. B; 7. A; 8. C; 9. B.

TERMS INTRODUCED IN THIS CHAPTER

Performance objective: is a description of an observable event that can indicate whether a student has learned a particular knowledge. A performance objective is not a description of the knowledge, but rather a description of a performance that shows whether the targeted knowledge has been learned.

Goal: is a desired instructional outcome, typically stated more broadly than a performance objective. A goal may be equivalent to a group of performance objectives. In the case of highly complex skills that cannot be broken down into observable statements of performance, a goal may be used as a substitute for performance objectives.

Declarative knowledge: is knowing that something is the case. It is information that can be conveyed in words; that is, knowledge that can be declared. Declarative knowledge varies considerably in complexity, ranging from very simple, such as dates of events, to very complex, such as trends in global climate change. Declarative knowledge can be assessed by having learners state or talk about what they know.

Procedural knowledge: is knowing how to do something. Procedural knowledge involves making discriminations, understanding concepts, and applying rules that govern relationships. Concepts, rules, and even discriminations can be very complex or very simple. Procedural knowledge is assessed by giving learners a task to complete that requires application of the procedural knowledge. The specific application must be one that the student has not applied earlier, and must be provided to the student rather than allowing the student to choose the application. Asking learners to explain a concept or rule provides a good indication of their declarative knowledge of the concept or rule, but not their procedural knowledge.

Problem solving: is involved when one has a goal but has not yet identified a means for reaching that goal. Problem solving requires the use of previously learned declarative and procedural knowledge. It may involve domain-specific strategies, suggesting that different strategies are employed when solving problems in different content areas, such as math and writing. Problem solving may involve a very simple or a very complex task. Complexity is not the distinction between procedural knowledge of a rule and problem solving. With a rule, the procedure, once learned, is established. With problem solving, the procedure for solving the problem is unknown and must be established. However, existing declarative and procedural knowledge helps establish an appropriate solution to the problem.

ENHANCE YOUR UNDERSTANDING

- A learner's outward performance may provide an inaccurate or misleading indication of that person's learned capabilities. Can you recall a recent situation where an instructor or other person made an incorrect conclusion about your knowledge based on your outward behaviors? What strategies might one use to reduce the number of inaccurate conclusions drawn from behaviors?
- This chapter (and most of the other chapters in this book) includes several "Apply What You Are Learning" exercises. These exercises actually are assessments. Look at some of them and try to identify which type of capability (information, discrimination, concept, rule, or complex skill) each exercise is assessing.
- Think of a capability you would try to teach your learners. (Do not confuse capability with performance. An example of a capability is knowing the concept of addition or knowing a rule, such as describing the relationship between the density of an object and its ability to float on water.) Identify by name the capability you have described. Then list learner performances that would be good indicators of whether this capability has been learned.

ADDITIONAL READING

Bloom, B. S. (Ed.). (1956). *Taxonomy of educational objectives: Handbook 1. Cognitive domain.* New York: McKay. Discusses the technique used to classify objectives, describes categories of the cognitive domain, and presents examples of objectives and test items within each category.

Gagné, R. M. (1985). *The conditions of learning* (4th ed.). New York: Holt, Rinehart, and Winston. Discusses the nature of learned capabilities and the conditions required for students to learn each capability.

Gronlund, N. E. (2004). *Writing instructional objectives for teaching and assessment* (7th ed.). Upper Saddle River, NJ: Merrill/Prentice Hall. This small book describes how to write objectives for attitudes as well as intellectual and performance outcomes. Suggestions are given for using objectives within instruction.

O'Donnell, A. M., Reeve, J., & Smith, J. K. (2007). *Educational psychology: Reflection for action.* Hoboken, NJ: Wiley/Jossey-Bass. Chapter 8 discusses cognitive theories of learning, including the relationship between cognitive and constructivist theories of learning.

3

Gathering Evidence of Validity

Validity pertains to the degree to which a test measures what it is supposed to measure. More than any other factor, the quality of a test, whether online or face to face, depends on its validity. If a test does not measure what it is supposed to measure, it is useless. Validity is the most central and essential quality in the development, interpretation, and use of educational measures.[1]

Validity is an abstraction. We cannot directly see validity any more than we can see the capabilities we wish to assess. Instead of observing validity, we depend on various types of evidence that indicate its presence or absence. Much like the strategy used by Agatha Christie's famous detective Hercule Poirot to solve a mystery, an instructor uses evidence to determine whether a test is measuring what it is supposed to measure. In educational measurement, validity evidence is typically grouped into three interrelated categories: *construct-related* evidence, *content-related* evidence, and *criterion-related* evidence.[2] As we will

observe, the distinctions among these categories are not always clear, and one type of evidence does not negate the need for other types. Validity is a unified concept based on available evidence (American Psychological Association, 1999). In this chapter, we will look at specific ways to develop and apply these three categories of validity evidence.

We will also observe that, unlike the classic Agatha Christie novel, validity evidence does not result in absolute verdicts. Instead, evidence establishes the *degree* to which a test is valid and the interpretations and uses for which the test has validity. Also unlike mystery novels, validity evidence is gathered both before and after a test is developed. The collection of validity evidence shapes the development of a test as well as its interpretation and use.

When assessment occurs online, and particularly when learners are at a considerable distance from the instructor, the conventional strategy for collecting validity evidence tends to be more restricted. As we will observe shortly, a particularly important strategy for collecting evidence involves simply looking around our physical neighborhood, seeing if what we observed through a test is substantiated by other indications of what learners appear able to do. When the instructor and learners interact face-to-face in the classroom, information provided through assessments can be corroborated, often continuously, by what the instructor observes through casual observations. When assessments are online, particularly in distance education situations, the frequency of the instructor's casual observations tends to be reduced.

---

[1] In this book, educational measurement refers to the process of determining a quantitative or qualitative attribute of an individual or group of individuals that is of academic relevance. Test refers to the vehicle used to observe that attribute, such as a written test, products that students produce, or an informal observation such as through an e-mail, phone conversation, or face-to-face observation.

[2] The most recent *Standards for Educational and Psychological Testing* (1999) both update and reorganize the discussion of validity evidence. Instead of the categories of construct-, content-, and criterion-related evidence, sources of validity evidence are grouped into five categories: test content, response processes, internal structure, relations to other variables, and consequences of testing. Discussion of validity within this book is contemporary, although the more traditional names for categories of validity evidence are used to facilitate communication.

To illustrate the importance of this corroboration, let us look at a scenario that is likely to occur in an introductory research methods course. The instructor wants to assess students' understanding of the importance of random assignment of individual people to treatment groups when conducting experimental research. To assess their knowledge, the instructor administers the following essay test:

> *Background provided the students:* A researcher wants to determine whether hormone replacement therapy prevents heart disease in women. To determine this, the researcher selects a large sample of women and categorizes them into two groups: those who have regularly taken estrogen over the past five years and those who took no hormone-replacement drug during that same period. The researcher found that the incidence of heart disease was lower among women who were taking estrogen, and consequently concluded that the use of estrogen does prevent heart disease in women.

> *Test question:* From this observation, the researcher concluded that the use of estrogen does prevent heart disease in women. What are alternate explanations for the results observed in this study? Explain what this researcher could have done to rule out your alternate explanations.

This illustration relates to an important finding a few years ago in medical research. Research originally had shown that women taking estrogen did have a lower incidence of heart disease. But later research established that, as a group, women taking estrogen were economically better off and more educated than women not using this therapy. The lower incidence of heart disease could be explained by these extraneous variables. In fact, in a subsequent study, when women were randomly assigned to two groups, with those in one group given estrogen and those in the other given a placebo, it was found that estrogen actually increased the incidence of heart disease.

Returning now to our original story, the instructor of this introductory research methods course gave students the above essay test and found that overall the students were able to identify alternate plausible explanations to findings in the original research. More central to the knowledge being assessed, students also recognized that random assignment of women to treatment groups would control for these alternate explanations. Through face-to-face casual conversations, our instructor continued to observe students to determine if, when talking about research designs, they continued to recognize the importance that random assignment plays in experimental research. Quite simply, if what the instructor observed through these informal conversations of students was similar to what was observed through the essay test, this corroboration would be evidence that conclusions drawn from the test were valid. On the other hand, if the informal conversations with students failed to corroborate what was observed on the test, this would cause the instructor to question the validity of what was concluded from the test. Later in this chapter we refer to this as *criterion-related validity evidence*—looking for relationships between performance on a test and criteria external to the test.

As the physical distance between instructor and learners increases with a corresponding decrease in opportunity for casual interactions, the number of opportunities for substantiating inferences drawn from the test through external criteria such as casual observation tends to drop, perhaps dramatically. This reduction in interaction increases the importance of each of the available interactions. This is analogous to the limited opportunity one has for making adjustments to the trajectory of a spacecraft sent to another planet as compared with adjustments to the steering of, for instance, an

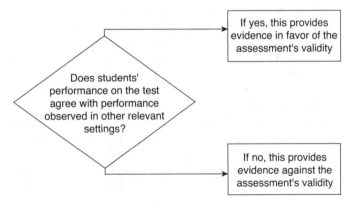

Figure 3.1
Establishing criterion-related evidence of validity

automobile. For somewhat different reasons, it is important to carefully control the paths of both spacecraft and cars. With automobiles, course corrections are made frequently, almost continuously. The consequence of the fact that fewer opportunities exist for correcting the path of spacecraft is that actions employed at each of these opportunities must be implemented very carefully.

The same applies to establishing validity evidence when learners are more removed from the instructor. The fewer opportunities to collect evidence for substantiating or questioning the validity of an assessment mean that each opportunity becomes more critical. When the instructor and learners are more distant, as in online learning, the opportunity to collect criterion-related evidence of validity is greatly diminished. The implication we will observe is that the two remaining types of validity evidence (construct-related and content-related) become more critical.

This chapter helps you achieve two skills:

- Recognize types of evidence used to establish validity, applying these types of evidence to situations where the instructor and learners are at a distance
- Recognize the role of validity in the interpretation and use of tests

CRITERION-RELATED EVIDENCE OF VALIDITY

Criterion-related evidence[3] *indicates how well performance on a test correlates with performance on relevant criterion measures that are external to the test.* Conceptually, criterion-related evidence of validity is quite simple. It essentially asks, "If a test is valid, with what other things should performance on the test correlate?" If, for example, an instructor's test is valid, performance on this test should be expected to correlate reasonably well with online learners' performance on other indicators of the same skill. If the test suggests that students understand the importance of random assignment within experimental designs, the instructor's casual observations of what students say when they discuss experimental designs should suggest the same thing. Figure 3.1 illustrates the simplicity of criterion-related evidence.

---

[3]The term *criterion-related evidence of validity* is sometimes confused with another term with which you might be familiar: *criterion-referenced test*. The meaning of these terms is distinct. Criterion-*referenced* refers to the frame of reference used to interpret performance on a test. It indicates that performance is given meaning by describing concisely the domain being measured by the test. In contrast, criterion-*related* validity is concerned with whether performance on a test correlates with other measures that should provide similar results. Chapter 6 addresses the important topic of criterion-referenced tests, including the interpretation of learner performance that these tests provide.

Because criterion-related evidence involves correlations, it is common to think in terms of statistical correlations. Criterion-related evidence for standardized tests such as the ACT, SAT, GMAT, LSAT, and GRE involve statistical correlations between scores on the test and scores on variables outside the test such as subsequent grade-point average in college. The degree to which the scores and later performance correlate helps establish the degree to which the test is valid. Their less than perfect correlations help establish limits to their validity.

However, the correlations used to establish criterion-related evidence are not always statistical. They may in fact involve qualitative descriptions and be based on judgments. As we noted in the introduction, with assessments used in courses taught in conventional classrooms, much of this evidence is obtained through frequent face-to-face interactions between instructor and learners.

With online assessment and particularly in distance learning situations, we are at a considerable disadvantage, at least with current technologies. The instructor still has important but often far fewer indicators with which test performance can be correlated. Using discussion and "chat" options can provide forms of validity evidence. Another vehicle is direct follow-up questions by e-mail especially with individuals who appear to need further opportunities to demonstrate their understanding.

Certainly, numerous comparisons are possible in which the level of informal interaction in an online course is equal to or even greater than that in some face-to-face classes. A large lecture class, even though students are in the same room as the instructor, generally does not allow the level of interaction available in many distance learning classes. The same can be true in small conventional classrooms when the instructor continually writes on the board, always facing away from the learners. In these situations, little criterion-related evidence of validity is being gathered. However, when comparisons between online and face-to-face settings involve equal ratios of instructors to learners with instructors devoting similar amounts of time to interactions with learners, the face-to-face setting allows for a greater amount of informal assessment that is essential to criterion-related evidence. In a tutorial setting, 20 minutes of face-to-face oral communication allows a greater degree of informal assessment than an equal amount of time devoted to reading and writing e-mails to these same students. An hour of discussion time face-to-face allows for more informal assessment than a one-hour chat session. Future technological developments, perhaps particularly higher-speed communication, will reduce or eliminate these differences. However, asynchronous interactions will always allow for fewer informal assessments than an equal amount of synchronous interactions. By no means does this cause online or distance learning to be inferior to face-to-face instruction in terms of learning outcomes. Online learning can achieve parity with face-to-face instruction in part because of the extensive up-front design and development of course material. One could devote the same up-front effort to face-to-face settings, but unlike online learning, one can often achieve good results in face-to-face settings by developing instructional elements while the course is underway. Similarly, the limited opportunity for gathering criterion-related evidence does not invalidate assessments, but it does establish the considerable importance that construct- and content-related evidence must play if those assessments are to be valid.

CONSTRUCT-RELATED EVIDENCE OF VALIDITY

Construct-related evidence establishes a link between the underlying psychological construct we wish to measure and the visible performance we choose to observe. There are many psychological constructs for which tests are developed, such as intelligence, interest, motivation, anxiety, and self-efficacy. In each case, the construct being measured is invisible. Measurement of the construct requires the use of some visible performance that provides an appropriate indication as to the status of the construct we wish to measure.

The constructs that are generally of greatest relevance to instructors are those of learned knowledge. As with any psychological construct, learned knowledge cannot be directly seen. We have previously noted that one cannot see what a learner knows or is thinking. Therefore, we need to establish whether the visible learner behaviors we choose to observe are legitimate indications of the learner knowledge we wish to evaluate.

In Chapter 2, we said knowledge consisted of declarative and procedural knowledge, and problem-solving skills. In that discussion, we established that very different types of performance are used to assess these different types of knowledge. As the name implies, declarative knowledge is demonstrated by learners declaring or stating what they know. In contrast, procedural knowledge involves doing something; that is, implementing a procedure. In this book, we are using *information* to refer to declarative knowledge. We have divided procedural knowledge into three subcategories: *discriminations, concepts,* and *rules;* although discriminations are typically not included in formal assessments except with young children. Problem solving builds on declarative and procedural knowledge and is demonstrated by asking learners to generate solutions to relevant and previously unused problems.

Again, construct-related evidence involves establishing a link between the invisible construct we wish to measure, that of the students' learned knowledge, and the visible performance we choose to observe and use as an indicator of that knowledge. As summarized in Figure 3.2, establishing this link can be subdivided into three steps:

- Step 1 involves establishing in your own mind a concise understanding of the knowledge you are going to assess. This does *not* mean establishing what you will see students do, although recognizing the differences in what knowledgeable versus unknowledgeable students do may be useful. This first step consists of establishing clearly in your own mind what it means to be knowledgeable within the specific area that is to be assessed.

- Step 2 involves establishing the type of capabilities embedded within this knowledge. What declarative knowledge (information) is involved? What procedural knowledge (concepts and rules)? And what problem solving? The assessment will likely include only a sample of this knowledge; however, establishing the types of capabilities involved is crucial to determining the types of performance that should be used within the assessment.

- Step 3 involves identifying specific examples of student performance that can legitimately serve as indicators of the knowledge that is to be assessed. The types of performance selected are based directly on the types of capabilities involved.

Perhaps obviously, the instructor must be knowledgeable in a content area to determine what is important for learners to learn, the type of

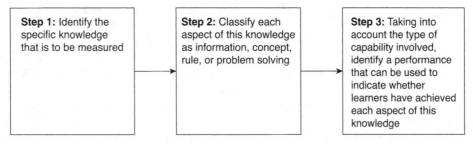

Figure 3.2
Establishing construct-related evidence of validity

capabilities each of these skills represent, and examples of performance that distinguish knowledgeable learners from individuals who have yet to achieve this knowledge. Some additional concerns are involved with instruction and assessment related to problem-solving skills. First, problem solving builds upon declarative and procedural skill. Therefore, the instructor must know what knowledge is prerequisite to solving a given problem and the techniques that help learners transfer that knowledge to the problem-solving situation. Second, solving problems requires the use of strategies that are often specific to a particular discipline. These strategies themselves represent procedural knowledge that has to be learned. The instructor must be knowledgeable about what strategies experts within the discipline use to solve problems and when it is appropriate to employ a particular strategy.

Illustration of Step 1: Identify Specific Knowledge to Measure

To illustrate the process of establishing construct-related evidence of validity, let us look at how it would apply to assessing learners' knowledge of some skills with which you are probably quite familiar—those associated with computing and interpreting the average of some numbers, such as the average age of a group of people. Technically, this numerical average is referred to as the "arithmetic mean."

As with most content, knowledge related to the arithmetic mean can vary from fundamental to highly sophisticated. For our illustration, let us identify the specific knowledge we are trying to measure as follows:

> The arithmetic mean provides a central tendency for numbers, such as ages of people. That is, it helps to establish where the center of the numbers is located. Computing the arithmetic mean involves first adding up all the numbers (the numerator) and dividing this total by the number of numbers (the denominator). We could use this formula to express the

division of the sum of scores (ΣX) by the number of numbers:

$$Mean = \frac{\Sigma X}{n}$$

The numerical value of the mean is somewhere between the highest and lowest of the numbers. It increases as overall magnitude of individual numbers increases; for instance, the mean age of a group of younger people is lower than the mean age of a group of older people. If the numbers are symmetrically distributed (each half of the distribution being the mirror image of the other), then 50% of the numbers will be below the mean and 50% will be above. The mean anticipates that numbers have an *interval* quality, that is, increasing any value by 1 has the same effect everywhere on the scale. Sometimes the shape of the distribution of numbers renders other measures of central tendency more appropriate than the mean. An example would be an extremely skewed set of numbers, such as the financial income of people; in which case the median provides a better measure of central tendency than the mean.

Professional judgment by the instructor ultimately determines what content is taught and assessed. For instance, one instructor might conclude that it is important for students to know how to interpret the arithmetic mean but not necessarily be able to compute it. Another instructor might believe it is important for students, when provided a description of data, to determine whether it is appropriate to use the arithmetic mean to describe that data. For our purposes, let us assume that the preceding narrative describes what students should know about the arithmetic mean.

Identifying the knowledge we are trying to measure (and each of the three steps to establishing construct-related evidence) often takes place entirely in the instructor's mind. For our illustration, we will write out the thought process.

Illustration of Step 2: Classify Each Aspect of Knowledge as Information, Concept, Rule, or Problem Solving

After identifying specific knowledge to be measured, which we did, the second step to establishing construct-related evidence is to classify each aspect of this knowledge as information, concept, rule, or problem solving. For our illustration, here are those classifications:

Information

- When the distribution is symmetrical, knows that 50% of the numbers are below the mean and 50% are above.[4]
- A formula that defines the arithmetic mean is

$$Mean = \frac{\Sigma X}{n}$$

Concepts

- Given that arithmetic mean is a measure of overall magnitude of numbers, knows what is meant by *overall magnitude*

Rules

- Can compute the mean for a set of numbers using the above formula
- Knows that the numerical value of the mean will increase as overall magnitude of numbers increases

Again, professional judgments are being made as to what knowledge will be assessed. For instance, another instructor might expect learners to be able to *declare* the mean as a measure of central tendency (information). Here we have decided not to include that knowledge, but instead to demonstrate *procedural* knowledge that the mean is a measure that reflects the magnitude of numbers

(a concept). We are expecting learners to *declare* the percent of numbers above and below the mean for a symmetrical distribution, but not asymmetrical distributions (both are information). Likewise, we are expecting learners to demonstrate both *declarative* and *procedural* knowledge related to the formula (information and a rule).

Although problem-solving skills are regularly taught in most courses of instruction, and are

---

3.1 Apply What You Are Learning

In the second step of our illustration, we have classified each aspect of knowledge related to the arithmetic mean as being information, concept, or rule. In the third step to establishing construct-related evidence, we must take into account the type of capability involved and identify a learner performance that can be used to indicate whether learners have achieved the knowledge. Recall that in Chapter 2 we established the following performance for assessing each of the three types of capabilities:

Information	Ask learners to state what they know
Concepts	Ask learners to classify diverse and previously unused illustrations as examples versus nonexamples of the concept
Rules	Provide learners a relevant but previously unused example and ask them to apply the rule

In light of the type of capability involved (information, concept, or rule), what should learners be asked to do to establish whether they have achieved each of the following aspects of knowledge? Be as specific as possible.

1. Knows that, with a symmetrical distribution, 50% of the numbers are above and 50% below the mean (information)
2. Knows the formula for computing the mean (information)
3. Knows how to compute the mean for a set of numbers (rule)
4. Given that arithmetic mean is a measure of overall magnitude of numbers, knows what is meant by overall magnitude (concept)

Answers can be found at the end of the chapter.

---

[4]Mathematicians, at least some of them, have fun with this statement. What happens if some of the numbers equal the mean? Then, literally speaking, less than half of all the numbers will be above and below the mean even if the distribution of numbers is symmetrical. For our purposes, we will (or at least your authors will) ignore this issue.

discussed with greater detail in later chapters, they are not included in our present illustration. An example of problem solving involving knowledge of the arithmetic mean would be determining how to accurately communicate to various audiences what averages within survey data do and do not tell us about the survey results.

Illustration of Step 3: Given the Type of Capability Involved, Identify a Performance to Indicate That Learners Have Achieved the Knowledge

As illustrated in Exercise 3.1, the third step to establishing construct-related evidence involves identifying a performance that can be used to indicate whether learners have achieved the targeted knowledge. The formal way to do this is to state at the outset what performance the learners will be asked to demonstrate; that is, establish our performance objectives.

Table 3.1 lists performance objectives relevant to our illustration involving the arithmetic mean. Notice how each objective specifies the learner behavior that will be observed. Whether or not one formally prepares performance objectives, one must always identify the performance that will be observed as part of establishing

construct-related validity evidence. A description of a performance should not require inference to determine whether an event has occurred; it must establish exactly what the learner will be observed doing. Whenever an instructor assesses students, the instructor is forcing the learner to display an observable performance. Through the construct-validation process, we are systematically establishing the performance that will provide a valid assessment *prior* to producing test items or other tasks that make up the assessment. We recognize that the observed performance is not an exhibit of a learner's knowledge, but only an indicator of the knowledge we wish to assess. Establishing construct-related evidence is our means of verifying that an appropriate indication of learner knowledge is being employed.

In summary, establishing construct-related evidence of validity within online settings largely precedes the development of an assessment. This is true for both written tests and the assessment of work on products. As was shown in Figure 3.2, three steps are involved: 1) identifying specific knowledge to be measured; 2) classifying each aspect of this knowledge with respect to the type of capability involved—usually information, concept, rule, or problem solving; and

Table 3.1

Performance objectives related to knowledge of arithmetic mean and numbers of items to be used to measure each objective

Objective	Number of Items
Information: State the percent of numbers that fall above or below the mean, if the distribution is symmetrical	1
Information: Write the formula that defines the arithmetic mean	1
Concept: Given a description of numbers, indicate whether or not the arithmetic mean provides the information that allows for this description	3
Rule: Given a set of numbers and its the formula, compute the arithmetic mean of the numbers	2
Rule: Given two sets of numbers, identify through inspection (not computation) the set that has the larger arithmetic mean	3

3) identifying an appropriate performance that will indicate whether learners have achieved the knowledge.

In later chapters, we will find that as long as appropriate behaviors are being elicited, any item format can measure information, concepts, and rules. However, to effectively assess problem-solving skills, one usually must evaluate products produced by the students. This is because the assessment of problem solving must allow learners to successfully solve problems with any of a variety of solutions. Conventional written tests, whether given online or on paper, generally provide better assessments when students' answers can be constrained. This constraint limits the usefulness of written tests when assessing problem-solving skills. Later chapters discuss the development of items for online written tests and the assessment of problem-solving skills of both individuals and collaborative groups.

Again, when establishing validity evidence, there is no substitute for knowing intimately the construct being measured. When measuring learned knowledge, the person developing the assessment must meaningfully answer the question, "How would I indicate to others that I have this knowledge?" Establishing a legitimate link between the invisible capability and an observable performance is the essence of construct-related validity.

CONTENT-RELATED EVIDENCE OF VALIDITY

Content-related evidence of validity establishes how well the content of a test[5] corresponds to the learner performance to be observed. We can think of content-related evidence as an extension of construct-related evidence. Through construct-related evidence, we determine what knowledge we need to assess and establish learner behaviors that will provide good indicators of that knowledge. Through content-related evidence, we determine how well our test incorporates those behaviors.

Poor planning or lack of planning by the instructor may result in a test that does not incorporate targeted behaviors. You probably are aware of some techniques instructors use that fail to control the content of tests in face-to-face as well as online settings. Examples include selecting items simply because they challenge or appear to make the learner think. The better planning strategy is what we are doing here: identifying specific content to be included in the test after first establishing what specific performances are to be observed through the test.

Another reason that a test may not incorporate targeted behaviors is that, because of lack of time and other resources, a test always involves sampling; that is, it includes only some of the behaviors that could be assessed. Some samples are better than others. For instance, including a representative sample of content in written tests or products that students are asked to complete is obviously better than using unrepresentative samples.

Content-related evidence of validity is typically established while an assessment is being planned. It involves a systematic analysis of what the test is intended to measure (such as we have already done in the previous section), and then uses this analysis to control the content of the test. Content-related evidence amounts to controlling the content of a test by establishing a content outline. It is analogous to controlling the content of an important paper that you write or speech that you give through the use of a content outline. Figure 3.3 identifies three techniques often used to control the content of assessments. The first two, the use of performance objectives or tables of specification, are used to control content of either online or paper and pencil written tests. The third technique, development of a

---

[5]Remember, a "test" refers to any activity through which the instructor establishes what it is a learner knows or can do. This can include online written tests, assessments of student work on products, and even informal assessments such as through e-mails, online chats, and face-to-face conversations.

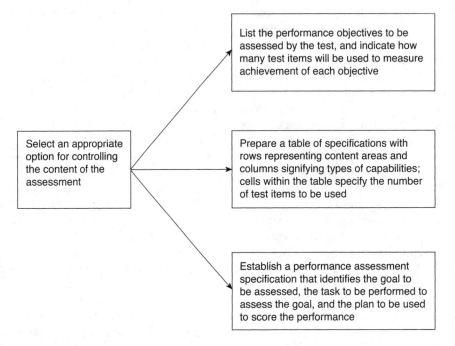

Figure 3.3
Options for establishing content-related evidence of validity

performance assessment specification, is used when products or other performance assessments are used to assess students' knowledge. Performance assessment specifications are discussed in Chapter 11.

Performance Objectives

If performance objectives have been formally developed, they can easily be used to control the content of a test. To do so, one simply indicates the number of test items that will be used to measure each objective. The *relative* number of items associated with each objective is proportional to the weights that respective objectives should have within the test. The total number of items on a test reflects the amount of time available for the test, which in turn is usually related to the perceived importance of the assessment. (In Chapter 5, we will look at the effect that the number of items has on the confidence with which the instructor assesses learners.)

Table 3.1 lists our performance objectives related to knowledge of the arithmetic mean. Each of these objectives clearly establishes what the test item will ask learners to do. For some of the objectives, the number of test items that can be generated is limited. For instance, only one or arguably two unique items can be created that ask learners to state the percent of numbers that are above and below the mean. Only one item can ask learners to write the formula for the arithmetic mean. Substantial numbers of items can be created for each of the remaining objectives. Nevertheless, listing performance objectives and specifying the number of items to be used to measure each objective is one way to tightly control the content of a written test.

Table of Specifications

Another common procedure for controlling test content is to develop a **table of specifications.** A table of specifications has two dimensions. The

Table 3.2
Table of specifications for a test related to knowledge of arithmetic mean

	Information	Concepts	Rules	Totals
Formula for arithmetic mean	1		2	3
Percent of scores above/below mean with symmetrical distributions	1			1
Information conveyed by mean		3		3
Identifying which set of numbers has larger mean			3	3

rows list the content areas to be addressed by the test. The columns list the types of capabilities the test is to measure.

Table 3.2 illustrates what a table of specifications might look like for our test related to the arithmetic mean. The rows list the content areas we have been identifying. The columns list the corresponding types of capabilities: information, concepts, and rules.

A list of performance objectives and a table of specifications are comparable techniques for controlling test content. The numbers within the table specify the number of items to be associated with each combination of content area and capability. For instance, one item will be used to measure *information* related to the formula for the mean, this being comparable to the performance objective that requires learners to write the definitional

formula for the mean. Two items will be used to measure a *rule* related to the definitional formula, this corresponding to the objective where learners compute the arithmetic mean of numbers. The *Totals* column simply indicates the total number of items within each content area.

Like the use performance objectives to control the content of a test, the numbers of items assigned are proportional to the emphasis or importance given to a particular content area and capability. To establish these numbers, the instructor should determine the following:

First, the total number of items to be included in the test

Then, the number of items to be associated with each content area, entering these numbers in the Totals column

Finally, the number of questions within a content area to be associated with each type of capability (information, concepts, and rules)

Performance objectives or a table of specifications is used to control the content of a test when the assessment involves a written test. In Chapter 11, we look at how the content of performance assessments is controlled when assessing problem-solving skills. With written tests, using a table of specifications is a more expeditious approach when performance objectives are not formally established. When a table of specifications is used, because learner performance is not identified, care must be taken to ensure a close match of test

---

3.2 Apply What You Are Learning

Based on the table of specifications in Table 3.2, answer the following questions.

1. What is the total number of questions in this test?
2. What is the total number of questions concerned with the formula for the arithmetic mean?
3. Of the questions that are concerned with the formula, how many should involve a rule?
4. How many questions on the overall test should measure rules?

Answers can be found at the end of the chapter.

content with the construct the test is supposed to be measuring. The behavior that a test item requires of a learner must correspond to the type of capability involved, whether it is information, concept, rule, or problem solving.

When developing written tests, many instructors do not systematically outline the content of the test before producing it. Instead, they simply create some good items that will challenge the students and that seem to ask important questions. As admirable as it is to challenge students and ask important questions, this loose control of the content of the test generally does not result in a good assessment. It is much like preparing a lecture or designing online instruction by simply asking what will challenge students and what are some important ideas that come to mind that should be addressed. In contrast, it is important to step back and outline what it is that content experts (the instructor included) find is important for one to know within the discipline. With respect to designing the assessment, one must establish a *representative subset* of the content that will be included in the test, including the types to capabilities that are to be addressed within each content area.

When instructors do not do this, the content of the test is more likely to be unrepresentative and will tend to address declarative knowledge but exclude procedural knowledge. When learning involves regular face-to-face interactions between the instructor and students, the failure to systematically outline content of a test will cause problems with the assessments. However, when assessments are online, and particularly when learners are at a distance, the situation is even worse. As noted earlier, when frequent face-to-face interactions are involved, the instructor has other indicators, outside the test, with which performance on the test is correlated. (We referred to this use of external criteria as *criterion-referenced* evidence of validity.) Without frequent face-to-face interactions, that evidence of validity is greatly diminished, and there is a substantially greater dependence on construct- and content-related procedures for ensuring the test is valid.

Should a test be invalid, even if its invalidity is unknown because of inattention to good validation procedures, the test is useless.

VALID INTERPRETATION AND USE OF TESTS

Discussions of validity have traditionally focused only on evidence of what a test measures. Messick (1989a, 1989b) has described how this perspective is limited. He reasons that test validation is inseparable from the interpretation and intended use of tests. As of 1999, his expanded perspective of validity is incorporated into the *Standards for Educational and Psychological Testing*.

Table 3.3 summarizes Messick's ideas. As illustrated in the table, Messick views validity in two dimensions, or facets. One dimension pertains to outcomes of a test; specifically, test interpretation (What do scores on the test mean?) and test use (What actions should result from having these scores?). The other dimension concerns justifications for the testing: evidence that justifies interpretations and uses of the test as well as consequences of these interpretations and uses of the test.

This two-by-two matrix results in four cells. The upper-left cell concerns evidence supporting interpretations of the test; that is, evidence of what the test measures. Included here are the types of evidence discussed earlier in this chapter: how well the test measures relevant constructs, descriptions of test content, and awareness of how performance on the test correlates with other measures. All this evidence facilitates interpretation of test performance.

The remaining three cells within the matrix address issues traditionally not included in discussions of test validity. The upper-right cell concerns evidence supporting proposed uses of a test; in other words, evidence that the test is relevant and useful for its intended application. This aspect of validity is relevant to instructors' tests since, as with any test, its intended use *must* control the development of the test. How a test is used must be compatible with the use for which it is designed.

Table 3.3
An expanded view of validity

	Test Interpretation	**Test Use**
Evidence	Evidence of what the test measures	Evidence that the test is relevant and useful for its intended application (*requires evidence of what the test measures*)
Consequences	Knowledge of appropriateness of what the test measures in light of society's values (*requires evidence of what the test measures*)	Consequences to society of using the test (*requires* (a) *evidence that the test is relevant and useful for its intended application,* and (b) *knowledge of appropriateness of what the test measures in light of society's values*)

Source: Adapted from "Meaning and Values in Test Validation" by S. Messick, 1989, *Educational Researcher, 18*(2), pp. 5–11.

Recall from Chapter 1 that the purpose of the vast majority of instructors' tests is to assess learners. Typically, this involves a formative or summative assessment. When, for instance, a formative assessment is the anticipated use, the test should help the instructor and learners determine what to do next regarding instruction. With face-to-face instruction, formative assessments are largely informal in nature, such as through the instructor's observations and various interactions with learners. Lorrie Shepard (2000) has an excellent discussion of this aspect of assessment, in which she describes the extensive role of informal assessments. However, when learners are not face to face, informal assessments are greatly diminished. Online tests fortunately can be incorporated into online instruction. Online tests can be set up so that feedback is provided individually as each learner completes a quiz. Online collaborative activities can play an important formative role. Nevertheless, when students are not face to face with the instructor, substitutes for the critical role played by informal assessments need to be established. Summative assessments, in contrast, occur at the end of a unit of instruction. They more typically rely on samples of content. Although online and distance learning involves both formative and summative assessments, compared with face-to-face settings, a greater reliance is going to be placed on summative assessments.

The key point here with both face-to-face and online situations is that the purpose of an assessment, that is, how it will be used, should be clearly in mind when the test is developed. In this sense, preparing an assessment activity is like planning for an important meeting. Not only does one want to prepare for what will happen during the meeting, one also must ensure that what happens during the meeting is heavily influenced by how the results of that meeting will be used.

The lower two cells of Table 3.3 pertain to *consequences* of test interpretation and use. The lower-left cell concerns consequences of test interpretation, specifically, knowledge of the appropriateness of what a test measures in light of society's values. Society's values include what instructors, other content experts, and learners, among others, perceive to be important and unimportant. At all levels of education, it is well known that what instructors and learners judge to be important strongly influences what is learned and what is assessed. As learners in higher education, particularly distance learners, become older and mature, their expectations and values are more developed and play a more significant role in determining the relevance and validity of instruction and assessments. Because of these mature expectations and values, project work and collaborative learning can be particularly effective assessment tools with distance learners. As long as instruction and assessments are consistent with perceived needs, distance learners are very willing partners in activities that are relevant to skills they know are important to achieve.

Likewise, mature learners are very responsive to the consequences of assessments in terms of how they are used. More than younger learners, they are motivated when sound decisions are made from tests. As the matrix associated with Messick's extended view of validity indicates (Table 3.3), the validity of consequences or outcomes associated with the use of assessments depends upon perceived values of what is being assessed that in turn rely on evidence that the assessments appropriately measure the appropriate constructs of learned knowledge.

SUMMARY

Validity pertains to how well a test measures what it is supposed to measure. It is the single most important quality in the development, interpretation, and use of any educational measure.

Validity is an abstraction. Instead of observing validity, we evaluate a variety of evidence pertaining to the interpretation and use of the test. Evidence associated with interpretation is conventionally grouped into construct-, content-, and criterion-related categories.

Criterion-related evidence of validity indicates how well performance on a test correlates with performance on relevant criterion measures external to the test. With instructors' assessments, criterion-related evidence is gathered by observing whether performance on an assessment agrees with other relevant indications of learner performance. In online settings, particularly when learners are at a distance, opportunities for establishing criterion-related evidence are greatly diminished, consequently increasing even further the importance of establishing construct- and content-related evidence.

Construct-related evidence establishes whether a test matches the capabilities or psychological construct that is to be measured. With instructors'

tests, learned knowledge is usually the construct of greatest relevance. Declarative knowledge, procedural knowledge, and problem-solving skills are the dominant types of learned knowledge.

Content-related evidence concerns how well elements of a test relate to the content domain being assessed. A table of specifications and list of performance objectives are two common techniques used to guide the establishment of content-related validity. Content-related evidence is gathered when the test is being developed.

Test validity applies not only to evidence of what the test measures, but also to evidence supporting applications for which the test is to be used. Validity also pertains to the appropriateness of what a test measures and to the consequences that result from use of the test. These dimensions of validity are interrelated. An evaluation of validity often indicates that a test is valid for some, but not all, applications for which it might be used.

ANSWERS: APPLY WHAT YOU ARE LEARNING

3.1 1. Because *information* is involved, learners can be asked to state what they know, for instance state the percentages of numbers above or below the mean, if the distribution is symmetrical; 2. Because *information* is involved, learners can be asked to state the formula, for instance write it out; 3. Because a *rule* is involved, learners need to apply the rule to a previously unused situation, for instance use the formula to compute the mean for a new set of numbers; 4. Because a *concept* is involved, learners need to classify previously unused examples of the concept, such as establishing whether or not an example of overall magnitude of numbers is being illustrated.

3.2 1. 1. 10 questions; 2. 3 questions; 3. 2 questions; 4. 5 questions.

TERMS INTRODUCED IN THIS CHAPTER

Criterion-related evidence: involves establishing how well performance on the test correlates with performance on a relevant criterion outside the test. With standardized tests, statistical correlations are often used. With an instructor's test, qualitative judgments are more common. Performance on the test is correlated with what is observed outside the test, often through informal observations that occur from e-mails, from performance on other projects and other assignments, and through discussions.

Construct-related evidence: involves establishing a link between the underlying construct being measured (knowledge to be learned) and the student performances that will provide visible indicators of what they have learned. Establishing this linkage involves understanding the knowledge to be assessed, identifying the types of capabilities embedded within this knowledge, and (given the types of capabilities involved) determining specific examples of student performance that can legitimately serve as indicators of that knowledge.

Content-related evidence: involves controlling the content of an assessment, usually by outlining its content. Performance objectives, a table of specifications, and performance assessment specifications are three common techniques used to outline the content. After identifying the appropriate performances to be observed through the assessment (see *construct-related evidence*), outlining the content of an assessment helps ensure that the appropriate knowledge and skills will be assessed.

Table of specifications: is an efficient way to outline and thereby control the content of a written test. The table consists of columns that list the content areas that are to be assessed by the test and rows that list the types of capabilities. Cells within the table identify the number of items within each content area associated with the respective types of capabilities.

ENHANCE YOUR UNDERSTANDING

- In a distance learning setting and for a subject area you currently teach or would likely teach, think of specific examples of knowledge you would try to help your learners learn. Try to think of separate examples for each of the following types of capability: information, concept, rule, and problem solving. For each example, describe what you might ask your learners to do to indicate what they have learned. Make sure each description takes into account the nature of the capability being assessed (see Table 2.2 in the previous chapter).

- Think of two specific assessments you might devise as a distance instructor—one that is clearly intended to play a formative role, the other a summative role. These assessments might be written tests, but could be any project or activity through which you observe learner performance. In light of its intended role, address these four questions:

  1. How would you establish what learners would be asked to do within the assessment (think construct-related evidence)?

  2. How would you ensure that the content of the actual assessment conforms to the content implied in your answer to the previous question (think content-related evidence)?

  3. With what could performance on this assessment be correlated to establish criterion-related evidence of validity?

  4. In what way is Messick's expanded view of validity relevant to the assessment?

Contrast the answers you gave to the formative versus summative assessments. Contrast assessments in conventional versus distance learning.

ADDITIONAL READING

Messick, S. (1989b). Validity. In R. L. Linn (Ed.), *Educational measurement* (3rd ed., pp. 13–103). New York: American Council on Education. This chapter provides an extended discussion of test validation, and one of the most frequently cited, beginning with a description of the historical development of concepts of validity.

4

Generalizing Observed Performance to Unobserved Performance

When students are assessed, the instructor observes only a small fraction of what might be observed. A written test incorporates only a portion of applicable items. A project involves completing one of many tasks that the learner might have been asked to perform.

The fact that assessment always involves only a small **sample** of potential observations raises an important question: Would the conclusions drawn based on what was observed be different if what was not observed were included? If, for example, a writing teacher assesses students' proficiency by having them write a paper in response to a prompt, what would happen if the teacher changed the writing prompt? Would students' performance on the writing assessment change? If so, the teacher's assessment of students' writing would not generalize. The conclusions concerning their writing proficiency would be useful only within the narrow context of the writing prompt that the teacher happened to use in the assessment.

This issue of **generalizability** is a sampling issue, not unlike sampling problems associated with **survey research.** When surveys are conducted, such as opinion polls, only a sample of potential respondents is participating. With surveys, a relevant question is whether or not the same results would have been obtained had different respondents been sampled.[1] If substantially

different results would have been obtained, either because the sample was small or because it was unrepresentative, then the usefulness of the survey diminishes dramatically. In contrast to surveys, assessments generally do not sample respondents; usually all learners are expected to participate in the assessment. However, specific content included within an assessment does represent a *sample* of content that potentially could have been used.

Chapter 1 introduced the potential problem that generalizability represents in online assessments. Beginning in the late 1970s and early 1980s, educational researchers began experimenting with written tests administered at computer terminals. Tests were scored immediately at their completion and students were provided feedback, often indicating where they excelled and where further study was necessary. However, results did not generalize very well. Because decisions within each content area were based on a small number of items, feedback reports would change dramatically when a different sample of items was used in a retest, even if students had done nothing to change their level of achievement.

The issue of generalizability creates a potentially serious problem. If a learner is judged proficient when asked to complete one task, but would have been judged not proficient had the assessment involved a different but equally appropriate measure of the same skill, one might as well flip coins to establish whether learners are proficient. Because the usefulness of assessments is substantially reduced if observations fail to generalize, it is important for us to be aware of

---

[1]With opinion surveys, the issue of whether the same results would have been obtained had the sample involved other respondents is different from the concern of whether the survey includes appropriate, well-worded questions. The appropriateness of questions is a very important issue in its own right, and is akin to validity concerns addressed in Chapter 3.

the conditions that reduce generalizability. This chapter helps you achieve two skills:

- Identify why observations often do not generalize
- Identify techniques for improving generalizability

Generalizability is a significant issue with all assessments, regardless of their format or context. However, resulting problems can be particularly acute when learners are at a distance because instructors do not have the same opportunity to interact casually with students and detect content sampling problems inherent in the tests. Discussions of the statistical aspects of generalizability are available elsewhere[2]; our focus here is on establishing a basic understanding of the nature of the problem, along with some practical techniques that reduce problems with generalizability.

WHY OBSERVATIONS DO NOT GENERALIZE

Observations within an assessment fail to generalize whenever there is some form of **inconsistency** influencing students' scores on the assessment. Identifying the sources of these inconsistencies is a good strategy for understanding where the problems are. Table 4.1 summarizes these sources and provides an example of each source of inconsistency.

Inconsistencies Between Tasks

Inconsistencies between tasks pertain to changes in scores that occur when learners are asked to do something different. These inconsistencies occur for several reasons. We will look at two that are particularly important: inconsistencies among test items that supposedly measure the same skill,

---

[2]Brennan (1992) developed a printed instructional module that introduces the statistical aspects of generalizability theory. Another way at looking at the inconsistencies within test scores is to compute reliability coefficients. Frisbie (1988) prepared an instructional module that addresses that approach. Both modules are available online at *http://ncme.org/pubs/items.cfm*.

and inconsistencies among alternative skills in the same content domain.

Inconsistencies Among Test Items That Supposedly Measure the Same Skill. Here is an example. When multiplying numbers, which of these do you find easier: multiplying numbers by 7 or 8, or multiplying the same numbers by 0 or 5? Most people find multiplication by 0s and 5s to be easier. In fact, students tend to score higher on a multiplication test that happens to include items involving 0 and 5, even though one might consider all the multiplication items to be measuring the same skill.

This type of inconsistency occurs with many skills. For instance, some quadratic equations are easier to factor than others. Which equations happen to be included in the test influences students' scores. Scores on a biology test involving terminology related to human anatomy are similarly affected by the selection of terms that happen to be included in the test. This phenomenon occurs on virtually every test; exchanging items that for all practical purposes are measuring the same skill changes the scores that students receive. This inconsistency among items that supposedly measure the same skill probably is something you expect, and some might consider it to be a natural characteristic of tests. However, this inconsistency can and often does pose a serious problem. For instance, Um (1995) examined a widely used high-stakes writing test where students provide a writing sample in response to a prompt. She found that by changing the prompt to which students' responded, significant changes occurred with respect to who passed the test. Yen (1997) found similar results within high-stakes tests in other content areas.

Learners perform inconsistently on items that supposedly measure the same skill, for a variety of reasons. One is that the learner's interest or prior experiences vary with respect to the task used in the assessment. Another is that many test items pose vague questions resulting in inconsistency in what students perceive is being asked. This results in inconsistencies in the

Table 4.1
Sources of inconsistency within assessments

Source	Description	Examples
Inconsistencies between tasks:		
Among test items that supposedly measure the same skill	Students' scores will likely change if different subsets of items, that for all practical purposes measure the same skill, are used	If one were to ask students to define a different subset of terms in a psychology test, scores would likely change If students are asked to demonstrate writing skills by responding to a prompt, their scores would likely change were a different prompt used
Among alternative skills within the same domain	Students' performance on one assessment does not generalize well to performance on another assessment when the two assessments measure different components of the same complex skill	Students who design the best page within a website for displaying products that are for sale are different from the students who design the best page for placing orders for the products, although both are components of the same complex task of designing a website Students who are best at describing the effects of high fuel prices on the economy are different from the students who are best at describing the effects high interest rates have on the economy, although both are components of the same complex task of understanding the effects of market forces on the economy
Inconsistencies between raters	Different raters vary in the scores they assign to a learner's performance	Different instructors reading the same students' answers to an essay question about ways to conserve gasoline will tend to assign different scores Different raters scoring the same musicians' performance on piano will tend to assign different ratings
Inconsistencies between occasions	Students' earlier performance is inconsistent from their later performance	Students' proficiency with converting temperature from Celsius to Fahrenheit, shortly after they learn this skill, is inconsistent from their proficiency when they later need this skill to interpret climate data from different countries

responses they provide. Still another reason is that with some test formats, learners often guess at the correct answer, and their guesses are inconsistently lucky.

Each of these examples is concerned with inconsistencies among test items that supposedly measure the same skill. The items are thought to be, for all practical purposes, interchangeable. If the skill being assessed involves multiplying single-digit numbers, multiplying 3 × 7 is thought to involve the same skill as multiplying 6 × 9. However, individuals who correctly complete the first multiplication problem may be somewhat different from those who successfully answer the second. If the skill involves the ability to write a persuasive paper in response to a prompt provided on the test, the various common-interest writing prompts one might use to assess this skill are often assumed to be interchangeable, even though altering the prompt is known to change which test takers write the most persuasive paper.

Inconsistencies Among Alternative Skills within the Same Domain.   The complexities of skills that are taught within most content areas contribute to inconsistency within assessments. We often combine distinct skills into a single performance objective or a single content domain to make instruction and assessment manageable. Alternatively, we might be unable to subdivide a complex skill into fully meaningful subparts. A learner who is proficient in one aspect of the skill may be less proficient in another. The particular set of activities sampled by an assessment affects the instructor's judgment of the learner's proficiency.

Solano-Flores and others (1997) present an interesting example of this. They describe a performance assessment used with fifth and sixth graders while investigating the use of performance assessments in science education. These children were learning methods of *observation,* the technique scientists use to create and test hypotheses when the variable under investigation cannot be manipulated. These researchers devised six separate performance assessments to determine whether the children were learning this skill. Each performance assessment involved making observations related to daytime astronomy, where the Sun is used to better understand astronomical properties. Children used a flashlight to represent the Sun and a globe to represent the Earth. In each of the performance assessments, children placed sticky miniature "towers" onto the globe and, using shadows created by the towers from the "sunlight," made and tested their hypotheses. In one performance assessment, for instance, children were shown a map like the one in Figure 4.1 that showed the shadows created by two towers, one north of the other. They were also shown the shadow of a third tower, away from the map, and through observation were required to establish where on the globe a tower with that shadow must be

Figure 4.1
The shadows of two towers viewed from above

located. Another one of the assessments required children to determine differences in how shadows change or move during the day in the Northern versus Southern Hemispheres.

Although all six tasks involved procedures one uses to make scientific observations, these procedures were never thought to be interchangeable. Locating an object on Earth based on the length and direction of its sunlight shadow involves a different procedure than that used to determine how shadows behave as the day progresses in the Northern versus Southern Hemispheres. As might be expected, they found that children who did best on any one of the performance assessments were different from those who did best on the other assessments. That is, the children's performance did not generalize, even though the six assessments were legitimate measures of the same problem-solving skill. Actually, these six performance assessments were homogeneous with respect to the content domain being assessed. Had the performance assessments not been limited to one specialized area within astronomy but instead reflected the broader range of science content for which observation is a method of inquiry, the generalizability of the children's performance might have been even lower.

For the most part, readers of this book are involved in the assessment of learners older than fifth and sixth graders. However, the finding of this particular study keeps showing up in research: learners' performance on one assessment does not generalize well to performance on another assessment when the two assessments measure different components of the same complex skill. For instance, students in a meteorology class who produce the best forecasts in the Great Lakes region of the United States will likely be different from the ones who produce the best forecasts in a mountainous region. Students in a business course who create the best business plans for a new restaurant franchise may not be the ones who would develop the best plans for a new computer-repair franchise. Unfortunately from an assessment perspective, learners perform

inconsistently on different skills within a complex domain. We say it is unfortunate because, had a different but equally legitimate task been used for a given assessment, quite possibly the conclusions we made as to which students are proficient would have changed.

In distance education, instructors often assess students' achievement relying heavily on papers, projects, and various other activities involving products. Each of these activities in essence is a performance assessment. In most cases, the instructor could defensibly have used a different project or focused on different tasks within the same projects. The fact that different activities and tasks could have been used means that the question is highly relevant as to whether the performances the instructor observed would have generalized had other equally defensible tasks been used for the assessment.

Similarly, when written tests are administered online, in most cases alternate test items could have been used to assess the same content. It is now more cost effective than it was in the late 1970s and early 1980s to use computers to administer tests and provide students with immediate feedback. However, the same issue of generalizability exists now as it did then: Would students' performance and likewise the feedback that is automatically given at the end of a test be the same had students answered a different sample of test items? In part because of the small number of items included in each test, students' performance likely would not generalize.

In summary, inconsistencies between tasks represent one important source of inconsistencies within assessments. This source of inconsistency appears in two forms. The first involves test items that *are thought to be interchangeable* even though learners do not perform the same from one item to another. For instance, we often find that students who can change one sentence from present tense to past tense are different from those who can perform the same task for a different sentence. The second form of inconsistency between tasks involves alternate tasks within the same complex domain that *are not thought to be interchangeable.* For instance, when working with a word processor, the format>paragraph feature contains a large variety of noninterchangeable features. Using format>paragraph to control the indentation of paragraphs is not thought to be the same task as using format>paragraph to make sure lines within a given paragraph are not split between two pages. Within this or any other complex domain, learners who successfully perform one task tend to be different from those who successfully perform an alternate task from the same domain.

Inconsistencies Between Raters

Subjectivity is often present in the *scoring* of assessments, particularly essay tests and papers, but also assessments like class projects. When subjectivity is involved, raters differ in the scores they assign to a learner's performance. Because a learner's performance on an assessment is completed prior to its being scored, the learner's performance certainly is not changing. Therefore, variability in the scores raters assign is due to something other than variability in the learner's performance. If a learner's performance does not change but the scores change as a result of inconsistencies between raters, something other than learner proficiency is influencing the scores. This is undesirable. With online assessments, usually only one person scores each learner's performance; however, this only hides the inconsistency that would become evident if multiple raters were involved.

When there is inconsistency between raters, we are saying that scores assigned by one rater do not fully generalize to those assigned by another. One way to improve generalizability across raters is to use multiple raters and to average their scores. Using multiple raters often is not practical. Fortunately, research has shown that, *when a scoring plan is carefully developed and implemented,* one obtains almost the same generalizability with one rater as would be obtained with multiple raters (Shavelson, Baxter, & Pine, 1992). In later chapters, we will look at ways to develop effective scoring plans.

4.1   Apply What You Are Learning

These questions concern generalizability. Some will require you to anticipate situations beyond those we have discussed. See how well you can answer each question.

1. If only one person is involved in scoring an assessment, there will be no apparent inconsistency between raters. Does this mean inconsistency between raters is not a problem as long as only one rater scores the students' performances?
2. Which of these options provides better generalizability? a) Using five test items, each of which is very similar to the other four; or b) Using five test items, each of which measures a different aspect of the skill being assessed
3. Does using a smaller or larger number of test items improve generalizability?
4. Which provides better generalizability? a) Asking all learners to answer the same five essay items; or b) Allowing learners to select from among 10 essay items the 5 that they will answer

Answers can be found at the end of the chapter.

Inconsistencies Between Earlier and Later Occasions

Inconsistencies are a problem only if generalizations are being made. Inconsistency between earlier and later occasions is a case in point. On the one hand, when a student begins a new unit of instruction, the instructor usually anticipates that the student's performance will be different from or inconsistent with performance that will be observed after instruction. For this reason, an instructor does not make generalizations about a learner's achievement after instruction based on what might have been observed before instruction. At the conclusion of instruction, an instructor assesses learner achievement. Because the instructor is not making a generalization, this inconsistency between earlier and later occasions is not a concern.

On the other hand, once a unit of instruction is completed, assessments of that content are often no longer continued. Because of problems with retention, learners' later performances will likely be inconsistent with their performances at the conclusion of instruction. This inconsistency *does* represent a problem if these skills are a prerequisite to later instruction. This inconsistency also represents a problem if learners are expected to apply these skills later within their profession after completing the course.

TECHNIQUES FOR IMPROVING GENERALIZABILITY

To improve how well the results of an assessment generalize, one must anticipate the conditions that cause inconsistency and then take actions to control those conditions. For example, the complexity within the content domain being taught is one major cause of inconsistency. A learner's score on a given test is influenced by the sample of specific tasks from the domain that are included on that test. One can generalize from the learner's performance on the test only to the extent that the test *adequately samples* relevant skills within the content domain being measured. One can improve assessments by increasing the number of observations included in the assessment (for instance by increasing the number of test items) and by improving the representativeness of skills measured by the test.

Four techniques for improving the generalizability of test scores are described here. The first includes a series of actions that can be used to improve the quality of learner performance observations. The second involves improvements in how a learner's performance is scored or judged. The third technique involves increasing the number of observations included in a test. The fourth is concerned with providing a sufficient sample of diverse tasks within the assessment.

Technique 1: Improving the Quality of Observations

Later chapters describe in detail a variety of techniques used to improve the quality of observations,

such as those that help establish more concise tasks for learners to complete. Chapters 7 and 8 describe specific techniques that apply to written tests, including those that involve completion, essay, and multiple-choice questions. Chapter 11 describes how to improve observations of learner performance obtained through project work. Chapter 14 addresses the same issue within the context of online collaborative learning.

Ambiguities in an assessment are a major threat to generalizability. When presented with a vague task, learners' reactions and responses are inconsistent. For instance, if an essay item states, "Describe the major distinctions between Yahoo! and Google," some test takers will describe differences in how the content of these websites is organized, others will address differences in the emphases of their content, and still others will discuss differences in how results of an Internet search are presented within each site.

Ambiguities within items tend to be more problematic with online tests. Although never desirable, ambiguities within classroom tests administered with the instructor present provides students the option of asking for clarity. In online settings, that interaction usually occurs only after a student completes the test. In a classroom setting, one can announce a correction to a test during its administration if it is absolutely necessary, although students usually dislike the interruption. With online tests software often disallows any change to a test or purges responses of students who have already completed the test if a change is made to any of its items.

Ambiguities within items can be reduced by a variety of means, depending on the test format. For example, with multiple-choice items, using options that are parallel in content can substantially reduce ambiguity. Particular words are problematic in multiple-choice items, and these can be avoided. Completion items perform much better if only a homogeneous set of words represent a correct response. We will look at techniques that help achieve this goal. With assessments involving projects, the specific nature of the product to be produced must be established and clearly communicated. Conciseness can work against the flexibility that is an asset of some test formats, such as essays and performance assessments. Our goal will be to determine which conditions must be specified or controlled while providing learners with flexibility in how to meet those conditions.

Technique 2: Improving the Scoring of Performances

Scoring plans are vital to the generalizability of essay questions and other subjectively scored assessments. Certainly an instructor would not produce an online multiple-choice test without also establishing for the computer how to score the items. Even though essays are much more difficult to score, many instructors construct essay items and sometimes even read answers without creating a scoring plan. In Chapters 7 and 11, we will look at procedures for developing effective scoring plans for essays and performance assessments.

Technique 3: Increasing the Number of Observations

We have noted that, with survey research, increasing the sample size decreases inconsistencies and consequently increases generalizability of results. With physical measurements also, increasing the number of observations is an effective way to improve consistency. For instance, when one uses a micrometer to measure the thickness of an object, multiple observations are obtained by repeatedly loosening and retightening the instrument's screw. These observations are then averaged to obtain one best measurement. Similarly, the pH of soil is established from several samples. With physical measurements, the degree of consistency among the repeated measurements is often used as evidence of the reliability of those measurements.

Increasing the number of observations likewise decreases inconsistency in educational

measures and consequently increases their generalizability. There are a number of ways to do this. One is to simply include more items in a test, which may be more practical when written tests are administered online as opposed to in the classroom, for instance. Another way is to have more than one person score each assessment when subjectivity is involved. Still another is to combine the observations of individual learners to obtain an overall assessment of performance for a *group* of learners rather than try to assess the proficiency of individual learners.

Increasing the number of observations improves generalizability because it tends to average out the randomness that is inherent in scores. For instance, including several multiple-choice items in a test averages out the difference in gains made from learners' guessing. Including multiple tasks within a project when the project is being used to assess student proficiency increases the generalizability of that assessment. Using multiple readers to score an essay test averages out the inconsistency among persons scoring the test, although a carefully implemented scoring plan is also effective at addressing this problem. Likewise, estimates of how the class as a whole is performing generalize better than do estimates of how individual learners in the class are performing. In each instance, consistency of the measure is improved by increasing the number of observations.

Technique 4: Expanding the Breadth of Observations

Another effective way to help ensure that performance will generalize to unobserved tasks is to expand the breadth of observations. Instead of using homogeneous items, use diverse items that broadly sample the domain. This is easier to do with completion, multiple-choice, and true-false formats because a test can include many items. Broadly sampling the domain is more difficult with essays and performance assessments. With essays, an effective way to increase the number of items is to *decrease* the scope of each item to allow an increase in the total number of items included in the test.

Expanding the breadth of observations is particularly problematic with performance assessments. Because of the high costs of performance assessments relative to written tests, there is a natural tendency to avoid reassessing a learner's performance of a particular skill in more than a single setting. However, the learner's performance observed within a single setting will probably not generalize to other settings.

4.2   Apply What You Are Learning

For each pair, indicate which strategy (A or B) improves generalizability.

1. A. Asking learners to perform a large number of tasks
   B. Asking learners to perform a small number of tasks
2. A. Based on an assessment, inferring what individual learners can do
   B. Based on an assessment, inferring what the class as a whole can do
3. A. Being flexible about which qualities will be scored in each learner's answer
   B. Being structured about which qualities will be scored in each learner's answer
4. A. Within the content domain being assessed, asking a learner to perform several very similar tasks
   B. Within the content domain being assessed, asking a learner to perform several diverse tasks

Answers can be found at the end of the chapter.

SUMMARY

Generalizability is the degree to which learner performances that are observed generalize to performances that are not observed. Only a small fraction of potential learner performances can be observed within an assessment. However, to be useful, assessments must be able to generalize beyond what has been observed. Generalizability is particularly an issue within distance learning settings or any online assessments where daily interaction with learners is restricted.

An instructor will have problems generalizing from assessments whenever certain types of inconsistencies are present in the performance being observed. These inconsistencies come from different sources. There are inconsistencies between earlier and later measures of learner performance, inconsistencies between raters, and inconsistencies across tasks that could have been included in an assessment.

Not all sources of inconsistency are relevant to a particular assessment. A source of inconsistency is problematic only if a generalization is involved. For instance, a learner's performance always changes over time. When an instructor assesses learners following instruction, the instructor is not making a generalization from assessments that occurred before instruction. On the other hand, if learned skills are prerequisite to later instruction and learners are not reassessed over the prerequisite skills, the instructor is making a generalization. In this latter situation, inconsistencies that occur over time restrict the instructor's ability to generalize.

An instructor can employ procedures that are known to improve generalizability. These are detailed in subsequent chapters.

ANSWERS: APPLY WHAT YOU ARE LEARNING

4.1 1. No, inconsistency is still a problem. The presence of just one rater hides potential inconsistency. However, *if* the scoring plan is carefully developed, the scores assigned by just one rater can be almost as consistent as those obtained by averaging the scores assigned by multiple raters; 2. Using five items that measure *diverse* aspects of the skill improves generalizability. Using our analogy to an opinion survey, which of the following samples will provide results that more likely generalize to the population: a sample of homogeneous respondents, such as individuals with very similar incomes; or heterogeneous respondents, such as respondents with diverse incomes? More diverse content samples within a content domain generalize better, just like more heterogeneous survey samples generalize better to the survey population; 3. Like opinion surveys, a larger number of observations generalizes better than a smaller number. This is true whether referring to number of test items or number of raters; 4. Requiring all learners to answer the same questions will generalize better. Given a choice, learners will tend to answer the items for which they know the answers. This will provide a less representative sample of performance than if learners are required to answer a specified set of five questions. Using our research survey analogy, which method will provide results that will more likely generalize to the population: carefully sampling five individuals and obtaining a 100% response rate, or carefully sampling 10 individuals but using responses from only 5 individuals who chose to respond?

4.2 1. A; 2. B. Increasing the number of tasks improves generalizability. This can be accomplished simply by using a large number of questions or by making inferences to the class as a whole rather than to individual learners; 3. B. Using a carefully structured scoring plan when scoring learners' answers considerably reduces error. With essays and product assessments, a structured scoring plan specifies what qualities will be scored, but provides learners flexibility in how they will demonstrate those qualities; 4. B. Selecting diverse rather than highly similar tasks from a domain to include in a test facilitates generalizability. The use of diverse tasks increases the chance that learner performances that were not observed are similar in nature to performances that were observed.

TERMS INTRODUCED IN THIS CHAPTER

Survey research: encompasses a broad area in which questionnaires are used to determine attitudes or opinions of people concerning a particular topic. For instance, survey research is used by manufacturers to evaluate consumers' awareness and opinions of their products, by politicians to determine constituents' attitudes towards various policies, and by the news media to examine the public's attitudes toward particular politicians and their actions. Surveys typically involve carefully selected samples of people.

Sample: refers to a subset from a larger population, usually with the intent of making inferences from the smaller sample to the larger population. A sample of respondents is typically involved in survey research; samples of approximately 1000 respondents are common. When carefully selected, samples of this size allow accurate inferences to the population being sampled. With assessments, the content being assessed is sampled rather than people. For instance, all students (rather than a sample of students) will complete a written test, but the test will include only a sample of items that could be drawn from the content area being assessed. The number of test items sampled from a particular content area is typically very small—far smaller than the sample of approximately 1000 people often used in survey research. The consequence is that scores on tests and other assessments often do not generalize very well to the scores that would have been obtained had a larger sample of items been included in the assessment.

Generalizability: is concerned with inconsistencies between different samples of student proficiency that are or could be included in an assessment. If the sample of students' performance that is observed will not generalize to other samples that could be observed, then conclusions are useful only within the narrow context of the observation.

Inconsistency: in assessments, as the name suggests, is a change in students' performance that is unpredictable and is caused by factors unrelated to students' level of achievement. These inconsistencies are related to sampling error. Major sources of inconsistency include inconsistencies among tasks that get included in a test and inconsistencies among raters when assessments have to be subjectively scored.

ENHANCE YOUR UNDERSTANDING

- At the beginning of this chapter, in the section titled "Why Observations Do Not Generalize," the following sources of inconsistencies are described:

    1. Inconsistencies between tasks involving test items that supposedly measure the same skill
    2. Inconsistencies between tasks involving alternative skills in the same content domain
    3. Inconsistencies between raters
    4. Inconsistencies between earlier and later occasions

List at least one example for each of the four. If possible, use specific examples from recent assessments administered to you or ones you administered to learners.

ADDITIONAL READING

Brennan, R. L. (1992). Generalizability theory. *Educational Measurement: Issues and Practice, 11*(4), 27–34. This instructional module introduces the conceptual and methodological aspects of generalizability theory.

Crocker, L., & Algina, J. (1986). *Introduction to classical and modern test theory.* Belmont, CA: Wadsworth. This book provides an excellent introduction to measurement theory, including discussion of procedures for estimating reliability.

Oosterhof, A. (2001). *Classroom applications of educational measurement* (3rd ed.). Upper Saddle River, NJ: Merrill/Prentice Hall. Chapter 5 discusses inconsistencies from the perspective of reliability, including the effect these inconsistencies have on the validity of an assessment.

PART II

Determining an Assessment Plan

Fundamental to the design of assessment is determining what to assess and how the assessment will be interpreted and used.

Determining what to assess in part is established by knowing whether training or education is involved. Instruction in most settings involves a combination of training and education. With training, the goal is for learners to be able to perform a particular task, often with a high degree of proficiency and consistency. Skills are narrowly defined and assessments are comprehensive. With education, the goal is to provide learners a framework for further learning and from which unanticipated problems can be solved. Assessments involve broader domains of knowledge, and issues as to how the assessments should sample those domains become highly relevant. Chapter 5 discusses how within an online environment to select content when training versus education is involved. The chapter also addresses other practical considerations including factors that influence the confidence one can have in assessment results and constraints imposed by the format of the test.

Determining how to interpret an assessment depends on the reference that will be used for that interpretation. With online settings, norm-referenced and criterion-referenced are the most common. We give particular attention to knowing when each of these two references is preferable, and conditions that facilitates the use of each reference.

Determining how to use an assessment for the most part involves anticipating formative versus summative evaluations. When used formatively, assessments are embedded within instruction. Their purpose it to monitor learning in order to determine whether instruction should continue, should be modified, or should cease. In face-to-face settings, this is accomplished largely through informal interactions with students. Online, a variety of options exists such as discussion board interactions, e-mail communications, and feedback embedded within assessments. Summative assessments occur at the conclusion of instruction such as at the end of a unit. They are used to certify achievement and typically provide the basis for assigning course grades.

Chapter 5 concludes with a discussion of procedures for assigning course grades. This includes selecting what assessments grades should be based on, determining the weight to be given each assessment, and setting performance standards.

5

Determining What to Assess

Determining what to assess is always a fundamental issue in any instructional situation, whether the context be online or in another setting. One fairly obvious consideration is the need to establish what learners must know and, consequently, what learning must be verified through each assessment. We will observe that this depends in part on whether learning a particular skill is considered training or education. With **training,** the goal is for learners to be able to perform a particular task, often with a high degree of proficiency and consistency. With **education,** the goal is to provide learners with a framework for further learning from which unanticipated problems can be solved.

As a result, with training, skills to be assessed are more narrowly defined than with education where assessments involve broader domains of knowledge. With these broader domains, it usually is necessary to select samples of knowledge and skills to assess, depending upon their criticality. It will also depend upon practical considerations, such as the number of skills that can be tested within a limited time and the other resources that may be available for assessment.

Some other practical issues indirectly related to resources also influence what is to be assessed. One is the degree of confidence one needs when interpreting the results of an assessment; higher confidence requires a greater number of observations. With a given amount of resources, the number of skills to be assessed must be limited if confidence in knowing what students can or

cannot do is to be high. Tolerating lower confidence allows the assessment of more skills.

Another factor indirectly related to resources pertains to the types of capabilities that are to be assessed and, consequently, the test formats that can be used within the assessments. For instance, item formats commonly used with written tests can measure declarative and procedural knowledge. However, these item formats cannot measure a student's ability to apply that knowledge in true problem-solving situations in which the specific means of achieving a solution is variable and has not been learned in advance. Performance assessments, including those that involve project work and homework assignments, have the potential to measure a learner's ability to solve problems. However, performance assessments usually require more time and resources to complete than do written tests. Consequently, as student evaluations rely more heavily on performance assessments, the number of skills that can be evaluated is reduced.

Because of differences in how one assesses training versus education, and practical considerations such as the level of confidence one wishes to have in the assessment results, determining what to assess is a complex issue involving compromises. Ultimately, the instructor relies heavily on professional judgment to decide what to teach and what to assess. This chapter helps instructors and instructional designers make these judgments by addressing two goals:

- Using the distinction between training and education to help establish what to assess

- Recognizing the implications that practical considerations have on limiting what can be assessed, especially in online and distance education settings

ESTABLISHING WHAT TO ASSESS WITHIN TRAINING AND EDUCATION

Our first consideration pertains to the types of skills emphasized in training versus education. Then we address procedures for selecting specific content to be included within an assessment.

Types of Skills Emphasized in Training and Education

Content of what learners must know is influenced by whether training or education is involved. A unit of instruction might consist exclusively of training or instruction, but more typically, elements of both are present.

Training is the process of developing competence in a set of specific skills in order to guarantee consistent and successful performance by individuals attempting to complete a particular task. For example, learning to drive a car involves training. A driver must achieve the set of skills that will ensure correct and safe operation of a vehicle. Assessments are used to determine the extent to which competence in each critical skill has been reached.

Other examples include training airplane pilots, department store clerks, and bank tellers. In schools, some of the basic computational procedures students learn in math involve training. Pre-med students are trained to identify parts of the human anatomy. Musicians are trained in how to play instruments. In each of these examples, specific tasks to be performed are identified and often levels of competency are set along with criteria for measuring each task. With training, learners are expected to demonstrate proficiency in each skill. If adequate proficiency is not reached, remedial or repeat training likely continues until the targeted performance level has been achieved.

Education involves broader domains of knowledge and attitude that are needed to function in society, to qualify for certain types of work, or to participate in further education. Unlike training, education does not and cannot anticipate even the majority of situations in which learned knowledge will be applied, but instead provides a foundation for a range of situations. For instance, prospective instructional designers enrolled in a course concerned with online assessment will learn only a fraction of the skills relevant to designing and using assessments. Most skills used by architects, engineers, writers, scientists, teachers, and parents are learned through education.

When training is involved, typically every skill and often every application of each skill are assessed. When skills are substantial in number and sophistication, training and assessments are broken into segments. Certainly, that is the case when training pilots, professional musicians, and other highly skilled professionals.

More so than with education, skills associated with training tend to include extensive motor skills. This is the case, for instance, with learning how to use a chemical balance or execute a golf swing. In fact, the assessment of skills and the training itself often incorporate simulation exercises or "hands-on" experiences. Even though declarative and procedural knowledge are involved in training, the design of instruction may focus heavily or even exclusively on the behaviors associated with a successful performance rather than the underlying cognitive skills. "Overlearning" is often used to ensure the automatic application of important concepts and rules. For example, pilots flying aircraft and surgeons diagnosing the cause of symptoms often must respond quickly, not taking time to analyze what conceptual knowledge and skills are needed to respond to, and solve, an immediate critical problem.

Education also involves declarative and procedural knowledge, but because the content domain being learned is broad, only a sampling of content associated with the domain is learned, and a small portion of that which is learned is actually assessed. Different instructors and even different students working with a given instructor will focus on different samples of content from a given domain.

In part, because only samples of content can be addressed, education must also include what we have referred to as *problem-solving* skills. We have define a problem as when one has established a goal but has not yet identified a means for reaching that goal. Problem solving is the process of establishing a means of reaching that goal. In situations for which training is applicable, one learns a procedure for handling each situation that is critical. Drivers of automobiles and pilots of aircraft usually do not want, and often cannot take time, to discover a means for reaching a goal. Training is intended to provide proficiency with all procedures that are essential to success. Education provides not only knowledge of information and procedures, but also strategies for solving unanticipated problems and a means of evaluating alternate strategies.

The distinction between training and education is relevant to both face-to-face and online settings, although the resulting implications have both similarities and differences. For instance, assessments in education sample but a fraction of the knowledge to be learned. Both face-to-face and online instructors will try to help learners generalize from skills assessed to the broader domain of skills not included in the assessment. Face-to-face instructors can more easily do this through interactive dialog with learners. Online instructors, when administering tests that are automatically scored by the computer, can provide written feedback immediately at the conclusion of the test. The face-to-face instructor has a greater interactive advantage. However, the more immediate feedback available online means that this feedback can build on what students had and still have in mind when answering items on the test. Feedback from a test administered in a face-to-face setting normally occurs hours or even days after the test is administered. By then, students have forgotten much of the reasoning they used during the test.

Selecting Content to Be Assessed When Training Is Involved

To select content where formal training is involved, a formal task analysis is used, particularly when

safety and other high costs influence the choice of skills to be learned. Task analysis is the process of breaking a complex performance into its component parts and establishing how these components function with each other. A task analysis is used, for instance, when designing instruction for training military personnel. Task analysis is similarly used in manufacturing to establish skills needed to operate various machines. Because of the significant financial savings that can be realized, task analysis is often used by large retailers to select skills that service employees will learn.

With the instructional situations that most readers of this book are likely to face, training is used for only a subset of the skills students are expected to learn. The remaining skills, although important, provide a foundation for later learning or for solving problems that cannot be fully addressed or anticipated during instruction. Instruction related to the latter skills would be considered education. For instance, instruction related to learning a computer programming language involves both training and education. Certain programming skills such as basic language commands used to receive input and write output are comprehensively taught and fully assessed. Other skills such as strategies for writing efficient and understandable computer code are given considerable emphasis, but cannot be taught comprehensively when students are learning a programming language. Therefore, the latter skills involve education rather than training, and consequently only a sample of skills related to programming strategies end up being assessed. On the other hand, students' ability to use common output commands involves training and often is fully examined.

Rather than using a formal task analysis, though, skills to be learned through training in these situations are established through professional judgment by individuals qualified to make these decisions. The individual might work alone, for instance, when one instructor designs a course. Alternatively, content might be established collaboratively, such as through a committee process.

Committees are typically used to establish professional standards for licensure exams. A committee will often incorporate input from consultants and conduct hearings through which stakeholders provide input. However, the established standards and resulting exams often blur the distinction between training and education. This is the case with certification exams for accountants. For instance, accountants are *trained* in how to use specific tax forms, but are *educated* on how to formulate audit objectives. A similar blurring of the distinction between knowledge gained through training and through education is likely to occur when a commission establishes state education standards for public schools. Without a careful delineation between training and education, the content of the exam becomes a set of skills in its own right for which students are trained. That is, considerable emphasis is placed on teaching to specific skills included in the test, separate from and, in some cases, substituting for helping learners to acquire an education.

In online instructional settings, the instructor has an advantage, in part, because any given assessment need not represent a **high-stakes comprehensive examination.** It is feasible to rely upon numerous assessments, each of which can be focused with respect to both content covered and purpose of the test. When assessments occur in classrooms, they tend to compete for instructional time. Although decreasing time spent on assessments provides more time for instruction, it also increases the stakes for each test and blurs the distinction between training and education.

In the more typical settings that involve online instruction, skills for which training is relevant are established through professional judgment, often by the instructor working alone. The instructor essentially identifies the core skills that all students must fully master to be successful. For instance, online instructors would expect their students to be adequately trained with certain computer skills, even if these skills were considered prerequisites that students should achieve prior to entering the course. These computer skills might include locating information on the web with a search engine, and creating documents using word processing software. If these were considered prerequisite skills, the instructor could indicate as much in the syllabus and expect students to assess their own proficiency. Or the instructor could formally verify that students have achieved these skills, and provide a means for gaining proficiency if need be. Either way, these computer skills would be an example of training, with every student's proficiency on each skill established through some kind of assessment.

When instruction involves training, it usually is not necessary to assess every instance in which the skill might be applied. Incorporating authenticity within the assessment may actually prevent or make impractical such exhaustive testing. For example, with geography, an elementary school teacher might consider knowing the names of the 50 states to be a skill in which students should be trained. One way students could demonstrate this proficiency would be to simply list from memory all 50 state names. An alternative and more **authentic assessment** would be for the teacher to provide a list that included familiar and unfamiliar city names along with the names of a significant *sample* of the 50 states. Students would be asked to identify the subset of names within the list that are state names. When assessing training, it is appropriate to thoroughly assess every skill; however, only a sample of instances in which each is applied need to be included within most assessments.

Similarly, when assessing a pilot's ability to land an airplane, the assessment would include a sample rather than all possible landing scenarios. When assessing a sales clerk's ability to conduct a cash transaction, the assessment would include a sample rather than all possible cash transactions. The size of the sample has to be large enough to provide adequate **confidence** with the assessment, an issue we address later in this chapter. All assessments involve samples of a task.

When training is involved, every skill being learned is assessed (although only a sample of possible applications of each skill may be assessed). With education, only a sample of skills to be learned is usually assessed. A second important distinction we have noted is that, with training, focus is on the specific behavior the learner is expected to perform. That behavior might be using a web search engine, filling in a tax form, landing an aircraft, or conducting a cash transaction. The underlying cognitive skills tend to be minimized. But with education, the cognitive skills, including the type of capabilities involved, are central to the development of an assessment. As with training, these cognitive skills—what a person knows or is thinking—cannot be directly observed by another person. But any of a number of behaviors associated with a particular skill might be relevant when this learned knowledge has to be applied. Therefore, with education, it is not sufficient to verify that a particular behavior can be performed. Instead, one must assess the underlying knowledge. The assessments must ask learners to perform a specific behavior that provides a good *indication* of what the learner knows or is thinking. When education is involved and we select content for our assessments, the selection of tasks that provide indirect observations of samples of knowledge becomes our focus.

Selecting Content to Be Assessed When Education Is Involved

In schools and colleges, most instruction is treated as education rather than training. Each course covers many topics with individual topics so broad that it often can be said, "One could write a book about that topic!" When topics covered by a course are that expansive, then certainly only a sample of content related to the topic can be addressed within the course, and education rather than training is involved.

In education, instruction and assessment are goal driven. Goals are fairly broad statements of target outcomes. The bulleted lists early in the chapters in this book are goal statements. Goals usually are established collaboratively, working at least informally with others within the content area.

An example of an instructional goal related to material addressed in this book is being able to electronically receive project work from students enrolled in an online course and to provide written feedback. In the discussion that follows, we will use this goal to illustrate how one selects content to be assessed when education rather than training is involved. Selecting the content can be thought of as involving the three steps presented in Figure 5.1.

Step 1: Select a Focus within the Goal. As with most goals, being able to electronically receive student work and provide feedback incorporates many skills and considerable content. This amount of content would be beyond what is practical to cover, particularly given that any course would also include a number of other goals. Therefore, some kind of focus must be given to this and every other instructional goal

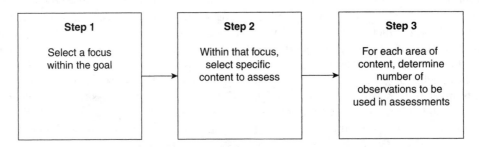

Figure 5.1
Steps for selecting content to assess when education rather than training is involved

associated with a course. The focus might be on students submitting assignments as e-mail attachments, with the instructor providing feedback to each student through an e-mail response. Alternately, the focus might be on working in an environment provided by an online course management system such as Blackboard to both receive students' uploaded files and respond electronically. A third possible focus, and the one we will use in our illustration, is a hybrid arrangement like the example discussed in Chapter 12. In this arrangement, students use Word to produce assignments and then upload the Word files in Blackboard. The instructor, using Word as an e-mail editor, provides feedback using Word's reviewing feature and e-mails the reviewed documents back to the students.

The instructor ultimately has to select the focus. Whatever focus is selected, it will probably not be the exact one that learners will eventually use, for example, after graduation. This, of course, is the nature of education. Unlike training, education provides a basis for problem solving and later learning. The specific focus that the instructor selects will be influenced by what foundation of knowledge will be most beneficial to students and what resources the instructor *and* students have access to during the learning process.

Step 2: Select Specific Content to Assess. After establishing a focus within a goal, the second step involves selecting specific content to include in the assessments. The focus within a particular instructional goal represents only a portion of the content that could be included within the broader educational goal. Furthermore, assessments can cover only a fraction of the content included in the scope of the instruction. In essence, then, assessments in education consist of small samples of skills selected from relatively small samples of content defined by the focus of the goal. That is, assessments involve a small sample of a small sample. To be effective and meaningful, one must select very

carefully and deliberately the specific content to include in assessments.

Various judgments come into play. For instance, one can typically identify a subset of content with which almost all learners are proficient. Except when particular content is crucial to subsequent learning, it is prudent to exclude from assessments any skills that virtually all students have mastered. Content in which virtually all students will be unsuccessful should also be excluded. In those cases, the assessment would provide relatively little information about the achievement of individual students that the instructor does not already know.

Another judgment involves the type of capabilities involved. Because different types of performance are used to measure achievement of the different types of capabilities, we have emphasized the importance of taking this into account when assessing student achievement. The basic capability types are declarative knowledge (information), procedural knowledge (concepts and rules), and problem solving. Chapter 2 describes these basic categories and discusses how to assess each. Table 2.2 within that chapter provides examples of goals that emphasize each type of capability and lists the type of student performance that is useful for assessing each.

Deciding what content should be assessed is somewhat analogous to planning meals; in both cases, a broad sampling facilitates interest and health. Much like the need to include more than just fruit in a diet even though fruit is an excellent source of nutrients, one should not limit assessments to capabilities involving only declarative knowledge or just problem solving.

Different test formats are particularly effective at assessing the various types of capabilities. For example, written tests can be used to assess declarative knowledge and much procedural knowledge. Performance assessments, which typically take the form of student projects for online courses, can also assess knowledge of rules *and* are uniquely able to assess problem solving. However, performance assessments require more time for students to complete and for instructors to evaluate. If capabilities to be assessed involve declarative or procedural knowledge instead of or in addition to problem solving, written tests can often help make assessments comprehensive and efficient. At the same time, relying exclusively on written tests will likely restrict the content that can be assessed.

The goal in our current illustration is to receive assigned work from students electronically and then provide written feedback. The focus is a hybrid arrangement in which students upload Word documents as assignments to Blackboard.

The instructor then uses the reviewing feature in Word to write comments directly in students' documents and e-mails them back. This focus includes declarative and procedural knowledge as well as problem solving. Table 5.1 proposes specific content to be included in the assessments. Because this selection of content involves professional judgment, it is likely that you would select a different combination of content or choose an entirely different focus for the educational goal.

According to Table 5.1, the assessments ask learners to describe how one accesses assignments from Blackboard's online gradebook, with

Table 5.1
Example of skills related to electronically receiving assignments and providing feedback in an online course

	Information	Concept	Rule	Problem Solving
1. Is able to describe how one accesses students' assignments from Blackboard's online gradebook	✓			
2. In Blackboard's online gradebook, is able to identify links to students' uploaded assignments		✓		
3. Is able to use Blackboard's gradebook features to access Word documents uploaded by students			✓	
4. Is able to describe capabilities of Word's reviewing feature	✓			
5. In Word documents, is able to identify a "mailto:" link		✓		
6. Is able to use Word as the editor when writing e-mail text			✓	
7. Is able to copy/paste material from students' Word documents to an e-mail editor			✓	
8. Is able to insert comments in an existing document using Word's reviewing feature			✓	
9. Given knowledge of the online gradebook features of Blackboard and the reviewing feature of Word, is able to review assignments that were uploaded to Blackboard and electronically provide students with feedback related to their assignments				✓

this being characterized as declarative knowledge, or information. Because this is declarative knowledge, our learners would be asked to verbally state what they know. An acceptable variation would be to use multiple-choice items where learners select correct statements about accessing a student's uploaded assignment file.

According to Table 5.1, the assessment will also determine whether learners have *conceptual* knowledge as to what a "mailto:" link is in a Word document. As a concept, this skill would be assessed by having learners distinguish between examples and nonexamples of "mailto:" links in a document. As noted in Table 2.2, asking students to verbally explain what a "mailto:" link is would be assessing knowledge of information rather than conceptual knowledge. Therefore, the assessment should not use that tactic. One way to assess this knowledge online would be to have students distinguish between examples and nonexamples of "mailto:" links in a Word document and define hotspots within the document, one of which is a "mailto:" link. Students would then demonstrate their conceptual knowledge by clicking on what they believe represents the "mailto:" link.

According to Table 5.1, we will also determine whether our learners can upload assignments and provide feedback electronically. Because this task involves problem solving, a performance assessment rather than a written test must be used to evaluate achievement of this skill. For instance, we might create a project involving a simulated Blackboard gradebook that includes uploaded assignments. Learners would then access some of the uploaded assignments and use Word to write feedback and return the edited assignments to their authors.

In summary, when selecting content to be assessed, the second step is to identify the specific sample of content to include. This must be done very deliberately because the content included in the assessments represents a small sample of the broader content one hopes students are learning. When selecting content, one should also identify the types of capabilities involved. This establishes the type of performance that can be used to assess the content and the test formats that can be used to assess the skill.

Step 3: Determine the Number of Observations to Be Used in Assessments. With written tests, the number of observations pertains to how many test items will be included in the test. With performance assessments, it pertains to how many different tasks learners will be asked to perform.

An obvious factor in determining the number of observations is the importance of the content. Skills that are more essential to the successful application of what is being learned will need to be emphasized more heavily. Probably a less obvious consideration is the confidence one has in the results of an assessment. Higher confidence is established by including more observations. However, increasing the number of observations per content area reduces the number of content areas that can be included in an assessment. That is, the number of skills sampled diminishes as the required confidence increases. In the next section of this chapter, we look in greater detail at the implications this and other practical considerations have on limiting what can be assessed. Here, though, is an overview of how one specifies the number of observations when planning an assessment.

In Table 5.1, we proposed content to include in an assessment. The goal of the assessment is to measure the ability to electronically receive project work from students enrolled in an online course and provide written feedback. To specify the number of observations, we will replace the checkmarks in Table 5.1 with the number of observations we will use to assess the specific skills our assessment will sample. This result will be something similar to that shown in Table 5.2. In Chapter 3, we referred to this table as a *table of specifications.*

One of the most obvious practical considerations when specifying the number of observations is the length of time it will take for students to complete the resulting written tests or performance assessments. As noted earlier, one

Table 5.2
Sample "table of specifications" related to electronically receiving assignments and providing feedback for an online course

	Information	Concept	Rule	Problem Solving
10. Is able to describe how one accesses students' assignments from within Blackboard's online gradebook	10			
11. In Blackboard's online gradebook, is able to identify links to students' uploaded assignments		2		
12. Is able to use Blackboard's gradebook features to access Word documents uploaded by students			2*	
13. Is able to describe capabilities of Word's reviewing feature	5			
14. In Word documents, is able to identify a "mailto:" link		2		
15. Is able to use Word as the editor when writing e-mail text			2*	
16. Is able to copy/paste material from students' Word documents to an e-mail editor			2*	
17. Is able to insert comments in an existing document using Word's reviewing feature			2*	
18. Given knowledge of the online gradebook features of Blackboard and the reviewing feature of Word, is able to review assignments that were uploaded to Blackboard and electronically provide students with feedback related to their assignments				0*

*It is deemed necessary to use performance assessments rather than a written test to evaluate these content areas.

advantage of online written assessments is that they are removed from the time constraints of the classroom. In classrooms, class times are fixed in terms of both when they occur and the number of minutes that are allotted to each class period. With online assessments, these constraints are less limiting, although there still are practical limits that restrict the number of items that can be included in a test. However, it is often possible to divide items across several smaller tests. In contrast, when performance assessments in traditional classroom settings take the form of student projects or assignments, they usually are completed outside class periods. Another advantage of being online is reducing or eliminating the physical handling of papers.

Table 5.2 proposes that 10 test items be associated with the first content area, and only two with the second. The second content area—identifying links in a webpage showing students' assignments that have been uploaded—is a very narrow skill, so fewer items are needed to test it.

Five items are associated with the fourth content area—describing capabilities of Word's reviewing feature. All of these numbers reflect professional judgments by the instructor. Therefore, the instructor may decide that less importance should be associated with the fifth than with the second content area since students will probably have had considerably more experience working with Word than with Blackboard's online gradebook. Although these judgments are quite arbitrary, they are not without reason gained through experience as to where emphasis needs to be placed and which content areas involve greater complexity.

The note at the bottom of Table 5.2 indicates that numbers marked with asterisks refer to content that is to be evaluated using a performance assessment, rather than a online written test. The second content area, for example, pertains to using Blackboard's gradebook features to access documents uploaded by students. Because this skill is judged to involve a rule, it should be assessed by having students apply the rule to a situation presented in the test. Because declarative knowledge is not the focus, having learners explain what they know would be an inappropriate assessment strategy. It is often possible to use written tests to assess rules. That would be the case, for instance, when assessing a student's ability to do algebra problems. However, it would likely be easier to assess the second content area listed in Table 5.2 by having learners complete a performance assessment in which they work directly with Blackboard's online gradebook to access some simulated uploaded assignments.

A table of specifications such as the one illustrated in Table 5.2 provides a reasonably detailed outline for the content of one's assessments. When instructors do not prepare similar outlines before constructing their assessments, their assessments have some surprise content. As students, we have all experienced tests that made us wonder where the content of the test came from. A practical advantage of a table of specifications is that it helps estimate the number of observations that will be included in an assessment. For instance, the num-ber of nonperformance assessment items specified in Table 5.2 (numbers without an asterisk) totals 19 items. If that is too few or too many items, the time to determine that is before the test is completed.

A total of eight observations have been specified and marked with asterisks in Table 5.2. If each one involves separate performance assessments, this would probably require too much time. It should be possible, though, to combine the four content areas associated with these eight observations into one student assignment or project, which would make the performance assessment more doable. However, doing so would approximate the ninth content area listed in Table 5.2—having learners review assignments that were uploaded to Blackboard and provide feedback on them electronically. This ninth content area involves problem solving and, if assessed literally as stated, would involve evaluating the adequacy of the feedback provided and not just assessing whether learners can go through the mechanics of uploading assignments and returning some kind of feedback electronically. In the table of specifications presented in Table 5.2, it was judged that insufficient time was available to include this ninth content area in the assessments. Consequently, the number of observations associated with this content area was set at zero.

Again, the basic implications of training versus education are the same in face-to-face and online settings with respect to determining what to assess. With training, the goal is for learners to perform a particular task, often with a high degree of proficiency and consistency. Skills are more narrowly defined and are fully assessed. Education, in contrast, provides learners with a framework for further learning from which unanticipated problems can be solved. Samples of knowledge and skills selected from broader domains of knowledge are assessed.

However, the respective constraints of face-to-face and online settings provide certain implications for selecting content. Face-to-face settings permit a higher degree of spontaneous interaction between an instructor and a student, making it more likely that errors in conclusions drawn from assessments will be detected. Although such errors are always undesirable, with online assessments it is essential that the content to be assessed by each test is selected deliberately. The instructor's opportunities for recovering from errors in an online assessment are more limited. On the other hand, online assessments allow more flexibility in the amount of time that is devoted to administering assessments. In face-to-face classroom settings, when additional time is used for assessment, less time is available for delivering instruction, at least within the context of the classroom. Although not unlimited, time associated with online activities is more negotiable. When education is involved, only a small portion of content can be assessed. Online settings allow these small portions to be larger.

OTHER PRACTICAL CONSIDERATIONS THAT DETERMINE WHAT TO ASSESS

In determining what to assess, the main consideration is whether training or education is involved. Online settings typically involve both, in which case procedures for selecting the content varies with the situation. Other practical considerations also influence what is assessed. We are going to review three of these considerations.

Establishing Required Confidence in Conclusions

One wants high confidence in conclusions drawn from an assessment. That is, one wants to be fairly sure that what is observed through an assessment is truly indicative of the learner's knowledge. However, as we have noted, assessments typically involve small samples of student performance. As we recognize from basic statistics, small samples tend to be associated with large sampling errors. Therefore, the confidence one can have in a particular assessment might be surprisingly low.

To illustrate this, let us assume that we consider 80% proficiency in a particular area of knowledge to be minimally acceptable. Let us further assume that some students in our class are 90% proficient and others are 70% proficient. That is, students in the first group could correctly answer 90% of the total universe of test items that measure this knowledge, and students in the second group could correctly answer 70%.

Of course, one would never include all of the possible test items that measure the content being assessed. Instead only a small sample of items would be included. Let us take this to an extreme. Can you anticipate what would happen if a test included the smallest possible sample—just one test item to assess a student's proficiency? The following exercise helps establish what would happen.

5.1   Apply What You Are Learning

Our illustration involves a situation in which 80% represents the minimum acceptable proficiency. One group of students is 90% proficient, and another group is 70% proficient.

1. If we use only one test item to judge whether a student is adequately proficient with a particular skill (one item sampled randomly from all possible test items that measure this skill), would a student *who correctly answers this item* be judged proficient or not proficient? What about a student who *incorrectly answers* this one test item?
2. Among those who are 90% proficient, what is the probability that a student will correctly answer the one item? What about those who are 70% proficient?
3. Still assuming that just one test item will be used, what is the probability that a student with a true proficiency of 90% will be correctly judged as proficient? (In our illustration, 80% proficiency has been judged as minimally adequate.) What is the probability that a student with true proficiency of 70% (below the required proficiency of 80%) will be judged appropriately as not being adequately proficient?

Answers can be found at the end of the chapter.

If you worked through the preceding exercise and verified your answer, you found that if judgments are based on just one test item, there is a fairly high probability (90%) of correctly classifying the student whose true proficiency is above the minimum performance standard. On the other hand, there is a low probability (only 30%) of correctly classifying the student whose true proficiency is below the minimum standard. Interestingly, with students whose true proficiency is somewhat below the minimum, flipping a coin provides a higher chance (50%) of correctly classifying them.

But are we likely to make judgments about students based on just one test item? Although not our preferred choice, instructors do something similar quite often. For instance, if a unit test has to assess 20 skills that are included in the unit of instruction (not an especially high number of skills considering the various pieces of information, concepts, and rules often included in one unit), and the unit test consists of 20 test items, then each of the assessed skills is being measured with just one test item.

Increasing the number of test items predictably increases the confidence of the assessment. There are various ways to achieve this. One is to assess fewer skills, allowing the use of more items for each skill. Oosterhof (2001) shows that three test items per skill can provide a fairly high confidence level in assessments.

Another option is to use assessments to make judgments about the class as a whole rather than about individual students. For instance, when one test item is used to judge the *overall* proficiency of a class of 25 students, 25 observations are involved in that judgment. Overall assessments about students in the class have much higher confidence than judgments about individual students in the class.

Although limits to the number of items that can be included in a test always cause a problem, online tests have the advantage over tests given face to face during class time. As noted earlier, one can devote more time to online testing and therefore use more test items in the assessment process.

Constraints Imposed by Test Format

Previous chapters have identified the types of knowledge and skills one needs to assess. These include declarative knowledge, which we are referring to as information; procedural knowledge, which we have subdivided into discriminations, concepts, and rules; and problem solving. Different types of performances are observed to assess these capabilities. (This is summarized in Table 2.2.) As will be addressed in subsequent chapters, each of the test formats has strengths and weaknesses regarding the types of tasks they can ask students to perform. Consequently, there are constraints on the types of capabilities each test format is able to assess.

In general, written test formats such as essay, completion, multiple choice, and true-false can measure declarative and procedural knowledge. However, a format we are referring to as *performance assessments* is uniquely able to measure problem-solving skills. Written test formats cannot measure problem-solving skills as they are defined in this book. (Chapters 10 through 12 are concerned with the assessment of problem solving and the design and use of performance assessments.)

Performance assessments are not unlike many class assignments that take the form of homework in face-to-face classroom settings, or projects or other activities in online instruction. The nature of performance assessments is detailed in later chapters. Not all assignments can be considered performance assessments. At a basic level, performance assessments require learners to perform a task that is valued in its own right. For instance, in a language arts course, a valued course outcome would be the learner's ability to write a paper on a given topic in a particular style. In a music theory course, one would value the learner's ability to compose music with particular chord progressions. In an assessment course, a valued outcome would be the learner's ability to produce an online written test.

Some are surprised that assignments can be treated as tests. Assignments are appropriately used online to facilitate learning or to provide learners with a particular experience. These assignments, however, can also be designed as a vehicle by which learners demonstrate achievement of important goals. Again, this is a topic for later chapters.

Each test format presents other constraints in addition to the type of capabilities it can measure. For instance, in varying degrees written formats are cost efficient in terms of the amount of material they can assess in a limited amount of time. Some online test formats can be scored automatically by the computer and can generate fairly detailed immediate feedback to the learner. These options will be addressed in the next chapters.

Need for Security

The need for test security indirectly affects the content that can be assessed. This is because security is less of a problem with certain test formats, particularly performance assessments. However, increasing the use of performance assessments versus written tests decreases the total amount of content that can be tested, and thus influences the choice of content that will be assessed.

Concern about test security is often expressed about online assessments. Security might be obtained by using proctors at testing centers, but this is not always practical or expedient. Unless security is elaborate, it can be breached fairly easily in almost any online or face-to-face setting. And it is unreasonable to expect an online assessment to be any more secure than an assessment administered in a typical classroom environment.

With written tests, particularly when relatively little weight is given to them in terms of course grades, it may be possible to establish adequate security by invoking an honor system. The perceived weight of written tests and therefore their need for security can be reduced by relying more heavily on performance assessments and assessments associated with collaborative activities, which for a variety of reasons tend to have fewer problems with security. For instance, students are typically given the scoring plan prior to completing performance assessments, whereas the scoring

key to a multiple-choice test must be kept secure. In Chapter 9, the issue of security with online assessments is addressed in detail.

SUMMARY

Selecting the content of a course involves judgments by the instructor. In deciding what parts of that content are to be assessed, the instructor must consider whether training or education is involved. With both face-to-face and online instruction, most units of instruction include elements of both training and education.

With training, one learns how to perform a particular task, typically with a high degree of proficiency and consistency. All critical knowledge and skills are assessed, although it usually is not necessary to assess every instance in which a particular skill is applied. Training tends to involve declarative and procedural knowledge, but not problem solving.

In contrast to training, education establishes a framework for further learning and for solving unanticipated problems. Assessments involve broader domains of knowledge but, out of necessity, only selected samples of knowledge or skills can be assessed. A three-step process for selecting these skills was addressed: selecting a focus within each goal; within that focus, selecting specific content to be assessed; and determining the number of observations to be used to assess that content.

When tests are infrequent and take on a high-stakes quality, the content of the test often becomes a set of skills in its own right for which students are trained. One of the advantages of online assessments is that tests can be administered more frequently, thus making it easier to maintain a distinction between training and education, and reducing the tendency to teach to the test.

Other considerations that determine what to assess include establishing the required confidence for the assessment. Greater confidence requires using more test items to measure each skill, which reduces the number of skills that can be assessed. Another consideration involves the constraints imposed by the test format. Written tests can measure declarative and procedural knowledge, but not problem solving; the latter requires performance assessments. A third consideration is test security and the impact it has on the selection of item format and, consequently, the amount of content that can be assessed.

ANSWERS:
APPLY WHAT YOU ARE LEARNING

5.1 1. If judgments are based on just one test item, a student who answers it correctly will be judged proficient, and one who answers it incorrectly will be judged not proficient. You are being appropriately cautious if you question whether one test item provides a sufficient basis to judge whether a student is proficient. 2. Among students who are 90% proficient, the probability that a particular student will answer the one item correctly is 90%. Among students who are 70% proficient, the probability is 70% that they will answer the one test item correctly. 3. The student with true proficiency of 90% has a 90% chance of correctly answering the one item. Therefore, the probability of correctly classifying this student as proficient is 90%. The student with true proficiency of 70% likewise has a 70% chance of correctly answering the item. However, because this student lacks the necessary 80% proficiency, a student with 70% proficiency will be correctly classified only if the student *incorrectly answers* the one test item. The probability of doing that is 100% − 70%, or 30%. That means there is a low probability that students with 70% true proficiency will be judged correctly as not proficient if the classification is based on only one test item.

TERMS INTRODUCED IN THIS CHAPTER

Training: the goal is for learners to be able to perform a particular task, often with a high degree of proficiency and consistency. Skills to be assessed are more narrowly defined and, proficiency with every skill is usually assessed.

Education: the goal is to provide learners with a framework for further learning from which unanticipated problems can be solved. Assessments involve broader domains of knowledge, and measure only samples of specific skills within these domains.

High-stakes examination: a written test or other assessment where performance on one test has significant implications for the person taking the test. Examples include professional licensure examinations or even unit tests when considerable weight is given to the exam. A great deal of planning and care is required when developing a high-stakes examination because of the considerable consequences of producing a defective assessment. Test security becomes a higher priority when high-stakes examinations are involved. The high stakes of assessments can be reduced by using a larger number of smaller assessments.

Authentic assessment: involves students demonstrating proficiency with a skill by performing a task similar to how that skill is used in real-world settings. For instance, an authentic assessment of using algebra to solve for one unknown would involve completing tasks similar to those encountered by surveyors or engineers.

Confidence: is the certainty with which one judges a student's level of proficiency with a particular skill. High confidence should be established for critical skills with lower confidence tolerated for noncritical skills, More test items, more products, or other observations are required to obtain high confidence in an assessment.

ENHANCE YOUR UNDERSTANDING

- In a content area you recently taught or course you recently completed, identify two significant examples of learning—one that involves training and the other, education. State the qualities that identify them as training or education. Describe differences in how one would assess these two content areas, given their classifications as training and education.

6

Determining How Assessments Will Be Interpreted and Used

The interpretation and use of an assessment is its primary purpose. Stated differently, the only justification for conducting an assessment is its eventual interpretation and use. In fact, the whole issue of validity and other foundational issues of assessment are closely linked with how the assessment is to be interpreted and used.

The *interpretation* of an assessment requires a frame of reference in order to become usable. Even with a clear understanding of what a test measures, a statement such as "your score on the quiz is 17" is of no use unless a reference is also provided. Answers to questions like the following help a learner (and instructor) establish that reference:

If my score is 17, how did others do?

Is 17 high or low with respect to what I can do?

Does 17 mean I have improved?

What does 17 mean I can and cannot do?

One always needs a frame of reference to interpret a score. This is true if the score is quantitative, such as a numerical score assigned to a quiz or project, or qualitative, such as an instructor's narrative description of strengths and weakness of a project submitted by a student.

We will observe that some frames of reference are more useful than others. This chapter emphasizes criterion-referenced and norm-referenced interpretations of performance, which typically are the most helpful references in instructional settings. Our discussion will look at conditions that must be present to make these two references viable. We will also briefly discuss two other frames of reference widely used with assessments.

The primary *use* of an assessment is to evaluate learners. As noted in Chapter 1, this evaluative role is typically formative or summative. Formative assessments occur during instruction. They help establish whether students have achieved sufficient mastery of skills and whether further instruction in these skills is appropriate. Summative assessments occur at the conclusion of instruction, such as at the end of a unit or the end of the course. Summative assessments are used to certify student achievement. The assignment of course grades is one outcome of summative assessments that we will address.

The interpretation and use of assessments are fundamental issues in both face-to-face and online settings. Although our focus is online assessment, it is essential that any discussion of assessment include the basics of how assessments will be interpreted and used. This chapter helps you achieve four skills related to this issue:

- Identify frames of reference that help interpret student performance

- Recognize the meaning of criterion-referenced and norm-referenced interpretations, and identify when each is preferable

- Select appropriate formative and summative uses of assessments

- Establish procedures for assigning course grades

FRAMES OF REFERENCE FOR INTERPRETING PERFORMANCE

In education, these four references are widely used for interpreting the performance of learners:

Ability-referenced, in which a learner's performance is interpreted in light of that individual's maximum performance

Growth-referenced, in which performance is compared with the learner's prior performance

Norm-referenced, in which interpretation is provided by comparing the learner's performance with the performances of others or with the typical performance of that individual

Criterion-referenced, in which meaning is provided by describing what the learner can and cannot do

Table 6.1 summarizes characteristics of these four frames of reference.

Ability-Referenced Interpretations

Ability-referenced interpretations are comparisons of a learner's performance with that individual's potential performance. Statements such as "That's about all this person can do" or "This person can do better if given more time" are examples of ability-referenced interpretations.

The key to using ability as the frame of reference is having a good estimate of the person's maximum possible performance. Therein is the problem. Instructors often have only tentative, broad ideas of what each learner can do. In online settings, the instructor usually has limited or possibly no direct contact with the learner, which further handicaps establishing ability. Although previous work and information from other instructors may provide ideas about a learner's ability, these estimates actually reflect what the learner was observed doing rather than the upper limit of the individual's capacity to perform.

Standardized aptitude tests, including those used in college admissions, also provide estimates of ability, but these estimates are general and of limited use in interpreting a learner's performance. Furthermore, standardized tests typically indicate which individuals will achieve the most rather than *how much* a particular person can achieve. As with any estimate of ability, scores on aptitude tests are usually confounded by other variables such as background, prior achievement, and motivation.

Perhaps the greatest limitation of ability estimates is that, for any particular skills we are trying to teach, we usually do not know precisely

Table 6.1
Four references commonly used for interpreting assessments

	Interpretation Provided by This Reference	Condition That Must Be Present for This Reference to Be Useful
Ability-referenced	How learners are performing relative to what they are capable of doing	Requires good measures of what each student is capable of doing; that is, knowing a student's maximum possible performance
Growth-referenced	How much learners have changed or improved relative to what they were doing earlier	Requires pre- and post-measures of performance that are highly reliable
Norm-referenced	How well learners are doing with respect to what is typical or reasonable	To whom learners are being compared must be clearly understood
Criterion-referenced	What learners can and cannot do	Content domain that was assessed must be well defined

which abilities are prerequisite to learning those skills and therefore limit what a learner is able to do. Because it is so difficult to obtain a good estimate of a learner's maximum possible performance, ability usually provides a weak frame of reference for interpreting learner performance and should be avoided.

Growth-Referenced Interpretations

Growth-referenced interpretations compare a person's present skills to prior performances. This is a natural frame of reference in instructional settings, since improvement in skills is highly relevant.

Growth implies change over time, that is, a change in performance between earlier and later measures of performance. For the measure of growth to be reliable, both the earlier and present measures must be reliable. If the earlier measure is simply an instructor's present recollection of each learner's earlier performance, this "measure" of earlier achievement will likely have very low reliability, and so will the growth-referenced interpretations.

Projects and other performance assessments that are widely used in online settings help get around this problem. When an individual's earlier project work is used formatively, when the earlier project involves the same skills as those being assessed in present work, and when both earlier and present products are reliably scored, then growth-referenced interpretations can be meaningful.

Growth-referenced and particularly ability-referenced interpretations of learner performance tend to be weak. Not knowing a learner's maximum possible performance restricts ability-referenced interpretations. The lack of a good assessment of earlier achievement often limits growth-referenced interpretations. These two references are best limited to formative assessments and then only when they are supplemented with norm and criterion references. For summative assessments, in which higher-impact decisions tend to be made, only norm-referenced and criterion-referenced interpretations should be used.

Norm-Referenced and Criterion-Referenced Interpretations

Norm-referenced interpretations involve comparing the learner's performance to a range of previously observed performances, usually those of students currently or previously enrolled in the class. In a variety of settings both in and outside of education, we often make comparisons with other individuals or events to help interpret what we see. How well a learner performed in creating a particular product is often described in terms of how others in the class did. Similarly, noneducational measures such as how much it rained, how fast you were driving, and how you feel today are often interpreted through comparison with similar events. It rained less than it usually does; I have never driven this fast; and so on. These are all norm-referenced interpretations.

For describing learner performance, norm-referenced interpretations are limited in that they do not define what a learner can and cannot do. However, they do help answer important questions such as what is typical and what is reasonable.

Criterion-referenced interpretations, in contrast, involve comparing a learner's performance with a well-defined content domain. Examples of content domains include the ability to locate a word in a Spanish dictionary; to associate famous composers of music with historical periods such as baroque, classical, and romantic; and to solve a set of algebraic equations involving two or more unknowns.

The key to making a criterion-referenced interpretation is having a well-defined domain. A criterion-referenced interpretation describes learner performance within that domain. That is, a criterion-referenced interpretation indicates what a person can and cannot do with respect to the content domain. However, unlike norm-referenced interpretations, criterion-referenced interpretations do not answer questions about what is typical and what is reasonable.

WHEN TO USE CRITERION- AND NORM-REFERENCED INTERPRETATIONS

Criterion-referenced means that a score is being interpreted in terms of the content domain the assessment measures. To permit a criterion-referenced interpretation, the description of what is being measured does not necessarily have to be elaborate, but it must be concise. Indicating that a person can use Google to locate the map of a city allows a criterion-referenced interpretation of an individual's performance because it clearly establishes what the person can (or cannot) do. So does stating that a person can run a mile in five minutes, list the elements in the periodic table, compute standard deviation, or convert temperatures from the Fahrenheit to the Celsius scale. Each of these examples establishes a specific skill that a learner can perform and, therefore, represents a criterion-referenced interpretation. Note, too, that the performances can be interpreted meaningfully with no reference to how other individuals performed.

In contrast, an assessment is norm-referenced if it compares a learner's performance with the typical distribution of performances. Indicating that a person can name more elements than 80% of the chemistry class represents a norm-referenced interpretation of performance, as does indicating that a person runs a mile slower than everyone on the track team, knows more Spanish vocabulary than half the class, or is the best violinist in the orchestra. The group of people with whom the person is being compared is the norm group.

Note that in these illustrations of norm-referenced interpretations, the person's skill is described in general terms. Saying that an individual is "the best violinist in the orchestra" indicates that the person performs better than other violinists in the orchestra but does not describe the violinist's specific skills—what this violinist can and cannot do. Norm-referenced interpretations can be made using more general descriptions of the content domain than criterion-referenced interpretations can. Stated differently, content domains that cannot be well-defined favor, or even require, norm-referenced as opposed to criterion-referenced interpretations.

Although norm-referenced interpretations can be made with more general descriptions of the content domain, they do require a well-defined norm group. A description of the violinist as the best in the orchestra provides meaningful information only if we have a clear understanding of which orchestra is being referenced.

6.1   Apply What You Are Learning

Does each of the following allow a criterion-referenced or norm-referenced interpretation of performance?

1. Tracey included more citations in her paper than any other student in our class.
2. Eric properly uses APA-style for references cited in his papers.
3. Austin scored near average on the computer technology quiz.
4. Tony can use an FTP-client software to move files between the server and his computer.
5. In geometry, David cannot bisect an angle.
6. Marie obtained the best score on the geometry test.

Answers can be found at the end of the chapter.

Both criterion-referenced and norm-referenced interpretations can be and usually are applied to a performance. For instance, we might observe that the student who types 45 words per minute on a computer keyboard is faster than 80% of the other students in the class. Both perspectives provide useful information.

It is possible for an assessment to be neither criterion-referenced nor norm-referenced. This condition is undesirable because, without a good reference, performance on the assessment lacks meaning. This was illustrated at the opening of the chapter, when we observed that a score of 17 had no meaning when given without reference, such as what the test measured or how others did on the test. This lack of a reference is so obvious that few instructors would report performance on an assessment in this manner without elaboration.

For less obvious reasons, however, many assessments, particularly conventional written tests, lack both criterion-referenced and norm-referenced interpretations. This situation typically occurs when an instructor wants to use a criterion-referenced test but does not understand that a criterion-referenced interpretation requires a well-defined content domain. The following examples illustrate this point.

Example 1:   Andrea scored 92% on the technology exam. This performance cannot be given a criterion-referenced interpretation because the specific skills measured by the exam are not detailed. Some educators believe that the use of percentage scores provides a criterion-referenced interpretation, perhaps because it suggests a degree of mastery. However, we do not know what Andrea can or cannot do. Nor is it possible to specify what instruction she should now receive. Scoring 92% may represent a high degree of competence if the exam measures difficult skills. Or it could represent low competence if the exam measures exceptionally easy skills. Converting scores to percentages does not in itself allow a criterion-referenced interpretation of a test. Andrea's performance cannot be norm-referenced either, unless comparison scores are also given.

Example 2:   Laura surpassed the criterion score of 80% and, therefore, passed the history test. Again, this performance cannot be given a criterion-referenced interpretation because the specific skills measured by the test are not described. Unless the specific history skills sampled by this test are known, we cannot tell whether scoring above 80% (or any other passing score) indicates a high or low proficiency in history. Establishing a passing score, sometimes called a criterion score, does not by itself allow for a criterion-referenced interpretation. For instance, norm-referenced tests such as the SAT or GRE often have passing or minimum scores associated with college admission. Interestingly, both norm-referenced and criterion-referenced interpretations can be given to test scores with or without specifying a passing score.

In online assessments, project work and other performance assessments usually play a more significant role than written tests. The scoring plans[1] for these assessments, when carefully constructed, establish a well-defined domain, and therefore facilitate criterion-referenced interpretations. Sharing the scoring plan when projects are evaluated is an effective way to communicate to learners what they can and cannot do.

Criterion-referenced interpretations began to gain popularity in the 1970s. This trend has been healthy because knowing what students can and cannot do is an important part of instruction. With the increased popularity of criterion-referencing, however, varying definitions of what makes an interpretation criterion-referenced have emerged—not all of which are appropriate. Some time ago, Nitko (1984) emphasized how important a well-defined domain of skills is to criterion-referenced interpretations. According to Nitko, the nature of a well-defined domain may be ordered or unordered. When a domain is ordered, a student's position within the domain also indicates what that individual can and cannot do. Here are examples of well-defined, ordered domains:

- A list of words ordered according to their spelling difficulty
- A series of pictures depicting finger positions on piano keys ranging from an untrained position through progressively more appropriate finger positions
- A series of math items ordered so that correctly answering each item (or group of items) requires mastery of a skill that is more complex than the one needed to answer the preceding item in the series

In the first example, noting the most difficult word a person can spell tends to identify specific words that an individual can and cannot spell. Similarly, identifying the picture that most closely

---

[1]Scoring plans include checklists, rating scales, scoring rubrics, and model answers.

resembles a music student's finger positions on piano keys indicates what the student must still learn. A similar interpretation can be given to a person's score on an ordered series of math items. When a content domain involves an "order," that is, when content within the domain represents a true hierarchy, then it is possible even within a quite broad domain to establish what a learner can and cannot do simply by knowing the point within the hierarchy that the learner has reached. In practice, however, domains tend *not* to represent perfect orders. For instance, a person may be able to spell some words that are more difficult and not be able to spell some easier ones. When a content domain is "unordered," each domain usually has to be narrowly defined or highly focused to establish what a learner can or cannot do.

Nitko (1984) pointed out that a large number of important skills taught in educational settings represent unordered performance domains. In a well-defined unordered domain, the skills cannot be ordered, although the skills included in the domain can be and are clearly established, or well defined. Likewise, the tasks that are used to assess the skills are clearly established. Here are examples of well-defined, unordered domains:

- Solving algebraic equations involving two unknowns
- Using a library's online catalog to determine whether the library has a particular book
- Copying music files to an iPod

These examples may require an individual to perform a particular sequence of behaviors; however, measuring the student's proficiency with these skills would probably not pinpoint the individual's performance on a continuum within the domain.

Nitko proposed various approaches to defining unordered domains. Two of them are specifying the stimulus and response attributes and

Note: Chapter 8 describes how to develop scoring plains.

specifying only the stimulus attributes of tasks that would be used to assess proficiency within the content domain. Performance objectives can be used to provide this specification. Another approach is to define a domain in terms of a common error made by learners, for example, erroneously inverting the letters *ie* when spelling words. Still another is to provide a concise plan for scoring learner performance.

Again, note that a passing score is not essential to a criterion-referenced interpretation of test performance. For either criterion-referenced or norm-referenced tests, however, a passing score may be administratively convenient and useful. For instance, tests used by a college admissions office to help select the best applicants tend to be norm-referenced. Cutoff scores are commonly used with these tests. An instructor who uses a mastery learning strategy establishes a cutoff

---

6.2   Apply What You Are Learning

Indicate whether each of the following allows a criterion-referenced interpretation, a norm-referenced interpretation, or neither.

1. William obtained a score of 100.
2. Using a periodic table, Victoria can name each of the elements.
3. Using graph paper, a ruler, and a protractor, Jamie can determine the sine, cosine, and tangent of angles.
4. Liang scored 90 on a history exam.
5. Using a map that displays geographic features but no political boundaries, Brian can show the location of Middle East countries.
6. Suzanne passed the geography test.
7. Jesse can set up Outlook Express to send encrypted e-mail messages.
8. In terms of grade-point average, Mark graduated at the median of his college class.
9. Donna passed the vocabulary portion of her Spanish final exam.
10. Nathaniel knows more vocabulary words than 80% of his second-year Spanish class.

Answers can be found at the end of the chapter.

score to determine which learners will be given further instruction. Unless the test measures a well-defined domain, however, the presence of a cut-off score does not facilitate a criterion-referenced interpretation. Educators often mistakenly believe that a cutoff score, rather than the well-defined domain, allows for criterion-referenced interpretations. Again, to be criterion-referenced, an assessment must concisely establish what a learner can (or cannot) do.

It is important to emphasize that the usefulness of an assessment depends largely on how well the domain being measured is defined or how adequately the norm group with whom students are being compared is known or described. Not all assessments are equal in these important qualities. The best criterion-referenced assessments determine within a very clearly defined domain exactly what each learner can and cannot do. The best norm-referenced assessments give a statement of a person's ability when compared with a very clearly defined and relevant group of other individuals. Many tests deviate from these ideal standards. Unfortunately, some performance assessments and particularly written tests provide no reference at all from which to interpret their scores.

CHOOSING THE APPROPRIATE INTERPRETATION

The type of interpretation to be used depends on the parameters available and the information needed from the results. Criterion-referenced interpretations are appropriate when content domains can be well defined and when it is important to determine what students can and cannot do. Norm-referenced interpretations are appropriate when a relevant and well-defined norm group can be established and when it is important to describe student performance in terms of what is typical or reasonable. As noted earlier, it is common to use both references, with one emphasized more than the other based on the situation.

The use of an assessment influences the reference used for the interpretation. For instance, assessments used for formative purposes must establish what individuals can or cannot do, and therefore emphasize criterion-referenced interpretations. On the other hand, assessments used for summative purposes tend to sample content more broadly and are less able to establish specifically what a learner can or cannot do. Summative assessments tend to favor norm-referenced interpretations. The concepts of formative and summative assessments were introduced in Chapter 1.

Interpretations of Formative Assessments

Formative assessments are embedded within instruction. Their purpose is to monitor learning to determine whether instruction should continue, should be modified, or should cease. Determining what an individual can and cannot do is central to formative assessments. Criterion-referenced interpretations are required.

In face-to-face classes, the vast majority of formative assessments involve the instructor's informal observations and questions. These informal assessments typically occur with greater detail in smaller classes. However, even in large classes, being face to face with learners allows an instructor to rapidly estimate what students comprehend just from interpreting body language and making other casual observations. In online situations, informal assessments are present but play a smaller role. They occur, usually asynchronously, by reading online discussions, responding to e-mails, monitoring group interactions, and so forth. Using chat software for "office hours" sessions can facilitate informal assessments. So can an unstructured online discussion forum where learners can raise questions and address issues.

In online situations, the instructional designer and the instructor often need to look for ways to offset the limited availability of informal assessments. One way is to set up conditions that allow online students to self-assess during learning. One option includes establishing and sharing with students concise scoring plans that will be used to evaluate their projects and other work.

This allows learners to self-assess their progress as they complete the work. Another option is to build item-by-item feedback into online quizzes that explains the reasoning behind correct responses and common incorrect responses. This allows learners to formatively self-assess their knowledge by comparing the reasoning they use to answer each item with the reasoning provided in the feedback. Most commercial online testing software allows the test developer to create feedback that is provided to students automatically at the conclusion of the quiz. Still another option is to have online discussion forums where discussion topics encourage learners to try out ideas or techniques they will later be asked to apply in projects or other activities.

Criterion-referenced interpretations are critical to assessments that are to be used formatively. The assessment, including learner feedback, must be designed to help learners answer the question, "What can I do and not do?" Alternately, learners must be able to establish concise distinctions between what they are doing and what the instructor expects them to do.

Interpretations for Summative Assessments

Summative assessments follow instruction and are typically used as unit tests, midterm and final exams, and projects or other end-of-unit assignments. Summative assessments usually involve general or global content domains. The broad domains being assessed include many specific skills; however, because of their number and complexity, only a sample of specific content domains are usually assessed in a summative assessment. Criterion-referenced interpretations are difficult to achieve because of the broadness of content involved. Summative assessments out of necessity emphasize norm-referenced interpretations.

More than with face-to-face classes, many end-of-unit online assessments play both a formative and a summative role, even though emphasis is on the latter. For instance, when automated narrative feedback is given at the conclusion of a written test administered online, the feedback provides formative information related to skills sampled by the test, even though the main role of the assessment is summative. Likewise, student project work is often used to assess performance of students towards the end of an instructional unit. If the project has significant deficiencies, feedback provided by the instructor is likely to be quite specific, establishing what the learner did and did not accomplish. The evaluation might result in the instructor asking the learner to revise the project. On the other hand, if it is of high quality, feedback provided by the instructor tends to be more general. The evaluation is summative in nature. As noted earlier, even while the learner is in the process of completing the project, as long as both the instructional goals and the criteria for scoring the assessment are clear, self-evaluation by the learner is formative in nature.

With both face-to-face and online instruction, criterion-referenced interpretations are generally preferred. It is always useful and important to establish what learners can and cannot do. However, providing a criterion-referenced interpretation usually requires assessing a very focused, well-defined content domain. However, when a summative assessment *samples* elements of a broader domain, it does not establish diagnostically what a student can and cannot do with respect to elements of the broader domain that were not included in the sample. Unlike criterion-referenced interpretations, norm-referenced interpretations can be made using more general descriptions of the content domain. As previously noted, content domains that cannot be well-defined favor, or even require, norm-referenced as opposed to criterion-referenced interpretations. Norm-referenced interpretations help evaluate a learner's overall performance in terms of what is typical and reasonable.

ESTABLISHING PROCEDURES FOR ASSIGNING COURSE GRADES

At most educational institutions, students enrolled in face-to-face as well as online courses are assigned a course grade when a class is completed. Sometimes pass-fail grades are used. More typically, letter grades are assigned.

In the United States during the early 1900s, percentage grades were the most popular grading system. Although that option is now seldom used, many instructors and some institutions associate percentages with each letter grade. Percentage grades assign each student a number between 0 and 100. One limitation of this reporting system is that the name itself is misleading. A student who receives a 100% probably has not mastered 100% of the course content in the sense that further improvement is impossible. Nor is it correct to state that a person who receives a 75% has learned three-fourths of the content. Simply changing the scoring plan or the difficulty of assessments will significantly alter students' percentage scores.

Letter grades consist of a series of letters, the most common being A, B, C, D, and F. As noted above, letter grades are often associated with percentage grades. For instance, the range of 90% to 100% might be equated to an A. Because percentage grades do not represent percentage of mastery and are heavily influenced by the difficulty of assessments, associating a range of scores with each grade, without a broader context, poorly defines letter grades. Unfortunately, this point is often ignored. Erroneously, an instructor or even an academic department within a college may be thought to have higher grading standards if higher percentages are associated with letter grades.

As with percentage grades, a limitation of letter grades is that they do not indicate what students can and cannot do. They provide only a general indication of performance.

Establishing Grading Criteria

Although most institutions use letter grades to report performance of both distance learners and students attending classes at the institution, the meaning of letter grades is often vague. In part, this is because a single letter is used to communicate very complex information. Instructors can offset this vagueness by carefully establishing grading criteria. Doing so involves 1) determining the nature and number of assessments on which to base grades, 2) selecting the weight to be given each assessment, and 3) setting the performance standard for each grade.

Nature and Number of Assessments. If the primary function of grades is to communicate students' academic proficiency, assessments on which grades are based must be measures of what students have learned. These assessments may involve diverse measures obtained throughout the term. However, only a content expert, typically the instructor, can determine the nature and number of assessments that should be used to establish proficiency. Here are some factors an instructor should consider.

1. As a whole, items included in grades should provide a representative sampling of all the instructional objectives covered during the term. Thus, a variety of measures, such as written tests and performance assessments can be included.

2. A grade should be based on multiple observations of achievement. The reliability of scores on one project or one written test is usually no better than moderate. Increasing the number of observations is one of the most effective techniques for increasing the reliability of grades or of any assessment.

3. Items that are unrelated to instructional objectives should be excluded from grades. For instance, unless neatness, promptness, and participation are specifically identified as instructional objectives, they should be excluded from grades, or at least their influence should be minimized when weights are determined for each assessment. This is not to suggest that qualities other than instructional objectives are unimportant. It is simply recognition that others who interpret grades typically assume that a

student receives a higher grade by achieving a greater number of course objectives. An instructor has the right and certainly the option to insist that students meet other expectations that are relevant to participating in the course, such as professionalism.

Determining the Weight to Be Given Each Assessment. The weight given to each assessment is also based on the professional judgment of the instructor. Quite obviously, more significant assessments are weighted more heavily. Weights should correspond to the relative importance of the learning outcomes being assessed. Particularly in distance learning environments, weights should not be based on the amount of effort or the time required to complete or evaluate individual assessments, beyond the degree to which time and effort are proportional to goals being assessed. Taken as a whole, the weights assigned to various assessments should make logical sense in terms of overall instructional goals.

When less than 10% of the overall grade is based on a particular assessment, that assessment has a minimal and usually negligible effect on the overall grade. For this reason, variables not directly related to instructional objectives, such as participation and promptness, can be included in the grading scheme without actually affecting the grades that are assigned. We are not encouraging inclusion of such variables—simply acknowledging that, to an extent, one can get away with it. (Authors also walk fine lines!) Watch out for cumulative effects. If, for example, participation and promptness are each given 10%, their cumulative effect becomes more substantial.

Establishing Performance Standards. Establishing performance standards for grades requires the selection of a standard to which student performance will be compared. Four standards are often considered:

1. A student's ability to learn
2. A student's prior performance
3. The performance of other students in the class
4. Predefined levels of performance

Instructors often try to combine standards (Nava & Loyd, 1991). For example, an instructor might use predefined levels of performance, such as 90% for an A, 80% for a B, and so on, but then adjust each student's grade based on an estimate of how much the student has improved. This procedure results in a grade that lacks meaning. By combining the two standards, the grade can no longer be interpreted in light of either standard. It no longer describes student performance in terms of the predefined levels, and it no longer describes how much the student has improved. It makes it impossible to interpret the grade. When assigning grades, select and use one reference exclusively.

A student's ability to learn. Using ability to learn as a standard is intuitively appealing, but as noted earlier it has some serious problems. It is appealing because all students have an equal chance of receiving a high grade. However, this grading standard has very serious problems:

- An instructor does not typically have reliable and valid measures of a student's ability to learn skills taught in the course.

- Without access to measures of ability, individuals outside the course cannot interpret the assigned grades.

A student's prior performance. Prior performance, or improvement, also provides an appealing standard. A student who begins with less achievement does not have to learn more to receive the same grade as a student who began with a higher level of achievement. However, basing grades on how much students have improved results in grades being controlled largely by the error that is inherent in every assessment. Here is why. If an instructor adjusts grades based on students' prior performances, this in effect removes the differences in grades that are associated with the real differences that exist among students. This adjustment does not remove errors inherent in each assessment. Consequently, by removing real differences among students, a much larger portion of differences in grades becomes associated with errors in the assessments. This problem becomes even worse when an instructor's measurement of a student's prior performances is based on a recollection of earlier performances rather than on a formal assessment of achievement prior to instruction. Grades should not be based on the improvement of each student's performance because of the substantial effect errors in assessment have on these grades.

Performance of other students in the class. Using the performance of others as the standard involves presetting the distribution of letter grades. For example, an instructor might assign an A to the top 15% of the students, B to the next 25%, and so on. This is sometimes called grading on the curve, but that is a misnomer since no particular curve is involved. Many, but not all, instructors are uncomfortable with this grading standard. Unless enrollment in the course is large, such as more than 200 students, the grades students receive can be influenced significantly by the characteristics of the students who happened to enroll in the course that term. Also, when collaborative learning is encouraged, which is often the situation with online courses, comparing students with each other to set grading standards can be counterproductive.

Predefined levels of performance. Assigning grades based on predefined levels of performance associates each grade with a fixed performance regardless of the distribution of grades ultimately assigned in the class. Often percentages are associated with each grade; for instance, 90% to 100% might correspond to an A, 80% to 90%, a B, and so on. However, recall that these percentages do not refer to percentage of mastery. Simply using easier or more difficult projects or tests significantly changes students' percentage scores. Therefore, instructors who associate the same percentages with each grade are not necessarily using the same grading standards. Instructors who are teaching similar courses and whose students end up with approximately the same distribution of grades are more likely to be using similar grading standards.

Although the distribution of grades is not the reference when grades are based on predefined levels of performance, the resulting distribution can help instructors determine whether they are using equivalent levels of performance for assigning grades. If grade distributions vary dramatically among instructors, this information can be used to help evaluate grading standards for the next term.

A second approach to defining performance standards is to associate adjectives with each letter grade. Common associations are A = excellent, B = good, C = satisfactory, D = poor, and F = failure. Institutions often use these or similar descriptions in published descriptions of their grading system. Certainly, these words are limited by their vagueness, but so are percentage scores, although less obviously so.

A third and superior approach to defining preset performance standards is to describe the characteristics of students associated with each letter grade. This is similar to establishing the descriptions in a scoring rubric. One technique for establishing these descriptions is first to identify which students were assigned each letter grade during the previous comparable term or year. Then, the subset of students who scored within the middle of each grade range is selected. Approximately the middle 50% of students within each grade range is appropriate. Finally, the performance of each of these subsets of students is described in terms of the broad instructional goals of the content being taught. As with a scoring rubric (see Chapter 8), it is best to use the same variables when describing the performances within each of these subsets of students. These descriptions become the preset performance standards for assigning grades to subsequent students.

SUMMARY

To be interpretable, performance on any assessment must have a frame of reference. Four interpretations commonly used by instructors are ability-referenced, growth-referenced, norm-referenced, and criterion-referenced. Of these, the norm-referenced and criterion-referenced interpretations tend to be the most useful. Norm-referenced interpretations require a clearly defined norm group. Criterion-referenced interpretations require a well-defined content domain.

Often both norm and criterion references are used to interpret student performance, although specific settings tend to emphasize one interpretation more than the other. Formative assessments emphasize criterion-referenced interpretations, whereas summative assessments emphasize norm-referenced interpretations.

A variety of standards are used when assigning grades. Some propose using each student's ability to learn, but it generally is not possible to establish any person's ability to learn. Improvement over prior performance represents another standard, but grades based on improvement often are influenced entirely by errors in the assessments. The performance of other students can be used as a reference for grading, but many instructors prefer not to use this approach. Also, unless large numbers of students are involved, the performance of the class may vary widely from one year to another. Assigning grades based on predefined levels of performance is generally the preferred option. These levels of performance might be established using percentages, although it is better to establish descriptions of performance associated with each letter grade, much like a scoring rubric.

ANSWERS:
APPLY WHAT YOU ARE LEARNING

6.1 1. norm-referenced; 2. criterion-referenced; 3. norm-referenced; 4. criterion-referenced; 5. criterion-referenced; 6. norm-referenced.

6.2 Items 2, 3, 5, and 7 allow criterion-referenced interpretations because each refers to a well-defined domain. From each of these items, one can indicate what the student can and cannot do relative to the domain. Items 8 and 10 allow norm-referenced interpretations. Although the specific skills that are referenced by these two items are not well defined (e.g., all that is known for sure about the vocabulary words is that they are

Spanish), they both relate student performance to the performance of others. Items 1, 4, 6, and 9 allow neither criterion-referenced nor norm-referenced interpretations. None of these latter items establish a well-defined domain. For example, the skills that are included in the geography test or the vocabulary portion of the Spanish exam are not specified. In addition, none of these latter items relate student performance to the performance of others.

TERMS INTRODUCED IN THIS CHAPTER

Ability-referenced interpretation: involves interpreting a learner's performance in the context of that person's maximum possible performance. Statements such as, "That's about all this person can do" are usually ability-referenced. (Statements such as "That's not typical of what this person does" is actually a norm-referenced interpretation.) Significant problems with ability-referenced interpretations include not having a good estimate of the person's maximum possible performance, and not knowing precisely which abilities are prerequisite to learning the skills being assessed.

Growth-referenced interpretation: involves interpreting a learner's performance relative to the learner's earlier performance. It requires good measures of the person's earlier and present performance.

Norm-referenced interpretation: involves comparing a learner's performance to a range of previously observed performances, such as those of students presently or previously enrolled in the class. Norm-referenced interpretations help establish typical and reasonable performance. Unlike *criterion-referenced* interpretations, a norm-referenced interpretation does not require a well-defined content domain to be useful, but does require a well-defined norm to which performance is compared.

Criterion-referenced interpretation: involves comparing a learner's performance to a well-defined content domain to establish what the person can or cannot do. A statement such as, "This person can create performance objectives" involves a well-defined content domain and is criterion-referenced. However, a statement such as "This person can design an online course" does not involve a well-defined domain, therefore it is not criterion-referenced and does not establish what specifically the person can do.

ENHANCE YOUR UNDERSTANDING

- Think of a written test you recently administered as an instructor or a test you took as a student. Was an ability-, growth-, norm-, or criterion-referenced interpretation used with this test? Why did you come to this conclusion? (Very often, more than one reference is used to interpret a particular test.) If an ability-referenced interpretation was used, was the ability of each student well understood? If a norm-referenced interpretation was used, was the group with which students were being compared clearly understood? If a criterion-referenced interpretation was used, was the content domain well defined?

- Think of written feedback that you either received or gave on a course project. What type(s) of reference did this feedback facilitate—ability, growth, norm, and/or criterion references? Using ideas discussed in this chapter, why do you come to this conclusion?

ADDITIONAL READING

Berk, R. A. (Ed.). (1984). *A guide to criterion-referenced test construction*. Baltimore, MD: Johns Hopkins University Press. Each chapter focuses on an issue important to criterion-referenced testing, such as describing alternative types of criterion-referenced tests, specifying what is to be measured by a test, determining test length, validating a test, and estimating the reliability of test scores.

Bloom, B. S., Madaus, G. F., & Hastings, J. T. (1981). *Evaluation to improve learning*. New York: McGraw-Hill. Chapters 4 through 6 provide a detailed discussion of formative, diagnostic, and summative evaluations.

Glaser, R. (1994). Criterion-referenced tests: Part I. Origins. *Educational measurement: Issues and practice, 13*(4), 9–11. Glaser introduced criterion-referenced testing in a 1963 address to the American Educational Research Association. In this article, the author reflects on that speech with respect to what has changed over the 30 years, and identifies anticipated problems that still remain.

Oosterhof, A. (2001). *Classroom applications of educational measurement* (3rd ed.). Upper Saddle River, NJ: Merrill/Prentice Hall. Chapter 18 includes an extended discussion of alternate grading systems and their use.

PART III

Producing and Administering Written Assessments

Items used within online tests can either require learners to construct responses, or can provide fixed responses from which test takers select an answer. Essay and completion items are familiar examples of the former and multiple-choice and true-false common examples of the latter.

When fixed responses are involved, a computer can easily score answers, display feedback previously created by the test developer, and automatically update records. Completion items can be scored by computer, but with varying success. It is increasingly becoming common for essay responses to be scored by computer, particular within large-scale testing programs.

Chapters 7 and 8 describe qualities important to include in written test items. Numerous illustrations are included to help explain these qualities. A separate section shows how to hand score answers to essay questions more efficiently and consistently.

Computers now allow for a number of variations to the more standard item formats. For instance, with multiple choice, students can reorder the options to match particular criteria or to illustrate a specific pattern. Test items can easily incorporate multimedia and links to external material on the web.

On the other hand, the design of software used with online testing often is poorly matched to the needs of instructors and instructional designers. Chapter 9 includes major sections that evaluate common characteristics of this software and propose standards against which the software should be judged.

Chapter 9 concludes with a discussion of issues and practical options for addressing security of online tests. This discussion is from the perspective of students as well as instructors and institutions.

7

Creating Constructed-Response Items

Items used in written tests are often categorized into two groups: those for which the learner must write out or construct a response, such as essay and completion formats, and those for which the learner chooses among options provided by the item, such as multiple-choice and true-false formats. Here in Chapter 7, we look at **constructed-response items.** The essay format, in particular, provides considerable flexibility in terms of gaining insight into a learner's thought process, whether we are talking about online or conventional paper-and-pencil tests. On the other hand, essay and other constructed-response items create special problems with respect to capabilities unique to online assessment, such as automatically scoring answers provided by learners. **Fixed-response items,** whose characteristics lend themselves to online assessments, are discussed in the next chapter.

Computer software that has been written for online testing, such as Blackboard and Question-Mark[1], varies in how it handles these item formats. For instance, with completion items, the software might automatically score responses written into a blank, but might be very restricted in what it recognizes as a correct response. Except in some large-scale testing programs, essays administered online are not scored by the computer. Software also varies with respect to simple things such as how much writing space is provided for answers and how well the written responses are managed for later scoring by a person.

Completion items are often used in instructors' quizzes and exams, and even in academic contests in which small teams of students from different schools compete against each other. Among tests administered using paper and pencil, completion items are used more often than items in all other formats. This may not be the case for tests administered online in distance learning environments because of the complexities sometimes associated with automatically scoring these items.

Because completion and essay items are used frequently, their characteristics are well-known including their advantages, limitations, and desired attributes. However, any review of constructed-response items used in both pencil-and-paper and online settings could reveal some major flaws. For example, many items present ambiguous questions for which diverse responses would qualify as appropriate answers. This chapter describes and illustrates the characteristics preferred in constructed-response items, beginning with the completion format. You will be asked to apply your understanding of these characteristics to evaluate some completion and essay items known to have some important flaws.

This chapter helps you achieve three skills that are relevant to using constructed-response items in online settings:

- Identify the advantages and limitations of completion and essay items

- Identify qualities desired in constructed-response items

- Evaluate completion and essay items for these qualities

---

[1]These systems and other software used with online assessments are discussed in later chapters.

COMPLETION ITEMS

Different names are used for this format. Sometimes it is called *fill in the blank* because that is what the student is often asked to do. Completion items can usually be rewritten as an equivalent question requiring a word or short phrase. For instance, this item

> The Italian artist who painted the ceiling of the Sistine Chapel is (Michelangelo).

can be rewritten as the following question:

> Which Italian artist painted the ceiling of the Sistine Chapel?

These variations of the completion format are interchangeable with respect to skills they measure.

Advantages and Limitations of Completion Items

Advantages. Completion items have three advantages over written items in other formats. First, completion items are easy to construct. Second, as with the essay format, completion items require students to produce an answer rather than to select an answer from alternatives. Third, unlike the essay format, many completion questions can be included in a single quiz or exam.

1. *Completion items are easy to construct.* The ease of constructing completion items is a function of two characteristics. First, completion items more readily measure recall of information than procedural knowledge, such as concepts and rules, and items that measure recall of information are easier to construct. Second, completion items do not require the detailed scoring plans of essay items or the options associated with multiple-choice items. For settings in which the completion format is appropriate, this efficiency in item construction is a major asset.

2. *Completion items require the student to supply the answer.* Multiple-choice, true-false, and other alternate-choice formats are negatively affected by guessing. Students often give the correct answer without solving the problem

presented. Because guessing lowers test-score reliability, completion tests tend to be more reliable than multiple-choice or alternate-choice tests that contain the same number of items.

3. *Many completion items can be included in a test.* The inclusion of many items allows one test to provide a more adequate sampling of content, particularly compared with the essay format. This ability increases the generalizability of test scores and potentially their validity.

Limitations. Completion items, however, have two significant limitations. First, as already noted, completion items are generally restricted to measuring recall of information. Second, they are more likely to be scored erroneously than are objectively scored formats, such as multiple-choice and alternate-choice tests.

1. *Completion items are generally limited to measuring recall of information.* You may have noticed that most completion tests you have taken or given examined knowledge of facts, such as names of people, places, and procedures. Because the student must answer items with a short phrase or often a single word, the skills that completion items measure are limited.

2. *Completion items are more likely to be scored erroneously than are the objectively scored formats.* Completion questions often can be answered with a variety of responses, any one of which might be the desired response. The question "Who discovered America?" could be referring to the name of a person, a nation, or a culture from any of a variety of historical periods. Errors are likely in scoring potentially correct but divergent responses to completion items. This is especially problematic when the computer scores the responses. Software is often very restrictive, unable to recognize a correct response that varies at all from the keyed response, including differences in spelling and capitalization. To minimize this problem, each completion item must be constructed so that knowledgeable students respond with homogeneous or even identical answers. Likewise, the computer must be

provided with all possible responses that will be considered acceptable, including tolerable misspellings and extra spacing when multiple words are involved.

Identifying Qualities Desired in Completion Items

This section examines specific criteria for evaluating completion items. In the next section, you will be asked to use these criteria to evaluate some completion questions.

1. *Does this item measure the specified skill?* For a test to have content validity, its items must collectively measure the skills that are specified in the performance objectives or outlined in a table of specifications.[2] An item should be selected or constructed only after the skill to be measured has been identified. Therefore, with every test item, regardless of format, it is essential to ask whether the item is measuring the targeted skill.

2. *Is the reading skill required by this item below the students' ability?* Unless the purpose of a test is to measure reading proficiency, the reading proficiency of students should not affect their scores. The level of reading skill required for understanding each item on a test should be *below* that of the students taking the test. Otherwise, you do not know whether incorrect answers are the result of a lack of knowledge or weak reading skills. When tests are administered online, because the instructor usually is unavailable to provide clarification during the test, one must be particularly careful to write items as directly as possible and certainly below the reading level of typical students.

3. *Will only a single or very homogeneous set of responses provide a correct response to the item?* The major cause of errors in scoring completion items is the use of questions for which there are

several legitimate answers. Constructing items so that only a single or very homogeneous set of responses represent a correct answer reduces this kind of error. Unless the item carefully restricts the correct answer, you may not be able to anticipate all the defensible answers when providing the key to the computer.

7.1 Apply What You Are Learning

Correct answers to two of the five items are restricted. Which two items are they?

1. A high-quality classroom test must be _____.
2. The item format that allows assessment of how well a student expresses ideas in writing is

   _____.
3. The difference between declarative and procedural knowledge is _____.
4. How long should a test be?
5. Which item format is generally limited to measuring a student's ability to recall information?

Answers can be found at the end of the chapter.

To develop items with restricted responses, a strategy that often works is to first determine the desired answer and then construct a question for which that answer is the only appropriate response. (Sounds like the popular quiz show *Jeopardy!*)

4. *Does the item use grammatical structure and vocabulary that is different from that contained in the source of instruction?* A common but unwise approach to constructing completion items is to select important sentences from a textbook or other source and replace a key word with a blank. Two problems are associated with this practice. First, it encourages students to memorize rather than to comprehend what is read. Second, and a more significant problem, is that most sentences derive some of their meaning from adjacent sentences. Extracting sentences creates vague test items. Note the vagueness of the following items. Each is an important sentence appearing earlier in this book.

---

[2]Chapter 3 describes how to use either performance objectives or a table of specifications to outline the content of a test before test items are selected or created. This is an important aspect of establishing valid tests.

The importance of declarative knowledge is often _____.

Performance objectives do not describe _____.

The intended answers are "downplayed" and "knowledge." What answers did you give?

5. *If the item requires a numerical response, does the question state the unit of measurement to be used in the answer?* Consider the following question:

What is the sum of 24 inches   <u>36</u> inches
and 12 inches?

Had "inches" not been specified to the right of the blank, correct answers would have included 3 (feet) and 1 (yard). You can score answers more quickly and accurately if students use a common unit of measure.

6. *Does the blank represent a key word?* If the blanks in completion items fail to represent key words, the test will measure reading comprehension more than knowledge of a particular content area. In fact, a technique for measuring reading comprehension is to have students fill in blanks representing every fifth word of a paragraph. Taylor (1953) named this procedure the "cloze" technique. Because blanks are substituted for every fifth word, rather than key words, the cloze technique does not (and is not intended to) provide an effective measure of the knowledge portrayed in the paragraph.

7.2   Apply What You Are Learning

To make a completion item, which underlined word in each sentence is the key word that could be replaced with a blank?

1. <u>Validity</u> is generally regarded as the most <u>essential</u> quality of an educational <u>test</u>.
2. A <u>test</u> that measures something <u>consistently</u> would be considered <u>reliable</u>.
3. More than any other <u>format</u>, it is difficult <u>measuring</u> a representative sample of content when using <u>essay</u> items.

Answers can be found at the end of the chapter.

---

7. *Are blanks placed at or near the end of the item?* The efficiency with which students answer completion items can be improved somewhat by placing blanks at or near the end of each item. This way, students can answer the items when they first come to a blank and avoid having to reread part of the item. Therefore, item 1 in the preceding examples should be rewritten as follows:

1. The quality generally regarded   1. validity
   as most essential in an
   educational test is <u>(1)</u>.

8. *Is the number of blanks sufficiently limited?* An excessive number of blanks in a completion item can cause problems. Too many blanks increases the amount of time required for students to determine what is being asked. If fewer blanks are used, more items can be included in a test, improving coverage of content and hence potential validity.

Another problem caused by using too many blanks is that the resulting test item often has a variety of unintended but legitimate answers. How many answers can you generate for this item?

A _____ is _____ of _____.

Some possibilities include the following:

A <u>gulf</u> is <u>south</u> of <u>Pensacola</u>.
A <u>mouse</u> is <u>kind</u> of <u>small</u>.
A <u>branch</u> is <u>part</u> of <u>a tree</u>.
A <u>great aunt</u> is <u>the sister</u> of <u>your grandparent</u>.

Although this example is rather extreme, completion items tend to have multiple solutions as the number of blanks increases. Software for many online assessment systems allows only one blank per item.

Practice Applying These Desired Qualities to Completion Items

The previous section examined eight criteria, which are listed in Table 7.1, for evaluating completion items. This section will help you apply them by looking at some examples.

Table 7.1
Criteria for evaluating completion items

1. Does this item measure the specified skill?
2. Is the reading skill required by this item below the students' ability?
3. Will only a single or very homogeneous set of responses provide a correct response to the item?
4. Does the item use grammatical structure and vocabulary that is different from that contained in the source of instruction?
5. If the item requires a numerical response, does the question state the unit of measure to be used in the answer?
6. Does the blank represent a key word?
7. Are blanks placed at or near the end of the item?
8. Is the number of blanks sufficiently limited?

The objective being assessed by the following items and the proposed correct responses are provided to help you evaluate each item. Each example fails to meet at least one of the criteria listed in Table 7.1. A critique follows each item. Numbers in parentheses preceding each critique indicate which of the criteria the example item has failed to achieve. Try to identify these problems before reading the critique.

Our three example items are intended to measure this objective:

Information: When given its definition, name the literary figure of speech being defined.

Completion Example 1

1. A (1) compares two different   1. simile
   things by using the word "like"
   or "as".

Critique for Example 1

(7) This completion item should be worded so that the blank appears near the end of the sentence. This improves the item's efficiency by allowing students to respond immediately. Here is an improved version of this item:

1. A comparison of two different   1. simile
   things by using the word
   "like" or "as" is called a(n) (1).

Completion Example 2

2. The statement "He eats like a   2. simile
   bird" illustrates what figure of
   speech? (2)

Critique for Example 2

(1) The problem with this example is serious, but it might be hard to find. The item is a good completion item *but* it does not measure the objective. Instead of giving the definition for a figure of speech, this item provides an example that the student must classify as to figure of speech. It measures students' knowledge of the concept of *simile,* which is procedural knowledge rather than declarative knowledge. (This item illustrates something that completion items have a difficult time doing—measuring procedural knowledge.) Again, the item is well written, and the knowledge being assessed is relevant; it just is not the knowledge the performance objective intends to target.

Completion Example 3

3. (3) imply resemblances such   3. metaphors
   as from human physiology to
   other objects, for instance,
   "the mouth of a river"
   or "the eye of a needle."

Critique for Example 3

(7) Again, this completion item should be worded so that the blank appears near the end of the sentence. Although the item includes examples of metaphors, they illustrate the definition of metaphors, which is included in the item. Here is an improved version of this item:

3. Implied resemblances such   3.   metaphors
   as from human physiology
   to other objects, for instance,
   "the mouth of a river" or
   "the eye of a needle"
   are called (3).

With online tests, it may be necessary to include both singular and plural versions as correct responses, if the computer requires a literal match for a response to be scored as correct. Again, this illustrates the need to construct word completion items so that correct responses are very limited.

ESSAY ITEMS

The essay question represents a very flexible test format for assessing distance learners. It can potentially measure any skill that can be assessed with other formats of written tests. An **essay item** is also uniquely able to assess a learner's ability to communicate ideas in writing. On the other hand, the essay format has a number of weaknesses that, if uncontrolled, can substantially reduce the usefulness of a test. For example, answers to essay questions are often scored differently depending on who does the grading. Also, a variety of characteristics other than the knowledge being assessed, such as the writer's grammar and the length of the written response, often affect essay scores.

This section describes characteristics typically associated with better-quality essay items. You will be asked to apply these characteristics by evaluating a series of essay questions. Many of the limitations of the essay format pertain to the scoring of responses. A variety of techniques that can improve scoring accuracy are described in this chapter. These include using a model answer, concealing the identity of learners, and grading all responses to one question at a time. Unfortunately, some of these techniques are impractical with present online assessment procedures.

Advantages and Limitations of Essay Items

Advantages. Essay items have three advantages over test questions written in other formats. First, essay items tend to measure more directly the behaviors specified by instructional objectives. Second, essay items examine the learner's ability to communicate ideas in writing. Third, because it allows test takers to explain their logic, the essay format helps instructors gain insight into the thinking that leads to students' answers.

1. *Essay items tend to measure more directly behaviors specified by instructional objectives.* All of the popular item formats can measure learners' knowledge of information, and as we will discuss later, many can also measure procedural knowledge. However, more than the other formats, essay items tend to directly measure the behavior specified by performance objectives. For instance, if the objective is for learners to describe situations where it is economically advantageous to lease rather than purchase a new automobile, the corresponding essay item might simply be

> Describe the situations where it is economically advantageous to lease versus purchase a new automobile.

Many well-written performance objectives can be restated as essay items with minor and sometimes no rewording. Other test formats, as illustrated by the following true-false items, get at the targeted behavior more *indirectly*:

> The shorter the time you expect to hold onto the car, the more it becomes advantageous to lease the car. (true)

> The more miles you expect to drive the car each year, the more it becomes advantageous to lease the car. (false)

As we will see later, the tendency for essay items to measure more directly the behavior specified by an objective is often the result of how we write performance objectives rather than any special characteristic of the essay format.

2. *Essay items can examine learners' ability to communicate ideas in writing.* Given the importance of writing skills, this quality is significant. However, when essay items are used to assess a learner's ability to communicate ideas, writing proficiency and comprehension of content should be reported in separate scores. Recall that the usefulness of test scores is reduced when a single score is used to simultaneously describe more than one outcome of instruction.

The advantage of using essay items to assess writing skills should not be overgeneralized. For example, the essay test does not represent an appropriate environment for training individuals to write. Learners are more inclined to develop their writing skills when their abilities are shaped through frequent writing experiences outside examination settings. The use of essay items as a means of improving writing skills is likely to fail because of examination pressure, such as the need to write answers quickly.

3. *Essay items allow test takers to explain their logic.* All test formats can measure declarative knowledge. Generalizations and knowledge of relationships make up much of our important declarative knowledge. An essay item can ask the test taker to explain where these come from. Multiple-choice items can measure procedural knowledge, such as when learners are asked to distinguish between examples and nonexamples of a concept. Essay items can ask test takers to make this same distinction, but then explain the logic used to establish the classification. With essay items, test takers are less able to provide a correct answer using the wrong logic.

Limitations. Essay items have three limitations relative to test items written in other formats. First, exams that use the essay format tend to provide a less-adequate sampling of the content being tested. Second, the scoring of essay items is less reliable. Third, essay items take longer to score.

1. *Essay items usually provide a less-adequate sampling of the content.* Time constraints usually allow inclusion of only a few essay items on one exam. As a result, one essay test will measure a relatively small portion of the skills that students are expected to learn. Many years ago, Posey (1932) established that when as few as 10 items are included in a test, scores are largely determined by whether these items happen by chance to sample content with which each learner is knowledgeable. One might use broad essay questions to cover a greater percentage of skills with each item. This strategy, however, tends to inflate existing weaknesses of the essay format. For instance, broad questions are very difficult to score accurately.

It is interesting to note that with essay tests learners spend most of their time writing out the answer rather than solving the problem posed by the question. If a learner is fairly knowledgeable about the concept being questioned, relatively little time is needed to read the essay item and formulate a response. If some way other than writing could be established for recording the learners' answers to essay questions, substantially more skills could be assessed by one test, although this would negate an advantage of the format—assessing one's ability to communicate knowledge in writing.

Because so few items can be included in an essay test, instructors often conclude that an advantage of the format is that less time is required to develop a test. The time required to develop one high-quality essay item, however, is generally greater than that required to develop a good item in any alternative format. The inclusion of fewer items in an essay test results from a limitation of the essay format and is *not* an advantage; time constraints allow for the measurement of only a few skills.

Furthermore, instructors often conclude that essay tests are easier to develop when they construct essay items without simultaneously creating a plan for scoring these items. This is a poor strategy that is discussed later in the chapter.

2. *The scoring of essay items is often highly subjective.* Because of the subjective aspect of scoring essay items, scores assigned to the students' answers are often inconsistent. This discrepancy results largely because the qualities being assessed by an essay question vary as a function of who reads the responses. Factors such as penmanship, expected achievement, and even sex and race of the learner have been found to significantly affect scores assigned to essays. With online assessments, keyboard entry will negate bias caused by quality of penmanship; however, the way online systems display the responses often makes it more difficult to conceal student identity.

The subjective scoring of essay tests, combined with the relatively small number of items that can be included in a test can substantially reduce generalizability of essays. Techniques described later in this chapter can help address this significant limitation of the essay format.

3. *Essay tests are more time-consuming to score.* Hand scoring of essay exams is obviously time consuming. No other written test format takes as long to score. If fairly detailed scoring procedures are followed and particularly if learner responses are graded by more than one reader (both techniques are desired), the amount of time required to score essay items can be considerable. Computer scoring of essay exams substantially reduces this limitation, although this capability is generally limited to large-scale assessments. Computer scoring of essays is discussed later in the chapter.

Computer scoring of essays is becoming an increasingly available option and has been the subject of ongoing research for a number of years (see, for example, Page & Paulus, 1968 1966). However, it has not yet become a practical option for most instructor-developed tests. The essay component in many large-scale assessments, including some college admission exams and statewide assessments, is scored exclusively by computer, or with the computer substituting for one of the human readers. Rudner and Gagne (2001), in an online reference included in the suggested readings at the end of this chapter, provides a synopsis of computer-scored essays.

Identifying Qualities Desired in Essay Items

Before considering specific qualities, a distinction should be made between brief-response and extended-response questions. Although extended-response essay items have unique assets, these same qualities limit their usefulness in online tests. An essay question usually qualifies as a brief-response item if learners can read and fully answer it within 10 minutes. The required length of the answer is generally established by the nature of the task presented to the learners. An extended-response item presents a broader task. The task may be broader simply because it asks learners to do quantitatively more rather than to do a qualitatively different kind of task. Alternatively, an extended-response item may allow learners to demonstrate such skills as creativity, selecting and organizing a number of ideas relevant to a given issue, and communicating ideas in writing. Either way, the appropriateness of using an extended-response essay question to achieve these characteristics should be evaluated.

If the purpose of using an extended-response question is to have learners demonstrate a greater number of skills, it can usually be broken into shorter questions that, individually, can be answered within 10 minutes. This tactic will significantly improve the consistency with which answers are scored and will typically allow assessment of a better cross section of skills.

Not all extended-response essay questions can be subdivided. To determine whether subdivision is possible, look at the types of capabilities that are being assessed. If they involve recalling information or demonstrating knowledge of concepts or rules, the extended-response question generally can be rewritten as a series of brief-response essays, and doing so will be advantageous.

On the other hand, if the extended-response question requires problem solving where learners can use diverse strategies to solve the problem, then brief-response questions may not suffice. Be careful here. A task does not involve problem solving simply because it is difficult, is academically important, or requires learners to do a lot. Problem solving involves but *does not* require learners to demonstrate their knowledge of information, concepts, or rules. If the extended-response question does require learners to do these things, it likely is not measuring what cognitive psychologists call problem solving. Problem solving requires learners to draw on and synthesize information, concepts, and rules. In solving the problem, the learners' recall of information and knowledge of concepts and rules generally is not documented in their written responses. Again, if the essay question is asking for a statement of knowledge of information, concepts, and rules, the essay question generally is not assessing a problem-solving skill and can be rewritten as a series of brief-response questions.

If a proposed essay question will require an extended response because it truly involves the complexity of problem solving, formats other than a written test should be considered. Usually, problem-solving skills are more adequately measured through performance assessments or even portfolios. Asking a learner to demonstrate a complex skill in the context of a brief written exam tends to be contrived and, more often than not, distorts and invalidates an important assessment. When essay tests are administered online, brief-response items are typically preferred.

This leads us to six specific criteria that characterize high-quality essay items. In the next section, you will be asked to use these criteria to evaluate a series of essay questions. The last section of this chapter describes techniques that can be used to facilitate accurate scoring of essay tests.

1. *Does the item measure the specified skill?* With every test item, regardless of format, it is essential to ask whether the item is measuring the targeted skill.

7.3   Apply What You Are Learning

Following is a performance objective followed by two essay items that were written to measure that objective. Which item (A or B) provides the best measure of this objective?

Concept: Given a description of a man-made object in space, state with explanation whether or not it is a satellite of Earth.

A. The mission of the Hubbell Space Telescope is to photograph far-away objects from its orbit above Earth. Is the Hubbell Space Telescope a satellite of Earth? Explain your reasoning.
B. What determines whether a space vehicle is an Earth satellite? Explain your reasoning.

Answers can be found at the end of the chapter.

Sometimes instructors allow learners to choose the subset of essay items they will answer. This practice lowers the content-related validity of the test, because the set of questions included is determined by learner preference rather than by a systematic plan. Allowing learners to select questions creates two additional problems as well. First, to the degree that learners avoid difficult questions, the test is less likely to detect areas with which they need help. Second, test scores based on subsets of items that measure different skills are difficult to interpret.

On the other hand, it often is appropriate to provide learners with options in how they respond to a question. For instance, learners might be allowed to write about the scientist of their choice to illustrate the scientific method of inquiry. The essay question might even list the names of scientists from which the learners may choose. Allowing learners a choice in how they respond to a question is appropriate as long as the same capability is being assessed regardless of a learner's choice, and the same scoring plan can be applied to all learners' responses.

Table 7.2
Three characteristics to be included in the scoring plan of each essay item

---

1. Total number of points assigned to the item based on its importance relative to other items
2. Specific attributes to be evaluated in students' responses
3. For each attribute, criteria for awarding points, including partial credit

---

2. Is the level of reading skill required by this item below the learners' ability? As with other formats, measures of reading ability and achievement will be confounded unless the reading skill required to understand the test item is below that of the learners taking the test. Each sentence in essay questions should use simple construction and words with which all learners are proficient.

3. Will all or almost all learners answer this item in less than 10 minutes? An essay question that requires learners to take more than 10 minutes to formulate and write a response is not a brief-response essay item. As discussed earlier, extended-response items should be avoided online assessments.

4. Will the **scoring plan**[3] *result in different readers assigning similar scores to a given learner's response?* Consistency in scoring is essential with all item formats. The need for consistency is more obvious for objectively scored items, such as multiple choice. For instance, if two people grade the same answers to a multiple-choice exam but derive quite different scores, the scoring process is likely to be judged inadequate. Consistency in scoring is equally important for essay items. If changing who reads answers to an essay item changes the score assigned, then something other than the adequacy of the student's answer is affecting the score. That is, the validity of an essay test is diminished when the possibility of inconsistent scoring exists. The scoring plan for each essay item must be designed so that different readers will assign similar scores to a given learner's response.

To facilitate reliable scoring, the scoring plan should incorporate the three characteristics listed in Table 7.2. First, the total number of points the item is worth should be provided to students when they take the test. Often the software used to administer online tests requires that points be specified for each essay item. This is good. *However, the points associated with each essay item should be proportional to the relative importance of the skill being tested,* and not be equated with the amount of time needed to answer the question. The increased time required to write a response to an essay item is a disadvantage of the essay format that cannot be avoided. It is not an appropriate reason for assigning more points to essay questions than to items in other formats.

Second, a scoring plan should specify the attributes to be evaluated. Figure 7.1 provides an example of how attributes should be specified. First, let us state the objective being assessed:

Concept: Given a description of a storm involving strong winds, state with explanation whether or not it is a hurricane.

Figure 7.1 shows an essay item that measures this objective and specifies the attributes in learners' responses that are to be scored. The essay question involves a concept, specifically that of hurricanes.

---

[3]The terms *scoring plan* and *scoring rubric* are sometimes used interchangeably, although technically a scoring rubric is one among several types of scoring plans. A scoring rubric establishes criteria for *holistically* scoring responses on multiple criteria. When essay questions are used to assess knowledge of *information* (rather than writing skills), **analytical** rather than **holistic scoring** is typically used. When numerical scores are used, analytical scoring assigns points to each of several qualities, with the points totaled for the essay question. Holistic scoring and consequently scoring rubrics are used more often with performance assessments and portfolios (see Chapter 11).

Figure 7.1
Illustration of attributes within a scoring plan

Test Item

A strong cold front approached Florida and a severe storm resulted. As the front approached, sustained winds from the southwest increased to 50 miles an hour with some gusts higher than 80. As the front passed, the wind switched to the northwest and then slowly diminished. Was this storm a hurricane? Explain your conclusion, briefly describing how <u>each</u> piece of information presented above was used in drawing your conclusion.

Attributes to Be Scored

1. Classifies the storm as not a hurricane

2. Identifies absence of a closed circulation around a calm center

3. Identifies absence of sustained wind above 74 miles per hour

4. Identifies two additional characteristics of this weather system that are not defining characteristics of a hurricane

---

If four attributes in Figure 7.1 are judged to be appropriate for scoring this essay item, misspellings or errors in grammar will not count. Information learners provide that is superfluous to the criteria specified in the scoring plan will not count, regardless of the accuracy of the information. (Such qualities would be scored only if included in the scoring plan.) Therefore, answers to essay items often will include errors that are not scored. This does not mean that such errors have to be or even should be ignored. Unscored errors can be marked, and learners can also be required to correct important errors after the test has been scored. Unfortunately, software used for some online tests only allows the instructor to assign points to a response, which makes it difficult to provide other useful feedback.

The third criterion to be included in a scoring plan pertains to how points will be awarded. In Figure 7.2, the points associated with each attribute, or combination of attributes, are specified.

A scoring plan must be precise enough for the reader to know when to award a point and when not to. If more than one point is associated with a given quality, the guidelines should indicate if and how partial credit is to be awarded.

When essay items are administered online, it is often possible to provide learners with a fairly detailed scoring plan immediately after the test is completed. Answers are formally scored later; however, providing the scoring plan at test completion helps learners determine how they did on the test and allows them to obtain some immediate feedback on their answers.

One might incorrectly conclude that a scoring plan prevents essay items from measuring more than factual knowledge. This conclusion would be justified if a scoring plan was simply a specification of the correct answer, but this is not what a scoring plan is. Instead of specifying the correct answer, the scoring plan specifies *attributes* of the correct answer. For instance, an essay item might ask learners to take a position on a controversial issue and defend that position. The scoring plan would not be concerned with the position the learners chose. Instead, the scoring plan would be concerned with the conciseness with which learners expressed their positions and the nature of the defense they gave in support of them. *The scoring plan delineates attributes that distinguish adequate from less adequate responses to the essay item.*

Figure 7.2
Illustration of a scoring plan

1 point	1. Classifies the storm as not a hurricane
2 points	2. Identifies absence of a closed circulation around a calm center (no partial credit)
1 point	3. Identifies absence of sustained wind above 74 miles per hour
2 points	4. Identifies two characteristics of this weather system that are not defining characteristics of a hurricane (1 point per characteristic)

7.4 Apply What You Are Learning

The preceding discussion identified three characteristics to use in developing a scoring plan. These characteristics are summarized in Table 7.2. Which of these characteristics has *not* been addressed in the scoring plans for each of the following essay items?

Item 1. In an orchestra, what are the differences between wind and string instruments?

Scoring plan for item 1: 1 point for each correct answer

Item 2. Support or critique this statement: "The reading level of a test should be equivalent to that of the average learner taking the test."

Scoring plan for item 2:
- Refers to need for reading level to be at or below that of all learners taking the test
- Refers to idea that a difficult reading level confounds measurement of reading ability with the skill being tested

Answers can be found at the end of the chapter.

How did your answers to this exercise compare with the answers given at the end of the chapter? Beyond problems with its scoring plan, notice how vague the first essay item is. A variety of differences between wind and string instruments could be listed, including some that the item writer probably did not anticipate. For instance, wind instruments are used in marching bands; they often are not made of wood; and they are always placed up to or partially into the player's mouth. Had the item writer thought through the scoring plan while developing the item, its vagueness would likely have been detected before the test was administered. You can probably recall encountering vague essay questions for which a scoring plan obviously had not been thought through. From the instructor's perspective, such items become somewhat embarrassing when even the best students are unable to establish what is being asked. From an assessment perspective, a concise scoring plan tends to significantly enhance the quality of an essay item, in part by helping to ensure that the essay question posed is concise.

5. *Does the scoring plan describe a correct and complete response?* The purpose of an instructor's test is to assess the learner's proficiency with a particular skill. This purpose can be realized only if test items are constructed so that learners who have acquired that knowledge tend to give a correct answer and learners who have not acquired that knowledge give an incorrect or incomplete response. This can be accomplished only if the person scoring the test can describe a correct and complete response. With an essay item, the correct response is described through the scoring plan.

Constructing a scoring plan that describes a correct and complete response is difficult if the essay item asks a broad question. This is a major reason for using essay questions that can be answered fully within 10 minutes, even if it involves breaking a larger question into a series of related smaller questions. Essay questions that require more than 10 minutes to answer tend to be too broad.

Colleagues who teach similar classes often can help each other develop or proof a scoring plan. One strategy is to ask a colleague to answer an essay question orally. If the colleague's response differs significantly from your own scoring plan, modify either the scoring plan or the item itself. An alternative strategy is to ask a colleague to score some of your learners' answers using your scoring plan. Usually, a colleague can quickly detect any significant problems that exist in the scoring plan.

6. *Is the item written in such a way that the scoring plan will be obvious to knowledgeable learners?* If learners who are proficient in the area being assessed are unable to describe how an item will be scored, the item cannot fulfill its role. The item will be unable to determine the proficiency of learners because it will not distinguish between learners who have acquired the knowledge and those who have not. Proficient learners will be able to give correct answers only if they can determine from the item the characteristics of a correct answer.

The same conditions that facilitate the development of a scoring plan also help communicate to learners the qualities desired in the answer. The essay item must pose a specific task for which the attributes of a correct response are not simply a matter of opinion. In addition to stating the essay question, it is sometimes helpful to state briefly the characteristics of a correct response, as well as how many points the essay item is worth.

Practice Applying These Desired Qualities to Essay Items

The previous section presented six criteria for evaluating essay items. Table 7.3 lists them. This section will help you apply these criteria through some example items.

Each example states the performance objective that is to be measured, an essay item designed to measure that objective, and the scoring plan that was proposed for scoring responses to the item. When administered, only the essay item would be shown to learners. Use Table 7.3 to evaluate each example. Each essay item and/or its scoring plan fails to meet at least one of these six criteria. Compare your evaluation to the critique that follows each example.

Essay Example 1

Objective: Concept: Given a description of heat being transferred, classify the heat transfer as predominantly conduction, convection, or radiation and provide logic behind this classification.
Essay item shown to learners: A pan of water is being heated on the stove. Although the water is not being stirred, the water can be seen moving around within the pan as the temperature of the water increases. Is heat being transferred within this water mostly by conduction, convection, or radiation? What is happening in this water that causes this transfer of heat? (3 points)

Table 7.3
Criteria for evaluating essay items

1. Does this item measure the specified skill?
2. Is the level of reading skill required by this item below the learners' ability?
3. Will all or almost all students answer this item in less than 10 minutes?
4. Will the scoring plan result in different readers assigning similar scores to a given student's response?
5. Does the scoring plan describe a correct and complete response?
6. Is the item written in such a way that the scoring plan will be obvious to knowledgeable learners?

Scoring plan: The learner shows that heat is being transferred by convection.

Critique for Example 1

The item, as written, is good. The scoring plan, however, does not provide criteria for awarding points. Without these criteria, different readers would likely assign dissimilar scores to each learner's response. Here is a better scoring plan:

1 point	States heat is being transferred by convection
1 point	Indicates that convection transfers heat by movement and thus mixing of the heated fluid
1 point	Indicates that convection movement is caused by fluid expanding when heated, thus becoming more buoyant and rising

Essay Example 2

Objective: Concept: When given an illustration of a change in a substance, classifies it as a physical change (i.e., altering the shape, form, volume, or density) or a chemical change (i.e., producing new substances with different characteristics).

Essay item shown to learners: Explain the difference between a physical and a chemical change in a substance. (3 points)

Scoring plan: Determine whether the learner correctly explains the difference.

Critique for Example 2

Example 2 fails to meet almost all the criteria in Table 7.3. Let us evaluate this item by examining each of the six criteria:

1. Asking the learner to explain the difference between physical and chemical change does not measure the objective. Notice that this objective involves a concept. To measure a concept, learners should be given an illustration they have not previously used in this context, and then be asked to classify the illustration. As worded, this essay item measures recall of

information, specifically, the distinction between physical and chemical change. A better essay item for measuring this objective would be the following:

A piece of wood has burned. Is this an example of a physical or a chemical change? Explain why.

2. To this item's credit, the level of reading skill needed to understand this question is appropriately lower than the reading level of those taking the test, assuming the item is directed at typical readers of this book.

3. Again to this item's credit, most learners can answer it within 10 minutes.

4. The scoring plan is vague, and different readers will likely assign quite different scores to a given learner's response. In essence, the scoring plan states that learners should give a correct answer without specifying attributes to be evaluated or how points are to be awarded. Here is an improved plan for awarding the 3 points associated with this item (although improving the scoring plan does not negate this item's other problems):

2 points	Associates physical change with altering shape, form, volume, or density (or 1 point if 3 of 4 are listed); otherwise, 0 points
1 point	Associates chemical change with producing a different substance

5. The original scoring plan does not describe a complete response, in large part because the scoring plan is not concise. As originally worded, content experts would differ in what they believe constitutes a fully correct response.

6. The essay item does not communicate to the learner how answers will be scored, mainly because the task presented to the learner is vague. Often, this is the result of having only a vague scoring plan in mind when the item is written. If the revised scoring presented in point 4 were used, here is how the essay item could be rewritten.

What changes in a substance, if they occur, would be classified as a physical change? Likewise, what change in a substance would be classified as a chemical change?

Essay Example 3

Objective: Rule: Given a constant force applied to an object moving through space, draw and explain the path this object will take through space as the force is continually applied to the object.

Essay item shown to learners: An object is initially moving through space from left to right. A constant force from above, perpendicular to its initial movement, is applied to the object. Draw the path the object will take over an extended period of time as a result of the force being applied. Explain why the object will follow the path you have drawn. (4 points)

Scoring plan: An appropriate path is drawn and explanation given.

Critique for Example 3

The item is well written, but its scoring plan is not. The item measures the objective and can be answered within 10 minutes.

This item is written so that the scoring plan probably would be obvious to knowledgeable learners even though, as it is presented here, it is carelessly written and, as a result, vague. Assuming the person reading the learners' answers is knowledgeable, the intended scoring plan might be implied from the item; therefore, we may not have a serious problem here. Regardless, creating a vague scoring plan is a bad practice because it encourages writing vague essay items. The scoring plan should specify the attributes to be evaluated in learners' responses, as well as criteria for awarding points for each attribute. Here is an improved scoring plan:

1 point	Drawing shows downward change in object's path
1 point	Change is smooth
1 point	From explanation, obvious that learner recognizes rate of motion

from left to right remains unchanged

1 point	From explanation, obvious that learner recognizes downward motion increases at a constant rate

Scoring Responses to Essay Items

Computer Scoring. Using a computer to score essay items sounds futuristic, and significant parts of it are. However, for some time there has been considerable interest in the possibility of computer scoring. Scoring answers by machine would reduce or eliminate some significant disadvantages of the essay format. For instance, the amount of time required to score answers would be reduced, particularly when large groups of learners were involved. Computer scoring of essays, if valid, would also help address the problem of inconsistency across readers.

As early as the mid-1960s, Ellis Page was experimenting with computerized essay scoring. He keypunched essays on cards for input into a computer, and then programmed the computer to search for characteristics such as the use of clichés and passive verbs that correlated highly with essay scores assigned by human raters. In this manner, the computer was able to assign scores to essays that correlated with human ratings to the same degree that the ratings of different humans correlated with each other. Research by Page and others has progressed to the point where a computer can now rate the quality of writing and check for the presence of conceptual ideas. In a number of large **standardized testing** programs that involve essays, a computer and a human independently read each essay. Additional human readers are brought in only when the scores assigned by the computer and the human are inconsistent. With some assessment programs, essays are scored only by a computer.

It is only a matter of time before computers can be programmed to, without human intervention, read and score essays typed into the computer by learners. For online essay tests produced by instructors and administered using Blackboard, technology is not yet at that stage. However, when computer scoring of such essays becomes widespread, it will likely occur in settings where learners enter their essays directly into a computer, such as through online assessments.

Reading Responses to Multiple Versus Single Items. With other formats, such as short answer and multiple choice, all of one learner's answers are read before reading the responses of the next learner. With essay items, all learners' responses to a given item should be evaluated before reading responses to the next item. From a practical perspective, working with one item at a time focuses the reader's attention and speeds up the scoring process—significant advantages in grading essay exams. More important, reading all responses to a given item improves scoring accuracy. Focusing on a single item helps the reader maintain a clear perception of the standards being used to evaluate answers to that particular essay question. Also, reading the responses of all learners to a single item reduces the tendency to bias the evaluation of one item in light of the quality of a learner's response to previous items.

Unfortunately, software that supports online testing generally does not permit reading all responses to one item at a time. Instead, the reader is essentially forced into reading one learner's responses to all items before going on to those of the next person. This substantially increases the amount of time required to score all of the tests and significantly increases inconsistencies in scoring. This is an unnecessary limitation and is a problem developers of online assessment software should address.

Reading Learners' Papers in a Variable Versus Consistent Order. It has been known for some time that the quality of a previously scored essay affects the score assigned to a subsequently read response. Daly and Dickson-Markman (1982) and Hughes, Keeling, and Tuck (1980) demonstrated that a high-quality essay deflates the score assigned to a subsequent paper. Hughes and Keeling (1984) found this to be true even when

responses were being judged against model answers. To reduce the cumulative effect this biasing might have across items on each learner's test score, the order of papers should be rearranged after each question is read.

Again, the developers of online assessment software should take this scoring consideration into account. Not only should readers be able to evaluate all answers to one item at a time, readers should also be able to ask for the order of responses to be randomized for each essay item. Unfortunately, most assessment software does not facilitate this, even though it would be fairly easy to program it to do so.

Concealing the Identity of Learners. Previously referenced studies by Chase (1979, 1986) found that factors such as expected achievement, as well as the sex and race of the learner, significantly affect scores assigned to essays. To prevent this biasing, learner identity should be concealed to the extent possible when scoring essays. Such techniques as having learners write their names on the back of their papers or using temporary identification numbers can be used for paper-and-pencil tests. With online assessments, concealing learner identity would be as simple as allowing the display of learner names to be turned off when responses were being scored. Again, the software developers usually fail to anticipate this need and may even display the learner's name adjacent to each response.

Using Multiple Readers. One would expect the reliability of scores on essay tests to increase when multiple raters read each paper and their scores are totaled or averaged. Although this is often the case, it is also impractical in most instructional settings.

In performance assessments, which share many scoring problems with essay items, research has shown that the reliability of scoring is *not* substantially increased by using multiple readers, *if* the scoring plan is well constructed and raters are adequately trained in its use (see, for example, Shavelson, Ruiz-Primo, Schultz, &

Wiley, 1998). This finding is applicable to the scoring of essays. Using multiple readers can only help. However, greater score reliability is likely when using carefully designed scoring plans for essay items, scoring responses anonymously, and reading all responses to one item before proceeding to the next.

Using Diversity of Responses as an Indicator of Item Ambiguity. Diversity of learners' responses, in which learners appear to be interpreting the essay question differently, should be viewed as an indication of item ambiguity. If an essay question is ambiguous, the instructor, in essence, is giving learners the option to interpret the question as they choose. This situation is similar to allowing each learner to select which questions to answer and usually causes the same problems with interpreting performance on the test. Essay questions that generate diverse responses should be revised before being used again.

SUMMARY

Completion items are a widely used format in written tests, but are used less often in online assessments because of difficulties in automatically scoring responses. There are three basic advantages to the completion format—ease of construction, student-generated answers, and the option of including many items in one test. Completion items have two basic limitations. They are generally limited to measuring recall of information, and they are more likely to be scored erroneously than are objectively scored items. Several desirable qualities of completion items were discussed and are listed in Table 7.1.

Essay items have some advantages over other written-test formats. They tend to measure instructional objectives more directly, and they help the instructor gain insight into the reasoning students use to derive answers. Essay items have basic limitations. They usually provide a less adequate sampling of content to be assessed, they are less reliably scored, and they are more time consuming to score. Six qualities that should be

incorporated into essay items were discussed and are listed in Table 7.3.

When constructing essay items, it is also important to simultaneously create a scoring plan. The scoring plan often specifies the characteristics as opposed to the content of a correct response. Other relevant scoring considerations include the desirability of scoring the responses of all learners to one item before scoring the next item, rearranging the order of learners' papers before reading the next item, and concealing the identity of learners when scoring responses. Unfortunately, software associated with online assessments generally does not facilitate efficient and effective scoring of essay responses.

ANSWERS: APPLY WHAT YOU ARE LEARNING

7.1 Correct answers to items 2 and 5 are restricted. Possible answers to item 1 include "valid," "reliable," "constructed from a list of objectives," and "a priority of all instructors." Possible answers for item 3 are "how they are learned" and "how they are assessed." Assuming that item 4 is referring to administration time, the answer depends on a variety of factors, such as the age of the students, the content area, and the purpose of the test.

7.2 1. validity; 2. reliable; 3. essay.

7.3 Item A provides the better measure. Notice also that item B is asking learners to recall information, whereas item A requires learners to determine whether or not an illustration is an example of a concept. Always be alert to the type of capability involved.

7.4 *Item 1 scoring plan:* Neither the total number of points nor the attributes to be evaluated is specified. *Item 2 scoring plan:* Neither the total number of points nor guidelines for awarding points is specified.

TERMS INTRODUCED IN THIS CHAPTER

Constructed-response items: represent one of the two categories of items used in written tests, and include the completion and essay formats. With constructed-response items, the learner enters or writes out the answer rather than choosing among options provided by the item.

Fixed-response items: are the other category of items used in written tests. The learner chooses among or manipulates in some manner response options provided by the item. The numerous variations of the basic multiple-choice and true-false formats are examples of fixed-response items.

Completion items: a type of constructed-response item; requires the learner to write words in one or more blanks embedded in the item. A computer can automatically score answers if it is given the correct responses.

Essay items: a type of constructed-response item; asks the learner to provide a narrative response to the test question. Computer programs have been developed that can automatically score essay responses; however, use of these scoring programs is generally limited to large-scale testing programs involving *standardized tests.*

Scoring plan: is a detailed description of how responses to an open-ended test item will be scored, whether it be an essay item, a performance assessment, or a portfolio assessment. A scoring plan is vital to ensuring that one rater's response will generalize fairly well to scores assigned by other raters.

Analytical scoring: is assigning points for each of multiple qualities, with a student's score on the test question being the total number of points received on the respective qualities. Analytical scoring tends to be more reliable than holistic scoring.

Holistic scoring: is assigning a score based on the rater's overall impression of each student's response. Holistic scoring usually can be accomplished more quickly than analytical scoring.

Standardized test: is typically administered to a large number of individuals and includes college admission tests and tests that are used in primary and secondary schools as part of a statewide assessment program. The term *standardized* refers to the fact that these tests are designed to be administered the same way or in a *standardized* way, even though they are administered to students at different times and locations.

ENHANCE YOUR UNDERSTANDING

- If you have access to some previously written completion items, use the qualities listed in Figure 7.1 to evaluate these items.

- Prepare some completion items that measure this objective and then use Figure 7.1 to evaluate them.

  Information: Given a geological feature, name the region of the country in which this feature exists.

- Similarly, if you have access to some previously written essay items, use the qualities listed in Table 7.3 to evaluate them, including the scoring plan.

- Prepare an essay item with a scoring plan that measures the following objective:

  Information: Using an actual example, describe the procedure Congress is to follow for attempting to override a presidential veto.

- Use Table 7.3 to evaluate this item. An essay item written to measure this objective probably can be answered in two to four sentences. Although this represents a minimal essay question, it provides a useful context for writing a concise essay item and scoring plan.

ADDITIONAL READING

Coffman, W. E. (1971). Essay examinations. In R. L. Thorndike (Ed.), *Educational measurement* (2nd ed.). Washington, DC: American Council on Education. This chapter provides a thorough discussion of advantages, limitations, and research issues related to essay questions as well as a description of procedures for improving the development and scoring of essay questions.

Daly, J. A., & Dickson-Markman, F. (1982). Contrast effects in evaluating essays. *Journal of Educational Measurement, 19,* 309–316.

Hughes, D. C., & Keeling, B. (1984). The use of model essays to reduce context effects in essay scoring. *Journal of Educational Measurement, 21,* 277–281.

Hughes, D. C., Keeling, B., & Tuck, B. F. (1980). The influence of context position and scoring method on essay scoring. *Journal of Educational Measurement, 17,* 131–135.

Page, E., & Paulus, D. (1968). *The analysis of essays by computer.* Final report submitted to Office of Education, Washington, DC Bureau of Research (ERIC Document No. ED028633).

Posey, C. (1932). Luck and examination grades. *Journal of Engineering Education, 23,* 292–296.

Rudner, L., & Gagne, P. (2001). *An overview of three approaches to scoring written essays by computer.* Retrieved from http://www.ericdigests.org/2002-2/essays.htm. This digest from the ERIC Clearinghouse on Assessment and Evaluation provides a synopsis of major research developments in computer scoring of essays, including recommended readings and URLs for related websites.

Wesman, A. G. (1971). Writing the test item. In R. L. Thorndike (Ed.), *Educational measurement* (2nd ed.). Washington, DC: American Council on Education. This chapter reviews the item-writing literature and discusses ideas for producing various formats of objectively scored test items.

8

Creating Fixed-Response Items

With online assessments, the most common fixed-response item formats are **multiple-choice** and **true-false.** The fixed-response format lends itself to online administration. For example, responses can often be scored immediately as each student completes the test, and the student's records can be updated automatically without the instructor's involvement. Fixed-response items also make it easy to automate feedback so that at the conclusion of a test, each learner receives an explanation of the logic behind the correct and incorrect **response options.** In particularly large-scale testing programs, fixed-response items are now being used in computer adaptive tests, in which specific items administered later in a test depend on the correctness of the examinee's answers earlier in that test.

You are familiar with limitations of fixed-response items. For instance, with multiple-choice items the correct response is always one of the options. True-false items in particular are very susceptible to guessing. Many individuals believe that fixed-response items are limited to measuring only the most basic forms of knowledge, but in this chapter we will challenge that perception. As with all item formats, fixed-response items have both significant limitations and unique advantages when it comes to online assessments. We will look at ways to minimize the limitations and capitalize on the advantages.

This chapter helps you achieve five skills relevant to using fixed-response items in online assessments:

- Identify the advantages and limitations of multiple-choice and true-false items
- Identify the qualities desired in items using these formats
- Evaluate multiple-choice and true-false items for these qualities
- Determine the optimal number of options to be included in a multiple-choice item
- Identify additional variations to the fixed-response format

ADVANTAGES AND LIMITATIONS OF FIXED-RESPONSE ITEMS
Advantages of Fixed-Response Items

Fixed-response items have four basic advantages. First, they provide a more adequate sampling of content. Second, they tend to structure the problem to be addressed more effectively. Third, they are easily scored by a computer. Fourth, computer-generated feedback to learners can easily be associated with responses to individual items.

1. *Fixed-response items allow a test to obtain a more adequate sampling of content.* There are two reasons for this. First, compared with essay items, many more items can be included in a given test. Learners can usually answer multiple-choice items at a rate of one per minute, and true-false items at a rate of two per minute. This is roughly comparable to the rates at which completion items can be answered, but of course it is far beyond what is possible with essay questions.

Second, compared with the completion format, fixed-response items can more readily measure procedural knowledge such as concepts and rules. Because completion items are usually answered with one or two words, they are generally limited to assessing declarative knowledge. In contrast, multiple-choice items can easily measure concepts by asking learners to classify the response options as examples versus nonexamples of a concept. True-false items can similarly propose examples of a concept, with learners being asked to classify each example as correct or incorrect. Multiple-choice items can also ask learners to apply a particular rule where the item's "wrong" response options represent common incorrect solutions resulting from the application of the rule. The multiple-choice options might also present descriptions of characteristics of the correct, and the common incorrect, solutions instead of the actual solution. Completion items usually cannot do this.

2. *Fixed-response items tend to structure the problem to be addressed more effectively.* Consider the following items:

Completion item: What should be the first step when constructing a test?

Multiple-choice item: Which of the following steps should be done first when constructing a test?

○ Determine the type of reliability to be computed.
○ Establish the number of items to be used.
● Identify the skills to be tested.
○ Review existing items.

With a completion item, a knowledgeable learner might anticipate several actions, any of which could occur first when preparing a test. For example, determining the need to schedule a test must occur before establishing a list of objectives to be tested. The options in the multiple-choice item define more adequately for the learner the time frame being addressed. A test item written in any format should clearly relay a problem to the learner. Items using the fixed-response format

achieve this goal more easily than do items that use the essay and completion formats.

Although fixed-response items can measure procedural knowledge, they usually cannot measure the most complex skill introduced in Chapter 2, that of problem solving. Solving complex problems requires learners to bring together numerous concepts and rules. Also, different learners will bring together different combinations of concepts and rules. A well-constructed fixed-response item carefully structures how one is to complete a particular task. This is not compatible with the flexibility inherent in solving problems. The difficulty in assessing problem-solving skills applies not only to the fixed-response item, but to all formats used with conventional written tests, including essays.

3. *Fixed-response items are easily scored by a computer.* Although computers are now being used to score essays for some large-scale assessments such as college admission tests, at this point essay tests developed for instructional use are invariably scored by human readers, even when the test is administered online. Although assessment products vary, some software is very inflexible with respect to how completion items are scored. Regardless of the software, learners often provide defensible answers to completion items that the instructor did not anticipate. At best, they cannot be scored automatically; at worst, the unanticipated correct answer is scored as wrong by the computer.

Computer scoring not only saves the instructor time, but also allows the answers to be scored immediately. Depending on the software, the instructor can see the pattern of students' responses, including where students are having difficulty, before all students have completed the test.

4. *Computer-generated feedback to learners can easily be associated with responses to individual items.* When multiple-choice and true-false formats are used, the software supporting the online tests typically allows the instructor to prearrange feedback to be provided at the conclusion of the test. This is not possible with

paper-and-pencil tests, which are scored later—often much later. Providing feedback immediately after the test is finished makes it more likely that students will recall the logic they used when answering items and will take advantage of that information when reading the feedback.

Often, different feedback messages can be provided for correct and incorrect answers, or even for each multiple-choice option, so that the feedback a student receives depends on which answer was selected. However, in general it is best to use one feedback message per item rather than separate messages based on students' responses. In part, this is because students often select a correct or incorrect response using logic different from what the instructor anticipated. The more basic reason is that feedback pertaining to the item as a whole matches the thought process better that students used when answering test items. For instance people answering multiple-choice items typically think through the test item and its options as a whole, rather than focusing their attention on only the option they end up selecting. The feedback provided at the end of the test should match as closely as possible the reasoning students used during the test. Instead of creating feedback tied to how the student responds, it is better to prepare just one feedback message for each item that explains the general logic of the answer and, in the case of multiple-choice items, why the wrong responses are incorrect. This allows the student to evaluate the logic he or she used to answer the item.

Limitations of Fixed-Response Items

Fixed-response items have three limitations. First, they are more susceptible to guessing. Second, they indirectly measure targeted behaviors more often than do essay items. Third, fixed-response items are time consuming to construct.

1. *Fixed-response items are susceptible to guessing.* This is a problem particularly with true-false items, where students will correctly answer 5 items on a 10-item test or 50 items on a 100-item test using blind guessing.

8.1 Apply What You Are Learning

Which item format is associated with each of the following advantages?

1. With this format, it is easier to write items that appropriately structure the problem that students are to address.
   A. Completion
   B. Essay
   C. Multiple-choice
2. With this format, students can answer more items in 30 minutes.
   A. Completion
   B. Multiple-choice
   C. True-false
3. With this format, students' ability to express ideas in writing can be evaluated.
   A. Completion
   B. Essay
   C. Multiple-choice
4. With this format, a computer can most easily provide students with feedback immediately after completing the test.
   A. Completion
   B. Essay
   C. True-false

Answers can be found at the end of the chapter.

This threat of guessing is more perceived than real. Learner knowledge should never be tested with just one item, regardless of format. And with the true-false item, if students really did guess blind, fewer than 10% of the students would correctly answer more than 7 of 10, 13 of 20, or 56 of 100 items on a test. Increasing the number of items included in a test controls the threat of guessing answers, which is feasible given the rate at which students can answer true-false items.

Nevertheless, guessing does reduce the reliability of fixed-response items. Increasing the number of items included in a test reduces, but does not negate, this problem. In general, when comparing tests that require equal amounts of time to administer, tests using completion items provide the highest reliability, followed by multiple-choice, alternate-choice, and essay tests, in that order (Frisbie, 1973; Oosterhof & Coats, 1984; Oosterhof & Glasnapp, 1974). However, even with guessing, tests that use the true-false format can obtain acceptably high reliabilities (Ebel, 1982). And although tests using completion items tend to be more reliable, as noted earlier, they are less able to measure procedural knowledge.

2. *Fixed-response items more often indirectly measure targeted behaviors*. Direct measures are always preferable to indirect measures. Indirect measures, however, are frequently used in many disciplines. An astronomer estimates the size and age of a star by measuring its color. Chemists measure the acidity of a liquid by judging the color of litmus paper. Similarly, an educator must often make judgments based on indirect observations. As long as the relationship is understood between a first quality that can be observed and a second quality that is of interest, the use of indirect measures is appropriate.

In instructional settings, we are often unaware that indirect measures are involved. Let us assume that we want to determine whether you, after reading this book, can establish evidence of validity for achievement tests. The most direct way to assess this skill is to observe whether you are able to develop a test from clear specifications that establish how the test will be used, the knowledge the test is to measure, and the learner behaviors that provide good indications of that knowledge. Better yet would be to observe you constructing several tests. However, asking someone to develop tests so that we can observe the person's ability to establish validity is usually impractical. As an alternative, we might indirectly measure this skill using the following essay item:

> Describe what an instructor must do to establish evidence of validity for an achievement test.

Often, we claim an essay item is a direct measure of our target skill by adjusting the wording of the performance objective. For instance, the previous essay item becomes a direct measure if our objective is written as follows:

Information: Describe how to establish evidence of validity for an achievement test.

Instead of the essay format, a series of multiple-choice items such as the one that follows might be used:

> When establishing content-related evidence of validity for an achievement test, an instructor must be most concerned with the
> ○ abilities of the learners.
> ○ adequacy of instruction.
> ● skills to be tested.
> ○ total number of items to be included on the test.

As with all test formats, fixed-response items do not allow instructors to observe directly what the learner was thinking or why the learner selected a particular wrong answer. Essay tests sometimes, but not always, provide an indication of the learner's thought process. As noted previously, fixed-response tests administered online may allow the instructor to create preset messages as feedback for each test item. Using this, learners can often, on their own, establish problems or errors in their reasoning. Nonetheless, neither essay questions nor test items using a fixed-choice format directly measure knowledge; one cannot see what a student knows or is thinking. All educational assessments, regardless of format, can only provide indirect measures of learner knowledge.

3. *Fixed-response items are time consuming to construct*. More time is required to build a test with fixed-response items than with completion items. This is particularly true with multiple-choice since considerable time is needed to develop effective alternatives for each item. Essay tests require less time to develop, primarily because fewer essay questions can be included in a test, but considerable time is needed to develop scoring plans for each item.

Usually, significantly more time is needed to develop fixed-response items that measure procedural knowledge than items that measure recall of information. This is generally true for all item formats. Because fixed-response and particularly multiple-choice tests are time consuming to construct, instructors often avoid them unless they have access to previously developed items or unless the number of learners makes scoring essay or completion items too formidable.

8.2   Apply What You Are Learning

Which item format is associated with each of the following limitations?

A. Completion
B. Essay
C. Multiple-choice
D. True-false

1. Least likely to measure procedural knowledge such as concepts and rules
2. Because of guessing, least likely for a learner's performance on one item to generalize to performance on other items
3. Because of inconsistencies in scoring, least likely for a learner's performance on one item to generalize to performance on other items
4. Because of the limited number of items used, least likely for a learner's performance on the overall test to generalize to other skills in the same unit of instruction

Answers can be found at the end of the chapter.

IDENTIFYING QUALITIES DESIRED IN FIXED-RESPONSE ITEMS

This section examines criteria for evaluating fixed-response items. In the next section, you will be asked to use these criteria to evaluate several test items.

1. *The item clearly measures the targeted skill.* As with any format, each fixed-response item must be constructed or selected to measure a specific skill. Often, several items are needed to assess a particular skill, with each item in the set measuring a different aspect or perspective of that skill.

2. *The level of reading proficiency required by the item is below the learners' ability.* Again, this concern is relevant to test items written in all formats. Unless the level of vocabulary and sentence structure are sufficiently low, a test item will confound the measurement of reading ability with that of the skill being measured.

8.3   Apply What You Are Learning

Listed below are pairs of items. In each pair, which item (A or B) is most free of extraneous words and content?

1. A. In miles per second, what is the speed of light?
   - ○ 186
   - ○ 1,860
   - ○ 18,600
   - ● 186,000

   B. Although it is believed physical objects cannot go this fast, the speed of light is
   - ○ 186 miles per second
   - ○ 1,860 miles per second
   - ○ 18,600 miles per second
   - ● 186,000 miles per second

2. A. In the United States, high-definition television uses
   - ○ analog signals
   - ● digital signals

   B. High-definition television, more so in the United States than some countries, uses
   - ○ analog signals
   - ● digital signals

3. A. One of the rules in volleyball is that a team scores points only when it serves the ball. (true)

   B. In volleyball, only the team that served the ball can score a point. (true)

Answers can be found at the end of the chapter.

---

3. *The item is stated as simply as possible.* The use of words or other content that are extraneous to the problems being presented might cause the item to measure how well learners can determine what the question is asking. Identifying what is

being asked represents an important skill. However, if that is not the skill being tested, including extraneous material in an item confounds the measurement of the intended skill. You will not know if learners missed the item because they did not comprehend the question or because they have yet to master the skill being tested. Each alternate-choice item should state its proposition as simply as possible.

Stating an alternate-choice item as simply as possible helps restrict the item to a single proposition. In the previous examples, when an item was not stated simply, multiple problems were created. To state items simply, clearly establish in your mind the problem to be addressed, and then include only words that are critical to conveying that problem.

4. *Adjectives and adverbs are emphasized when they reverse or significantly alter the meaning of an item.* Whenever a single word significantly changes the meaning of a sentence or phrase in a test item, that word should be underlined or capitalized to draw attention to its presence. Otherwise, a learner may read over the word and misinterpret the item. Here are some examples in which a word has been underlined because it alters the meaning of the phrase:

> Which of the following conditions <u>least</u> affects the speed at which wind blows?
>
> All of the following represent a field of science <u>except</u>
>
> Which of the following is <u>not</u> a major cause of forest fires?

With online testing, the software used to input the test items often makes it difficult to underline words, or to use other formatting controls such as bold and italics. If the software is generating HTML code, which it usually is, underlines and some other formats can be inserted using *tags*. For instance, if you enter

> Which of the following conditions <u>least<u/> affects the speed at which wind blows?

the word *least* becomes underlined. Substituting *b* or *i* for *u* in these tabs starts and stops bold and italics, respectively. If these tags do not work, an alternative is to simply use uppercase for all the letters in the word or words that need to be emphasized.

The third previous example includes the word *not*. This word is particularly troublesome and should be eliminated from test items, especially fixed-response items. Because most phrases make grammatical sense whether *not* is included or omitted, it is easy to misread those items even though the meaning of the sentence changes dramatically. Potentially, then, the test item becomes a measure of how carefully learners can read rather than a measure of the skill that the item was designed to target. The same problem occurs with conjunctions involving *not* such as *cannot* and *can't*. Demonstrate the problem to yourself. Which of the following statements are true?

> Decreasing the number of items does *not* increase test reliability.
>
> A test is *not* necessarily reliable if it is valid.
>
> More true-false than essay items *cannot* be included in a given test.

Only the first statement is true. Note how much easier these items become when the word *not* is deleted:

> Decreasing the number of items increases test reliability. (false)
>
> A test is reliable if it is valid. (true)
>
> More true-false than essay items can be included in a given test. (true)

5. *Each wrong answer is plausible.* Ideally, fixed-response items should be constructed so that

> Learners who are proficient with the skill select the correct answer.
>
> Every learner who has yet to achieve the skill selects a wrong answer.

This ideal, however, is unrealistic. Most academic skills are complex enough that learners cannot simply be classified into two groups—those who have mastered the skill and those who have not. The elusive perfect item cannot divide learners into such distinct groups because this grouping does not exist.

The perfect fixed-response item is elusive for a second reason. Learners who have not achieved the intended proficiency often select the correct answer by guessing, by detecting fallacies within the item, or by observing something in the correct response that is compatible with their misconception. Fixed-response items can be substan-tially improved by making sure that each wrong answer is at least as attractive as the correct response for learners who have not learned the skill being measured.

Techniques that make wrong answers more plausible are illustrated in Figure 8.1. First, dis-tractors in multiple-choice items can represent common misconceptions, as seen in items 1 and 2. In item 1, *orange* and *red* represent common

---

1. When bicycling at night, which of the following colors of clothing is it best to wear?
   - ○ Blue
   - ○ Orange
   - ○ Red
   - ● White

2. Although the duration of a lightning bolt is very short, the resulting sound of thunder usually lasts for several seconds. Why does the duration of thunder last so much longer than that of the lightning?
   - ● Some parts of a lightning bolt are closer to the observer than other parts.
   - ○ The heat generated by lightning requires time to dissipate.
   - ○ Thunder echoes off nearby objects such as buildings and hills.

3. Multiple-choice items should contain at least four options.
   - ○ True
   - ● False

4. In the majority of collegiate sports, the grade-point average of athletes is lower than that of students in general.
   - ○ True
   - ● False

5. Which among the following represents the highest Pearson correlation coefficient?
   - ○ 0.00
   - ● 0.80
   - ○ 100
   - ○ 1,000

6. In educational testing, what term refers to how well a test measures the skills it is supposed to measure?
   - ○ Authenticity
   - ○ Conformity
   - ○ Objectivity
   - ○ Reliability
   - ● Validity

Figure 8.1
Illustrations of plausible wrong answers

misconceptions because these colors, in daylight, are so bright. White clothing reflects more light and is the best choice when bicycling at night. With respect to item 2, many people believe that echoing causes thunder to linger. In reality, because a lightning bolt is several miles in length, the sound of thunder caused by closer parts of the lightning bolt reaches an observer several seconds before thunder caused by more distant parts. The wrong answer to item 3 is plausible because multiple-choice items commonly use four or five options. Deviating from this norm seems inappropriate. With item 4, the wrong answer is plausible because it tends to be true among athletes in the more visible sports, even though it is untrue among athletes in the majority of varsity sports.

Wrong answers also can be made more plausible by making them sound correct to the untrained reader, as illustrated by items 5 and 6. In item 5, uninformed learners will likely find options 100 and 1000 attractive since they sound like perfect or high scores; however, 1.00 is the highest value of the correlation coefficient. In item 6, the words *authenticity, conformity,* and *objectivity* sound like labels one might associate with a test that measures what it was designed to measure. These distractors do not represent common misconceptions. Learners would select *authenticity* because of ignorance rather than because of a misconception.

Multiple-choice distractors are often made plausible simply by being reasonably close to the correct answer. With items involving numerical answers, distractors will be more attractive if they represent common errors that are fairly close to the correct response. Learners who can approximate but not correctly solve the problem will consider such options. Although the use of distractors similar to the correct response improves their plausibility, care must be taken so that knowledgeable learners continue to select the intended answer as the correct response.

Writing items so that the wrong choice is plausible may seem devious. This perception is inaccurate when the purpose of the test item is kept in focus. To the degree possible, each item should distinguish between those learners who have gained a relevant skill and those who have not. If knowledgeable learners perceive the wrong answer as a correct response, an item loses its usefulness. Similarly, if learners who have not yet learned the relevant skill are more attracted to the correct response than to the wrong choice, the item again loses its usefulness.

Desired Qualities Specific to Multiple-Choice Items

The following desired qualities are unique to the multiple-choice format.

6. *The stem clearly presents the problem to be addressed.* When the stem to a multiple-choice item is not self-explanatory, learners end up reading the options without knowing what problem they are supposed to solve. The stem by itself should communicate what the learner is expected to do.

8.4   Apply What You Are Learning

Listed below are pairs of item stems. In each pair, which stem more adequately presents the problem to be addressed?

1. A. Validity is....
   B. A test is said to be valid if it....

2. A. When riding a bicycle at night....
   B. Which color of clothing is best to wear when riding a bicycle at night?

3. A. Which one of the following scales is used to measure the magnitude of an earthquake?
   B. Earthquakes are often very powerful and can be measured by seismographs over long distances. The Richter scale....

Answers can be found at the end of the chapter.

A useful technique for improving the clarity of the stem is to present it as a question rather than as an incomplete sentence. Notice how this technique improved the clarity of the stems in items 2 and 3 in the previous exercise. Individuals who have had limited experience in constructing multiple-choice items find that writing the stem as a question helps formulate the problem being addressed and tends to improve the clarity of the entire item.

7. *All options are parallel in type of content.* When options vary in type of content, the item is asking learners to make a single judgment about two or more distinct qualities, like comparing apples to oranges. Note in the next example that because the options are not parallel in content, more than one alternative may represent the correct response.

Which of the following represents the warmest temperature?

○ 100 degrees Celsius.
○ 200 degrees Fahrenheit.
○ 300 degrees Kelvin.
○ an oven set at medium.

The first three options are all specific temperatures on well-defined scales. The fourth option represents a range of temperatures and uses an undefined scale (e.g., is this a drying oven used by a chemist or a food-baking oven?). The correct answer conceivably could be either "100 degrees Celsius" (the highest temperature among the first three options) or "an oven set at medium."

It is common for wrong answers to become defensible if all options are *not* parallel in content. This happens because the unparallel options cause test takers to evaluate the merits of the multiple-choice options on qualities other than what the item writer had in mind. Before constructing alternatives to a multiple-choice item, first think of the characteristics that all options will have in common. Then write options that match those characteristics. This approach helps maintain a focus for the item and reduces the chance of distractors' inadvertently becoming correct responses. Usually, options fail to be parallel in content because the stem does not present a concise problem.

8. *The options avoid repetitive words.* The following item would be more efficient if the words repeated in each option were relocated to the stem:

Physics is

○ the science that deals with the structure of matter.
○ the science that deals with the composition, structure, and properties of substances.
○ the science that is more concerned with solids than liquids.

Not only would this editing result in a more efficient use of words, but the modified stem would state the problem more clearly. Sometimes, a limited amount of repetition across options helps reinforce the idea presented in the stem or makes the options easier to read. However, excessive repetition should be avoided.

9. *The grammar in each option is consistent with the stem.* In the next illustration, can you identify the correct answer even though you may not know the concept being tested?

In item response theory, the one-parameter model assumes that each test item

○ discriminates equally well.
○ learners perform equally well.
○ learners score the same across items.
○ guessing affects all items the same.

In this item, the stem grammatically matches only the first option, which happens to be the correct answer. The correct answer sounds correct.

When responses do not match the stem, the item provides clues to the answer that are not relevant to learner achievement. A grammatical mismatch usually occurs when the stem represents an incomplete sentence but one or more of the options do not adequately complete the sentence. This problem can be avoided by writing the stem as a question rather than as an incomplete statement. Whenever incomplete statements are used as a stem, each of the options should be checked for grammatical consistency with the stem.

10. *The item excludes options equivalent to* all of the above *and* none of the above. Phrases such as *all of the above* and *none of the above* are often included in multiple-choice items. Their

typical role is to increase the number of options. *None of the above* is sometimes used to avoid giving clues to learners when their incorrect solutions are not consistent with any of the options included with the item. Although the rationale for using such options is good, their effect on test items is not beneficial.

When *all of the above* is used, a multiple-choice item actually behaves as if the number of options has been reduced. If any two of the options can be identified as correct, the learner can be quite certain that *all of the above* is correct, in effect eliminating the role of the remaining responses. Similarly, if just one option can be identified as incorrect, the *all of the above* option can be eliminated.

Sometimes, each of the distractors in a multiple-choice item contains a degree of truth, often unintentionally. When *all of the above* is used in this context, learners are placed in an unfair situation by being expected to select between the superior option or *all of the above.*

None of the above has similar problems. If a fallacy can be seen in each option, *none of the above* represents the logical response. Learners, however, usually have difficulty determining whether the erroneous qualities were intentional and serious enough for the instructor to judge the option wrong. The only way to avoid this problem is to use options that are unequivocally correct or incorrect, and developing such options is difficult.

Spelling and computation skills do lend themselves to unequivocal statements. *None of the above* is often used in multiple-choice items that test these skills so learners will not assume that the correct solution is among the options. The effect of using *none of the above* with computational items was investigated by Oosterhof and Coats (1984). Replacing the last option with *none of the above* was actually found to lower reliability. *None of the above* served as an effective option only when it was the correct answer. Because less knowledgeable learners seldom selected *none of the above,* it became an effective distractor only when it was the correct response. However, constantly using *none of the above* as the correct response is obviously not recommended.

11. *Unless another order is more logical, options are arranged alphabetically.* Correct answers should be distributed evenly among the alternative positions in multiple-choice items. Because items often are constructed before they are assembled into a test, this may be difficult. Another approach is to alphabetize the options within each item. This strategy will counteract the tendency many instructors have of favoring a particular location for the correct response.

Sometimes, arranging options in an order other than alphabetical makes it easier for learners to contrast the options. For example, options representing numerical values, dates, or points along a scale should be listed sequentially from low to high.

8.5   Apply What You Are Learning

The options in each of the following items are alphabetized. In which of these items should the options not be alphabetical?

1. What is the minimum number of alternatives that can be used in a multiple-choice item?
   - ○ five
   - ○ four
   - ○ one
   - ○ three
   - ● two

2. Which best describes the relationship between reliability and validity? High validity is associated with
   - ● high reliability
   - ○ low reliability
   - ○ moderate reliability
   - ○ zero reliability

3. Which item format will likely produce the highest reliability if used to construct a 30-minute test?
   - ● completion
   - ○ essay
   - ○ multiple-choice
   - ○ true-false

Answers can be found at the end of the chapter.

Desired Qualities Specific to True-False Items

The following desired qualities are unique to true-false items.

12. *The item is unequivocally true or false.* This quality is particularly difficult to achieve because it requires creating a proposition from a single statement that, in isolation, is unequivocally true or false. A technique that often eliminates the problem is to contrast two ideas. The following true-false item has been improved through such a contrast:

Without contrast: The reliability of short-answer tests is unaffected by guessing.

With contrast: The reliability of short-answer tests is less affected by guessing than is the reliability of multiple-choice tests.

Because the short-answer format is generally not affected by guessing, the first item is basically true. Sometimes, however, learners do get correct answers on short-answer items by guessing. An example would be correctly guessing the spelling of a word on a spelling test.

True-false items must function as unequivocally correct or incorrect propositions *from the perspective of learners with whom the items will be used.* It may be unrealistic to write items that content experts, for instance, would judge to be unequivocal. If your knowledgeable learners consistently answer an item correctly, this is evidence that the item is constructed appropriately. If, however, some learners present defensible explanations for selecting the wrong response, you have reason to believe the item is deficient.

13. *The item presents a single proposition.* A true-false item becomes ambiguous when it contains two propositions, one that may be true and the other false. To avoid this source of ambiguity, true-false items should always state a single proposition.

14. *Adjectives and adverbs that imply an indefinite degree are excluded.* Words such as *frequent, often,* and *sometimes* specify indeterminate quantities. These and similar words have a broad range

of meanings. The sentence, "Learners *often* spelled the words correctly," could mean they correctly spelled several out of 100 words or almost all of 100 words. Words with indefinite meanings should be excluded from alternate-choice items. They prevent items from being classified as unequivocally correct or incorrect. Which of the following true-false items can be answered unequivocally?

Alternate-choice tests *usually* include *many* items.

Multiple-choice items *frequently* have three options.

Instructors *typically* use short-answer items.

None of these items can be answered unequivocally; because the italicized words have indefinite meanings. Here is how each of these items could be made unequivocally true or false:

A 20-minute test can include more questions if short-answer items are rewritten as alternate-choice items. (true)

A multiple-choice item can contain three options. (true)

Instructors use more short-answer items in classroom tests than any other format. (true)

15. *Adjectives and adverbs with absolute meanings are avoided.* Statements containing words such as *all, always, every, never,* and *no* are usually found to be false. Students who have

not learned the concept being tested answer such items as incorrect because an exception to *always* or *never* probably exists. Therefore, these words increase the effectiveness of true-false items that are true because learners unfamiliar with the concept anticipate the presence of exceptions. Conversely, these words lower the effectiveness of false statements and should not be used when the statement poses a false proposition. However, if absolute words are used too frequently in true statements, students soon learn to reverse common logic. For this reason, you might occasionally use words with absolute meanings but, in general, should avoid their use in true-false items.

PRACTICE APPLYING THESE DESIRED QUALITIES TO FIXED-RESPONSE ITEMS

Table 8.1 lists the 15 criteria for judging fixed-response items that we have just discussed. This section will help you apply these criteria by examining some example items.

The objective being assessed and the proposed correct response are provided to help you evaluate each item. Each example fails to meet at least one of the criteria addressed in this checklist. A critique follows each item. Numbers in parentheses preceding each critique indicate the criteria in Table 8.1 that the item failed to achieve. Try to identify these problems before reading the critique.

The first examples pertain to a rule in astronomy that states objects in lower orbit travel faster than objects in higher orbit. Examples 8.1 through 8.3 are intended to measure knowledge of the following objective:

Rule: Given smaller objects in orbit around a substantially larger object, uses the relative height of orbits to identify which object is traveling fastest in its orbit.

Table 8.1
Criteria for evaluating fixed-choice items

1. Does this item measure the specified skill?
2. Is the level of reading skill required by this item below the students' ability?
3. Is the item stated as simply as possible?
4. Are adjectives or adverbs emphasized when they reverse or significantly alter the meaning of an item?
5. Is each wrong answer plausible?

Desired qualities specific to multiple-choice items
6. Does the stem clearly present the problem to be addressed?
7. Are all options parallel in type of content?
8. Do the options avoid repetitive words?
9. Is the grammar in each option consistent with the stem?
10. Does the item exclude options equivalent to *all of the above* and *none of the above*?
11. Unless another order is more logical, are options arranged alphabetically?

Desired qualities specific to true-false items
12. Is the item unequivocally true or false?
13. Does the item present a single proposition?
14. Are adjectives and adverbs that imply an indefinite degree excluded?
15. Are adjectives and adverbs with absolute meanings avoided?

Example 8.1

The artificial satellite with the highest orbital speed

○ is the most recently launched satellite.
○ is the satellite in the higher orbit.
● is the satellite in the lower orbit.
○ is the satellite with an orbit closest to the equator.

Critique for Example 8.1

(Table 8.1 criteria not achieved: 6, 7, and 8)

The stem does not clearly describe the problem that learners are to solve. This is partly because each option repeats a significant amount of information that should be included in the stem. Because the stem fails to present a clear problem, the options are not parallel in content. The options also use the same words repetitively, although that may make this particular item easier to read. Here is an improved version of the item:

Does the artificial satellite in higher or lower orbit have the higher orbital speed?

○ The satellite in higher orbit.
● The satellite in lower orbit.
○ The satellites have the same orbital speed.

Example 8.2

Ganymede and Callisto are moons of Jupiter with approximately equal mass. Ganymede orbits 1.1 million miles above Jupiter, whereas Callisto orbits 1.9 million miles above the planet. Ganymede has

● the faster orbital speed.
○ more impact craters.
○ will fall out of orbit sooner.

Critique for Example 8.2

(Table 8.1 criteria not achieved: 6, 7, 9, and 11)

Again, the stem does not clearly describe the problem learners are to solve and the options are not parallel in content. Recall that the problem with using options that are not parallel in content is that more than one of the options often is unintentionally correct. That has happened here. For instance, more impact craters tend to exist on the moon that is closest to a planet because the planet's gravity attracts small objects in space. If the item writer had first constructed a stem that clearly established the problem to be addressed, the options would likely have become parallel in content.

This item has two other problems. Notice that the third option is not grammatically consistent with the stem. When the grammar of an option does not match the stem, it provides clues to the answer that are not relevant to learner achievement. The remaining problem with this item is that options are not ordered alphabetically. Unless another order is more logical, arranging options alphabetically helps randomize the location of the correct answer.

Here is an improved version of Example 8.2. The stem more clearly presents a problem, which in turn forces the options to be parallel in content. Although options are not listed alphabetically, they are in a logical order.

Ganymede and Callisto are moons of Jupiter with approximately equal mass. Ganymede orbits 1.1 million miles above Jupiter, whereas Callisto orbits 1.9 million miles above the planet. Which moon has the faster orbital speed?

● Ganymede has the faster orbital speed.
○ Both moons have the same orbital speed.
○ Callisto has the faster orbital speed.

Example 8.3

When a planet has more than one moon, which of the following best explains why the moon closest to a planet has the highest orbital speed?

● The closest moon has to travel faster to offset the greater gravitational pull of the planet.
○ The closest moon tends to be the youngest moon and has maintained more of its original speed.
○ The closest moon usually is smaller than the other moons and therefore travels faster.

Critique for Example 8.3

(Table 8.1 criteria not achieved: 1)

The problem with this item might be harder to detect, but it is very basic. Mechanically, this item is well constructed, but it does not measure the specified objective. Because the objective pertains to a rule, the item should ask learners to apply the rule to solve a previously unused problem. Instead, this item is measuring declarative knowledge, or knowledge of information. The item asks learners to identify correct statements of factual information. Declarative knowledge is important and learners must be able to state what they know; however, the present performance objective is concerned with knowledge of a rule, not declarative knowledge.

Items in Examples 8.4 through 8.6 are intended to measure the following objective:

Information: Identifies basic characteristics of instruments commonly used in a symphony orchestra.

Example 8.4

Which of the following characteristics is not a difference between a trumpet and a trombone?

- ● Both are made primarily of metal.
- ○ Both can play notes an octave below middle C.
- ○ Both change pitch primarily with valves.
- ○ All of the above.
- ○ None of the above.

Critique for Example 8.4

(Table 8.1 criteria not achieved: 4 and 10)

When a word significantly changes the meaning of the item, emphasis should be drawn to it, such as by underlining. Although *not* is such a word, it should be excluded from items because it is so easy to misread, and also tends to confuse the problem being presented by the item. One way to remove "not" from the item is to change the stem to a positive statement, as

illustrated in the revision. The item also includes *all of the above* and *none of the above* as options, which should be avoided. Here is an improved version:

Which of the following is true of <u>both</u> trumpets and trombones?

- ● They are made primarily of metal.
- ○ They can play notes an octave below middle C.
- ○ They change pitch primarily with valves.

Example 8.5

A symphony orchestra includes many instruments. They can be classified into strings, brass, woodwinds, and percussion sections. The percussion section:

- ○ includes the chimes.
- ○ includes timpani which can be tuned to different pitches.
- ○ involves drums as well as other instruments.
- ○ is where you place the glockenspiel.
- ● All of the above.

Critique for Example 8.5

(Table 8.1 criteria not achieved: 3, 6, and 10)

The stem contains extraneous content and could be stated more simply. Once again, the stem does not clearly establish the problem to be addressed. The intended answer, *All of the above*, becomes the obvious answer to learners who know that any two of the preceding options are correct. *All of the above* also causes problems if the options for the item vary from being fully correct to partially correct. Here is an improved version of this item:

Within a symphony orchestra, the percussion section includes all of the following instruments <u>except</u>

- ● bassoon.
- ○ chimes.
- ○ drums.
- ○ glockenspiel.
- ○ timpani.

Example 8.6

Which one of the following instruments uses reeds to make sound?

- ● Oboe.
- ○ French horn.
- ○ Glockenspiel.
- ○ The conductor.
- ○ None of the above.

Critique for Example 8.6

(Table 8.1 criteria not achieved: 5, 10, and 11)

Most learners, even without knowing what a reed is, will recognize that the conductor is not an instrument; that option is not plausible and should be replaced. *None of the above* is more acceptable here than in many items, because each of the options is unequivocally correct or incorrect. However, research cited earlier in this chapter indicates *none of the above* usually does not work as well as an option that directly answers the stem. Finally, unless there is another more logical order, the options should be alphabetized. This helps randomize the location of the correct response. Here is an improved version of the item:

Which one of the following instruments uses reeds to make sound?

- ○ Flute.
- ○ French horn.
- ○ Glockenspiel.
- ● Oboe.
- ○ Vibraphone.

OPTIMAL NUMBER OF CHOICES FOR MULTIPLE-CHOICE ITEMS

With multiple-choice items, the most important factor in determining the number of options is the number of appropriate distractors that can be created. Incorporating distractors that are not plausible or that are not parallel to the content of other options will contribute to the ambiguity of items. Software used with online assessments usually allows more than the five options per item that is often associated with paper-and-pencil tests.

However, the optimal number of choices to be included in an item might be less than expected. Lord (1977) compared four approaches for establishing this optimal number. Results varied somewhat, depending on the theoretical assumptions being made. In general, however, three options per item were found to produce the most reliable test scores *as long as the total number of options across items in the test was constant.* For example, 20 items involving three options tend to provide more reliable scores than 12 items involving five options. Two options per item were found to be the next best. Four and then five options per item were found to be less effective.

This research into the optimal number of choices per item made one assumption that often is not true—that the total number of options a learner can complete is the same regardless of how the options are grouped into items. It was expected that the same amount of time would be required to answer 60 alternatives divided into 30 two-option, 20 three-option, 15 four-option, or 12 five-option items. Budescu and Nevo (1985) investigated the appropriateness of that assumption with vocabulary, mathematical reasoning, and verbal comprehension tests. Each item in the vocabulary test could be read and answered quickly. The stems of the mathematical reasoning tests, however, required examinees to solve a computational problem before responding. The verbal reasoning items required examinees to read a paragraph before answering questions. Therefore, more time was required to administer 30 two-option mathematical reasoning items than 12 five-option mathematical reasoning items. The same was true with the verbal reasoning items. Adjusted for different amounts of testing time, five-option mathematical and verbal reasoning items were more reliable.

When a significant amount of time is required to solve the problem being addressed by the item, using fewer items with more options per item is the best strategy. If items can be answered quickly, it is preferable to use more items with fewer options per item.

VARIATIONS OF FIXED-RESPONSE ITEMS

There are a number of variations of fixed-response items, most of which have little resemblance to traditional multiple-choice and true-false formats. Several of these variations are described here. Some software used with online assessment may not support all of these variations.

Matching Items

Matching items are a special case of the multiple-choice format in which several items share one set of options. With paper-and-pencil tests, a common approach is to format matching items into two columns, presenting the items or questions in the left column and the shared options to the right. With online tests, matching items are sometimes formatted like a traditional multiple-choice item, with the set of options repeated after each question.

A more efficient approach is illustrated in Figure 8.2 where the set of options is presented once, to the side of the questions, much like on paper-and-pencil tests. In this illustration, learners are asked to identify the role played by individuals in the development of the U.S. Constitution. An answer is selected from the list using the drop-down menu to the left of each question.

As with all multiple-choice items, options for matching items should be parallel in content. In Figure 8.2, all the options represent the names of individuals associated with establishing the Constitution. Unfortunately, instructors sometimes lengthen the list of answers, ostensibly to reduce guessing, by combining heterogeneous content into one set of matching items. If necessary, subdivide matching items into separate groups to ensure that the list of options is homogeneous for each group.

Option Ranking Items

Learners can be asked to rank multiple-choice alternatives on a number of qualities. In Figure 8.3, learners are asked to rearrange a list of historical events in the order they occurred. Using

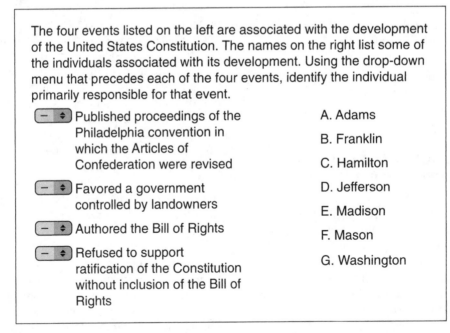

Figure 8.2
Illustration of matching items

The eight events listed below are associated with the development of the United States Constitution; however, they are listed out of order. Reorder these events so that they are listed in the order they occurred, with the earliest event placed at the top. To reorder the events, use the drop-down menu that precedes each event.

(– ↕) Articles of Confederation are ratified

(– ↕) Articles of Confederation are written

(– ↕) Articles of Confederation revised in Philadelphia

(– ↕) Bill of Rights is written

(– ↕) Constitution of the United States is ratified

(– ↕) Constitution of the United States is written

(– ↕) First Continental Congress is convened

(– ↕) Second Continental Congress is convened

Figure 8.3
Illustration of ranking options involving historical events

the drop-down menu to the left of each event, the learner changes the order in which the events are displayed on the screen. In Figure 8.4, learners are asked to estimate or calculate distances of various cities from Chicago, and then order the list of cities with respect to these distances. Again, as with all multiple-choice items, options should always be parallel in content. If a set of options represents more than a single dimension, knowledgeable learners may use a defensible but unanticipated criteria for ranking the options.

Multiple True-False Items

Figure 8.5 illustrates a multiple true-false item. A conventional multiple-choice item consists of a stem and a list of options with one of the options being correct and the others serving as distracters. With multiple true-false, all, some, or none of the options can be correct. Multiple true-false is a good name for this format since it should be thought of as a series of true-false items. For instance, for the item to work each option must present a proposition that by itself is unequivocally true or false. (In contrast, conventional multiple-choice items allow learners to select the best answer among a series of options, all of which may contain some truth and some falsity.) Another common name for the multiple true-false format is multiple answer.

Embedded-Choice Items

A series of what are essentially true-false items can be embedded in a paragraph. The spelling test illustrated in Figure 8.6 illustrates this approach. Each item consists of an underlined word or group of words. Learners are asked to indicate whether each underlined element represents a particular

Listed below are four cities. Order these cities with respect to their distance from Chicago. Place at the top of the list the city that is closest to Chicago, and at the bottom the city that is the furthest. To reorder the city names, use the drop-down menu that precedes each name.

[− ◆] Boston

[− ◆] Detroit

[− ◆] Kansas City

[− ◆] San Francisco

Figure 8.4
Illustration of ranking options involving distances between cities

Read each option and indicate which are correct.

In comparison with multiple-choice items, advantages of the true-false format are
- ● more items can be administered within a single test.
- ○ higher reliability is obtained from a given number of test items.
- ● each test item can be developed in less time.
- ○ students will select the correct answer only when they have achieved the skill being tested.

Figure 8.5
Illustration of multiple true-false items

In the next paragraph, click on each underlined word that is **misspelled.** When you click on an underlined word, it changes color. To unselect a word, click on it again and it will return to its original color. Some words are **misspelled** because the wrong but similar sounding word has been used by mistake.

Construct validity is the most <u>relavent</u> type of validity if <u>their</u> is a need to determine whether a <u>particuler</u> test, in <u>affect</u>, measures a psychological construct. Examples of psychological constructs include <u>intelligense</u>; <u>various</u> specific aptitudes, such as math aptitude, music aptitude, and <u>creativity</u>; and <u>personelity</u> traits, such as <u>anxiety</u> and <u>motivation</u>.

When finished marking the **misspelled** words, click on the submit button.

[SUBMIT]

Figure 8.6
Illustration of embedded choice items measuring spelling skills

In the next paragraph, click on each underlined word that is used as a **verb.** When you click on an underlined word, it changes color. To unselect a word, click on it again and it will return to its original color.

Sailing <u>has</u> many advantages <u>as</u> a recreational sport. You <u>can sail</u> by yourself or <u>with</u> others. You can <u>participate</u> in leisurely day sailing or competitive <u>racing</u>. You <u>need</u> not be physically strong to enjoy the sport. And <u>while</u> important basic <u>techniques</u> can be <u>learned</u> quickly, you can <u>spend</u> a lifetime developing your <u>sailing</u> skills.

When finished marking the words used as a **verb,** click on the submit button.

SUBMIT

Figure 8.7
Embedded items measuring knowledge of the concept of a verb

quality such as a correctly spelled word or a factually correct statement. By listing words in the context of a paragraph, the test becomes a more authentic assessment of what learners are expected to do; that is, check the spelling of words within a context rather than in isolation. As illustrated in items 2 and 4, this spelling test also requires learners to verify that the appropriate word is being spelled.

Figure 8.7 illustrates embedded items used to determine if learners can identify verbs within sentences. Because students are required to classify numerous examples, this format is a particularly effective way to assess whether students have learned a concept—in this illustration, the concept of a verb.

SUMMARY

Unlike the completion and essay formats, fixed-response items provide more than one answer option and learners must choose which is correct. The most widely used fixed-response items are multiple-choice and true-false. Several variations of multiple-choice and true-false items were also described.

The fixed-response format has certain advantages. Many items can be included in one test, and declarative as well as procedural knowledge can

be assessed. This means that a test using fixed-response items can assess a relatively substantial amount of content. With fixed-response items, one can more easily structure the problem that learners are to address. Responses to fixed-response items can easily be scored by the computer immediately after a learner completes the test. Computer-generated feedback associated with responses to individual items can also be given. However, fixed-response items are more susceptible to guessing and, more than with essay items, must indirectly measure performance objectives. Tests that use fixed-response items usually require more time to construct. Fifteen qualities that should be incorporated into fixed-response items were discussed and are listed in Table 8.1.

ANSWERS:
APPLY WHAT YOU ARE LEARNING

8.1 1. C; 2. C; 3. A; 4. C. *Item 1:* With multiple-choice items, the options often help structure the problem presented in the stem. *Item 2:* Students can usually answer true-false items at twice the rate of completion or multiple-choice items. *Item 3:* With written tests, only the essay format can assess learners' ability to communicate ideas in writing. *Item 4:* Software that allows the instructor to provide feedback on items at the conclusion of a test is more readily available with the multiple-choice and true-false formats.

8.2 1. A; 2. D; 3. B; 4. B. *Item 1:* The short response required by completion items usually limits this format to measuring declarative knowledge, rather than procedural knowledge such as concepts and rules. Unlike completion items, the learner's response to multiple-choice items (usually an A, B, C, D, or E) is not the actual solution to the problem presented by the item. Instead, answers to multiple-choice items provide an indirect indicator of whether the learner has solved the problem presented by the item. *Items 2 through 4:* Guessing significantly affects the reliability or generalizability of multiple-choice and particularly true-false items. However, inconsistency in scoring even more significantly reduces the generalizability of essay items. Reliability of test scores can be improved by increasing the number of items included in the test, but this is more difficult to accomplish with the essay format. Completion items are least affected by guessing, and a test can include a substantial number of completion items. Therefore tests that use completion items tend to be the most reliable. However, as noted earlier, it is most difficult to measure skills involving procedural knowledge using completion items.

8.3 1. A; 2. A; 3. B.

8.4 1. B; 2. A. Note that the stems with extraneous material are longer than necessary. This extraneous material may also unintentionally provide information that learners can use to answer other questions in the test.

8.5 1. Options in item 1 should be ordered numerically, from one to five. Options in item 2 should be ordered from zero reliability to high reliability, or possibly the reverse. In item 3, listing options alphabetically should be sufficient, although some writers may prefer a particular grouping of the item formats.

8.6 1. yes; 2. no; 3. yes. *Item 1:* The two propositions are "essay tests require less time to construct" and "essay tests require more time to score." This is a poor true-false item

because conceivably one statement could be true and the other false. *Item 2:* Although this item involves a contrast (short-answer versus multiple-choice formats), only one proposition is stated: Guessing affects the reliability of short-answer items less than multiple-choice items. *Item 3:* Two propositions are presented in this item. The first proposition is true: Classroom tests should be reliable. The second proposition is false: Scores on a given classroom test should not be expected to remain constant across time. (If learner achievement changes, scores on achievement tests should reflect that change.)

TERMS INTRODUCED IN THIS CHAPTER

Multiple-choice: items the most frequently used fixed-choice option. In its most traditional form, it consists of a statement that describes a task that learners are to complete, often referred to as the stem, and a series of response options that provide possible responses to the stem. A number of variations to the traditional multiple-choice item are available. For instance, instead of selecting the correct response among incorrect distractors, learners can be asked to rank order the options based on criteria given in the stem.

True-false: items typically consist of a statement or proposition that learners are asked to classify as a true or false statement. Considerable variation from this basic format is possible. For instance, learners can be asked to determine whether each highlighted word in a paragraph is a true or false instance of some quality, such as being correctly versus incorrectly spelled, or being an example or nonexample of a verb or another part of speech.

Response options: are the list of choices a learner has to work with when responding to fixed-response items. With *true-false* items, the options are simply true and false, but they are more involved with other variations of fixed-choice items. With traditional *multiple-choice* items, the response options include one correct response, and one or more incorrect answers that are often referred to as the distractors. With *option ranking* items, the learner re-orders or ranks the options according to criteria specified in the item.

ENHANCE YOUR UNDERSTANDING

- If you have access to some previously written multiple-choice or true-false items, use the qualities listed in Table 8.1 to evaluate them.
- Prepare some multiple-choice or true-false items that measure each of the following objectives:

    Information: Distinguish between safe and unsafe bicycling practices.

    Rule: Identify the effect that Earth's latitude has on the relative length of a winter day and a summer day, for different locales.

    (Remember, to assess knowledge of a rule, the learner should be asked to apply the rule to situations or examples to which they have not previously applied that rule. In the Northern and Southern Hemispheres, locales closer to the poles have longer days in their summer and shorter days in their winter than do locales closer to the equator. For example, the North Pole has continuous daylight at the beginning of its summer.)

    Use Table 8.1 to evaluate these items.

- Write and then evaluate several items for an objective within your academic specialization.

ADDITIONAL READING

Carlson, S. B. (1985). *Creative classroom testing.* Princeton, NJ: Educational Testing Service. This book discusses types of objectively scored test items that instructors often overlook when constructing classroom tests. Several of the types described are variations of the multiple-choice format. A number of examples and worksheets are provided in the discussion.

Frisbie, D. A. (1973). Multiple-choice vs. true-false: A Comparison of reliabilities. *Journal of Educational Measurement, 10,* 297–304.

Haladyna, T. M. (1999). *Developing and validating multiple-choice test items* (2nd ed.). Mahwah, NJ: Lawrence Erlbaum. This book provides an extended discussion of developing multiple-choice items and validating item responses.

Osterlind, S. J. (1998). *Constructing test items: Multiple-choice, constructed response, performance, and other formats* (2nd ed.). Boston: Kluwer Academic Publishers. This book provides an extensive treatment of constructing test items, particularly those using the multiple-choice format. Emphasis is on methods for identifying and minimizing measurement error during item construction and later review.

Wesman, A. G. (1971). Writing the test item. In R. L. Thorndike (Ed.), *Educational measurement* (2nd ed., pp. 113–128). Washington, DC: American Council on Education. This chapter reviews the item-writing literature and discusses ideas for producing various formats of objectively scored test items. See pages 113–120 for a discussion of the construction of multiple-choice and matching items; see pages 122–128 for the construction and characteristics of multiple-choice items in interpretive exercises.

9

Administering Written Tests on the Web

A recent World Series in major league baseball involved two New York City teams, the Mets and the Yankees. Many sports enthusiasts referred to these (and some of the subsequent games between the Mets and Yankees) as the "Subway Series." During one World Series game, two women were eating dinner at a New York restaurant, each carrying the very latest Internet-enabled cell phone. Conversation naturally turned to the game, but then took on the form of a challenge. Which one of them, using her portable phone, could most quickly find out the score of the game? The first woman turned on her phone, zipped through menus on its display screen, connected to a sports website, and got the score in two minutes flat! Then the other woman took out her phone, called her husband who was watching the game at home, and had the score in 20 seconds.

There are lessons to be learned here, and most of them also apply to administering written tests on the Web. Online testing is truly a high-tech endeavor that uses capabilities not available to paper-and-pencil tests. The underlying software of online systems is sophisticated, but their menu-driven features make them easy to learn. In spite of and partly because of their sophistication, online testing often requires more time to set up and use than the paper-and-pencil alternative, particularly with respect to producing the tests. Procedures engineered into many of the online testing systems require learners, and particularly instructors, to be creative if they are to fully realize the high efficiencies these systems can provide.

In this chapter, you will become acquainted with characteristics of online testing procedures.

Most, but not all, are associated with software designed specifically for online learning settings. We will look at features that are available with many of these systems, including the item formats they support and the capabilities they provide for administering tests, scoring answers, and reporting results. We will also introduce standards we believe represent reasonable expectations for this assessment component of Web-based systems.

Unlike pencil-and-paper tests, many computer-administered assessments can be scored immediately after the student completes the test. Depending on the options provided by the instructor, students can review items on the test at its completion and even receive fairly detailed diagnostic feedback such as explanations of the logic behind each item's correct response. At their convenience, learners can also check their own scores on the tests and other assignments through the instructor's online gradebook. The instructor can diagnose problems by looking for patterns in students' responses to test items, even while the test administration is in progress. These response patterns not only facilitate formative evaluations of achievement, they also help identify deficiencies within test items.

Web-based testing is not fully secure. But then neither are paper-and-pencil tests when administered in the conventional classroom. Item pools can be compromised. A person other than the one whose name is on the test might be providing the answers. The resources to which the student has access during the test are not fully controlled. We will look at these issues, recognizing that test security in online-learning settings is largely a function of how students perceive the intended use and consequences of these tests.

This chapter helps you learn three skills related to the assessment of online learners:

- Recognize common characteristics of software designed to help create, administer, and score online written tests
- Establish standards for this software
- Identify issues and practical options for addressing security of online tests

The focus for this chapter is on administering written tests on the Web. Of course, this includes building the online test as well as administering the items and scoring students' answers. When building the test, it is critical that the content of the test be controlled. Chapter 3 discusses this issue in some detail in the context of establishing content-related evidence of validity. This important aspect of validity is achieved by first outlining the content of the test and only then establishing test items that are consistent with that outline. Simply writing test items and making them available online does not control the content of a test adequately. Chances are very high that you have taken a number of tests in which content did not correspond closely to the objectives of instruction. Those tests were built without first establishing a framework to control test content. Many believe they can construct a test without working from a content plan, but it simply cannot be done. Please keep this in mind as we discuss the online administration of tests. A test is worthless or even dangerous if it lacks validity. Controlling the content, typically through performance objectives or a table of specifications, is an essential aspect of producing and administering valid online tests.

COMMON CHARACTERISTICS OF SOFTWARE FOR ONLINE TESTS

There are two basic types of software through which an instructor can produce, administer, and score online written tests. In online learning settings, the more dominant type manages instructional materials, maintains student records, and facilitates communication with students. Online assessment is an integral component or indirect feature of these systems. Blackboard is a widely used management system. The second type of software allows one to produce and then administer a test using a computer; computer-administered testing is its primary function. QuestionMark[1] is an example of the second type of software. It might be used by an individual computer, a group of computers connected through a local area network (LAN), or any computer with access to the Internet. It is also used to administer online surveys to a broad audience, but it tends not to include communication features often used in online learning such as online discussion, chat, and gradebooks.

This section discusses characteristics of software used for online testing, including descriptions of the item formats they accommodate, feedback they can provide to learners, records they maintain, and techniques to improve the efficiency of their use. As with any software, you will increase your understanding substantially by actually working with these systems. Many systems, such as Blackboard, allow you to look at existing websites that use its software, but better yet, let you create a website for your own course using their servers. The QuestionMark website referenced at the end of this chapter allows you to work with tests involving the large variety of item formats that this system can accommodate. Working online with these software systems is time well spent.

Available Item Formats

All systems support variations of the basic item formats, including completion, essay, multiple-choice, and true-false. All systems go well beyond what

---

[1]Internet links to Blackboard, QuestionMark, and some other software used to assess and manage records of online learners are listed at the end of the chapter in "Enhance Your Understanding."

one typically sees in printed tests. For instance, items in online tests can easily accommodate photographs and other images, sounds, and even movies. In essence, almost any content and format in a website, even links to external sites, can be incorporated into items used in online tests.

The variations within the basic formats differ across systems, both in terms of choices provided and creativity in their implementation. For example, some fairly predictable variations of the multiple-choice format include matching and ranking of options. Matching, in essence, is a series of multiple-choice items that share a common set of options. Ranking of options requires the student to order the multiple-choice options with respect to criteria established within the item stem. Figure 8.4 in the previous chapter illustrates one such item, in which students reorder the names of cities to reflect their respective distances from Chicago.

One creative variation of multiple-choice requires the student to click on an area within a photograph or other image. The image is electronically subdivided into a series of sections, often called **hotspots.** The student cannot see the boundaries of the hotspots but the boundaries establish the options of the multiple-choice item. By clicking on a specific area within the image, the student selects the correct or an incorrect option for each item. Learners might be asked to identify locations on a map, or medical students might be asked to identify indications of a particular disease on an X-ray.

When a test is administered online, all variations of multiple-choice items can be scored automatically upon completion of the test. If desired, students can also be allowed to review items and their answers when the test is finished. The instructor can also prepare narrative feedback for each item.

Online testing systems vary considerably in how effectively they implement the completion format, particularly the scoring of answers. Primarily because of problems with automated scoring of answers, the completion format is used less often with online tests than with paper-and-pencil alternatives. For online learning, automated scoring

may be a necessity and not just an advantage. This is because an online test might be available to students for a period of days, or even longer. It is impractical to manually score each test as it is completed, and the value of feedback to students is greatly diminished if scoring is delayed until the end of the testing window.

As we will discuss later, some online systems are needlessly restrictive in how they score completion items. For instance, if the correct answer to an item is *dog* but a student capitalizes the first letter, the answer might be scored as wrong. If the answer to a completion item involves two words, such as *New York* and a student inserts an extra space between the two words, the answer often would be scored as wrong.

Given that word processors and many other programs involving text entry can respond to spelling and even grammatical errors, it is reasonable to expect online testing software to have a considerable amount of intelligence built into the scoring of items written in the completion format. Completion items are a viable format. They also are relatively easy to construct—certainly much more so than multiple-choice items. Developers of online assessment systems could help reduce the load of online instructors by improving the sophistication of scoring algorithms used with the completion format.

Essay items can also be included in online tests. Large-scale standardized tests can be scored by computer, but essay tests developed by instructors and administered online have to be manually scored later. It is only a matter of time, however, before these essays are also scored automatically. As we will discuss later, developers of online testing can design more efficient scoring software.

As illustrated in Figures 9.1a and 9.1b, when essay items are administered online, students see the essay question and are provided a space to type their answer. Many students (and instructors) appreciate typed answers, because typing is often quicker than writing and is usually easier to read. At the completion of the test, online systems can redisplay the student's answer along

You are knowledgeable about what a bird is. You know that eagles, hawks, sparrows, chickens, turkeys, ostriches, and penguins are all birds, and that butterflies, bats, bees, and kangaroos are not. As with many skills, knowledge of what a bird is involves both declarative and procedural knowledge. To demonstrate that you know how to assess declarative and procedural knowledge, do the following:

Explain how you would assess a learner's declarative knowledge of a bird (INFORMATION), and also a learner's knowledge of the CONCEPT of a bird (a type of procedural knowledge). Each of your two explanations (information and concept) should be illustrated with a specific example.

Limit your response to two to five sentences. (Item worth 4 points)

Normal ▾	3 ▾	Times New Roman ▾	**B** *I* <u>U</u>	≡ ≡ ≡	≣ ≣ ⫤ ⫤

To assess knowledge of INFORMATION, one asks learners to declare what they know. For instance, one might ask learners, "Why are eagles and chickens birds whereas butterflies and bats are not?" To assess knowledge of a CONCEPT, learners are provided a number of diverse and new illustrations and asked to classify each as an example or nonexample of the concept. For instance, learners could be shown previously unused pictures of hawks, sparrows, penguins, bees, bats, and kangaroos and asked to indicate which are examples of birds.

Figure 9.1a
Illustration of how an essay item is displayed, with a student's written response appearing in blue on the computer screen

with the scoring plan[2] that will be used by the instructor. Displaying the scoring plan this way represents a fairly helpful form of feedback that allows students to estimate their score.

---

[2]The development of scoring plans for essay tests is discussed in Chapter 7. Often, the term *scoring rubric* is used instead of or interchangeably with scoring plan. Technically, a scoring rubric is a particular type of scoring plan in which student responses are scored holistically. Rubrics, which are often used when scoring performance assessments, are discussed in detail, in Chapter 11.

Producing the Test

Online testing software uses templates through which instructors build tests. Figure 9.2 illustrates a template that would be used with a multiple-choice item to enter the stem, response options, and feedback to students. The nature of these templates varies considerably depending on the item format involved, as well as whether graphics or other nontext material will be included. Other test-related information also has to be entered, including the number of times a student can complete the test, whether items and answers can be reviewed at the completion of the test, the amount of time allowed for completing the test,

You are knowledgeable about what a bird is. You know that eagles, hawks, sparrows, chickens, turkeys, ostriches, and penguins are all birds, and that butterflies, bats, bees, and kangaroos are not. As with many skills, knowledge of what a bird is involves both declarative and procedural knowledge. To demonstrate that you know how to assess declarative and procedural knowledge, do the following:

Explain how you would assess a learner's declarative knowledge of a bird (INFORMATION), and also a learner's knowledge of the CONCEPT of a bird (a type of procedural knowledge). Each of your two explanations (information and concept) should be illustrated with a specific example.

Limit your response to two to five sentences. (Item worth 4 points)

Selected Answer: To assess knowledge of INFORMATION, one asks learners to declare what they know. For instance, one might ask learners, "Why are eagles and chickens birds whereas butterflies and bats are not?" To assess knowledge of a CONCEPT, learners are provided a number of diverse and new illustrations and asked to classify each as an example or nonexample of the concept. For instance, learners could be shown previously unused pictures of hawks, sparrows, penguins, bees, bats, and kangaroos and asked to indicate which are examples of birds.

Correct Answer: √After the window for completing this quiz closes, the following scoring plan will be used to manually score responses to this essay item. Points you receive for your response will be added to your total score on this quiz.

1 POINT: The response establishes that information (or declarative knowledge) is assessed by asking learners to state what they know
1 POINT: The illustration for "information" involves the learner stating what is known
[Example of both of the above: "Information is assessed by asking students to tell what they know, for instance stating what characteristics an animal must have to be classified as a 'bird'."]

1 POINT: The response establishes that a concept is assessed by providing diverse unused examples and nonexamples of the concept and asking learners to establish which of the illustrations are correct examples
1 POINT: The illustration for "concept" involves the learner classifying examples versus nonexamples of the concept
[Example of both of the above: "Concepts are assessed by providing students diverse and previously unused examples of the concept and asking students to identify which of the illustrations are correct examples. For instance, students might be asked which among the following are birds: butterflies, bees, eagles, kangaroos, sparrows, chickens, and penguins.]

Figure 9.1b
Illustration of how displaying the scoring plan provides feedback at student's completion of an essay test (student's answer will appear in blue on computer screen)

the dates on which the test will be available, and where within the course website a hyperlink to the test will be established.

Characteristics of the templates greatly affect the efficiency with which an instructor can build the test. Unfortunately, the design needs of the computer programmer are sometimes better represented in the template than are the needs of an instructor. For instance, as illustrated in Figure 9.2, the template for a multiple-choice item may consist of a small window for the item stem followed by a series of even smaller windows for each of the options. In this template, the windows for each option are so small that only a few words can be viewed at a time. Likewise, the windows at the bottom for entering feedback to students allow viewing only one or two sentences. To read the contents of an item, the instructor has to scroll the text in each window. In addition, quite often, no spell checker is provided to help catch typographical errors. From the instructor's perspective, building the test on a computer likely will be more time consuming and more frustrating than building a paper-and-pencil test. *The sophistication available through technology should decrease, not increase the workload of instructors.*

The creativity of instructors can offset some of the inefficiencies built into test item templates. One strategy is to construct and edit test items in a word processing program and then copy/paste

❶ Multiple Choice Question

Question Text:

> You wish to determine whether students can determine the distance of a lighting strike given the time delay of the thunder. This knowledge is classified as a RULE. Which of the following is the best way to assess knowledge of this rule?

❷ Answers

Select the number of possible answers, fill in the fields with possible answers, and check the answers that will create a correct response.

Number of Answers: 3

Correct Answer	Answer Values
○	Ask students to describe how to calcul[(Remove)
⊙	Ask students to specify the distance of (Remove)
○	Using an essay test, ask students to ex (Remove)

❸ Options

Enter a response to a correct answer and a response to an incorrect answer.

Correct Response:

> To test knowledge of a RULE, provide students a relevant but previously unused

Incorrect Response:

> To test knowledge of a RULE, provide students a relevant but previously unused

Figure 9.2
Illustration of a template used to produce multiple-choice items for an online test

material into the template. Text can be entered and edited more quickly and the full item stem, all of the options, and the feedback for one and sometimes multiple items can be viewed simultaneously. Figure 9.3 illustrates how multiple-choice items might be formatted in a word processor. (The terms *ITEM, STEM,* and *FEEDBACK STATEMENT* are included in the figure for clarity of the illustration. It would be expedient not to use these identifiers when building the test.) The correct answer is identified with bold type. A blank line separates the options from the stem and the feedback. Extra blank lines visually separate items from each other. With the word processor, spelling and grammar can be quickly checked. When the

test is finished, it can be pasted into the template one paragraph at a time. (Preferably, the online testing software would automate the transfer of text from the word processor, or alternately, provide its own built-in editor.)

The process of moving text from a word processor to an item template can be further expedited by using keyboard commands or **hotkeys** that are built into personal computers. For instance, the sequence of steps listed in Box 9.1 expedites moving text for multiple-choice items from a word processor file (Figure 9.3) to a web-based template (Figure 9.2). This sequence is repeated for each of the multiple-choice options, using **Ctrl-C** to copy the text of one option at a time, **Alt-Tab** to toggle over to the template, and **Ctrl-V** to paste the text into the template. As illustrated in Figure 9.3, using bold type to identify the correct multiple-choice option allows you to quickly identify the correct response without rereading the test item. If you have access to a computer, try this procedure to see how it helps you enter test items more quickly.

A word processor can facilitate entry of test items for any written test. By using copy/paste, the item text can then be moved quickly into whatever template is used for entering items for an online test.

With many programs used for building online tests, one can also enter content as HTML code. Doing so provides considerable control over the

---

ITEM STEM: Which of the following best describes the relationship between capability and performance?

Capability is the potential to learn, whereas performance is what actually was learned.
Capability is a person's knowledge, whereas performance is used as an indicator of that knowledge.
Capability is declarative knowledge, whereas performance is procedural knowledge.

FEEDBACK: One cannot see what another person knows. Almost always, performance is only an indication of a person's capability (i.e., knowledge).

ITEM STEM: Which type of capability is involved in the following skill? "When shown previously unseen books, determining whether or not the book is a dictionary."

Information
Concept
Rule
Problem solving

FEEDBACK: Knowing a concept involves being able to classify previously unused illustrations as examples versus nonexamples of the concept.

ITEM STEM: You wish to determine whether students can determine the distance of a lighting strike given the time delay of the thunder. This knowledge is classified as a RULE. Which of the following is the best way to assess knowledge of this rule?

Ask students to describe how to calculate the distance of a lightning strike from the delay of the thunder.
Ask students to specify the distance of the lightning for each of several time delays of thunder you provide.
Using an essay test, ask students to explain why thunder is heard after a lightning strike occurs.

FEEDBACK: To test knowledge of a RULE, provide students a relevant but previously unused example and ask them to apply the rule. For example, with the present rule, a new example can be created simply by using an illustration with a previously unused time delay for the thunder. Asking students to describe how to calculate the distance, or to explain why thunder is heard after a lightning strike, are measures of declarative knowledge.

Figure 9.3
Illustration of text within a word processor used to build a test

Box 9.1

Illustration of steps used to expedite moving test items from a word processor file to a web-based template

---

1. Open the template used to input test items into the online assessment program, such as the one illustrated in Figure 9.2. Also open your word processing file that contains the test items, such as shown in Figure 9.3. With both windows open, you can quickly toggle back and forth between the template and the word processor by pressing **Alt-Tab** (that is, holding down the Alt key, pressing the Tab key, and releasing both keys). To provide more working room, maximize both the template and word processor windows so that each fills the screen.

2. In the word processor, highlight the text to the stem of the first multiple-choice item. Press **Ctrl-C** (Control and C keys) to copy the highlighted text.

3. Press **Alt-Tab** to toggle to the template.

4. After clicking on the space where the stem is to be written, press **Ctrl-V** to paste the text of the stem into its space. Press **Alt-Tab** to toggle back to the word processor.

Additional strategies that facilitate transferring text:

Double-click anywhere on a word to quickly highlight the entire word.

Ctrl-click on any word to quickly highlight all words within the sentence.

Double-click anywhere in the left margin to quickly select all words within one paragraph.

---

format of text and other material. One can easily learn some basic HTML commands, but it is much easier to use a What-You-See-Is-What-You-Get (WYSIWYG) editor, and then copy/paste the generated HTML code into the template. For basic formatting such as bold, underlined, and italic text, the test-building software should not, but often does, require the user to insert the HTML tags.

When building tests, some software will allow the instructor to create links to material needed to support a test item, such as an external graphic or table of data. Care should be taken when using links within a test, since each access increases the amount of time required to complete the test and the probability that network errors will interrupt the test administration.

Administering and Scoring Items and Providing Feedback

In addition to most students being more familiar with the format, paper-and-pencil tests have a number of other advantages over the same tests administered online. For instance, students can easily mark items they want to review before completing the test, and they usually can jump from item to item more quickly. Carefully designed online software, however, can match these advantages. For instance, a small separate window listing item numbers can be displayed on the monitor, so students can click on a number to jump to the corresponding item. Item numbers can be marked in different colors, such as green and red, to indicate whether or not the item has been answered. If a student is interested in coming back to an item after answering it, he or she can click on a button that will change the color of the item number to yellow.

As noted earlier, advantages of online testing include incorporating color, graphics, and multimedia in tests; scoring tests immediately and updating gradebooks automatically; and providing feedback and scores when tests are finished.

Test security, which is a greater issue with online tests, is addressed later in this chapter.

It is possible to limit the amount of time students have for completing a test; however, this has special implications when a test is administered online. Because time limits are in terms of elapsed time, network delays and other problems are not taken into account. Because factors beyond the student's control affect how quickly a test can be completed, imposed time limits can be very frustrating for students. Time delays can help maintain test security, but unless speed of response is a critical component of the skill being measured, the varying degrees of anxiety caused in students by setting a time limit can actually confound what the test is measuring. In conventional classroom tests, time limits are often set simply because students must leave at the end of the period to make room for the next class. And instructors often compound this problem by including too many items in the test for the time allowed. Because online learners have some flexibility as to when they take the test, setting time limits creates an unnecessary burden on students. Again, unless speed of response is one of the elements being assessed, any time limits that are imposed should allow students sufficient time to answer all items and to review their responses.

As we have noted, online assessments allow the instructor to create feedback for each item that is displayed when the student completes the test. Usually, different feedback can be established for both correct and incorrect answers to an item, but generally it is sufficient and often better to establish just one explanation for each item. Feedback that explains the reasoning behind the correct response (and even logic for avoiding an incorrect response) can reinforce the reasoning of knowledgeable students and provide instruction to others. However, many correct responses to multiple-choice and particularly true-false items are the result of lucky guesses. Only the student knows what logic was used to answer a given item. Providing distinct feedback for both right and wrong responses can convey misleading information to students who select the right answer for the wrong reason. Again, we recommend including only one feedback message for each test item. It should explain the logic behind the correct answer, and possibly the incorrect logic leading to the wrong responses.

Providing feedback messages in online tests also helps the instructor spot faulty test items. When assessments are administered face-to-face, students can easily raise questions about ambiguous questions during or at the conclusion of the test. This does not happen as readily with online

tests. If items are misleading or contain other significant problems, online learners are more likely to bring this to the instructor's attention when the logic presented in feedback by the instructor is inconsistent with their own. Learners are also likely to alert the instructor to unanticipated but legitimate answers to items; for instance, a miskeyed multiple-choice item or answers to a completion item that the computer fails to recognize as a correct response. When narrative feedback is not provided, learners and instructors are less likely to detect problems within tests.

Managing Records

A major asset of many online assessment systems is that they also manage student records. When items can be scored by computer, the computer is also able to automatically record scores in a gradebook. When the test includes items that must be manually scored, such as essays, the score the instructor or reader assigns to these items can be automatically added and recorded in the gradebook. This is an asset for instructors, particularly since online learners complete tests at various times. Learners can also check their own records in the gradebook at any time.

Record management systems typically can display scores for one student or scores for all students on one variable, such as a test or assignment. They can also display a spreadsheet, where all scores for all students are listed. Usually the instructor has control over how scores are grouped and ordered.

The online system might also allow the instructor to export records, so they can be read into another program such as Excel. This allows the instructor to control how scores are aggregated. Many management systems simply total points for each student. When this is the case, unless scores are exported to another program, the only control an instructor has over the weights of tests might be the number of items associated with each test.

Record management systems are not always accurate in how they handle records for tests and assignments that have not yet been completed. Often when computing a student's overall percentage score, they count as zero any test that has not yet been completed. This is roughly equivalent to the weather service recording the temperature as zero whenever the reading is missing. Recording an extreme score when information is missing greatly distorts totaled or averaged scores and frustrates students.

STANDARDS FOR ONLINE TESTING SOFTWARE

We propose here a set of standards for online testing software. These are personal standards based on personal experiences; however, we believe they represent a useful framework for extending our discussion of online testing.

Many online systems conform to most of these standards, although no system presently achieves them all. Therefore some represent goals, albeit goals we believe to be reasonable and relevant. You may want to use them as criteria when evaluating online testing software

Standards Related to Supported Item Content and Formats

1. *At a minimum, all common item formats should be supported.* Common items are generally assumed to include completion, brief-response essay, multiple-choice, matching, and true-false. Software often supports a much wider range of formats, which is good. For instance, some online testing programs allow embedded hotspots that students point to and click in response to directions given in the item. As an example, the item might read "Click on the noun in the following sentence," with hotspots electronically identifying the individual words within the subsequent sentence that are and are not used as nouns.

2. *All item formats should allow inclusion of symbols, equations, charts, tables, clip art, photographs, and sound files.* Although most items on written tests contain text, many items need to include formatted tables and figures, math formulas, or pictures. For instance, a math instructor

should be able to properly display equations in test items rather than relying on representations using standard ASCII text. Art instructors should be able to display photographs of several paintings and ask students to click on the one by a particular artist. Instructors in auto mechanics should be able to ask students to listen to several sounds and identify the one that most clearly indicates that the engine valves need to be adjusted. Software should make it easy for instructors to include objects within test items.

3. *The instructor should be able to enter test content as HTML code.* Web browsers use **HTML** code. The software that generates online tests, in essence, creates HTML code corresponding to material entered by the instructor. Instructors who are proficient in using editors that create HTML code often have more flexibility in the content of test items if the online testing software allows them to be entered directly as code. It should not be necessary for instructors to use HTML code, but if that is their wish, the software should allow the substantial increase in flexibility that directly creating code provides.

Standards Related to Ease with Which a Test Is Produced

4. *Without knowledge of HTML code, the instructor should be able to specify bold, underlined, and italicized text; font choice; and linefeeds.* These format options are widely used in text. With most assessment software they can be inserted using relatively simple HTML code, but that should not be required. Instructors should always be able to insert these format features in the same manner as with even the most basic word processors.

5. *The full content of the entire item should be continuously visible when the instructor is creating or editing the item.* With word processors, one depends upon seeing adjacent text when creating or editing a document. This is no less true when working with test items. It is unacceptable, for instance, to have the stem and each option of a multiple-choice item individually displayed in a small window, with only a portion of each visible to the instructor. If it is impractical to continuously

display the full text of an item while it is being edited, then the software developer should provide an alternative, such as uploading a Word document file containing the full test into the online testing system. Piecemeal copy/paste such as moving one stem and option at a time is troublesome. A preferred alternative would be for the online testing software developer to create **styles** for use with the most widely used word processors such as Word. The styles could preset formats for item components, such as the multiple-choice stem, and the options. When imported into the testing software, style identifications could be used to appropriately code the item components in the online testing program.

6. *A spell checker should be included if direct text entry is used.* If the software expects the instructor to enter the text directly into the system, a spell checker should be provided. This is less critical if text can be copied from a word processing file.

7. *While creating a test, the instructor should be given warning messages when it is likely that information is missing or has been input incorrectly.* With any online testing system, there are a number of points at which the instructor can easily make errors when building a written test. The software should anticipate and identify probable errors when they occur. This includes the instructor failing to identify the correct answer for automatically scored items, or failing to specify the number of points associated with an item, especially when zero points is the default value set by the software. Another common problem is providing a number of multiple-choice options that does not match the number anticipated by the software. For instance, if the software anticipates four options, but the instructor only includes three options for a particular item, problems can result if a student accidentally clicks on the blank fourth option. In this case, the software should ask the instructor whether the number of options provided by the computer should be set at three, or, preferably, the software should automatically adjust its own parameters so that the number of options matches what the instructor is using.

8. *For each test, the instructor should be able to provide a description of the test and directions to students.* The description of the test would typically be posted on the website when the test becomes available. Directions would be displayed when a student begins the test.

9. *The instructor should be able to preview the test exactly as it will appear to students.* Some but not all software systems allow the instructor to view tests and related material exactly as students will see it. This is critical so the instructor can anticipate and prevent problems that students will experience when they take the test online at a location away from the instructor.

Standards Related to Controlling Students' Access to a Test

10. *The instructor should be able to specify the date and time that the test will automatically start and stop being available.* In online learning settings, a test is often made available for a period of time. Once those times are established, the instructor should not have to manually start and stop the quiz or exam. Often it is impractical to do so, for instance, when the instructor is in a meeting. Or the instructor might be preoccupied with other tasks and neglect to start the test, resulting in needless frustration on the part of the students. The same issues apply when the test is to be made unavailable. Students taking tests online often have limited options for interacting with the instructor during the test and appreciate predictability, particularly with events affecting course grades. It is reasonable to expect developers of software to allow instructors to automate the start and stop times of tests.

11. *The instructor should be provided an efficient means for making a test available later to students requiring a makeup.* It is often necessary to allow some students to take a test outside the regularly scheduled time. The problem is establishing an efficient way to selectively open the test after it is no longer available to others. Creative workarounds are sometimes possible, although a better solution is a software option that allows the instructor to specify an additional window of time

for which the test will be open to selected students for makeup.

12. *The instructor should be able to specify time limits for completing a test.* This might be done in cases where it is important for students to demonstrate that they can complete tasks within a specified period of time, or simply to help ensure that students are not relying on external resources. When time limits are imposed, this information needs to be communicated to students. The software should provide options for helping students keep track of time. Depending on circumstances, though, students might find no display to be the least frustrating, which is why that option should be available. Time limits are often not necessary and should be used judiciously. They tend to increase anxiety, sometimes substantially, and unlike classrooms where students are face-to-face, there is no need to worry about students completing a test before the next class starts!

13. *The instructor should be able to establish a password for accessing each test.* The option of using passwords allows the instructor to open a test to the class, but limit access to students who have met prerequisite conditions, such as completing a reading or turning in an assignment. When the condition has been met, the instructor provides the password through e-mail or some other communication option built into the software.

14. *The instructor should be able to allow students to take the test multiple times.* Particularly when a test is being used for drill and practice or for formative assessments, the instructor may want to allow students to take the test more than once. The program should allow the instructor to specify the maximum number of times, with the default set to one. A value such as zero could be used to denote an unlimited number of accesses.

Some online testing systems allow the software to automatically sample items from a larger pool. Unless items are carefully stratified in terms of both item content and item difficulty, this procedure is discouraged, particularly when tests are used for summative evaluations. Particularly when less than 10 items are included,

even a random sampling of test items results in scores being highly influenced by the items that happen to be included in the test. If other security precautions addressed later are taken, it generally is not necessary to vary test items among students when tests are administered online.

If, for purposes of formative assessment, an instructor wants to expose students to different sets of items, one option is to create several equivalent forms of the test that are controlled as much as possible with respect to item content and difficulty. Students can then complete as many versions of the test as they find necessary, but only one attempt is allowed per test form.

15. *When students are permitted only one attempt, any access by a student to the test constitutes an attempt.* This helps sustain test security. Once the content of the test is accessed, the software should be able to prevent a student viewing the content, backing out, and reaccessing the test later. From a programming perspective, this usually is accomplished by inserting a verification check as soon as the student clicks on a link to the test. In the verification check, the student is asked whether he or she wants to take the test now. If the answer is no, the student is returned to the previous page. If the answer is yes, the program immediately records the action as an access to the test and the opening page of the test is displayed.

16. *The instructor should be able to reset a student's test attempt if its administration is aborted prior to completion.* If a student's Internet connection is interrupted during a test, the test administration is often aborted. If students are limited to one attempt, they may not be able to restart the test even though their answers were lost in the abort. Software should be designed so that the instructor can intervene and reset the computer's record without having to rely on systems-level support.

17. *To help keep a test secure, the instructor should be able to prevent students from saving or printing test items and related material.* It is very easy to print or electronically copy material

displayed on a computer screen. If students are so inclined, this could quickly compromise test security. Software can be designed so that instructors are able to control whether students can print or electronically copy test material. Doing so does not ensure test security, but does eliminate a serious electronic leak within the system.

Standards Related to How a Test Is Displayed to Students

18. *Material should be displayed for students in an easy-to-read format that is aesthetically pleasing.* This is a reasonable expectation in both what the instructor sees when creating the test and what the students see when the test is administered. This is particularly important during the test administration since test validity is potentially threatened if factors other than achievement are affecting a student's performance. Aside from readability, the appearance of a test should suggest a high degree of professionalism, if for no other reason than to help instill confidence in the software by both the students and the instructor.

19. *Students should be able to quickly scroll through items and change responses prior to completing the test.* The worst situation regarding standards is with systems that do not allow students to return to previous items, requiring a response to each item before moving on. The best situation is where students can quickly mark items they wish to look at later, and can answer items in whatever order they wish.

This flexibility is not possible with *computer adaptive tests*, where a computer selects the next item to be administered based on the student's answers to prior items. However, adaptive tests are mainly used with large-scale testing such as the Graduate Record Examination, and are typically inappropriate for use with course-based assessments.

Standards Related to Scoring Tests and Providing Feedback

20. *The instructor should be able to allow students to review their answers to items immediately after the test is scored.* Many assessments administered online can be scored immediately. If the instructor is willing to create feedback for individual test items, a computer can easily share this feedback with each student as soon as answers are submitted. Feedback generally consists of an explanation of the correct answer and may include explanations related to common incorrect responses. (As noted earlier, creating distinct feedback for correct versus incorrect responses is discouraged.) With essay items, feedback can be in the form of the scoring plan, which in turn allows students to immediately determine at least an approximation of their scores on these items.

21. *The instructor should be able to obtain a summary of students' responses to items, during test administration as well as at the end.* With multiple-choice items, the percent of students selecting each option should be provided. With completion items, answers given by students should be listed in two groups—those scored as correct and those scored as incorrect, with the number of students giving each answer provided. Responses to essay items cannot be easily summarized; however, written responses can be displayed sequentially by item, just as they should be presented for scoring. When a summary of item responses is provided, an instructor can quickly get a sense of how students are performing. This in turn greatly facilitates formative evaluation.

22. *Scores on tests should be recorded automatically in the gradebook.* In cases where the computer is able to score the items, students' scores should be recorded without instructor intervention. When the test includes items that are scored by a reader, scores should be automatically calculated and recorded as soon as the items have been scored.

23. *The instructor should be able to override scores assigned to items at any time.* This allows the instructor to fix unanticipated problems, such as correct answers that were not expected.

24. *To facilitate accuracy of scoring essays, the software should allow for scoring of all responses to one test item at a time.* Essays can be scored

much more consistently and also more quickly if all students' responses to one item can be read before going to responses associated with the next item. Scoring all items for one student is less accurate and efficient, since it requires repeatedly cycling through the scoring plans for each student's test. Ideally, software should randomize the order in which student's responses are read for a given item. When responses are read, the scoring plan for the test item should always be visible or easily accessible.

25. *The instructor should be able to set the points for each item.* This is particularly relevant for essay items, where points should reflect the relative importance of content assessed by each item. A warning message should be displayed whenever the instructor enters a score that exceeds the points specified for the item.

ISSUES AND PRACTICAL OPTIONS FOR ADDRESSING SECURITY

Security of assessments is a natural concern in any setting, but it seems particularly important with online assessments. Reasons include reduced visibility of learners who are online rather than face-to-face, and the fewer interactions that typically result. The response to security needs should, however, be from the perspective of learners as well as from that of instructors and institutions.

Security from the Perspective of Students

One aspect of security from the perspective of learners pertains to privacy. As in face-to-face classes, learners have a right to privacy with respect to answers on a test, scores and evaluation resulting from those answers, and personal communications with the instructor. Information available to individuals other than the instructor should be on a need to know basis. And when it is decided that individuals other than the instructor need access to this personal information, a student should be aware of who these individuals are.

With online testing, it is much easier for others to gain access or even unintentionally be provided with access to information that in other settings would be secure. An instructor's access can easily be shared with teaching assistants, other faculty, guests, and website developers. Learners should know who is seeing their information and what information they are allowed to see. The computer and network systems staff, and the administrators they report to, can and sometimes do have full access to students' records, even to the extent of being able to intervene and adjust records without the instructor's knowledge. This type of access is similar to allowing computer systems personnel in banks to access and change financial records of customers without authorization, or providing systems personnel in hospitals similar access to patient records. On the Internet, it is possible for individuals unaffiliated with the educational institution to invisibly intercept records and other information transmitted to and from learners. Therefore, any data that would be considered private should be encrypted at an appropriate level.

Another aspect of security that is important to learners pertains to dependability. In face-to-face classrooms, relatively rare events such as fire alarms might disrupt test administrations. Online settings are different. It is probable that during any one administration of an online test, one or more learners will be unable to complete the test due to network or server problems or glitches in a student's local computer. Even a careless error by the instructor when assembling an online test can compromise its administration; in a face-to-face classroom, the same error would be resolved quickly. When students are allowed just one test administration, an interruption locks the student out of the test.

Software that supports online testing should be designed to reduce the problems that learners face when inevitable disruptions occur. For instance, instructors can be given the means to reset records so that the student can restart a test. Students may have to restart the test from the beginning because answers are usually uploaded at the end of a test rather than after each item. Doing otherwise slows the test administration and makes it more difficult for students to move around within a test. Other software solutions tend to interact negatively with security concerns of instructors. For instance, instructors can encourage students to print out and work with a paper copy of the test so that work is not lost if there is a computer failure. But this opens the possibility for students to distribute tests to others. The only real solution is to design software and systems that are stable. Just as with cars, televisions, and personal electronic organizers, usefulness increases as simplicity and intuitiveness increase along with stability. With online tests as with other online transactions where privacy is a reasonable expectation, stability and predictability influence security both indirectly and directly.

Security from the Perspective of Instructors and Institutions

It is reasonable to expect students to act in an honorable way, and the majority of students do. However, security of assessments needs to be addressed by instructors and their institutions, not only because of problems with a minority of students, but also because other online instructional activities often make assessment policies confusing to learners.

With online instruction, we encourage students to communicate with each other and the software we use is designed to facilitate that communication. The electronic nature of this medium also allows wholesale copying and pasting. In some situations, learners are encouraged to copy and share material in this manner; however, in other situations, this is regarded as plagiarism. We sometimes encourage learners to work collaboratively on assessments, whereas we generally assume learners are working by themselves on written tests. We encourage learners to help each other with problems, including those experienced during a recently completed test, but the discussion sometimes takes place on public forums that might be open to those who have not yet completed the test. The Internet fosters communication among learners. Assisting a person who is not physically visible may seem less blatant than passing a paper copy of answers or test questions to another individual in person.

With online instruction, we encourage students to rely on external sources, and the Internet facilitates the process. During written tests, as with performance assessments, learners often are encouraged to work at their own pace, emphasizing knowledge over speed when demonstrating what has been achieved.

Learners generally welcome clear statements of policy and expectations when taking tests. An instructor can often use the institution's honor code as a framework for communicating expectations. A formal honor code also helps to convey the seriousness of expectations.

Features designed into online software can increase security. Some software can prevent students from using electronic copy and paste of test material, and similarly prevent students from using a printer. Tests can be timed to make it more difficult to access material outside the test. Other options include using electronic signatures, or using testing centers where students go to a designated site and are required to present identification.

One should not expect higher security in online settings than in face-to-face classrooms. While recognizing that compromised test security is not desirable or even acceptable, there are limits to how secure a test can be. At some point, the price we pay for achieving a higher level of security becomes too high both financially and in terms of the effects it has on the beneficial qualities associated with online assessments and online learning activities.

Emphasizing performance assessments and collaborative assessments, which are discussed in later chapters, can reduce the dependence on written tests and likewise the need for their security. Performance assessments usually do not have the same security concerns as written tests. With performance assessments, instructors usually can tell learners in advance exactly what tasks they will perform. Also, one can and usually should distribute the scoring plan in advance, a practice not compatible with most written tests. Learners typically can use external resources with performance assessments. As noted in Chapter 12, learners can also review each other's work and provide suggestions. For purposes of course grades, by placing the majority of weight on performance assessments and the minority on written tests, and by increasing the frequency of written tests and decreasing the length of each, the likelihood that students will compromise the security of the written tests is diminished.

Establishing test security is accomplished initially through clear communication of expectations. It is further established by taking actions that reduce students' options for compromising security along with actions that reduce their perceived need to do so. Except by taking extreme measures, perfect test security will not be realized in online settings. The goal should be that of establishing security consistent with that offered in face-to-face settings, and avoiding actions that undermine the significant educational benefits one is able to provide learners through online activities.

SUMMARY

Computer software incorporated in course management and other systems, combined with the Internet, makes online assessment feasible. This software is often highly sophisticated and easy to learn; however, its use often requires significantly more time on the part of the instructor, particularly with respect to building a test. Software generally provides a template for setting up and entering the items for a test. It also administers the test online, often scores items immediately at the conclusion of the administration, and provides the learner any feedback the instructor created for individual items. The software facilitates the manual scoring of items such as essays, and maintains electronic gradebooks that the instructor and individual students can access.

A set of standards is proposed for online-testing software. These standards pertain to how test material is entered and displayed, issues related to automating the administration and

scoring of tests, scoring of essays, providing students feedback at the conclusion of the test, and facilitating test security.

Issues and practical options that instructors have for addressing security are described. Security needs should be addressed from the perspective of learners as well as that of instructors and institutions. With respect to learners, this includes respecting privacy and providing dependability. Both can be problematic because of the open and complex nature of the Internet. A number of issues related to security are addressed in part through clear communication of expectations. Security is a greater concern with online learning because of reduced face-to-face interaction, and also because many online learning activities involve collaborative work and the use of external resources. Online testing software can help maintain security through controls on copying and printing test material. Emphasizing performance assessments can reduce reliance on written tests. One should not expect higher security than that typically achieved in face-to-face classrooms.

TERMS INTRODUCED IN THIS CHAPTER

Hotspot: is a defined area in a graphic or picture containing a hyperlink. Clicking anywhere within the area results in the action associated with the hyperlink, such as opening another image, playing a sound, or making a record within a database. A page within a website can contain multiple hotspots. Within a test, this allows creation of test items in which students click on various parts of a graphic or picture in response to prompts provided by the test item. A person can tell that a hotspot is present because the mouse pointer changes appearance when moved over the hotspot.

Hotkey: is a combination of keyboard strokes built into software programs to save the user time. An example of a hotkey is Ctrl>S (pressing the Ctrl key and prior to its release pressing the S key), which often saves the file being edited. Other examples are Ctrl>C to copy and Ctrl>V then paste material from one place to another. In Windows, Alt>Tab allows the user to jump from one window to another when multiple programs are running.

HTML: is the acronym for Hypertext Markup Language, which is a language in which web pages are written. Often, developers of websites use a specialized editor that generates HTML code corresponding to the text, graphics, hyperlinks, and other material entered using the editor.

Style: is a software tool available in word processors and other editors that helps the user format a document. For instance, styles can be created for titles, headings, and various paragraphs within a document. For example, once a style is created for a heading, a single action by the user changes the font and paragraph formats of text to those preset for that particular type of heading. Many styles usually come preprogrammed with editors, however users and programmers can create their own additional sets of styles. For instance, with multiple-choice items, a style can be created for an item's options that sequences letters at the front of each option, establishes a hanging or negative indentation for the first line of every option, and controls paragraph spacing. Online course management systems should use styles to expedite importing text from widely used editors such as Word.

ENHANCE YOUR UNDERSTANDING

- Listed here are product names and websites for various online assessment and course management systems. Go to the websites and view their descriptions and demonstrations. Web addresses can change, but can often be reestablished using an Internet search engine.

Blackboard	*blackboard.com*
ClearLearning	*clearlearning.com*
CPS	*einstruction.com*
Education to Go	*educationtogo.com*
Hot Potatoes	*hotpot.uvic.ca/*
IntraLearn	*intralearn.com*
Respondus	*respondus.com*
QuestionMark	*questionmark.com*
Quia	*quia.com*
WebCT	*blackboard.com/webct/*

- Some course management systems allow you to develop a course website on their server. Individually or as a class, go to the website for one of the above systems, set up a demonstration course or lesson, and then produce some tests. There usually is no cost for setting up a demonstration. If a group is involved in this activity, share your reactions with each other.

- Using a format similar to that illustrated in Figure 9.3, build a test using a word processor. Then copy/paste items over to the course management system. How does this compare with entering items directly into the system?

- This chapter proposes a set of standards for online testing software. Categorize each standard as critical, highly desirable, or preferred, along with brief notes to yourself as to why you selected the particular category for each standard. Form a small group and exchange views as to how each standard should be categorized. From the discussion, see if additional standards can be identified that would be judged as either critical or highly desirable.

ADDITIONAL READING

The EduTools website (www.edutools.info) provides descriptions of various course management systems, reviewing each product in terms of a set of 40 product features.

PART IV

Producing and Administering Performance Assessments

When one talks about assessments, it typically is about written tests. Within major course management products like Blackboard, when one reads the user's manual, the section concerned with assessment again focuses on written tests.

On the other hand, when one looks at how instructors working within online environments try to determine what learners can do and what they know, most often they use vehicles *other than* written tests. This is particularly true within distance learning situations. Rather than written tests, instructors use projects and various other assignments to establish what has been learned. Yes, these projects and activities often involve techniques used to facilitate learning. However, it is these procedures and not written tests that actually provide the dominant basis for establishing what learners are able to do.

From an assessment perspective, these procedures are called performance assessments. A performance assessment requires the learner to perform actions that are an explicit objective or goal of instruction. As Linn, Baker, and Dunbar (1991) indicate, the performance involves tasks that are valued in their own right rather than valued as indicators or correlates of other valued performances, a characteristic more typical of written tests.

Instructors often do not think of projects and other activities as assessments, but that is what they are when used to establish what learners can do. Recognizing their assessment role is important because of the significant implications this has to considerations we have been addressing, such as validity and generalizability of observations.

These performance assessments are not particularly effective at measuring declarative knowledge. Performance assessments are very effective at measuring procedural knowledge, particularly when *rules* are involved. Performance assessments are uniquely able to measure what we have referred to as *problem solving*; a situation where a goal has been identified but a means of reaching the goal has yet to be established. Written tests cannot measure problem-solving skills when so defined.

Chapter 10 is concerned with issues associated with using performance assessments. This includes their advantages and limitations, and techniques used for scoring these assessments. Chapter 10 also discusses actions one should take before creating a performance assessment. Chapter 11 focuses on the actual creation of performance assessments. As with any assessment, this includes establishing the capability to be assessed, the performance to be observed, and the means for scoring students' work. The chapter includes numerous illustrations of performance assessments.

Chapter 12 focuses on managing online performance assessments. This includes a discussion of features within web-based systems that facilitate using these assessments. The chapter provides an extend treatment of how instructors can significantly improve the efficiency with which student work is handled.

10

Considerations When Using Performance Assessments

Performance assessments are probably one of the oldest forms of evaluation. For example, one person learning from another how to weave or how to make pottery, skills that date back earlier than 7000 B.C., surely involved performance assessments. In the history of mankind, written tests are relatively new. And the multiple-choice item represents the newest format for a written assessment, with a history measured in decades rather than centuries or millenniums.

Unlike written tests, performance assessments have always involved a *direct* observation of learner behavior, or of a product resulting from that behavior. Performance assessments do what written tests cannot; they measure acquisition of *problem solving;* a set of skills that goes beyond the knowledge of concepts and rules. With performance assessments, one can evaluate a learner's ability to write a persuasive letter, complete a tax return, program a computer, use the scientific method to test a research hypothesis, play a musical instrument, deliver a speech, or pitch a baseball.

Many course assignments and learner activities that occur in both face-to-face and online settings can be used as performance assessments, as long as *performing the activity* is an explicit objective or goal of instruction. Let us illustrate this with both a nonexample and an example of a performance assessment. This is an activity that would *not* be used as a performance assessment:

For students majoring in library science, asking them to complete a reading

assignment through which they learn how to organize periodicals in the library would *not* represent a performance assessment, because the act of completing a reading assignment is not an instructional objective for these students, although it probably is a means of helping the students achieve an objective of instruction.

In contrast, here is an activity that can be used as a performance assessment:

Observing library science students actually creating an organizational plan for periodicals (or observing the completed plan) would be an example of a performance assessment since the ability to perform this task is an instructional objective or goal for these students.

Any course activity can be used as a performance assessment as long as the ability to execute the particular process or produce the resulting product is an explicit goal of instruction. However, as emphasized in this and the next two chapters, when an activity is used as a performance assessment, considerations such as validity and generalizability of performance become critical considerations. We will find, for instance, that changing somewhat the task that students are asked to perform to demonstrate that they have learned a particular skill will often significantly change how well the students perform the task. That is, when an alternate but equally legitimate task is used to assess student proficiency, different conclusions about students' competence will often emerge.

We will find that in online learning settings, performance assessments have some special advantages over written tests, but also some significant limitations. One advantage is that observing a learner's work in a performance assessment often provides insights into the learner's knowledge that are lacking when the learner is not face to face with the instructor. Another advantage is that performance assessments can, to a degree, make up for the lack of test security that is often a concern when learners are assessed online. Security needs of performance assessments are reduced, in part, because the scoring plan can be provided to learners before the assessment, and learners can be given model products in advance to guide their own work. A disadvantage of performance assessments is they tend to be less efficient than written tests. Other things being equal, performance assessments require substantially more time and resources. Also, many complex skills are presently difficult and sometimes impossible to assess fully online, such as the ability to work with volatile chemicals in a lab or to perform certain nursing skills such as treating a burn.

Performance assessments are typically used in conjunction with written tests. Although performance assessments are often needed to measure problem-solving skills, written tests tend to be more efficient when assessing information, concepts, and rules that provide the fundamental knowledge for problem solving. For example, before a performance assessment asks learners to create hypotheses about the behavior of binary stars, written tests can be used to establish learners' knowledge of concepts and rules related to gravitation, mass, and centrifugal force. This knowledge is prerequisite to understanding the characteristics of binary stars as they spin around each other.

Performance assessments are sometimes referred to as *alternative assessments,* however Nitko and Brookhart (2007) point out that "alternative assessment usually means in opposition to standardized achievement tests and to multiple-choice [and other fixed-response] item formats" (p. 253). Performance assessments are also referred to as *authentic assessments* because they involve performing an activity that is an explicit goal of instruction. In our discussion, we will address the importance of performance assessments involving authentic tasks, but we will resist the temptation of referring to the use of these tasks as an authentic assessment. Doing so begs the question as to whether other important assessments are not authentic. We have been careful in our discussion to recognize that *all* educational assessments involve a performance that provides indirect indications of what a person knows and is thinking. With cognitive skills, performance assessments are no more authentic than written tests. However, performance assessments provide indicators of very important types of knowledge and thinking that written tests are unable to assess. For instance, only performance assessments effectively evaluate what cognitive psychologists refer to as problem-solving techniques—situations in which a goal has been identified, but a means of reaching the goal has yet to be established.

The next chapter describes how to create performance assessments in the context of online learning. In this chapter, we will examine some important characteristics of performance assessments and discuss their implications. We will also describe four procedures for scoring performance assessments: comparison to models, checklists, rating scales, and scoring rubrics. We conclude by discussing some tasks that should precede development of a performance assessment. This chapter helps you achieve three skills:

- Identify characteristics of performance assessments

- Recognize qualities desired in a performance assessment

- Recognize the characteristics that models, checklists, rating scales, and scoring rubrics should have when used to score performance assessments

CHARACTERISTICS OF PERFORMANCE ASSESSMENTS

Specifying the characteristics of performance assessments depends in part on deciding exactly what a performance assessment is. The qualities associated with written formats such as multiple-choice and essay are more established. The nature of performance assessments is highly diverse and may include observation and evaluation of lab experiments, artwork, speaking, work habits, social interactions, and opinions about issues. For our purposes, a performance assessment will be limited to those situations that meet the following criteria:

1. Specific behaviors or outcomes of behaviors are to be observed

2. The behaviors represent performance objectives or goals of the course

3. It is possible to judge the appropriateness of learners' actions or at least to identify whether one possible response is more appropriate than some alternative response

4. The behavior or outcome cannot be directly measured using a paper-and-pencil test, such as a test involving a multiple-choice, essay, or other written format

Defining performance assessments in this manner narrows our focus. For example, determining whether an individual can "apply instructional design principles" does not establish specific behaviors or outcomes of behaviors to be observed; it is too global to be evaluated through a performance assessment. However, determining whether a person can produce essay items and a scoring plan for a test, or can use commercial software to produce an online written test is specific and thus would represent a performance assessment. Writing a research paper that compares current theories of learning would not be a performance assessment unless *being able to research and write a paper* on such a topic is a performance objective or a goal of the course. Determining whether a learner is more likely to listen to jazz or rap would not be a

performance assessment because one response is no more appropriate than another. Narrowing our definition of performance assessments in this way does not mean that observing general behaviors and providing learning experiences are inappropriate, or that providing learners with experiences for which there are no correct or preferred solutions should be avoided. Our definition is restricted to focusing on procedures other than written tests to which educational measurement principles can be readily applied.

Categories of Performance Assessments

Performance assessments can be categorized in several ways. This section contrasts performance assessments that measure a process versus a product, use simulated versus real settings, and depend on natural versus structured stimuli.

Process Versus Product Measures. A process is the procedure that a learner uses to complete a task. A product is the tangible outcome that results from completing the process. For example, using word processing software to produce a document is a process; the document is the product. Generally, a performance assessment is concerned with only the process or the product, or at least emphasizes one over the other. For instance, in evaluating an artist's work with watercolors, the completed painting might be assessed, but not the learner's technique in producing the painting. In online settings, it is easier to work with products than with the process that produces them. It is easier to evaluate the product, such as the word processor document or the watercolor painting, than it is to evaluate the process used to create the document or painting. Electronic images are often used to convey products from the learner to the instructor. If the process rather than the product is to be evaluated, indirect methods for observing the process usually must be employed. A common indirect method is for learners to submit a journal that describes the process in writing. Chapter 9 illustrates several performance assessments and includes examples of both process and product measures.

Simulated Versus Real Settings. Many performance assessments involve simulations because the real situations are too expensive or dangerous to use, unavailable, or impractical for other reasons. Some simulations are so realistic that they unquestionably represent adequate substitutes for the real thing. Sophisticated flight simulators can train and examine student pilots so thoroughly that they can safely pilot basic aircraft solo without prior in-flight experience.

Performance assessments in both online and face-to-face settings often depend on simulations. The realism of the simulation might represent an important quality of the performance assessment or may represent nothing more significant than superficial appearance. The need for realism must be judged in light of the reason for giving the assessment. For instance, if the principles that affect stock prices are being taught, a performance assessment need not have any consequences associated with learners' investing wisely or poorly. Although the assessment may seem more realistic and exciting if the exchange of money is simulated, doing so would have little benefit and might even hamper the instructor's ability to determine whether learners know how to work with factors that influence stock prices. On the other hand, including information in the simulation about changes in interest rates and the price of bonds would represent important aspects of the assessment, because these significantly affect the price of stock.

Natural Versus Structured Stimuli. A stimulus is natural when it occurs without the intervention of the observer. For instance, a learner's social skills are typically evaluated without prompts. In online settings, much like in written tests, the stimulus— what the learner is told to do—is structured to ensure that the behavior being evaluated will occur quickly or will occur in a particular setting. Examples of structured stimuli include asking a learner to program a computer to perform a

particular task, to create a specific PowerPoint presentation, or to prepare a sampling plan for selecting individuals to be included in a particular research study.

Natural stimuli facilitate the observation of a typical performance, whereas structured stimuli tend to elicit maximum performance. Therefore, natural stimuli are preferred for assessing personality traits, work habits, and willingness to follow prescribed procedures such as safety rules. Structured stimuli are needed to determine how well a learner can explain a concept orally, write a paper, play a musical instrument, or perform other tasks. This of course means that learners are demonstrating what they are capable of doing rather than what they can be expected to do.

Structuring the stimulus also ensures that the performance to be observed will occur. Observation time can be reduced by asking a learner to do something, rather than waiting for it to happen naturally. Structuring also helps determine whether the lack of a particular performance results because the learner is avoiding a behavior in which he or she is not proficient or because the appropriate condition for eliciting that behavior has yet to occur. Again, online performance assessments tend to be structured.

Advantages of Performance Assessments

Performance assessments have significant advantages and limitations when compared with written tests. Some are relevant to all instructional settings, whereas others pertain specifically to online situations. Here we look at five advantages.

1. *Performance assessments can measure skills that written tests cannot.* This is the most significant advantage of performance assessments. Many skills fall into this category because they rely heavily on motor skills, such as those involved in speech, writing, foreign language, science labs, music, art, and sports. Present technology limits the assessment of motor skills online, this being a major factor that determines which content areas can and cannot be taught through distance learning. Other skills can be

measured only by performance assessments because of constraints posed by written tests; these skills, as mentioned earlier, are problem-solving skills. Problem solving draws on previously learned information, concepts, and rules and involves problems that can be solved in a variety of ways. A written test can measure learners' understanding of grammar rules; however, a performance assessment must be used to determine whether learners can apply these rules when writing. Parallel examples exist in every academic area. Learning how to implement problem-solving strategies is often the ultimate justification of most formally taught courses. Without performance assessments, proficiency with these skills generally cannot be evaluated.

2. *Performance assessments influence what is taught and learned by expanding what is assessed.* If, for example, you and I are learning grammar rules, the way we expect these skills to be tested will probably influence what we learn. We will be motivated to learn the difference between the active voice and passive voice if we anticipate being asked to make this distinction on a written test. However, we will more likely learn to write in the active voice if our writing performance is also going to be assessed. Furthermore, the instructor is more likely to teach learners how to write in the active voice if the performance assessment is part of the instructional plan. The effective use of performance assessments encourages the teaching and learning of complex skills both in face-to-face and online settings.

3. *Performance assessments facilitate the assessment of a learner's process, rather than a product resulting from the process.* This third advantage pertains particularly to face-to-face settings. Whereas written tests focus on the product that results from performing the task, the focus of a performance assessment is often on the process a learner uses to get to that product. As we have noted, often the only option when not face to face is to indirectly observe the process, such as through student journals. Online learners do not benefit as much from formative assessments since, compared with summative assessments, a formative assessment relies very heavily on observing the process students use when completing a task. Being able to observe students' process is a significant advantage of performance assessments. The fact that online learners are less able to make use of this advantage is a constraining factor of online learning, not of performance assessments.

4. *Performance assessments tend to provide better insights into a learner's knowledge.* Direct observation of learner behavior, a characteristic of performance assessments more than of written tests, often provides insight into the learner's reasoning and understanding. For instance, an instructor will gain more insight about a meteorology student's comprehension of weather systems by evaluating a weather map produced by the student than by scoring the student's answers on a written test. Similarly, reviewing a profit/loss report prepared by a business student shows more about the student's knowledge of the accounting process than having the learner answer multiple-choice or even essay items related to the procedure. In face-to-face settings, many insights into what students know are obtained casually. In online situations, the instructor relies much more heavily on insights that are provided through the formal assessments. Performance assessments can be designed to provide these insights more easily than can written tests.

5. *Performance assessments can better tolerate settings with low test security.* Many instructors are understandably concerned about administering written tests in the unproctored settings that are prevalent when students are online. With performance assessments, this is less of a concern. When students are asked to produce a product or report the process they used to produce the product, it is usually possible or even desirable to include the scoring plan along with directions to the assessment. As we will note later, the instructor might even provide models that illustrate the qualities of a good response. In some situations, students are encouraged to work together. With performance assessments, one usually does

everything possible to ensure that the characteristics of a student's response are desirable. With written tests, this assistance usually will nullify the utility of the assessment.

Limitations of Performance Assessments

Three limitations of performance assessments are their lower efficiency, their subjectivity in scoring, and the problems they have with generalizability.

1. *Performance assessments are less efficient.* Compared with written tests, they generally require more time to produce, administer, and particularly score. Item for item, setting up a performance assessment requires more time than setting up an essay item and its scoring plan. However, once set up, the performance assessment can be used repeatedly across subsequent school terms. One cannot continue to reuse written tests with impunity. Students require more time to complete performance assessments than written tests. The substantial amount of scoring time associated with performance assessments never lets up. The computer can automatically score many written tests when students submit their answers and even record the scores. Not so with performance assessments.

2. *Scoring of performance assessments is subjective.* Like with essay tests, the scoring of performance assessments is susceptible to rater error. Bias, expectations, and inconsistent standards can easily cause instructors to interpret the same observation differently. As with essay tests, this problem can be controlled by developing and employing a careful scoring plan.

3. *Performance assessments have problems with generalizability.* Will the instructor's conclusions about students' proficiency be the same if the performance assessment involves a different, equally defensible task from the same content domain? Will a meteorology student who can create a two-day precipitation forecast involving a cold front also produce a two-day precipitation forecast involving a tropical storm or hurricane? Will a physics student who is able to create a demonstration of factors affecting electrical voltage also be able to demonstrate factors affecting amperage? Will an instructional design student who can create a good multiple-choice test also be able to create a good performance assessment or essay test? Performance often does not generalize across alternative skills of a domain. The way to resolve this problem is to observe the learner performing each task. However, doing so is often not possible because performance assessments are time consuming to administer.

OPTIONS FOR SCORING PERFORMANCE ASSESSMENTS

As with essay tests, performance assessments can be scored analytically or holistically. With analytical scoring, the appropriateness of a learner's response is judged on each of a series of attributes using checklists and rating scales. The scoring of many performance assessments, however, cannot be broken into distinct attributes. Instead, an overall or holistic judgment is made. Scoring rubrics and comparisons to a model are used with holistic scoring.

Scoring amounts to making a summary statement concerning a learner's performance. This summary may (but does not have to) involve numbers. Although numbers are convenient, the actual descriptions provided by a checklist, rating scale, or scoring rubric are generally more useful than numbers generated through the scoring process. Numbers are helpful when summative judgments are involved, such as when grades are to be assigned. The number is recorded in the gradebook; however, the qualitative feedback along with the numerical score is provided to the learner. With formative assessments, the verbal descriptions of the scoring plan provide a framework for discussing results with learners.

Scoring Option 1: Comparisons with a Model

Comparing each learner's performance with a model is the most efficient method for scoring performance assessments, and is quite compatible with the online environment. When coupled with narrative feedback, **comparison with a model** is a particularly effective means of providing feedback to learners. It works best when the focus of the performance assessment is on the product rather than the process.

To compare learners' products with a model, the instructor creates a sample product that fully complies with qualities that should be present in products produced by the learners. Each learner's product is then compared with the model using a scale such as the one illustrated in Figure 10.1. In addition to the scale rating, the instructor typically provides comments explaining the nature of the problems observed in the product. The narrative also provides suggestions for addressing these problems, along with comments about positive aspects of the product. Chapter 12 describes Internet-based options for providing this narrative feedback to learners.

Care must be taken to ensure that the model is fully consistent with the directions given to learners prior to completing the product. The instructor should be able to produce a product superior to most if not all of the learners. However, the purpose of the model is not to show what the instructor can do, but instead to illustrate a product that is fully compliant with the directions. When scoring performance assessments, it is inappropriate to give less than full credit to a performance that is fully consistent with the directions for the assessment. The overall quality of

products produced by the most capable students often will exceed specifications given in the directions. Learners should be encouraged and complimented for exceeding expectations.

The model with which comparisons are to be made is often shown to learners prior to their producing the product. When this is done, the model "amplifies" the directions to learners; it illustrates what is expected. Providing the model in advance does not provide learners the "answer" in the way a scoring plan or key would for a written test. Particularly when problem solving is being assessed, any number of different models could be produced that would fully satisfy the requirements for the model product. Providing learners with a model product in advance illustrates only one of the possible models. For instance, a model given to students in library science for how periodicals can be set up in the library would be different from the products produced by the learners, particularly if they are working with a different set of periodicals or are asked to produce a plan for a library with different physical dimensions and other properties.

A technique that is particularly effective is to use as models exemplary products produced by learners who were enrolled in previous sections of the course. With the learner's permission, products are typically displayed with the learner's name and often with other identifying information such as the learner's academic major. Again, one uses as models only products that are fully compliant with the directions for the performance

20	Your project is basically equivalent to the model project
18 or 19	A minor problem somewhere
16 or 17	Several minor problems, or a significant problem somewhere
14 or 15	A few significant problems, but overall OK
10	Not OK. A redo will be accepted if done right away
0	Nothing received (a zero does terrible things to the average!)

Figure 10.1
Illustration of a scale used to compare products with a model

assessment. Using products produced by a variety of prior learners has several advantages: the diversity of models will increase, learners are more motivated when the models represent work of their peers rather than the instructor, and there is less justification for producing products that are inferior to those that their peers are able to produce. Many current learners are also more motivated because, if their own products are exemplary, they might be used as future models.

Regarding the scales in Figure 10.1, the numerical values within any scale are arbitrary in that there are no absolute values that should be assigned. The fact that these values are arbitrary does not mean that they are chosen without logic or that their choice has no consequences. If the numerical scores are included in the computation of grades, using values that meaningfully correspond with grading criteria can expedite the assignment of grades (and also help learners anticipate course grades from the ratings). For instance, if 70% represents the break point between a passing and a failing grade, then the 14 out of 20 points used in Figure 10.1 provides a convenient break between "OK" and "not OK" ratings. In this rating scale, 10 points are associated with the "not OK" or unsatisfactory rating, along with a "redo" option for the learner. The strategy here is to use a score that is sufficiently below the 70% level to get the attention of the learner and provide impetus to improve performance on the project. Were the learner to choose not to redo the project, a 10 point score is not extreme and will not have undue consequences to the course grade as long as the learner's overall performance is satisfactory. On the other hand, a zero rating does represent an extreme score and its use for work not completed can have significant consequences that are inconsistent with using grades to indicate achievement of course goals (see Chapter 6). A zero score in Figure 10.1 can be used largely as a bluff, but a serious one, to make it clear to the learner that missing work is unacceptable. Particularly when learners are not face-to-face, rating scales play a role in facilitating communication.

Scoring Options 2 and 3: Checklists and Rating Scales

A **checklist** is a list of actions or descriptions. The rater (usually the instructor) checks off items as the behavior or outcome is observed. Checklists can be used in a variety of settings to establish the presence or absence of a series of conditions. They also help structure complex observations. Pilots use a preflight checklist to structure the complex observations that occur before takeoff. A checklist can similarly structure observations of a learner in a performance assessment.

The checklist in Figure 10.2 is from part of a performance assessment related to using a word processor, specifically skills associated with formatting paragraphs. In this assessment, learners were given both an electronic and a printed copy of a short paper. Changes that the learners were to make were handwritten on the paper copy. The checklist was used to observe each learner's use of a word processor to make the required changes. Using a checklist is appropriate here because each attribute can be reported as satisfactory or unsatisfactory. Notice that an option is provided for recording a "did not observe."

Rating scales are similar to checklists, except they provide a scale or range of responses for each item. Figure 10.3 illustrates a series of rating scales. These scales are associated with rating a speech. In this example, learners are assigned a score between 1 and 7 on different qualities associated with delivering a speech. Again, the values are arbitrary. Ratings of 3, 4, and 5 are used the most in these scales, with extra numerical space separating the 1 and 7 from the other ratings to denote their exceptional nature.

The numerical values in the rating scale (Figure 10.3) may not convert to percentages for grading purposes as readily as the values in Figure 10.1. For instance, is 7 to be treated as 100%? If so, with 3 out of 7 representing a point near the bottom of an acceptable performance range, would a percentage of approximately 40% represent the difference between a passing and failing grade? If grades are also based on other assignments, does 40%, also represent a passing score on those

Y = Yes
N = No
? = Unobserved

Y N ? 1. ENTER key used only at end of paragraphs (not to wrap text)
Y N ? 2. Shift-ENTER used when needed to force line break
Y N ? 3. ALIGNMENT CENTER used to center title
Y N ? 4. KEEP WITH NEXT used to prevent page break between heading and following text
Y N ? 5. SPACING BEFORE or SPACING AFTER (not extra Enter) used to provide space between
          paragraphs
Y N ? 6. INDENTATION FIRST LINE (not Tab) used to indent first line of paragraph
Y N ? 7. INDENTATION LEFT used when needed to indent paragraph

Figure 10.2
Checklist for scoring techniques for formatting paragraphs with a word processing program

7 = Exceptional, an uncommon level of achievement at this point
5 = Very good, superior to what is usually achieved at this point
4 = Good, typical of what is usually achieved at this point
3 = Acceptable although somewhat below what is often achieved at this point
1 = Below class standards

1	3 4 5	7	OVERALL RATING
1	3 4 5	7	1. Establishes initial interest
1	3 4 5	7	2. Sustains interest
1	3 4 5	7	3. Organization
1	3 4 5	7	4. Persuasiveness
1	3 4 5	7	5. Dependency on notes
1	3 4 5	7	6. Enunciation
1	3 4 5	7	7. Grammar
1	3 4 5	7	8. Posture
1	3 4 5	7	9. Gestures

Figure 10.3
Illustration of a rating scale

assignments? If not, how are scores on various assignments combined? Questions such as these can make the use of rating scales problematic when assigning grades, although experience gained over time usually establishes solutions to these problems.

Rating scales can assume a variety of forms. For instance, the scales in Figure 10.3 use words

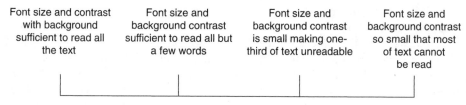

Figure 10.4
A scale that is incorrectly constructed because it rates two distinct qualities

involving comparisons among learners. Chapter 6 refers to such comparisons as *norm-referenced* interpretations, in contrast to *criterion-referenced* interpretations. Descriptors such as "exceptional" and "good" work quite well when a scale is to be norm-referenced, because the meaning of descriptions is gained partly through practice, through which typical and reasonable performance standards are established. In Figure 10.3, elaborations such as "superior to *what is usually achieved at this point*" help establish common meanings.

With any rating scale, words used to describe the meaning of various points on the scale should be carefully chosen so that they have the same meaning to different raters. The words must also describe only one dimension or characteristic per scale. Note that the scale shown in Figure 10.4 has two dimensions that are simultaneously addressed with respect to the quality of Power-Point slides. This scale should be divided into two separate scales, one concerned with the size of fonts and the other with contrast between the fonts and the background.

Each rating scale should have four to seven divisions. Words do not have to be used at each point within the scale but should at least define the scale at its two extremes. Preferably, intermediate points within the scale, especially the midpoint, should also be defined.

There is a tendency for raters to use only a portion of each scale, for example, to rate more individuals as above average than below average. This practice negates the usefulness of part of the scale and reduces the reliability of scores. To minimize

this problem, verbal descriptions used throughout the full range of a scale should depict plausible behaviors or levels of performance that actually do occur among the learners being observed.

The efficiency of a checklist or rating scale has a major impact on how complex the performance assessment can be. The following characteristics improve efficiency:

• The fewest words possible should be used within each item of the checklist or rating scale. Similarly, the fewest words possible should be used to define points on a rating scale. Minimizing the words increases the speed with which the items can be read. Telegraphic phrases that represent incomplete sentences but clearly communicate ideas to the rater are appropriate. Using a redundant phrase in each item, such as "the learner will," is inappropriate.

• Key nouns and verbs that indicate the essence of the quality being addressed should appear early in each item. This helps the practiced rater recognize each item within the checklist or rating scale simply by reading the first few words. Notice that a rater with some experience using the checklist in Figure 10.2 will recognize each statement by reading just a few words.

• Items should be grouped in the order they are likely to be rated. When evaluating a process, the order should correspond to the sequence in which behaviors are likely to be observed or addressed within the learner's journal. When evaluating a product, items of similar content or various stages of the evaluation should be grouped together.

- All items should have the same polarity. For checklists, all items should describe either a desired quality or an undesired quality. For rating scales, the left end of scales should always describe either the most desired or the least desired performance.[1]
- The checklist or rating scale should be easy to mark. Usually a space for placing the mark should be located consistently to the left or the right of each item in the checklist. The rating scales, along with words used to define points on the scales, should similarly be listed vertically down the side of the page. Any narrative used to describe what is being rated is located to the side of each scale.

A numerical score for a learner's performance can be obtained from a checklist by adding up the points associated with each item for which the learner received credit. With rating scales, a numerical score can be obtained by associating points with each scale, such as 1 through 5, and then summing these points across items. In many situations, such as providing feedback to learners, ratings on individual items are more informative than is a totaled score. As long as items in a checklist or rating scale identify specific qualities that a learner is or is not able to perform, they are providing criterion-referenced interpretations of performance. (The same applies to scoring rubrics, which are discussed in the next section.)

As illustrated in Figure 10.3, it is often useful to provide an overall or holistic rating in addition to ratings on more narrowly focused items. It is common to place the overall rating after the other items, although it is actually better to place it at the beginning. When placed at the end, overall ratings are heavily influenced by ratings on the preceding items. In essence, it becomes an averaged or totaled rating, which, if that is desired, can be obtained more reliably by simply summing points across the items. If the overall rating is meant to be holistic, it is better to place it ahead of the other items, when the instructor is more likely to make a holistic judgment rather than one influenced by the more analytic elements of the other ratings.

Scoring Option 4: Scoring Rubrics

Like comparisons to a model, **scoring rubrics** involve holistic ratings.[2] Performance assessments sometimes are scored holistically even when a number of distinct qualities are being assessed. Often this is done because it is not possible to separate a product or performance into a series of individual attributes. Sometimes holistic scoring is used simply because it is faster than analytical scoring; it is quicker to obtain an overall impression than to make a series of judgments. Scoring rubrics are often included when several attributes are being used simultaneously to make a holistic judgment. In a way, a scoring rubric is like a rating scale, with descriptions of performance that range from higher to lower. Unlike a rating scale, though, a scoring rubric addresses several qualities simultaneously within the same scale.

A restaurant uses a scoring rubric, in essence, to describe how meat can be cooked. In the series of descriptions shown in Figure 10.5, notice how the same set of variables—in this case, color and temperature—is present at each level of the rating. Each variable changes from lower to higher

---

[1] In contrast, when developing opinion questionnaires, one should reverse the polarities of some items so that respondents will carefully read each question before answering. Unlike questionnaires, a checklist or rating scale is used repeatedly by the same observer. Once experienced, the observer does not read through items sequentially or in great detail. Reversing the polarity of some items slows down the experienced observer and increases the risk of marking incorrectly.

[2] The term *scoring rubric* is used by some to represent any specification of scoring procedures. More typically, a scoring rubric refers to a series of holistic descriptions, in contrast for instance to the analytical descriptions used with rating scales or in a checklist. The term *scoring plan* is used to denote how a particular performance is to be scored. A scoring plan might involve comparisons with a model, a checklist, rating scales, or scoring rubrics.

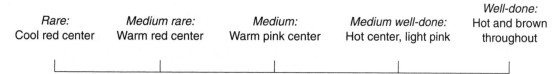

| Rare:
Cool red center | Medium rare:
Warm red center | Medium:
Warm pink center | Medium well-done:
Hot center, light pink | Well-done:
Hot and brown
throughout |

Figure 10.5
Descriptions of cooked meat

as the overall rating changes from one end of the continuum to the other. This use of the same set of variables across the full range of the continuum is a common characteristic of scoring rubrics.

With performance assessments, a scoring rubric provides a series of holistic descriptions of performance. The rater observes the learner's performance and then assigns the learner to the category that best describes her or his performance.

Figure 10.6 illustrates a rubric for scoring writing samples. Notice, again, that the same set of variables is used across the range of the continuum. When developing a scoring rubric, it is important first to list the variables that are to be judged and then to establish specific descriptions of these characteristics for each point along the continuum. These characteristics should fit together at each point. That is, it is not sufficient for each variable to change from lower to higher across the continuum. Instead, the description of all variables should match what is typically seen in learners performing at a particular level. For instance, in the previous rubric describing how meat is cooked, meat that is light pink in the center will also be expected to have a hot temperature in the center. In Figure 10.6, a learner who uses ample supporting ideas or examples (listed in the highest category of the rubric) will typically use words precisely and exhibit few errors in spelling. A learner who includes but does not develop supporting ideas (fourth category in the rubric) will likely also demonstrate an adequate but limited word choice and misspell common words. If descriptions of variables at a particular point on the continuum represent a combination that is

unlikely to be seen in learners, the scoring rubric will be difficult to use and inconsistencies in scoring will increase. If desired, numerical values can be associated with each category in a scoring rubric, although it is the verbal descriptions within the rubric that provides the interpretable rating of a performance.

ACTIONS TO TAKE BEFORE CREATING A PERFORMANCE ASSESSMENT

As we have noted, in online learning, performance assessments take on a variety of forms. They include many, and in some cases, all course activities in which learners submit a tangible product of some type for review by the instructor. In face-to-face classroom settings, these might represent homework assignments or even products produced through an in-class activity. To be a performance assessment in either a face-to-face or online setting, the activity must represent a process or produce a product that directly illustrates a degree of accomplishment of an explicit goal of instruction. In essence, the behavior exhibited is an intended outcome of instruction within the course. The product is not just documentation that learners participated in a prescribed activity. Instead, the performance is a behavior that the course is designed to instill in students—an intended outcome of learning.

The next chapter describes how to create performance assessments. Before beginning that discussion, it will be useful to identify other tasks that should be completed before a performance assessment is produced. Performance

Writing is focused on the topic
Logical organization pattern
Ample supporting ideas or examples
Demonstrates sense of wholeness
Word choice is precise
Few errors in spelling
Various kinds of sentence structures used

Writing is focused on the topic
Organization pattern has some lapses
Supporting ideas or examples used
Demonstrates sense of wholeness
Word choice lacks some precision
Errors in spelling uncommon words
Various kinds of sentence structures used

Writing is generally focused on topic
Organizational pattern evident, with lapses
Occasional supporting idea or example
Demonstrates sense of wholeness
Word choice adequate
Errors in spelling mostly uncommon words
Different simple sentence structures used

Writing contains ideas extraneous to topic
Organization pattern attempted, with lapses
Supporting ideas not developed
May lack sense of wholeness
Word choice adequate but limited
Common words misspelled
Different simple sentence structures used

Writing slightly related to topic
Little evidence of organization pattern
Supporting ideas inadequate or illogical
Limited sense of wholeness
Word choice limited or immature
Common words frequently misspelled
Simple sentence structure used

Figure 10.6
Illustration of a rubric for scoring a writing sample

assessments are very valuable tools. They can assess skills that written tests cannot. These skills tend to represent the ultimate goals of instruction. At the same time, performance assessments are our most expensive assessment tool. They should be implemented judiciously. Here are some strategies that can be useful in this regard.

Identify Authentic Tasks

Performance assessments should focus on authentic tasks. Here are qualities that make a task authentic:

- The task is an actual performance outcome that learners are to achieve through instruction. It is not a convenient substitute for that performance or an indirect indication that learners have achieved that performance.
- The task requires learners to draw on previously learned knowledge.
- The task clearly involves important themes and ideas associated with the content being taught.
- The task involves a real-world application of the content being taught.

This last point is often confusing. Involving real-world applications does not necessarily refer to activities in which learners will directly participate later in life. Much is learned through education that learners do not specifically use later in their profession. Instead, real-world applications involve direct applications of knowledge that are highly relevant to situations outside the course. Authentic tasks in science, for instance, relate to real-world situations in which the science is applied or discussed. Likewise, authentic tasks in math relate to real-world situations in which mathematicians or other consumers of mathematics use math knowledge. Particularly in professional schools, authentic tasks parallel closely what learners will eventually perform in their work. However, in its broader meaning, authentic refers to authenticity with respect to how targeted knowledge is used within a discipline to solve problems in the world.

Identify Concise Goals That Will Be Assessed

Performance assessments are based on concise instructional goals. Prior to creating a performance assessment, the goal to be assessed must be identified. Whereas a performance objective identifies the specific behavior, a goal is stated more broadly. Performance assessments normally are used to evaluate broader objectives or goals. To illustrate the contrast, an example of a performance objective is

Information: Identify qualities desired in essay items.

An example of a goal is

Produce an essay item.

A goal is often the equivalent of several objectives. Goals rather than performance objectives typically have to be used with performance assessments, because the task often cannot be meaningfully expressed as a series of specific behaviors. Alternatively, listing the full series of specific performances associated with the task may be impractical.

Nevertheless, to develop a performance assessment, a goal must be expressed in operational terms. For instance, "understands how knowledge of energy is fundamental to all the scientific disciplines," refers to important knowledge, but fails to establish the type of tasks learners are expected to perform. To ascertain the validity of a performance assessment, the goal must be written so that one can unequivocally judge whether the task used is a legitimate instance of what the goal suggests learners should be able to do. However, even with concise goals, a specific task typically represents one of several options for indicating proficiency with the goal.

When constructing performance assessments, there may be a temptation to increase realism by involving associated skills irrelevant to the goal being assessed. For instance, if the goal is "establishing an economical means to travel between two distant locations," the simulated expenditure of money could be associated with the task, but is not essential to determining whether a person can establish an economical means of travel. Including unessential associated skills in an assessment may increase realism, but it is equivalent to including irrelevant information in a written test item. Extraneous information tends to confuse learners and, more important, confounds the assessment. The use of concise goals reduces the tendency to include extraneous material in the assessment.

Determine Whether the Assessment Will Focus on Process or Product

As we have noted, a performance assessment is uniquely able to evaluate the process that a learner uses as well as the product that results from completing the task. An example of a process would be determining which computer best matches one's needs. An example of a product would be successfully ordering a particular computer online. Generally, a performance assessment focuses on either process or product, not both. For some tasks, the way a learner tackles the problem is more relevant to the instructional goal than is the specific solution the learner derives. When interactions between the instructor and learner are asynchronous, which they usually are in online settings, observing the process is difficult. Therefore, if the focus of the assessment is to be on the process, the instructor must devise a way for the learner to document the process that was used. For instance, the process of selecting a computer that meets one's needs can be described in writing.

Tell Learners What Will Be Expected of Them

One advantage of performance assessments is that you usually can tell learners exactly what is on the test. This cannot be done with a written test. With performance assessments, telling learners what they will be asked to do, right down to the actual scoring criteria, is a very effective way

of communicating instructional goals. (This also is an effective way to help assure that your instruction is consistent with your goals!) Telling learners what they are to do increases the likelihood that they will successfully perform the task. Given that performance assessments are time consuming to score, you can save yourself and your learners considerable time by explaining what you expect them to accomplish. Performance assessments on which learners have performed well are scored much more quickly than performance assessments with which learners have had significant problems.

Determine That Learners Have Mastered Prerequisite Skills

When used appropriately, performance assessments require learners to integrate prior knowledge. Obviously, without knowledge of prerequisite information, concepts, and rules, learners will usually not succeed with the performance assessment. Considerable time will be saved if prerequisite skills are identified and learners' achievement of these skills is evaluated before the performance assessment is administered. Again, performance assessments on which learners perform well are much more quickly scored.

SUMMARY

A performance assessment is the only way to measure many skills. A performance assessment is authentic when the performance to be observed consists of actual versus indirect indications that a learner has achieved an instructional goal, and involves a direct application of knowledge that is highly relevant to situations outside the course. Performance assessments can be used to evaluate a process or a product. They can assess behaviors resulting from natural or structured stimuli. Performance assessments are more time consuming than written tests to develop, administer, and score. They can be used to effectively communicate instructional goals to learners and can assess capabilities, including problem-solving skills, that cannot be evaluated through written tests.

Comparisons with models, checklists, rating scales, and scoring rubrics facilitate judging and recording observations from performance assessments. Checklists are appropriate when the process or product can be broken into components that are judged to be present or absent, adequate or inadequate. Comparisons with models and scoring rubrics are used when performance is to be scored holistically. Holistic scoring is usually quicker, although the resulting scores tend to have lower reliability than when checklists or rating scales are used. Usually, qualitative scoring of performance assessments is preferable, although numerical scores can be derived when needed, such as for assigning course grades.

TERMS INTRODUCED IN THIS CHAPTER

Performance assessment: is a measure of a learner's competence where the performance to be observed (or the product resulting from the performance) is an explicit goal of instruction. Performance assessments are uniquely able to measure problem solving. The measurement of many skills other than problem solving requires the use of performance assessments because of the motor skills involved, such as in speech and language, science labs, the performing arts, and sports.

Comparison with a model: is a scoring strategy in which each student's performance or product is compared with a previously produced model that would receive full credit when scored. These models often are the products of prior students' performances on the same assessment. Scores are assigned by comparing each student's performance with the model using a scale such as the one in Figure 10.1. Comparison with a model is an example of holistic scoring.

Checklists: are used for scoring performance assessments when the correctness of a process or product can be judged in terms of the presence or absence of a series of conditions. Figure 10.2 illustrates a checklist used for scoring an assessment. The use of a checklist is an example of analytical scoring.

Rating scales: are similar to a checklist in that performance is judged in terms of a series of separate qualities. As illustrated in Figure 10.3, unlike a checklist, rating scales associate a range of values with each item. They are used when judgments need to be made as to the degree to which each characteristic is present, rather than simply the presence or absence of each quality. The use of rating scales is an example of analytical scoring.

Scoring rubric: is a type of scoring plan used when holistic judgments are to be made simultaneously on a series of interrelated qualities. As illustrated in Figure 10.6, a scoring rubric typically involves the same set of qualities described at different levels of proficiency.

ENHANCE YOUR UNDERSTANDING

- List three instructional goals for a course you might teach that would be assessed with a performance assessment. Do you believe that the performance of learners who achieved each of these goals would be considered authentic? Why or why not?

ADDITIONAL READING

Messick, S. (1994). The interplay of evidence and consequences in the validation of performance assessments. *Educational Researcher, 23*(2), 13–23. This article provides a detailed discussion of validity issues related to performance assessments. Topics addressed include the need for targeting the underlying capability when designing an assessment rather than focusing on learners' outward performance. The article also discusses the role of structured assessments such as objectively scored tests.

Shavelson, R. J., Baxter, G. P., & Pine, J. (1992). Performance assessments: Political rhetoric and measurement reality. *Educational Researcher, 21*(4), 22–27. This article summarizes research studies by the authors related to performance assessments. Issues addressed include factors affecting learner performance on the assessments, reliability of scores, and correlation of scores on performance assessments with traditional written tests. Their research involved fifth- and sixth-grade students participating in a special hands-on science curriculum, but it is reasonable to expect their findings to generalize to online settings involving older learners.

11

Creating Online Performance Assessments

The previous chapter discussed considerations when using performance assessments, including options for scoring results. This chapter uses this information to describe how to create an online performance assessment. As noted earlier, online performance assessments include almost any product that learners submit to demonstrate a particular proficiency. In face-to-face instruction, one might characterize many of these products as homework assignments, because they often are an extension of instruction through which students apply what they are learning. In online settings, the products students produce play a critical role in establishing what they have learned. For purposes of our discussion, online performance assessments do not include written tests such as those that involve multiple-choice, true-false, completion, and essay items.

As we discuss the creation of online performance assessments, there are two issues to keep in mind. First, although performance assessments play a dominant role in online learning, they pertain only to situations where the learners' actions are being used to directly measure an explicit goal of instruction. This excludes course activities that are being used primarily to provide experiences or to facilitate learning. For example, a writing assignment where the purpose of the activity is to expose the learner to important ideas within the discipline would be a learning activity and not an assessment. To be a performance assessment, it must involve an explicit behavior

that the instruction is designed to establish, or the product being observed must be a direct result of this explicit behavior.

The second important issue is that, although the performance being observed is an explicit outcome that is expected to result from instruction, this performance is not the *knowledge* we hope the learner is achieving. What a learner knows or is thinking is internal to the person's mind and cannot be observed. The performance we observe is *only an indication* of the learner's knowledge. This fact results in our need to address critical concerns that have been discussed throughout the book and are highly relevant to this chapter. Specifically, we must be aware of the types of knowledge that exist (declarative and procedural knowledge, and problem solving) and the types of performance that provide good indicators of each type of knowledge. We must also recognize that any performance that is observed is only a sample of what could have been observed, and that other performances that could be sampled might result in different inferences about a learner's knowledge.

Online performance assessments can be used to measure any type of capability, however the time required to evaluate students' products and provide meaningful feedback requires us to use them judiciously. In online settings, performance assessments are rarely used to measure declarative knowledge; that is, knowledge of information. They are frequently used to measure procedural knowledge, specifically concepts and rules. Performance assessments are uniquely able to measure problem-solving skills. Measuring knowledge of a concept or rule will be called **single-task performance assessment.** These assessments are usually easy to produce, although they require more time to administer and score than do their written-test counterparts. When a problem-solving skill is involved, the assessment will be called a **complex-task performance assessment,** because the learner is being asked to apply a complex of information, concepts, and rules to solve the problem. These assessments tend to be more difficult to create. Written tests cannot measure the skills that are assessed with a complex-task performance assessment.

As we discuss the creation of performance assessments, we must keep in mind the considerations that precede their development. As with all systematic instruction, our assessments of learner performance must be goal driven. We also should limit performance assessments to tasks that are authentic; that is, these assessments should involve real-world applications of the content being taught. Because using online performance assessments is time intensive, we should identify prerequisite skills that can be assessed through more economical written tests.

Figure 11.1 outlines a specification we use in this chapter to structure the development of performance assessments. This **performance assessment specification** takes into account the considerations addressed in Chapter 10, and organizes creation of a performance assessment into three basic steps. Step 1, identifying the capability to be assessed, involves establishing the goal to be assessed and the type of capability it involves. Step 2, establishing the performance to be observed, includes identifying prerequisite skills and establishing whether focus will be on the process learners use or the product they produce when they employ the process. Step 3 is concerned with development of a plan for scoring performance.

In this chapter, we initially talk through each of the three basic steps, illustrating how they are used to develop a complex-task performance assess-

---

CAPABILITY TO BE ASSESSED
- *Goal to be assessed*
- *Type of capability involved*

PERFORMANCE TO BE OBSERVED
- *Summary descriptions of tasks associated with goal being assessed*
- *Description of tasks to be performed*
- *Focus on process or product?*
- *Prerequisite skills to be verified*
- *Instructions to learners*

SCORING PLAN

Figure 11.1
Performance assessment specification

---

ment. We then use the three steps to describe the development of four additional assessments. This chapter helps you achieve two skills:

- Recognize the three basic steps to producing a performance assessment that can be used online

- Apply these steps to the creation of single-task and complex-task performance assessments

STEP 1: ESTABLISHING THE CAPABILITY TO BE ASSESSED

In both face-to-face and online settings, specifying the capability to be assessed is the most fundamental step in creating a performance assessment. Throughout this book, a very deliberate distinction has been drawn between the learner's capability and the learner's performance. The capability is the learner's knowledge that we would like to assess but cannot observe directly, whereas a performance is the learner's outward behavior used to obtain an indication of what the learner knows or is thinking.

A performance assessment is used to systematically observe this performance. The selection of the performance to be observed must be based on a clear awareness of the capability being assessed. Identifying that capability helps us determine the type of behavior we should observe and how broadly our observation must generalize. For instance, if we want to know whether a learner can find information about the geography of another country without the help of others, we might ask the learner to obtain the information using the Internet. However, we may want our observations to generalize to what can be found through specialized electronic and non-electronic resources available through university libraries. We might want the learner to be able to obtain this information in a variety of contexts, such as locating an interesting place to visit or understanding particular habits of people living in that country. One must clearly establish the capabilities we are trying to assess and use that framework to control the content of our performance assessments.

With performance assessments, the capability is usually expressed as a goal. Goals involve statements such as these:

1. Using online resources provided by the U.S. government, establish the influence that the geography of a given country has on crops grown in that country.

2. Summarize the main idea expressed in a poem.

3. Select the appropriate statistical technique for testing the significance of the difference between control and treatment groups.

4. Calculate the volume of irregularly shaped objects.

5. Determine when and where astronomical objects will be visible in the sky.

As noted in earlier chapters, goals may incorporate several performance objectives. Goals give clear direction as to where the learner is expected to go, but generally do not identify the specific behavior the learner will exhibit in the process of accomplishing that goal. An instructional goal often represents a summary statement or a title for the capability we are trying to assess. For example, the first of the listed goals expects learners to find out some reasons why particular crops are grown in a given country. But unlike a performance objective, this goal does not identify specific behaviors the learner will be observed performing while establishing why the particular crops are grown there. In fact, any of a number of behaviors could be observed to assess this goal. For instance, a learner might be observed using an Internet search engine, evaluating the relative merits of several websites in terms of the information they provide, or trying to find information about a particular crop that is unknown to the learner but commonly grown in the specified country.

This goal is relevant to content discussed earlier in this book: *Create items for a written test.* We are going to develop our first performance assessment specification using this goal. If the book you are presently reading is a text for a class in which you are enrolled, this goal could easily be one you are expected to achieve. As with our earlier examples of goals, this one gives direction as to what you or other learners are expected to achieve, but it does not establish the specific behaviors you would be observed performing in the process of accomplishing this goal. As with other goals, this one encompasses a number of different behaviors. We will identify these behaviors during the process of developing the performance assessment specification presented in Figure 11.2.

Along with establishing the goal, one must establish the type of capability involved: information, concept, rule, or problem solving. Our present goal, "create items for written tests," represents problem solving—a complex action involving the recall of information and the use of concepts and the rules to achieve a particular outcome. For instance, if creating completion items is involved, one must apply procedures such as wording the item so that the blank is placed at the end, and constructing the item so that only a very homogeneous set of answers represent a defensible response. Additional procedures would also have to be employed to create good completion items, and somewhat

CAPABILITY TO BE ASSESSED
- *Goal to be assessed:* Create items for a written test
- *Type of capability involved:* Problem solving

PERFORMANCE TO BE OBSERVED
- *Summary descriptions of tasks associated with goal being assessed:*

  Given performance objectives, create items using variations of completion, essay, multiple-choice, and alternate-choice formats that measure those objectives

  Create scoring plans for essay items

  Create test items and scoring plans in various content areas

  Verify that items are consistent with criteria for evaluating the respective formats

- *Description of tasks to be performed:* Each learner will create 10 completion items that measure a performance objective they previously established. The performance objective will be relevant to content with which the individual learner is highly proficient. Learners will be asked to verify but not document that the ten items are consistent with the eight criteria for evaluating completion items (Table 7.1 in Chapter 7).

- *Focus on process or product?* Product

- *Prerequisite skills to be verified:*

  Learners can identify the logic for each of the eight criteria for evaluating completion items

  Learners can create performance objectives relevant to their individual expertise, which can be measured using completion items

- *Instructions to learners:* Using a performance objective you have previously established, create 10 completion items that measure that objective. If 10 items cannot be constructed for the one objective, use additional performance objectives you have established. Each item must be consistent with the eight criteria for evaluating completion items (Table 7.1 in Chapter 7).

SCORING PLAN

Y N ?   1. Does this item measure the specified skill?

Y N ?   2. Is the level of reading skill required by this item below the students' ability?

Y N ?   3. Will only a single or very homogeneous set of responses provide a correct response to the item?

Y N ?   4. Does the item use wording that is different from that contained in the source of instruction?

Y N ?   5. If the item requires a numerical response, does the question state the unit of measure to be used in the answer?

Y N ?   6. Does the blank represent a key word?

Y N ?   7. Are blanks placed at or near the end of the item?

Y N ?   8. Is the number of blanks sufficiently limited?

Figure 11.2
A performance assessment specification in the area of achievement testing

Table 11.1
Techniques for assessing various capabilities

Capability	Assessment Technique
Declarative knowledge	
Information	Ask learners to state what they know
Procedural knowledge	
Concept	Provide learners with diverse and previously unused illustrations and ask them to classify them as examples versus nonexamples of the concept
Rule	Provide learners with a relevant but previously unused example and ask them to apply the rule
Problem solving	Ask learners to generate solutions to a previously unused problem that is inherent to the targeted instructional goal

---

11.1   Apply What You Are Learning

For each of the following goals, which among these types of capability is involved?

  A. Information
  B. Concept
  C. Rule
  D. Problem solving

1. Serving as a banker, calculating the monthly payment due on loans with a given interest rate
2. Serving as an accountant, calculating for your clients the taxes they must pay
3. Serving as a meteorologist, determining the direction of wind when shown high- and low-pressure areas adjacent to each other on a weather map (In the Northern Hemisphere, air flows clockwise around high-pressure centers and counterclockwise around low-pressure centers. The reverse is true in the Southern Hemisphere.)
4. Serving as a writer, using widely available word processing software to produce a manuscript document
5. Serving as yourself in this exercise, identifying the type of capability involved for each of several goals

Answers can be found at the end of the chapter.

overlapping procedures would be used to create items using the other item formats.

Establishing the type of capability involved is very important because, as we have learned, different types of learner behavior serve as indicators of the various types of capability, which in turn establishes the behaviors that should be included in the performance assessment. Table 11.1 lists the types of capability that have been discussed in this book, along with the technique that is effective at assessing the various types of capability.

STEP 2: ESTABLISHING THE PERFORMANCE TO BE OBSERVED

Online assessments favor performances that result in a product. Performance assessments can and often do focus on the process learners are using. However, because of the asynchronous nature of most online assessments, if the focus is to be on the learner's process, a means must be established for learners to document the process they use. Therefore, when the assessment is online, a performance assessment is going to result in learners creating a product—whether or not that product is the outcome of the goal—or a document that establishes the process used in achieving that outcome. In *Step 2*, we establish the performance to be observed, and in so doing, define the product (or documentation of the process) that the instructor will subsequently use to evaluate the learner's performance.

Establishing the performance to be observed is subdivided into several actions. The specification in Figure 11.2 shows that the first action is to provide summary descriptions of tasks associated with the goal being assessed. That is, one needs to identify all significant learner behaviors that *could* be used to assess the instructional goal.

Identifying Summary Descriptions of Tasks Associated with Goal Being Assessed

Recall that the behavior observed through a performance assessment is usually only one of many behaviors that might be used. One has to anticipate that if a performance assessment involved a different sample of behaviors, a different conclusion might be drawn regarding a learner's achievement of the goal. This question has continually concerned us in our discussion of performance assessments: Would the performance we choose to observe generalize to other performances that could be used to assess the same goal? Unfortunately, research clearly indicates that the answer usually is "No." (See, for example, Shavelson, Baxter, & Pine, 1992; Solano-Flores, et al., 1997; Um, 1995; and Yen, 1997.) In online settings, this is particularly problematic. It is complicated further with online learning because, compared with face-to-face settings involving the same ratio of students to instructional staff, online instructors have fewer opportunities to casually observe learners, and thus fewer opportunities to cross-validate conclusions through casual observation.

Because performance often will not generalize across various tasks associated with a given instructional goal, the online instructor must anticipate which significant behaviors can be used in the assessment. The ideal action would be to develop performance assessments to observe each significant behavior and empirically determine where generalization does and does not occur. In both online and face-to-face settings, an empirical approach to determining generalizability is unrealistic. The second best option is to logically rather than empirically address the generalization issue. That is, identify significant behaviors that could be used to assess the goal and then make an informed judgment as to where generalization will and will not occur.

The specification in Figure 11.2 lists summary descriptions of tasks associated with our present goal. To assess whether learners can create items for written tests, this would include creating written test items using variations of the major formats such as essay and multiple-choice. In the case of essay items, knowing how to develop scoring plans would also be relevant. One would want learners to be able to create test items and scoring plans in diverse content areas. One would expect the created items to have qualities consistent with good test items, such as those addressed in Chapters 7 and 8.

As is usually the case, this means that conceivably a very large number of performance assessments could be developed to measure a person's ability to create items for a written test. Certainly, the potential number of assessments is larger than what is practical to administer. Through logical reasoning, choices have to be made about which to include in the assessment. For instance, it seems logical that if a learner can create good test items using a particular item format in one content area, the learner will similarly be able to create good items with that same item format in other content areas, as long as the learner is knowledgeable in each content area. Therefore we would conclude that this particular performance *will* generalize and there is no need to observe the creation of items in multiple content areas.

On the other hand, a learner who is able to create good completion items may not be able to create good multiple-choice items. To establish that the learner is proficient with both formats (and similarly in other formats such as essay), separate performance assessments must be developed to measure each relevant format.

It usually is not possible to develop perform-ance assessments for all significant behaviors associated with a given goal. Choices have to be made. One way to do this is to understand restric-tions on the goal. For instance, instead of assum-ing learners are proficient in all item formats, we might allow learners to make a judgment as to which item formats are most relevant to their sit-uations and select the formats with which they individually will demonstrate proficiency.

The generalization issue, however, must be taken seriously. Performance typically does not generalize across various behaviors that might be used to assess achievement of a particular goal. The prudent instructor anticipates this problem and makes conscious choices with respect to the practical limits of generalizability.

It is useful to emphasize the importance of the process we are going through here. As noted in our discussion, particularly in face-to-face settings, many performance assessments are thought of as homework assignments or exercises. In online settings, a product being used as a performance assessment to determine whether learners have achieved a particular instructional goal must sys-tematically follow the steps we are discussing to ensure that the assessment is valid, and that the performance will generalize adequately to tasks that the learner could have been asked to com-plete. With single-task performance assessments, the steps discussed here often can be completed quickly in one's mind. For complex-task assess-ments such as the one we are now discussing, a formal performance assessment specification must usually be developed. If this process is not followed the likelihood is greatly increased that the assessment of what students know and what they can do will be invalid, and that the perform-ance observed will not generalize beyond the specific task that learners are asked to perform.

Describing the Tasks to Be Performed

After summary descriptions of tasks associated with the instructional goal are identified, the next action in the development of a performance assessment is to describe the tasks learners will be asked to perform in the present assessment. The assessment of a given goal, as we have noted, will usually involve more than a single performance assessment. To be practical, a subset among pos-sible behaviors must be selected and a perform-ance assessment developed for each.

For a given instructional goal, development of the initial specification is the most time consuming. For instance, the specification illustrated in Figure 11.2 pertains to the development of completion items. If it is determined that for generalizability purposes it is appropriate to also assess learners' ability to create multiple-choice items, then a performance assessment specification needs to be established for that task. However, doing so would be quite easy since much of the specification could be copied and modified somewhat from the initial specification. For instance, the same summary descriptions of tasks associated with the goal could be used. Although the description of tasks to be performed would change for each specification, parallel content of that description can often be used across performance assessments that measure the same goal.

The performance assessment specified in Figure 11.2 is concerned with creating good completion items. In the specification, the description of tasks to be performed establishes what exactly we will see the learner do. According to the present spec-ification, each learner will create 10 completion items that measure a performance objective that was previously established. This objective will be relevant to content with which the learner is proficient. Learners will be expected to verify but not document that each of the 10 completion items are consistent with criteria established earlier in this book.

Here are two issues to take into account when describing the tasks learners are to perform:

1. *Does this performance focus on authentic tasks?* To be authentic, the task will involve ac-tual performance outcomes that learners are to accomplish through the instruction. The tasks are not to be convenient substitutes for that

performance, or an indirect indication that learners have achieved the performance. The tasks are also to involve real-world applications of the content being taught.

2. *Are the number and nature of qualities to be observed sufficiently limited to allow accurate scoring?* Just like with essay questions, overly comprehensive performance assessments are difficult to manage. Largely because the scoring becomes less focused, scores on an essay test consisting of three items, each requiring 20 minutes to answer, usually results in less reliable scores than an essay test consisting of six items, each requiring 10 minutes to answer. The same is true with performance assessments. Breaking a comprehensive performance assessment into a series of more focused assessments tends to improve accuracy in scoring. For instance, instead of using one comprehensive performance assessment to determine whether learners can create test items and build an online test, it is better to use one assessment that requires them to create completion items, a separate assessment in which they similarly create multiple-choice items, and a third assessment that involves assembling these items into an online written test.

Establishing Whether the Focus Is on the Process or Product

A *process* is the procedure that a learner uses to complete a task. A *product* is the tangible outcome that results from completing the process. Generally, a performance assessment is concerned with only the process or only the product, or at least emphasizes one over the other. It is easier to work with products than with the process that produces the product; therefore, if the focus is to be on the process learners use, indirect methods for observing the process usually must be employed. Typically, learners are asked to document their process in writing—in essence, learners "think aloud" in writing. When the focus of the assessment is on process, directions given to the students must establish expectations concisely.

Generally, if there is a particular or preferred process to be followed in the performance, or if whatever process is followed must have specified qualities, then the focus of the performance assessment should be on the process. If the outcome of the process is more important, then focus is placed on the product. For conciseness, the focus of a performance assessment should be on either the process or the product, but not both. The focus of the performance assessment specified in Figure 11.2 is on a product—a set of 10 completion items.

Identifying Prerequisite Skills to Be Verified

Identifying prerequisite skills as part of a performance assessment specification can be quite beneficial, because substantially more time is required to score an assessment and provide feedback when a learner's performance is deficient. This is particularly true as the number and significance of deficiencies increases. With online assessments, providing feedback is particularly laborious because, unlike face-to-face settings, it usually has to be written out rather than conveyed orally. If a performance is particularly deficient, the learner may be asked to repeat the assessment, which adds further to scoring time. Performance assessments require substantially more time to score than do online written tests. This increases dramatically if a student's performance assessment is deficient.

Identifying and verifying the achievement of prerequisite skills increases the likelihood that learners will succeed with the assessment. In Figure 11.2, two prerequisites are listed. One pertains to knowing the logic for the eight criteria for evaluating completion items, and the other involves having previously created a relevant performance objective for which the completion items will be written.

Of course professional judgment is used to determine which prerequisites will be listed. Most prerequisite skills *do not* need to be included. For example, the learner's ability to converse in the language being used, or the learner's ability to use a computer and the Internet to convey answers are either safely assumed or assessed much earlier. Many skills directly associated with the goal being assessed also need not be listed when experience indicates that learners will have already mastered the skills. Only prerequisite skills that experience suggests may be problematic are listed here in the specification.

Again, if prerequisite skills are not verified, learners who attempt the performance assessment without these skills are at high risk of performing poorly. Their poor performance subsequently increases time that will be required to score the assessment and provide feedback.

Establishing Instructions to Learners

The last action in establishing the performance to be observed is preparing the instructions that will be provided to the learners. This amounts to writing out what learners will be told to do. These instructions obviously have to be pertinent to the performance being observed. That is, the directions must be consistent with the description of tasks being performed, the focus on process or product, and the skills known to be prerequisite.

In Figure 11.2, instructions given in the specification tell learners to create 10 completion items that measure an existing performance objective. They indicate that more than one objective can be used, if necessary. They advise learners to evaluate their items using criteria presented earlier in the book.

Taking time to systematically establish what students will be told to do, along with identifying prerequisite skills, represent wise investments. Both actions improve the likelihood that learners will successfully complete the task they are expected to perform. This, in turn, helps address one major limitation of performance assessments—the cost and time required to score them.

STEP 3: ESTABLISHING THE SCORING PLAN

As with essay items, the scoring plan is an integral part of a performance assessment. Chapter 10 identified four options for establishing a scoring plan. Two options involve holistic scoring, these being a *comparison to a model* and the use of a *scoring rubric.* The other two options, *checklists* and *rating scales,* involve analytical scoring. Among the four options, *comparisons to a model* and *checklists* are the ones most often used in online settings. The scoring plan in Figure 11.1 involves a checklist.

The content of a scoring plan is heavily dependent on whether the process or the product of a learner's response is to be scored. As noted earlier, the process will be scored if generally accepted procedures for completing the task have been taught, and a learner's departure from these procedures can be detected. However, the product will be scored if a variety of procedures are appropriate, particular procedures have not been explicitly taught, or the procedures a learner uses cannot be documented. With the scoring plan illustrated in Figure 11.2, the checklist is focusing on products, specifically the characteristics of the items that are to be produced.

Three issues should be considered when establishing any scoring plan.

1. *Is each quality to be measured directly observable?* A process or product can be measured only if it can be observed. When possible, qualities to be scored should be described so that no inference is required to determine that the quality being scored does in fact exist. Note that most of the descriptions given in the scoring criteria in Figure 11.2 are directly observable. For instance, one can determine, without inference, whether the blanks are at or near the end of an item. Some inference is required, however, to determine whether the reading skill required by the item will be sufficiently low, or whether the item uses wording different from that contained in the course of instruction.

2. *Does the scoring plan delineate essential qualities of a satisfactory performance?* The importance of this characteristic to a scoring plan is obvious. Particularly with complex performance assessments, it is easy to accidentally exclude some essential qualities in the scoring plan. A way to reduce this problem is to ask a colleague to

11.2   Apply What You Are Learning

Following are descriptions used to judge the adequacy of learner performance with various skills. The first five descriptions pertain to process assessments and the second five to product assessments. Within each group of five, three of the descriptions require substantial inference, because the specified qualities are not directly observable. Therefore, those descriptions are less desirable as scoring criteria. In each set, which three descriptions require an inference?

Process Assessments

1. The learner demonstrates good sportsmanship.
2. The learner uses fingertips to depress valves on the trumpet.
3. The learner knows how to sand a piece of wood.
4. The learner places a lighted match next to the burner before turning on the gas.
5. The learner correctly views the needle on the voltage meter.

Product Assessments

1. The painted piece of wood is free of brush marks.
2. The chair is solidly constructed.
3. The steak is properly cooked.
4. The fingernails are free of dirt.
5. The learner understands the directions.

Answers can be found at the end of the chapter.

look at your performance assessment and independently list important qualities to be scored, or at least provide feedback to your scoring criteria.

3. *Will the scoring plan result in different observers' assigning similar scores to a learner's performance?* Once the desired characteristics of a performance are established, the scoring plan should result in independent observers' giving consistent ratings to a particular performance. If they do not, ratings of one instructor will not generalize to those of others. Creating scoring plans for which no inference or limited inference is required for judging performances substantially improves the consistency with which raters score a learner's performance.

In both online and face-to-face settings, multiple instructors do not typically score performance assessments. The issue of generalizability of ratings across instructors, however, is still a very relevant concern. One wants scores on a performance assessment to be a function of learner performance, rather than an effect caused by which person happened to be the learner's instructor. Research shows (for example, Shavelson, Baxter, & Pine, 1992) that if a scoring plan is well constructed and utilized, performance ratings will generalize quite well across instructors.

It is useful to note that a scoring plan often does not result in a numerical score. Instead, qualitative descriptions, such as those established through a checklist, provide a qualitative scoring of performance. Numerical scores can be derived, for instance, by associating points with each item in a checklist and summing the points. However, particularly when assessments play a formative role, qualitative feedback is more useful to the learner. A carefully devised scoring plan helps establish what qualities will be observed and then communicated through feedback to the learner.

This completes a specification and the construction of a performance assessment. The performance assessment still has to be put online so that it can be administered to the learners. Likewise, a means has to be established for learners to display or otherwise convey their performance, and for the instructor to score and provide feedback related to that performance. We look at these issues in Chapter 12.

A specification shows that creation of a performance assessment involves more planning than simply thinking of a task that learners will be asked to complete. It is quite natural to question whether it really is necessary to use a specification to create a performance assessment. An analogy that comes to mind is that of a building project. For a simple project, like constructing a birdhouse or doghouse, one probably can visualize the plans adequately without creating formal plans for the project. For a more complex project, such as constructing a deck for a house or constructing the house itself, formal plans are in order. Some builders feel confident enough to construct a deck or even a house without formal plans, and sometimes succeed. Depending on the magnitude of the construction project, the cost of not succeeding can be substantial. You can anticipate where this analogy is taking us.

With single-task performance assessments such as those used to assess knowledge of a concept or rule, it is often possible to create the specification in the mind rather than writing it out. The three basic steps of the specification must still be completed, even if only done mentally. When creating a performance assessment, it is critical that the capability to be assessed, the performance to be observed, and the scoring plan to be used all be established as integral parts of the performance assessment. However, when a complex problem-solving skill is being assessed, rather than knowledge of a concept or rule, then the performance assessment specification should be formally established as part of the process of creating the assessment. One may be tempted to construct complex performance assessments without formal specification. Some succeed, but others do not. Particularly with the reduced opportunity to verify through face-to-face interaction what learners have achieved, the cost of performance assessments not succeeding can be substantial.

ADDITIONAL EXAMPLES OF CREATING PERFORMANCE ASSESSMENTS

The preceding sections divided the creation of a performance assessment specification into three basic steps:

1. Establishing the capability to be assessed.

2. Establishing the performance to be observed.

3. Establishing the scoring plan.

These three steps were illustrated with a performance assessment specification related to the creation of items for a written test. In the last section of this chapter, we will use these three steps to create specifications for four additional performance assessments. Three of the assessments involve knowledge of a concept or rule, and therefore are *single-task* performance assessments. The fourth example involves a problem-solving skill, and therefore is an illustration of a *complex-task* assessment.

Example 2: Classifying Knowledge as Declarative or Procedural

Establishing the Capability to Be Assessed. As with our first illustration, our next specification involves a skill that is very relevant to you—that of distinguishing between declarative and procedural knowledge. One's knowledge of this skill can be determined using a performance assessment. A specification for that assessment is presented in Figure 11.3. Distinguishing between declarative and procedural knowledge involves knowing a concept.

Establishing the Performance to Be Observed. The performance assessment specification in Figure 11.3, in its *Description of tasks to be performed,* indicates that learners will be asked to read the various "Apply What You Are Learning" exercises in this book and classify them as assessments of declarative or procedural knowledge. This corresponds to the behavior used to assess knowledge of concepts (Table 11.1) in that learners are being given diverse and previously unused illustrations and asked to classify each as an example or nonexample of declarative or procedural knowledge. As is the case here, the illustrations need not be unknown to learners. They do need to be unused for the present classification purpose, which is the situation here as long as a reader was not previously asked to determine whether these exercises involved declarative or procedural knowledge. However, it is questionable whether performance on the present assessment will generalize adequately to the goal being assessed. The summary of tasks associated with the present goal (Figure 11.3) indicates that one should be able to appropriately classify illustrations of knowledge from any of

CAPABILITY TO BE ASSESSED

- *Goal to be assessed:* Classify examples of knowledge as declarative knowledge (information) or procedural knowledge (discrimination, concept, or rule)
- *Type of capability involved:* Concept

PERFORMANCE TO BE OBSERVED

- *Summary descriptions of tasks associated with goal being assessed:*

    Whenever provided a relevant illustration of knowledge, classify the knowledge as being declarative or procedural knowledge

    The description of knowledge may refer to any of a number of diverse circumstances; for instance, it might describe what learners are about to be taught, skills that learners have acquired, or knowledge implicit in completing mental exercise

    When assessed, learner may be asked to document the reasoning used to classify the described knowledge

- *Description of tasks to be performed:* Learners will identify two exercises in this book, one that requires declarative knowledge to complete, and one that requires procedural knowledge. Learners will document the reasoning used to classify the exercise as requiring declarative or procedural knowledge.

- *Focus on process or product?* Process

- *Prerequisite skill to be verified:* Learners can identify the distinguishing characteristics of declarative and procedural knowledge

- *Instructions to learners:* Chapters in this book contain a number of exercises titled *Apply What You Are Learning*. Each exercise requires you to use either declarative or procedural knowledge. Identify one that requires declarative knowledge and another that requires procedural knowledge. For both examples, describe how you determined the type of knowledge involved. Your explanation should convince the reader that you use correct logic when classifying descriptions of knowledge.

SCORING PLAN

10	Explanation is basically equivalent to the following model
9	Explanation has a minor problem somewhere
8	Explanation has several minor problems, or a significant problem somewhere
7	Explanation has some significant problems, but overall is OK
5	Explanation is not OK; please redo incorporating the attached suggestions

Model Answer

Answering "8.1 Apply What You Are Learning" in Chapter 8 requires the use of declarative knowledge. Declarative knowledge is used when one recalls information, and can be assessed by having learners state what they know. To answer the questions in exercise 8.1, the reader has to recall factual information, specifically the characteristics of various item formats, and then state what they know. Unlike procedural knowledge, this exercise does not require learners to demonstrate ability to perform a process, such as classifying examples not previously encountered. Instead, learners are required to recall information that had been presented earlier.

Answering "8.4 Apply What You Are Learning" in Chapter 8 requires the use of procedural knowledge. Procedural knowledge involves using a learned process (concept or rule) to respond to a situation not previously encountered. The questions in exercise 8.4 present pairs of illustrations that the reader has not previously encountered. The reader has to use knowledge pertaining to multiple-choice items; specifically that the item stem should adequately present the problem to be addressed. Unlike declarative knowledge, readers are not being asked to recall and state previously learned information.

Figure 11.3
A performance assessment specification in the area of learning theory applications

several diverse circumstances, such as in content that students are about to be taught, and in skills students have acquired. If it is judged that the restrictive setting of the current assessment does not generalize, then additional performance assessments will have to be created so that the assessments collectively measure the broad instructional goal adequately.

The present goal, classifying illustrations as examples of declarative or procedural knowledge, is more concerned with a process than a product. It is true that ultimately the action associated with this goal leads to a "classification," which clearly is a product. However, it is the process leading up to this classification that is of particular interest here. Therefore, as indicated in Figure 11.3, our focus in this performance assessment is on the process rather than the product. With online learners, observing the process is often problematic. Instead of observing how a learner completes the task, the instructor usually must rely on documentation of that process provided by the learner. That is reflected in the present specification; learners are asked to document reasoning that they used to classify the illustrations.

The performance assessment specification also establishes the prerequisite skills to be verified and the directions to be provided to learners. To ensure that learners will succeed with this performance assessment, it makes sense to include as a prerequisite the ability to identify the characteristics of declarative versus procedural knowledge. The *instructions to learners* in Figure 11.3 establishes specifically what learners will be asked to do.

Establishing the Scoring Plan. One option for scoring this performance assessment would be to create a checklist. Because the focus is on the process rather than the product, the checklist might itemize qualities that should be present in the learners' descriptions of their logic. However, instead of a checklist, the scoring plan in Figure 11.3 uses a comparison with a model answer. Take a moment to read through the

model. Notice that it is responsive to the instructions to learners. It identifies from the exercises one example each of declarative and procedural knowledge. More importantly, it documents the reasoning that was used to classify these two examples. The 10-point scale that accompanies the model answer simply asks for a judgment regarding how close each learner's response is to the model answer. The numerical values included are useful for recording the ratings in a gradebook. With respect to feedback to learners, the instructor would typically write brief responses explaining the nature of any problems in the learner's logic and options for resolving them.

With performance assessments, the scoring plan often is given to learners in advance of the assessment. When the scoring plan involves a *checklist,* the checklist tends to amplify directions provided to learners, identifying qualities that should be included in their performance. When *comparison to a model* is used as the scoring plan, the model illustrates an appropriate response, and in turn helps establish expectations and standards for learners' performance.

Example 3: Using *Word* to Provide Feedback on Projects

Establishing the Capability to Be Assessed. Our next example involves a set of simple tools within Microsoft Word that will be shown in the next chapter to help provide online learners with feedback on their projects. These tools were not designed specifically for online instruction, but were intended for groups of individuals working collaboratively on a written document. They make it easier for one individual to review, comment, and even edit a document created by another. This, of course, parallels what an instructor does when reviewing a student's paper. One tool makes it easy for the instructor to edit a student's narrative by deleting and inserting text, all of which is automatically tracked so that the student can see the changes the instructor has suggested. Another tool allows the instructor to select a portion of text within the document, such as a sentence or paragraph, and insert a comment related to that selection. This is much like writing a comment in the margin of a paper. In our next chapter, we will look at this and a variety of other tools that can facilitate the management of online performance assessments.

In a workshop or course designed for individuals who are prospective online instructors, it would be useful to show participants how to use this tool to provide feedback to learners, *and* then to assess their ability to use it. The specification shown in Figure 11.4 could be used for that assessment. The type of capability involved in this performance assessment is a rule or, perhaps more accurately, a set of highly related rules. The ability to use these particular tools to review student projects represents a set of rules in the sense that, once learned, they can be used quickly and repeatedly in other settings where they are relevant. That is, once learned, the tools can be used to help provide feedback to any of a number of documents created by online learners.

Establishing the Performance to Be Observed. As indicated in Figure 11.4, the tasks to be performed in this assessment are essentially the full set of tasks associated with the goal. Our goal is to be able to use the tools available in Word to provide feedback on projects submitted by online learners. The tools are conveniently grouped together in Word's *Reviewing* toolbar. It would be practical to incorporate the full set of tools into one performance assessment. The assessment specified in Figure 11.4 asks learners to use the *Track Changes* toolbar to automate the tracking of any edits to a student's document that involve deleting or inserting text, to use the *Insert Comments* to insert a comment that is linked to a portion of the student's text, and to also use highlighted text to make a more general comment that pertains to the student's overall document. Because all tasks associated with the present goal are included in the performance assessment, there is no need for concern about generalization. We will not be making a generalization, because we will have observed the full set of performances associated with the current instructional goal.

The specification in Figure 11.4 establishes the instructions to learners that would be provided with this assessment, and notes that the focus of this performance assessment is on a product rather than a process. The specification identifies one prerequisite skill that is important to verify—a learner's ability to open the *Reviewing* toolbar. This prerequisite skill is easy to learn, but without that skill, a learner is likely to fail the present performance assessment. As with all performance assessment specifications illustrated in this chapter, this one systematically addresses three questions critical to creating a performance assessment: 1) What is the capability that is being assessed, 2) what performance can be used to indicate whether learners have achieved that capability, and 3) what procedures will be used to score that performance.

Establishing the Scoring Plan. The scoring plan in Figure 11.4 involves a checklist. As should be the case, all items in this checklist have the same polarity; that is, all checklist items represent positive qualities that a learner's performance should include. Also, each item describes a quality that can be observed directly, or that at most requires a limited inference to establish whether the performance exhibits the particular quality. For instance, little inference is required to determine whether the *Track Changes* tool was used to mark deleted text. The results of using that tool would be plainly visible within the edited document. It would be possible and desirable to rewrite each item in this checklist as a more telegraphic statement. For clarity, that is not done in Figure 11.4, but it could easily be done in a checklist designed for personal use. Telegraphic statements make it easier to score a learner's performance.

Example 4: Evaluating Assumptions When Selecting a Statistical Technique

Establishing the Capability to Be Assessed. Our last two examples broaden our illustrations to

CAPABILITY TO BE ASSESSED
- *Goal to be assessed:* Using tools available in Microsoft Word, provide feedback on projects submitted by online learners as electronic documents.
- *Type of capability involved:* Rule

PERFORMANCE TO BE OBSERVED
- *Summary descriptions of tasks associated with goal being assessed:*

   Using *Track Changes* tool to suggest text that should be deleted or added to a learner's document

   Using *Insert Comment* tool to add a comment about a selected portion or statement within a learner's document

   Using highlighted text to add a comment about a learner's document
- *Description of tasks to be performed:* A Word document, representing an online learner's work on a project is provided electronically. Using functions available within Word, feedback is added electronically to the document. The feedback includes the following elements:

   Suggested addition and deletion of text displayed in the document using the *Track Changes* tool

   A comment made concerning a selected portion of text within the document, displayed using the *Insert Comment* tool

   A comment made concerning the overall document, using highlighted text
- *Focus on process or product?* Product
- *Prerequisite skills to be verified:*

   Ability to open the *Reviewing* toolbar

- *Instructions to learners:* You are being asked to demonstrate the use of functions available within Word to provide feedback on a project submitted electronically by an online learner. The learner's project is already in the form of a Word document file. After reading the learner's document, provide the following feedback:

   Using the *Track Changes* tool, suggest text that should be deleted and added to the document

   Using the *Insert Comment* tool, add a comment about a selected portion of text within the document

   Add an overall comment about the learner's document, being sure that the appearance of this comment is visibly distinct from text provided by the learner and distinct from highlighting that resulted from using the *Insert Comment* tool

SCORING PLAN

Y N   Text suggested for deletion is marked using *Track Changes* tool

Y N   Text suggested for addition is underscored using *Track Changes* tool

Y N   Placing cursor on highlighted text reviews its embedded comment

Y N   Appearance of overall comment distinct from text in original document

Y N   Appearance of external comment distinct from highlighting associated with embedded comment

Figure 11.4
A performance assessment specification in the area of providing feedback to learners

other content areas. Our next example is from the area of applied statistics, and our final example will be from astronomy. If you have completed an undergraduate or graduate course in statistics, you will relate fondly or otherwise to the performance assessment specified in Figure 11.5. In a basic statistics course, one is typically taught that assumptions are involved when statistical tests are used to help infer from a sample to the population. An informed consumer of statistics will evaluate consequences of possible violation

of these assumptions. Some statistical assumptions are robust under certain conditions. That is, within the constraints of certain conditions, even a gross violation of the assumption does not affect the interpretation of results. The purpose of our present performance assessment is to determine whether learners can select an appropriate statistical test in light of the possible violation and robustness of these assumptions.

The type of capability involved with this skill is a *rule*. One might be tempted to classify this

---

CAPABILITY TO BE ASSESSED

- *Goal to be assessed:* In light of possible violation and robustness of assumptions, select the appropriate technique for testing the statistical significance of the difference between two sample means
- *Type of capability involved:* Rules

PERFORMANCE TO BE OBSERVED

- *Summary descriptions of tasks associated with goal being assessed:* A learner is faced with a situation where the statistical significance of the difference between sample means is to be tested. In light of possible violation of assumptions and robustness of available statistical tests, the learner selects an appropriate test.

    Situation may involve two sample means, more than two sample means but within one dimension, and two or more sample means with multiple dimensions wherein interactions can be observed

    Situation may involve data and/or a research situation provided by the learner or the instructor

    Robustness of the assumption pertaining to normality will be evaluated in light of sample sizes

    Robustness of the assumption pertaining to homogeneity of variances will be evaluated in light of sample sizes within groups, and also relative variability of scores as indicated with any common numerical index (e.g., standard deviation) or any common graphic display of scores (e.g., histogram)

    Possible violation of assumption pertaining to independence of observations will be evaluated from description of the dependent variable and research methodology

- *Description of tasks to be performed:* The learner is provided a summary description of a research study in reading education, where one group of students is taught using phonics and the other using a whole-language approach. For the phonics and whole-language groups respectively, the sample sizes are 60 and 30. When the samples were given a reading test at the end of instruction, the respective score means were 55.2 and 48.1 and the score standard

Figure 11.5
A performance assessment specification in the area of applied statistics

(*continued*)

deviations were 7.1 and 4.3. Histograms show both distributions of scores to be close to symmetrical with a single mode. Using this information, in light of possible violation and robustness of assumptions, the learner selects the technique for testing the statistical significance of difference between the two sample means. The selection is from three choices provided in the assessment: *t*-test where equal variances are assumed, *t*-test where equal variances are not assumed, and the Mann-Whitney *U*-test.

- *Focus on process or product?* Process
- *Prerequisite skills to be verified:*

   Ability to state statistical hypotheses associated with the *t*-test where equal variances are assumed, the *t*-test where equal variances are not assumed, and the Mann-Whitney *U*-test

- *Instructions to learners:* Select one of the following three techniques to test the statistical significance between the sample means of scores on the reading test.

   t-test where equal variances are assumed

   t-test where equal variances are not assumed

   Mann-Whitney *U*-test

Taking into account the two assumptions pertaining to normality and homogeneity of variance, provide the logic you used in selecting the technique.

SCORING PLAN

Y   N   States that since *only scores in the samples are observed*, it is not possible to establish whether scores are normally distributed in the *populations* from which samples were drawn

Y   N   States that assumption of normality is robust because sample sizes are larger than 25

Y   N   States that robustness of normality assumption means probabilities of Types I and II error rates will be close to values set for α and β

Y   N   Avoids selecting Mann-Whitney *U*-test because of robustness of normality assumption

Y   N   States that since *only scores in the samples are observed*, it is not possible to establish whether variability of scores is the same in the *populations* from which samples were drawn

Y   N   States that assumption of equal variances is not robust because of substantial difference in sample sizes (60 to 30 not smaller than 1.5 to 1, which is necessary for assumption to be robust)

Y   N   States that *lack* of robustness of equal variances assumption means probabilities of Types I and II error rates could depart significantly from values set for α and β

Y   N   Avoids selecting *t*-test where equal variances are assumed because of lack of robustness of homogeneity of variances assumption

Figure 11.5
Continued

skill as problem solving. It certainly can involve a somewhat complicated and difficult process. But it is a rule since the selection of the appropriate statistical test can be accomplished by following a prescribed procedure. This procedure does not have to be created by the learner. The present performance assessment would be used to establish whether an individual has learned and therefore can apply the prescribed procedure.

Establishing the Performance to Be Observed. As with each specification, the *Summary descriptions of tasks associated with goal being assessed* defines the possible performances we could use to assess the present instructional goal. You may recognize many of the tasks summarized, such as the statistical assumptions of normality and equal variances, and the use of numerical indexes like standard deviation and graphic displays like the histogram.

As is usually the case, it is not practical to include all possible tasks in one performance assessment. Look at the *Description of tasks to be performed* in Figure 11.5 to see what is to be included in the present assessment. The specification indicates that learners will be given a description of a research study in reading education involving phonics and whole-language treatment groups. Other details are provided such as sample sizes, sample means and standard deviations, and the names of three statistical tests that might be used to analyze the data. The specific task described here would almost certainly not generalize to the larger set of tasks summarized earlier in the specification. Additional performance assessment would have to be specified and administered to obtain that generalizability.

As in our earlier examples, the specification illustrated in Figure 11.5 also establishes specific instructions to be given to learners, identifies prerequisite skills that should be verified to help ensure learners' successful performance on the assessment, and indicates that the focus of the assessment is on learners' process, not the product.

Establishing the Scoring Plan. Because the focus is on the process use, learners would have to document the process they use since, particularly in online situations, the process generally cannot be observed directly. The scoring plan must pertain to this process.

The scoring plan in Figure 11.5 uses a checklist. A checklist usually involves telegraphic sentences to expedite its use. As is often the case, this checklist could, but does not, associate numerical values with items. As with other performance assessments, this scoring plan can be distributed to learners in advance. Unlike written

tests, one does not have to secure the key to the correct answers. The scoring plan often amplifies instructions provided to learners and, if they have the skill being assessed, helps ensure learner success on the assessment. We have noted before that when learners do well, the amount of time required to score assessments and provide feedback is substantially reduced.

The checklist in Figure 11.5 incorporates qualities proposed in Chapter 10 for improving the efficiency with which the checklist can be used. For instance, items in this checklist are grouped by the order in which they likely will be rated. Also, key nouns and verbs that indicate the essence of the quality being addressed appear early in each item so that, with some practice, the instructor can recognize each item simply by reading the first few words. All items in the checklist have the same polarity.

Example 5: Establishing Strategies to Locate Astronomical Objects in the Sky

Establishing the Capability to Be Assessed. An important skill that astronomers learn early is how to locate objects in the night sky. With computers, this is often done quickly and automatically using software. But as with many disciplines, it is still important to understand the logic behind predicting what will be visible, and where and when it will be visible in the sky. Our last performance assessment pertains to this skill. Its specification in Figure 11.6 identifies it as involving *problem solving*. As with other such situations, it involves a problem that can be solved in a number of ways using different combinations of information, concepts, and rules. Also, the learner is presented with a goal, but not a means for reaching that goal. To successfully solve the problem, a learner will need to invoke previously learned information, concepts, and rules.

Establishing the Performance to Be Observed. A number of tasks go into locating astronomical objects in the sky. Summarized in Figure 11.6, they include, for instance, the local clock time of the observer, the darkness of the local sky, and the apparent brightness of the astronomical object.

CAPABILITY TO BE ASSESSED

- *Goal to be assessed:* Identify a specific strategy (including variables that need to be taken into account) to establish when and where in the sky astronomical objects will be visible from a specific point on Earth within a specified 24-hour period of time

- *Type of capability involved:* Problem solving

PERFORMANCE TO BE OBSERVED

- *Summary descriptions of tasks associated with goal being assessed:*

  Time of visibility will be expressed in terms of local clock time and take into account darkness of the local sky, apparent brightness of the object, and time of rise and set of the object with respect to the observer's horizon

  Location at a point in time in the sky will be expressed in terms of the object's altitude in the sky and azimuth (relation to true north) apparent to the observer

  For artificial Earth satellites in low orbit, because of their relatively quick apparent movement, location will describe their trace across the sky

  For objects outside the solar system, visibility will be established using the apparent brightness of the object, the object's relative location in space (right ascension and declination), the observer's latitude/longitude, local clock time and apparent sidereal time, and darkness of the local sky

  For natural objects within the solar system (e.g., planets and asteroids), the orbital elements of the object will be taken into account in addition to the above

  For artificial Earth satellites, the Earth's shadow will be taken into account in addition to the above

- *Description of tasks to be performed:* Learners will be asked to describe how they would establish when and where in the sky the International Space Station is visible where they live. Specifically, they will be asked to identify variables that are relevant to this task, and to explain why each variable is relevant.

- *Focus on process or product?* Process

- *Prerequisite skills to be verified:*

  Familiarity of learners with the celestial object used in the assessment

  Knowledge of the astronomical concepts of orbital elements, apparent brightness, right ascension and declination, and apparent sidereal time

  Knowledge of how to obtain for a celestial object data related to its orbital elements, apparent brightness, and right ascension and declination

  Knowledge of local latitude/longitude

- *Instructions to learners:* You have been asked to determine when and where in the sky the International Space Station (ISS) will be visible at the location where you live. The ISS is in low Earth orbit and when spotted, appears to move slowly across the sky much like an airplane. Therefore, its location would be described in terms of when and where it first appears in the sky, when and where it is at its maximum height in the sky, and when it disappears. For purposes of this assessment, you need not establish the actual time and where in the sky the ISS will be visible. You are to

  Identify each of the variables that must be taken into account

  Provide a clear explanation as to why each variable is relevant

Figure 11.6
A performance assessment specification in the area of astronomy

SCORING PLAN

        0 = No reference is made to this variable

        1 = Variable referenced, but without relevant explanation

        2 = Variable referenced, but relevant explanation contains critical flaws

        3 = Variable referenced, but relevant explanation contains significant noncritical flaws

        4 = Variable referenced, with relevant and sound explanation

1. Orbital elements of ISS	0 1 2 3 4
2. Right ascension and declination	0 1 2 3 4
3. Apparent sidereal time	0 1 2 3 4
4. Latitude/longitude for observer	0 1 2 3 4
5. Local clock time for observer	0 1 2 3 4
6. Altitude and azimuth for observer	0 1 2 3 4
7. Apparent brightness of ISS	0 1 2 3 4
8. Darkness of local sky	0 1 2 3 4
9. Trace of ISS from first appearance, maximum height, and disappearance	0 1 2 3 4

Tasks to be employed depend in part on the nature of the object to be observed. For instance, locating planets in our solar system requires information about their orbits, but locating stars does not.

As with every performance assessment, the number of specific tasks must be limited. Figure 11.6 provides the *description of tasks to be performed* in this assessment. Learners will be asked to describe how they would establish when and where in the sky the International Space Station is visible. A learner's performance on this task probably would generalize to establishing the time and location when other artificial satellites in Earth's orbit are visible. However, separate assessments would likely be necessary for the planets, moons of planets, comets, and objects outside our solar system such as stars.

Notice the pattern that applies to the specification of each performance assessment. The tasks associated with the goal must be identified, albeit in summary form. A detailed specification of the sample of tasks included in the present assessment is then identified. This detailed specification narrows the assessment to something manageable that can be scored effectively. Because only a sample of possible tasks is included in the assessment, one must anticipate whether or not the performance observed in the present assessment would generalize to the performance of tasks not sampled. Usually, the conclusion is that generalization requires creation and administration of additional performance assessments to ensure generalizability. As we noted earlier, when performance assessment specifications are used, such as those illustrated in this chapter, the development of the additional assessments for the same instructional goal is efficient. However, the time required to administer and score some or all of the additional assessments may prevent their use, in which case one must be restrained with respect to generalizing learner performance from what was observed.

The specification in Figure 11.6 indicates the prerequisite skills that will be verified and the instructions that will be provided to the learners. Look through the prerequisite skills. Even if you have no familiarity with astronomy, you will probably recognize the relevance of several of these skills, such as knowing the latitude and longitude of the observer, the orbit of the space station, and the station's apparent brightness. Online written tests or quizzes (discussed in Chapters 8 through 10) can be used to verify many of these skills. Not doing so would likely substantially increase the amount of time needed to score learners' responses on the present performance assessment.

Establishing the Scoring Plan. The focus of the present assessment is on the process. Again, in online settings, this means that learners must document, usually in writing, what they did since the instructor cannot directly observe what is being done. The scoring plan in Figure 11.6 involves a series of rating scales. In this case, the same descriptors are used for all scales. Therefore, the descriptors can be listed at the top as a separate scoring key and represented by numbers—in this case 0 through 4. Again, the numbers are arbitrary, although the numbers chosen may have significant consequences to subsequent assignment of course grades if used for that purpose.

SUMMARY

The creation and scoring of a performance assessment is divided into three basic steps. First, one establishes what capability is to be assessed. Although an assessment ultimately requires observation of learners' performance, that performance provides only an *indication* of the learners' capability. Our understanding of the content and type of capability being assessed guides our selection of behaviors to be observed through our performance assessment. We have identified three basic types of capability. If the capability involves declarative knowledge, we have referred to it as information. Procedural knowledge has been divided into three subcategories: discriminations, concepts, and rules, although discriminations are generally not formally assessed except with young children. The third basic type of capability is problem solving. Table 11.1 lists the behaviors used to assess the various types of capability.

The second step in developing a performance assessment is establishing the performance to be observed. This performance must be relevant to the capability being evaluated and must be practical in terms of the number and nature of qualities that must be scored. Conditions under which the performance will occur must be clear, and instructions to the learner must be concise and complete. To help ensure success, critical prerequisite skills should be verified before the performance assessment is administered. Usually, only a sample of tasks that should to be observed can be included in one assessment. This affects generalizability of results and must be addressed by including additional assessments or restricting the interpretation of what is observed.

The third step in developing a performance assessment is creating a scoring plan. This plan should involve qualities that are directly observable and that collectively represent the essential qualities of a satisfactory performance. The scoring plan should result in different observers' assigning similar scores to a learner's performance. A scoring plan typically involves a checklist, rating scales, comparison to a model, or a scoring rubric.

ANSWERS: APPLY WHAT YOU ARE LEARNING

11.1 1. 1. C; 2. D; 3. C; 4. D; 5. B. The banker uses a formula, or more likely a table, calculator, or small computer to calculate the monthly payment due on a given loan. Regardless of the tool used, this would involve a rule, since the same procedure can be replicated with each loan to calculate the monthly payment. Except for the simplest cases, various accountants would employ different combinations of information and rules to optimize taxes for a given client. The meteorologist has a simple rule to apply; in the northern hemisphere the wind goes clockwise around high pressure and counterclockwise around low pressure areas; the reverse is true in the southern hemisphere. Knowing the location of dominant high- and low-pressure centers establishes wind direction. The writer employs problem-solving skills to use the word processor. Various information, concepts, and rules are combined to enter and format text for a particular manuscript. The specific combination varies from one manuscript to another, and among different writers. In this exercise, you are demonstrating knowledge of a concept. You are classifying new illustrations into categories.

11.2 2. Among the process descriptions, items 1, 3, and 5 require an inference about what is being observed. The following alternatives directly describe what is to be observed: Item 1: The learner helps teammates score points. Item 3: The learner sands the wood parallel to the grain. Item 5: The learner views the voltage meter in a way that will eliminate parallax error. Among the product descriptions, items 2, 3, and 5 require inferences. Alternatives to these items include the following: Item 2: The chair supports 500 pounds. Item 3: The steak is pink in the center. Item 5: The broom was placed (as directed) in the closet.

TERMS INTRODUCED IN THIS CHAPTER

Performance assessment specification: is used to help plan and ultimately define a performance assessment. It includes three basic elements: the capability to be assessed; the performance to be observed; and the scoring plan. Performance assessment specifications are illustrated in Figures 11.2 through 11.6.

Single-task performance assessment: is a performance assessment used to measure knowledge of a concept or a rule. Single-task performance assessments are usually easy to produce, although they require more time to administer and score than do their written-test counterparts. The *specification* for a single-task performance assessment often can be developed in one's mind, without writing it down. However, addressing each of the components of a performance assessment specification remains an important procedure.

Complex-task performance assessment: involves problem solving, in which the learner is asked to apply a complex of information, concepts, and rules to solve a problem. Complex-task performance assessments tend to be more difficult to create. Written tests cannot measure skills assessed with a complex-task performance assessment.

ENHANCE YOUR UNDERSTANDING

- Devise a performance assessment for assessing this instructional goal: Determine the density of a solid object. (Density can be defined as an object's mass relative to water. An object with twice the mass of water would have a density of 2.0. Similarly, an object with half the mass of water would have a density of 0.5.) Using criteria addressed in this and the preceding chapter, select a task that is authentic through which one can assess a learner's achievement of this instructional objective.

- Identify an instructional goal involving problem solving that is relevant to a content area in which you are proficient. Prepare a performance assessment that assesses that goal. Use the specification format provided in Figure 11.1.

ADDITIONAL READING

Berk, R. A. (Ed.). (1986). *Performance assessment: Methods and applications.* Baltimore, MD: Johns Hopkins University Press. This book includes several chapters on the development and use of performance assessments. Specific chapters discuss listening, speaking, and writing assessments.

Fitzpatrick, R., & Morrison, E. J. (1971). Performance and product evaluation. In R. L. Thorndike (Ed.), *Educational measurement* (2nd ed., pp. 237–270). Washington, DC: American Council on Education.

This chapter discusses the development and production of performance assessments. Examples are provided in a variety of content areas. Issues such as the reality of simulations, reliability, validity, and cost factors are addressed.

Moskal, B. M. (2003). Recommendations for developing classroom performance assessments and scoring rubrics. *Practical Assessment, Research & Evaluation,* 8(14). Available online at *pareonline.net/getvn. asp?v58&n514*. This article provides an easy-to-read and useful set of recommendations for developing course-based performance assessments including the writing of goals; developing, administering, and scoring the actual assessment; and interpreting and using the results.

12

Managing Online Performance Assessments

In face-to-face settings, the instructor often devotes considerable time to presenting material to learners through lectures and other means. In online settings, learning tends to be more student-centered. A greater portion of the instructor's time is devoted to facilitating learning, and providing opportunities for learners to demonstrate what they know and what they can do. Although we often equate student assessments with written tests, student projects and other activities play a vital assessment role in online settings in determining what learners can do. It seems reasonable to assume that instructors involved with online learning devote a large portion of their time to assessing learner performance, not only to certify student achievement, but also to provide the basis for formatively guiding subsequent learning.

In the preceding chapters, we noted that many learner activities that occur in both face-to-face and online settings represent a performance assessment, as long as *performing the activity* is an explicit objective or goal of instruction. Many projects completed by individual learners can be treated as assessments. This alerts us to the need for addressing fundamental assessment issues such as whether the work students submit represents a valid indication of their knowledge, and whether the sample of performances that are observed will generalize to alternate indicators that could have been used.

We noted that in online-learning settings, performance assessments have some special advantages. For instance, their direct measure of instructional outcomes provides insights into a learner's knowledge that are more difficult to obtain when the learner is not face-to-face with the instructor. These insights are not readily obtained through online written tests, particularly those that are objectively scored. Another advantage is that performance assessments can, to a degree, make up for the lack of test security that often is a concern when learners are assessed online. The authentic nature of performance assessments reduces the need for assessments to occur in a secure environment. Similarly, plans for scoring a performance assessment typically do not need to be secured since learners are usually given the scoring plan prior to the assessment.

In face-to-face instruction, as enrollment in a class increases, the demands on the instructor also increase, but not proportionally. With larger class sizes, more time is required to evaluate homework and read essay tests, but not so much for classroom presentations or objectively scored tests. In fact, demands associated with increased class size are often compensated for by decreasing the use of homework and essays. In contrast, when learners are online, any increase in class size tends to result in a proportional increase in demands on an instructor's time. The heavier reliance on project work for assessing performance is a major contributor to this increased demand. Consequently, careful and efficient management of online performance assessments is important in making the assessment of online learners practical.

Online performance assessments involve four elements: 1) communicating tasks and expectations to learners, 2) conveying products and other responses from each learner to the instructor and often to other learners, 3) providing feedback to each learner, and 4) maintaining records that summarize what transpired. In this chapter, we discuss these four elements, with particular attention to techniques that help make the management of assessments more efficient.

Our focus in this chapter is on projects completed by individual learners that serve as formative and summative assessments. We will also describe techniques that facilitate sharing products of this work among learners, and sharing feedback to projects across learners. In Chapters 13 and 14, we address assessment in collaborative settings. The present chapter helps you achieve the following three skills related to assessing online learners:

- Identify issues that affect the choice of an electronic system to manage performance assessments
- Identify options for conveying products and feedback between learners and the instructor
- Select techniques that improve the efficiency of managing online performance assessments

ISSUES AFFECTING CHOICE OF MANAGEMENT SYSTEM

In Chapter 11, several integrated online course management systems were identified. Although specific features vary, any one of these systems allows the instructor to administer written tests to students or to at least maintain records. Often these Web-based systems also allow students to participate in chat sessions, interact through asynchronous discussions, and electronically send material back and forth between the student and the instructor.

The manuals that accompany these course management systems, in their discussion of assessment, tend to focus on the components that administer written tests. This is ironic in the sense that one

distinction between face-to-face instruction and online learning is the latter's heavy reliance on assessments other than conventional written tests. Without directly stating it, the manuals imply that electronic communications between instructor and learner represent "nonassessment" activities. In reality, most of the assessment of online learners occurs through these types of activities. Although many features of course management systems are not specifically designed for facilitating assessments, they can play a significant role in doing so. For instance, "digital drop boxes" and other software features allow learners and instructors to pass computer files containing project work back and forth. These interactions can represent formative evaluations, where the instructor's assessment (or that of other students) guides subsequent actions and learning. These interactions can also represent summative evaluations, where the instructor uses learners' products to establish, for grading purposes, the degree to which each learner has achieved course objectives. Clearly, as with face-to-face interactions in a classroom, online discussions provide a means through which learners build knowledge through shared experiences, are exposed to multiple perspectives, formulate awareness of issues where there is no one answer, and develop interest and gain motivation. These collaborative issues are addressed in Chapters 13 and 14. However, one must not discount the importance of an instructor's formative and summative evaluations of individual students and the role technology plays in facilitating performance assessments that lead to these evaluations.

Later in this chapter, we will look at features in Web-based systems that facilitate management of online performance assessments. We will also look at techniques for improving the efficiency of these assessments. In this section, we will look at several issues that influence what system or features one uses. These include the type of material used in the assessments, whether privacy is maintained between the student and instructor or information is open to other learners enrolled in the course, whether feedback from the instructor is detached from or integrated into the products produced by students, and whether records of student performance are maintained separately or become an integral part of the management system.

Type of Material

With present technology, most assessments and other interactions between an instructor and online learners are asynchronous. The learner submits something to the instructor, and sometime later the instructor replies, or vice versa. Much material that is sent between instructor and student takes the form of computer files or at least material that can be transmitted and saved as files. This encompasses a wide range of material including text, graphics, sound files, and files that can be played or viewed with software that both the instructor and students possess.

Whenever the learner uses software to produce a file, the instructor has the option of using that same software to send feedback to the learner. For instance, if a student submits a document file created with a word processor, the instructor can use the same word processor not only to read the student's file, but also to efficiently work with and edit that file. Later we will note that some software, such as Word and Excel, are designed to facilitate online collaborative work. These features were not designed with online learning in mind, but they can be used effectively to work interactively with students and to provide instructor feedback to students.

Private or Public Handling of Material

In traditional settings, especially in postsecondary education, material developed by students is given directly to the instructor, reviewed, and then returned to the student. Although many students may simultaneously submit material to the instructor, the process is usually closed or private between the instructor and each student.

A more public way of handling student material, used particularly in elementary and middle school grades, is to place completed work in binders or folders, often referred to as portfolios. The instructor accesses and reviews material in each portfolio. Although students are usually allowed to look at each other's portfolio, the process still functions largely as a closed system between the instructor and each student.

When material is submitted electronically, a student can share material with other students just as easily as with the instructor. Of course, it is still possible to pass material privately between student and instructor, but now one has a choice. Later, we will look at options for electronically sharing materials openly. This public handling of material provides several potential benefits, although the benefits realized depend to a large degree on expectations established by the instructor. One benefit is that students often get ideas and discover broader applications by viewing each other's work. Also, if online learners perceive one another as peers, sharing work can motivate students to perform at higher levels. Many students are more concerned about making positive impressions with peers than with the instructor.

Private handling of material between the instructor and the student may be more comfortable for some students. In fact, the added anxiety of openly sharing work with classmates might be so high that it becomes counterproductive. Similarly, when the instructor's feedback to a student can be viewed by others, diplomacy within the feedback becomes very important. E-mail also can be used to privately communicate any significant negative concerns to a student.

Detached or Integrated Feedback

Feedback to a student from the instructor can be either detached from or integrated into material produced by the learner. With conventional classroom settings, **integrated feedback** is typical. Comments are written on students' papers rather than on a separate page that is then attached to each paper. The instructor circles words or phrases in a student's paper or draws arrows to points being referenced. Within online settings, **detached feedback** is often used. Feedback is detached when it is external to the student's document. This might consist of an e-mail sent by the instructor

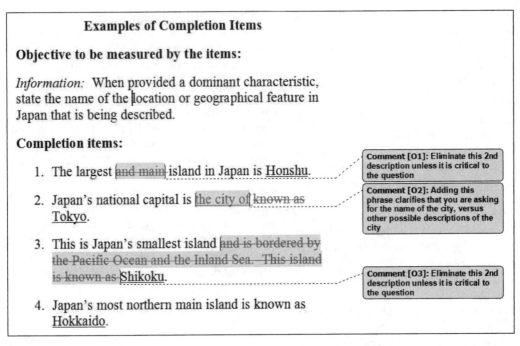

Figure 12.1
Illustration of feedback integrated into a student's word document

in response to material submitted by the student. Or course management software might be used to write comments that become linked to (yet remain visually separate from) each student's product.

Integrated feedback tends to be more efficient than detached feedback. For instance, if the instructor uses e-mails to provide feedback to a set of products, the text of the e-mails typically has to include supporting information that identifies what is being referenced. Had the instructor been writing feedback on a paper document, simply drawing an arrow could identify more efficiently the material being referenced. Unfortunately, most Web-based course management systems allow only the less-efficient detached feedback. They also tend to make the process of accessing and returning students' files more laborious than is necessary. Given the significant time-saving abilities and other efficiencies that computers should provide, it is unfortunate that Web-based systems have not addressed this issue more effectively.

To provide integrated feedback, an instructor can often take advantage of the sophisticated

software students use to generate their products. For example, Figure 12.1 illustrates feedback that was integrated into a student's Word document. Using the *Reviewing* function in Word, deletions and inserts suggested by the instructor are automatically marked. Also, comments written in the document are visually linked to text selected by the instructor.[1] In Word, this reviewing feature can be accessed by opening the Reviewing toolbar in the View menu.

Student Records

In both conventional and online settings, student records are increasingly being managed electronically. A number of stand-alone electronic gradebooks are available, but vary considerably in their sophistication and ease of use. Many of

---

[1]Edits and comments are displayed somewhat differently in various versions of Microsoft Word. When using this feature, it is prudent to determine which versions students are using to and establish what students will see when comments are displayed.

these programs are available for a nominal cost and can be located using a search engine like Google or Yahoo! General-purpose spreadsheet and data management software such as Excel and Access also can be used to manage student records; however, some sophistication with such programs is required to use them most effectively. Blackboard and other course management systems have built-in systems for maintaining student records, although they tend to be the most restrictive in terms of how scores are aggregated and how their data is displayed.

Software designed to administer online written tests, including Blackboard and QuestionMark, will automatically grade objectively scored tests and update student records. This saves considerable instructor time. Most systems, however, require manual scoring of other types of tests, particularly performance assessments. Later in this chapter, we look at techniques that significantly improve the efficiency of the process when performance assessments are involved.

TRANSFERRING PRODUCTS BETWEEN STUDENTS AND INSTRUCTOR

In this section, we look at the standard online options for transferring products between students and the instructor, when products are in the form of computer files. In the next section, we describe ways to improve the efficiency of this transfer and of online performance assessments in general. We will find that the utility of a particular file-transfer option is related to the issues addressed previously, such as the type of material involved, whether this material is to be handled privately or publicly, and whether feedback from the instructor is to be integrated into or kept separate from the product produced by the student.

File Transfer Protocol

File transfer protocol (FTP) is a procedure for transferring files between two computers, typically using the Internet. Unless a client program is used, FTP involves UNIX text commands that are not intuitive for most individuals. Inexpensive client

programs are available[2] that use familiar computer mouse actions such as click and drag to activate FTP commands and quickly move files between, for instance, a local PC and a remote central server.

FTP can be (but seldom is) used to transfer files between instructors and students. This is understandable because much of its supporting software does not closely match the needs of online learners and instructors. On the other hand, the FTP framework offers significant possibilities. For instance, FTP provides an efficient means of quickly moving numerous files between students and instructors, as well as allowing students to access each other's files with or without editing privileges. But for FTP to be widely adopted in online learning, specialized client programs need to be created that better meet the needs of instructors and learners.

Several years ago, Oracle Corporation developed an Internet File System called Oracle iFS[3] and demonstrated how an FTP-based file-sharing system can facilitate collaborative work in a business environment. Its features evolved in a direction that does not match the needs of online learning; however this system shows how FTP can provide a cost-effective means of collaboration and file sharing. We will examine this option in more detail later in this chapter when we discuss options for improving the efficiency of working online with performance assessments.

E-mail

Instructors and students involved in online learning are obviously familiar with e-mail and its ability to include file attachments. With attachments, students and instructors can send anything to each other that can be represented as a computer file.

---

[2]WS_FTP LE, a popular free FTP client, can be downloaded from *www.FTPplanet.com*. A demonstration version of its commercial version, WS_FTP Pro is available from *www.ipswitch.com*. CuteFTP, a popular commercial FTP client is available at *www.cuteftp.com*.
[3]Oracle iFS (Internet File Server) was replaced by Oracle Content Management SDK, a more comprehensive and scalable run-time and development platform for content-oriented applications.

E-mail allows either public or private communications between the instructor and students. When students' material is to be handled publicly, e-mails could be copied to others in the class, although each student opening every other student's e-mail and attachments would be tedious and not likely to occur without strong encouragement from the instructor. E-mail sent between an individual student and the instructor is sufficiently secure to be considered generally private, although not in an absolute sense.

In terms of receiving student's products as e-mail attachments, the task of opening every student's e-mail is just as tedious for the instructor as it is for students. This problem can be reduced through advance planning. One technique that helps is to require all students to include, in the subject line of their e-mail, previously agreed upon words or characters. E-mail clients such as Eudora, Outlook, and Mail allow the user to set up rules for processing incoming e-mail. For instance, if students are directed to include the course number somewhere in the subject line, a rule can be created that places incoming e-mail into a special directory set up for that course. Allowing the e-mail reader to automatically sort incoming e-mail into folders expedites processing and reading the mail.

Establishing protocols for names of attached files expedites working with those files. One option would be to require students to name each file *Project00-Lastname,Firstname* where *00* is the project number, and *Lastname* and *Firstname* are the student's last and first name.[4] With this protocol, files can easily be grouped by project and ordered alphabetically by student name in the instructor's computer. Later we will describe how this ordering of students' files can help expedite evaluating work and record keeping.

When students submit projects as word processing files, consider requiring them to provide their e-mail address at a prescribed location, such as at the beginning or end of the document. Word processors typically change e-mail addresses into a link. When the instructor has finished reviewing the file, clicking on this e-mail link usually opens a return e-mail with the student's address already entered, thereby saving the instructor some time.

E-mail can also be used to distribute gradebook records and other information to online learners. If a Web-based course management system is used, records are usually available to students through an online gradebook. If that option does not exist, Oosterhof (2000) describes a way this information can be distributed through automated e-mails.[5] In essence, features in Word and Excel are combined to generate e-mail messages. Word and other word processing programs can create form letters, that include specific information retrieved from a database. Excel can serve as a database, and as the instructor's gradebook. Word is, of course, able to send output to a printer, but it is less widely known that this output can also be sent by the Internet in the form of e-mail. This allows the instructor to efficiently send e-mails that contain information retrieved from the Excel gradebook to each student.

Course Management Systems

The most widely used Web-based course management system is Blackboard; however, many alternative systems are available, including those listed at the end of Chapter 11. Course management systems typically provide a means for

---

[4]It is important for the file naming protocol to be specific. For instance, one might insist that file names include no spaces, that a hyphen separate the project number from the name, and a comma separate the student's last and first name. Following a specific protocol helps ensure files will sort appropriately and are easier for the instructor to work with. For instance, if some but not all students insert a blank between project number and last name, their files will list out of order since blanks sort high within a list. Also, if more than 10 projects are involved, assigning two-digit numbers to each project (e.g., Project09 and Project10) ensures that Project 9 will sort above Project 10.

[5]A version of this paper is available at *garnet.fsu.edu/~aooster/papers/email.pdf.*

students to upload assessment products in the form of computer files to the Web server. The instructor can then use a compatible program to view the content of the files. The instructor can also work with each file, for example, inserting edits and comments if it is a word processor document. The instructor can return the edited file to the student, along with a text message separate from the file. The instructor can record a score for the student's product in the online gradebook. This entire process is private between the instructor and each student.

This approach to receiving products from students, providing feedback, and recording scores in a gradebook is appealing. However, the actions the instructor must complete in reviewing each student's product can be very time-consuming, even to the extent of being woefully unacceptable. For instance, while some management systems allow for batch downloading of student files, many systems require downloading files individually, a process that can be task intensive and aggravatingly long regardless of whether a broadband connection is being used or not. More time may be required to access and resend each student's file than to view the student's work and create feedback. Depending on features, using e-mail to receive work from students and provide feedback may actually be faster than working in some Web-based course management systems.

Course management systems generally provide some variation of a discussion tool like ListServ, where participants in a public forum contribute what becomes strings of written comments or discussion on a particular comment. In online settings, a discussion board typically is used to facilitate asynchronous discussion among learners; however, it can be adapted to receiving and reviewing student work.

When used for asynchronous discussion, the instructor might set up a number of conferences or forums. Each forum can be configured so that students can initiate a string of conversations, with all students able to view and respond to comments made by others. Computer files can be attached to comments much like

they are to e-mails. To use a discussion tool for transferring products between students and instructors, instead of posting a comment for discussion, each student posts the product resulting from the project or performance assessment.

Using a discussion tool to post students' products and feedback from the instructor has certain limitations. Some would regard the public nature of the forum to be one limitation, but that is not our position. Other limitations, however, are more problematic. Unless files are attached, products posted to the discussion board are limited to unformatted text unless HTML code is used. This excludes common features like paragraph indentation and spacing, bold and underlined text, tables, graphics, and many other formatting features that are commonplace in a word processor.

On the other hand, because discussion boards function in a Web environment, they usually can interpret HTML code that controls the formatting of material in Web browsers. Some discussion boards handle the generation of HTML code transparently, allowing users to format much as if they were using a word processor. Otherwise, if students have access to a WYSIWYG HTML editor, it can be relatively easy to copy HTML code from the editor to the discussion board. Word processors such as Word will also create HTML code if the document file is saved as an HTML or Web file, although the process is somewhat clumsy.

As noted earlier, a discussion tool usually will accommodate file attachments. This allows considerable flexibility in the type and format of assessment products that a student can post. The use of attached files, however, reduces significantly the efficiency with which assessment products can be evaluated.

Another product, called WebBoard,[6] functions much like a discussion tool. It provides discussion board features for online courses that are not

---

[6]Information about WebBoard is available at *webboard.com*.

part of a Web-based course management system. WebBoard has a built-in spell checker and other useful features.

IMPROVING EFFICIENCY OF PERFORMANCE ASSESSMENTS

Because of the one-to-one interaction between the instructor and learner, assessment of students in an online environment can be very time-consuming for the instructor. This problem is often further aggravated by inefficiencies, such as those just discussed, in Web-based systems. It is well worth an instructor's time to design techniques into the learning system that improve the efficiency of assessments. This section describes some of these techniques; Oosterhof (2006) provides further discussion.[7]

Ensuring High Performance Levels

It is common knowledge among instructors that significantly more time is needed to review lower-quality student work than high-quality work. A student product that has numerous problems is going to require more comments to address the specific issues. It is also more difficult to explain what is wrong to a student who is experiencing problems than it is to explain what is right to a student who has successfully completed a task.

An effective way to improve efficiency of assessments is to take steps that help ensure that a student will succeed. Although quality of performance is affected by what the student can and will achieve, there are actions that an instructor can take to encourage quality. One such action is to clearly communicate what is expected of the student. Certainly an advantage of a well-designed performance assessment is that expectations and often even the scoring plan are made public to students in advance.

Another technique that improves efficiency is for the instructor to be alert to prerequisite skills. As noted in the previous chapter, identifying

prerequisite skills is part of specifying a performance assessment. Because performance assessments in general and online instruction in particular are time-intensive, being sure that prerequisite skills have been accomplished adds significantly to the efficiency of assessments. When possible, breaking projects into a sequence of smaller products can make it easier to communicate expectations and help ensure the mastery of prerequisite skills.

Providing Models of Completed Work

Providing examples of superior work help amplify instructions to students and provide information about the scoring plan. They also help to set standards. Models by previous class members can be particularly effective because they establish what peers have done and, therefore, what is reasonable for the student to accomplish. Students can also be enticed to produce superior work by knowing that their own work and that of classmates is being selected for use as models for future students. Including the student's name, with permission, is usually a particularly effective inducement. It is important to use models for students to emulate, not imitate. Figure 12.2 illustrates how a model project is presented, embedded within the online directions to the assignment and its scoring rubric.

Helping Learners Improve Readability of Work

Attractive work is not only more enjoyable to review; it is easier and quicker to review. Look at qualities that you find contribute to the attractiveness and readability of documents. This includes the use of paragraphs to help establish organization of ideas, indentation of the first line or spacing between paragraphs, and correct grammar and spelling. Establish these as expectations, and build them into models, even if this involves reformatting models generated by students.

Encourage, or even require, learners to use software that facilitates correct spelling and appropriate formatting when producing documents. When

---

[7]A version of this paper is available at *http://garnet.fsu. edu/~aooster/papers/Strategies.pdf*

Project 6: Illustrate how to measure different types of capabilities

First step: As a reference for the next step, state the kind of task a student should be asked to perform to demonstrate knowledge of each of the following types of capability:

- Information (declarative knowledge)
- Concept (a type of procedural knowledge)
- Rule (a type of procedural knowledge)
- Problem solving

Second step: Select one benchmark or grade level expectation from the Florida *Sunshine State Standards* that you would likely teach (<u>click here to access the Standards</u>).

Final step: Identify two specific skills you would expect students to learn. One skill should involve declarative knowledge and the other procedural knowledge (a rule or concept). Both skills should be obviously relevant to the benchmark or grade level expectation that you selected. (Most benchmarks and grade level expectations within the *Standards* are quite broad and encompass several skills.) For each of the two skills you identified:

1. State the type of capability this specific skill represents
2. In light of how you indicated knowledge of this type of capability should be demonstrated (see your first step), describe what you would ask your students to do in order to assess their achievement of this capability

The focus of Project 2 is on declarative and procedural knowledge. Exclude skills that involve problem solving.

Target Performance	• In your first step, the kind of task a student should be asked to perform for information, concept, rule, and problem solving is clearly equivalent to that stated in the reading. • Selected benchmark or grade level expectation from the *Sunshine State Standards* is stated verbatim and is identified by content area and grade level • The skill involving declarative knowledge obviously involves *information;* the skill involving procedural knowledge obviously involves a *concept* or *rule.* • That which students would be asked to do in order to assess their achievement is <u>obviously</u> <u>consistent</u> with • the specific skills involved • the type of capability each of the skills represent

Figure 12.2
A model by a previous student bundled with directions and scoring rubric

Acceptable Performance	• First four criteria are the same as above • That which students would be asked to do in order to assess their achievement, <u>with inference</u>, <u>appears consistent</u> with the specific skills, including the type of capability involved

Example produced by Lisa Stanley
Teacher, Riversink Elementary School

Kind of task a student should be asked to perform to demonstrate knowledge of each of the following types of capability:

<u>Information (declarative knowledge).</u> The student will state what they know about specific facts, principles, trends, criteria, and manners in which to organize events.

<u>Concept (a type of procedural knowledge).</u> The student will classify physical objects or abstract concepts using previously unused illustrations of examples and nonexamples.

<u>Rule (a type of procedural knowledge).</u> The student will apply principles of a rule to unused examples of the rule that have relevancy.

<u>Problem solving.</u> The student will be given a previously unused example of a problem (nonmathematical) and will be asked to generate a solution to the problem.

Language Arts — Grades PreK–2: Reading

Standard 1: The student uses the reading process effectively.

Benchmark 2 for this standard: Identifies words and constructs meaning from text, illustrations, graphics, and charts using the strategies of phonics, word structure, and context clues.

Example of Declarative Knowledge and How It Would Be Assessed

<u>Description of Knowledge:</u> The student will state the effects of a silent "e" found at the end of the word on the first vowel in the word

<u>Assessment:</u> Tell me what happens to the sound of the first vowel in a word, when a silent "e" is found at the end of the word. (Students state that the silent "e" makes the first vowel say its name.)

Example of Procedural Knowledge (a rule) and How It Would Be Assessed

<u>Description of Knowledge:</u> The student will apply the principles of using illustrations to construct meaning from the text.

<u>Assessment:</u> Using only previously unread books, look at the illustrations in the book and draw a picture that summarizes the story.

Figure 12.2 (*continued*)
A model by a previous student bundled with directions and scoring rubric

a discussion tool with limited capabilities is used to submit products, require students to use a word processor to create text, and show them how to copy and paste work from a word processor into their Web browser. Publicly compliment student work that is particularly professional in its presentation. Express concern to students who fail to check spelling before submitting work, even to the extent of asking for the work to be resubmitted.

Incorporating Peer Reviews

When assessments require considerable time to review, having students assist with a peer review can help improve the quality of products prior to the instructor's review. Peers often are able to identify especially the more basic problems, particularly when directions and scoring plans are clearly stated. Students also learn from each other.

Contingencies can enhance the effectiveness of peer reviews. For instance, two other students might be assigned to review a given student's product. In turn, that student can be asked to show in the revised product how recommendations from peers were incorporated, or explain why a suggestion was not used. Scores assigned by two peers might be averaged with the instructor's subsequent score. Chapters 13 and 14 address the use of peers in assessment.

Streamlining Scoring and Score Recording Process

An effective way to reduce the enormous amount of time required to review student work is to streamline the scoring and recording procedures. A goal when processing student work should be to devote a large percentage of time to interpreting what students have produced and communicating evaluative judgments to the student. Minimal time should be required for activities such as retrieving a student's work, writing comments, recording scores, and electronically returning reviewed documents to the student. Described here are a series of strategies we have found to be effective at streamlining the scoring and score reporting process.

Use software other than Web-based course management systems to access student work. As noted previously, this software contributes substantially to inefficiencies. Using other procedures, including some options identified earlier, can help streamline the scoring and scoring reporting process. For example, using e-mail attachments to transfer student products is generally more efficient than using systems included in some Web-based systems. If students' products can be handled publicly, using a discussion tool such as a discussion board is usually more efficient than downloading and opening a computer file from each student, and then uploading the reviewed file.

Oracle iFS, referenced earlier in the chapter, provides an alternate option for managing students' products. Oracle iFS is a Web-based system designed for situations where individuals at various sites work collaboratively with material contained in computer files. To access the iFS system, users simply enter a prescribed URL in their Web browser. The Oracle iFS system allows a remote server to become a virtual extension of each person's personal computer, with access and other controls placed on the transfer and use of these files. In online-learning settings, the iFS system can facilitate the transfer of students' projects to a remote server, and control who has access to these projects.

Figure 12.3 illustrates one way that Oracle iFS can be set up. In this illustration, the left panel lists subdirectories that have been created for the respective projects. As shown in the figure, clicking on one of these subdirectories open a list, in the right panel, of files that are currently posted on the server within that subdirectory. A file naming convention has been used in which the project number and student name are displayed. By clicking on any of these file names, the instructor or other students can view the contents of that file. The icons at the top of the right panel facilitate working with the files. For instance, clicking on the "Upload" icon allows the user to upload a file from her or his personal computer to the subdirectory selected on the

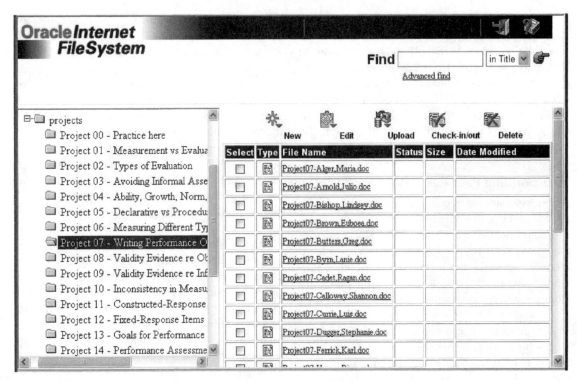

Figure 12.3
Screen image from oracle iFS listing project files posted by students

remote server.[8] Similarly, clicking on the "Delete" icon allows the removal of selected files. Through its access controls, Oracle iFS can be set up so that students are able to view each other's project files, but only the instructor and owner of a given file can edit or delete it.

The Oracle iFS is built on an FTP framework, so the procedures illustrated here could readily be applied to an FTP client-type program if it were adapted to the needs of online learning. Figure 12.4a illustrates a screen display provided by such a client program. The left panel lists directories and files that have been established on the instructor's personal computer and the right panel lists directories and files on the remote server. Using a mouse to select and drag any subset of directories from the right panel to the left panel causes these directories *and* their contents to be downloaded to the instructor's computer.[9] For instance, through a single one-step select-and-drag action, the instructor can download (or upload) all student files associated with one or more projects. Figure 12.4b displays material from the same course; however, now individual student files for one of the assignments is displayed.

---

[8]Clicking on a file name downloads a copy of that file from the server to the user's personal computer and opens it in the associated program, such as a word processor. The user's computer must have appropriate software to work with the file. From the perspective of the user, the download is transparent; it appears as if a local file was being accessed.

[9]Files can similarly be uploaded from the instructor's computer to the remote computer, by selecting those files in the left panel and dragging them to the appropriate directory displayed in the right panel.

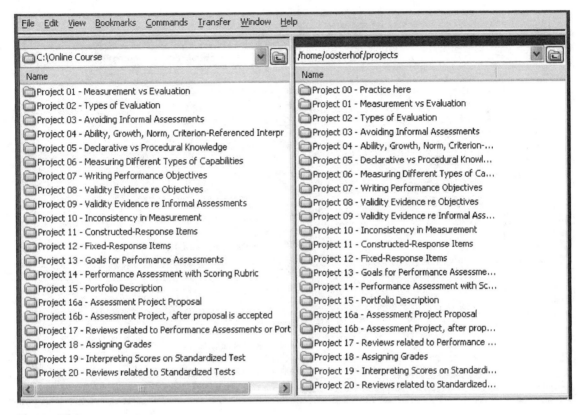

Figure 12.4a
Screen image from an FTP client program listing project folders

When evaluating students' projects, a strategy we have used is to modify the file name of projects as they are reviewed. As illustrated in Figure 12.5, we add the prefix "Reviewed" to show that a project has been evaluated. This way, it is easy to keep track of which projects have yet to be reviewed. Likewise, when evaluated projects are uploaded back to the server, students can quickly determine that their work has been reviewed by the presence of the preface. As soon as evaluated projects have been uploaded to the server, we delete students' original files. That is, the "reviewed" files with our comments and edits replace the original files. If a student submits project work after projects of other students have been reviewed, the absence of the "Reviewed" prefix makes it obvious to the instructor that additional projects have been posted, which now need to be evaluated.

Require students to use a prescribed convention for naming files. As noted earlier, depending on the protocol used for transferring students' files, we may establish a file naming convention that students must follow when posting their project work. As illustrated in Figure 12.4b, we might require the file name to be

Project00-Lastname, Firstname

where *00* is the two-digit project number, *Lastname* is the student's last name, and *Firstname* is the student's first name. We also stipulate no spaces within the file name, and a hyphen and comma embedded within the name as shown. Students sometimes joke about this regimented practice, but significant practical benefits are realized. For instance, this protocol causes students' files to be listed alphabetically by students'

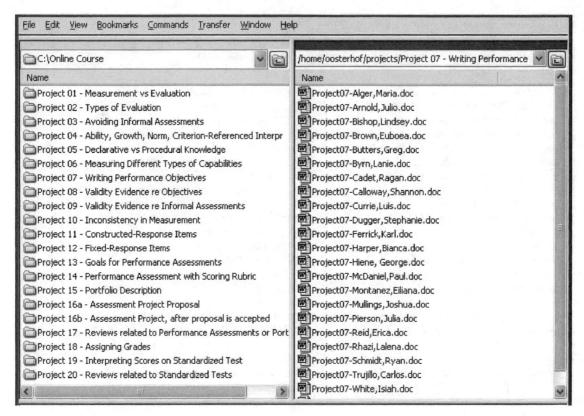

Figure 12.4b
Screen image from an FTP client program listing project folders and students' project files

last names, the same order that they appear in our electronic gradebook. This makes it easier to enter scores in the gradebook when evaluating projects. This alphabetical listing also makes it easier to determine if projects from any of the students are missing. Including the project number makes it easier to spot projects that students have uploaded to the wrong subdirectory. Students will grudgingly admit that the naming convention sometimes helps them search for lost project work on their own computer when their organization has been less than optimal!

Explore the course management system for imaginative workarounds. It sometimes seems that most course management systems are designed by software developers who are far

removed from online instruction and assessment. To illustrate, Blackboard includes a feature called the Digital Drop Box that allows students and the instructor to exchange files. Although conceptually appealing, using this drop box to access, review, and provide feedback to students' documents involves a series of time-consuming steps. The time required to review a set of products for the whole class is absurd.

However, in Blackboard's Control Panel is a section titled "Content Areas." Using the Manage Course Menu link in the *Course Options* section, one can create a new content area and give it a name such as "Upload a Product." Then, by moving through the Control Panel into the new content area and looking closely (real closely!)

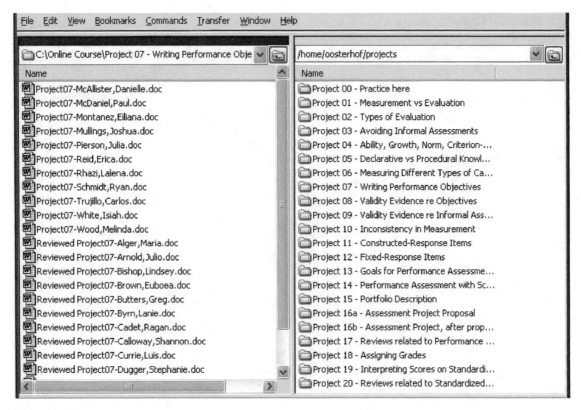

Figure 12.5
Screen image from an FTP client program illustrating use of a prefix to identify projects that have been reviewed

one finds a pull-down menu where one of the options is "Assignment" (see Figure 12.6). Selecting "Assignment" allows the instructor to create a location for students to upload files containing project work. The illustration in Figure 12.6 indicates that four assignment areas have already been created, and named products 1 through 4. When a new assignment area is created, a corresponding entry is created in the online gradebook. When students upload their files, the instructor can go to the online gradebook to retrieve their files.

With Blackboard, a particularly efficient way to retrieve students' files is to use the "Item File Cleanup" option in the gradebook. (The cleanup feature is accessed by clicking on one of the names in the gradebook related to the assignment.)

Ironically, the purpose of the "cleanup" option is to delete students' files. However, it also presents a list of students' names along with the files they have uploaded. Clicking on a file name opens that file for viewing.

Explore options outside the course management system to expedite reviewing student products. One can often use software other than a course management system to significantly increase the efficiency with which students' work is reviewed. This is unfortunate because, by definition, a well-designed management system should minimize the management workload of instructors (and students). Given the tremendous processing power of computers, the use of electronic documents rather than physical documents should *reduce* the amount of time needed to review student work

Upload a Product

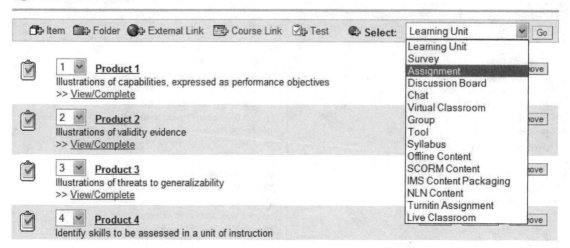

Figure 12.6

An illustration of adding an assignment to content areas within Blackboard's control panel

and provide narrative feedback. Sadly, many course management systems actually increase the amount of processing time. Following is an example of other software that can expedite the review of student work; the sequence of steps described here is summarized in Figure 12.7.

This example assumes that students' documents were produced using Word, and that the instructor is using Outlook from the Microsoft Office suite as the e-mail client. (In Outlook, Word must be selected as the e-mail editor.) When using a course management system, students' document files are often downloaded first to the instructor's personal computer, either individually or in a batch. If files are downloaded in a batch to a directory in the instructor's hard drive, going to that directory and clicking on a student's file opens the file in Word. If files for a project are downloaded individually, going to the server or management system directory that contains the files and clicking on a file name opens the student's document.

If students have been required to include their e-mail address in the Word document, clicking on that address activates Outlook and opens

Word as its e-mail editor in a second Word window (see Figure 12.8). The editor automatically inserts the student's e-mail address as the "To" entry. Using copy/paste, the instructor moves a copy of the student's entire document into the Word e-mail editor. Because Word is functioning as the editor, the instructor can use Word's reviewing functions to insert comments and edit text. Clicking on the "Send" button sends the reviewed document to the student with embedded comments and edits. If so configured, Outlook automatically saves as "sent mail" a copy of each student's reviewed document. As long as the student's e-mail client handles HTML code (most clients do), the student can view the instructor's edits and comments in the original and fully formatted document. The process is repeated with each student's file, each time initiating the process by clicking on the file name of the next student's document.

With practice and the use of hotkeys (see the next section), the process of opening a student's document, copying it to Outlook's editor, reviewing and inserting feedback, and sending the reviewed document back to the student can

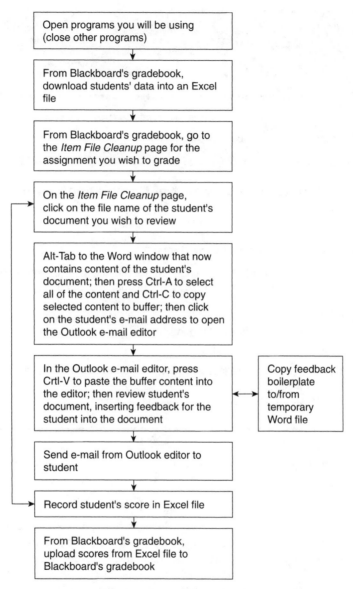

Figure 12.7
Hotkeys used to expedite work among multiple windows

proceed very quickly. Aside from the time required to read and insert comments, our experience is that the overhead associated with retrieving and subsequently returning reviewed documents to students requires less than 10 seconds per student. This does not include the time required to evaluate each student's document; however, reviewing student work and providing feedback is where instructors should spend time—opening, manipulating, and returning student files. Many instructors can now write more quickly by keyboard than by pen, so evaluating

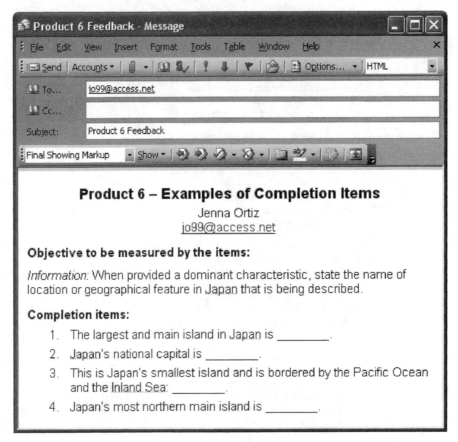

Figure 12.8
Screen image of word being used as the e-mail editor with a student's product pasted into the editor

students' electronic documents should be more efficient than working with physical documents.

When reviewing assessment products, use your computer's hotkeys to move quickly within and between your software. Much of the software used in online learning settings has built-in hot keys, reserved for quickly executing common tasks. Taking advantage of selected keys can significantly increase the efficiency with which students' projects are reviewed. Summarized in Table 12.1 and described here are some common and particularly useful hotkeys:

Within much of the software used by Macintosh and Windows machines, the X, C, and V keys, when pressed while holding the Control key, will cut, copy, and paste whatever text is highlighted. For instance, if you anticipate writing the same or similar comment in feedback to several students, you can highlight your comment in the first student's project, press Control-C to copy it, and then Control-V when you are ready to paste the comment as feedback in the second student's project. The pasted comment can be edited as necessary. If a series of comments are being used repeatedly, they can be written into a temporary Word document and then copied and pasted as needed when reviewing a student's project.

Table 12.1
Hotkeys used to expedite work among multiple windows

Hotkey	Function
Alt-Tab	Jump between active programs
Ctrl-A	Select-All, for example, selects all the text within a student's document; can be used in Word to select everything before using copy/paste to move the text to Outlook
Ctrl-C Ctrl-V	Ctrl-C copies selected text into buffer, and Ctrl-V pastes the contents of the buffer to wherever the cursor is active; can be used to quickly copy/paste the contents of a student's document from Word to Outlook, or similarly to copy/paste boilerplate to and from the document where you store the various boilerplates (Ctrl-X cuts rather than copies selected text into buffer)
Alt-Backspace	Undoes what you just did; often can be pressed more than once to undo several steps (Shift-Alt-Backspace often undoes an undo)
Ctrl-click	In Word and some other programs, holding the Ctrl key down when you click the left mouse button selects whichever sentence the mouse pointer is resting on; this and the following technique are particularly useful for moving boilerplate into feedback messages
Double-click	In Word and some other programs, double-clicking the left button selects one word in the text; double-clicking with the mouse pointer located in the left margin, however, selects one paragraph

In Word and other programs, various hotkeys or keystrokes quickly highlight particular text within a document. For instance, double-clicking on any word highlights that word. Holding down the Control key and double-clicking on a word highlights the full sentence containing that word. Double-clicking in the margin to the left of a paragraph highlights that paragraph. Control-A highlights everything in the document. Take time to look through the hotkeys documented in your software manuals. Learning the hotkeys for tasks you perform repeatedly will likely be time well spent.

Pressing the Tab key while holding the Alternate key toggles you between two programs. For instance, if you are using Word to review projects and a Web browser to display your online gradebook, you can expand both the Word program and the browser to full-screen, and use Alternate-Tab to toggle quickly between Word and the gradebook. This can help you quickly record a score in the grade-book as you complete the review of each project in Word. If you have more than two programs active at one time, continuing to hold down the Alternate key as you repeatedly press the Tab key allows you to move quickly from one program to another.

SUMMARY

In online settings, more than in face-to-face classroom settings, a substantial amount of an instructor's time is used for asynchronous interactions with learners. Much of this time is for reviewing products the learners have produced and using these evaluations as a formative or summative assessment of student's achievement of targeted instructional outcomes. Given their one-to-one nature, these interactions can be very time-consuming; therefore, it is important to evaluate options for making them efficient.

Choosing a system for managing interactions depends on several issues. For example, when material is sent to the instructor and then back to the student, can it be handled publicly or must it be private? When the instructor reviews the material and provides feedback, can the comments be sent to the student detached from the product or integrated into the product much like instructors in conventional classes write comments *on* papers before returning them to students?

When students' products can be handled publicly and feedback can be detached from their text-based documents, then a discussion tool such as a ListServ or a discussion board often provides an efficient means of receiving, reviewing, and returning products being assessed. Except for attachments, a discussion tool is usually limited to simple text, making many common tasks difficult, such as formatting text or inserting tables or diagrams, unless one is willing to use an HTML editor. When students submit products as computer files or if products are to be handled privately, files attached to e-mails typically are a more efficient option than those provided through Web-based course management systems.

A variety of strategies reduce the amount of time needed to review student products. One of the most important is taking steps to ensure a high level of student performance. This includes clearly communicating what students are to do, ensuring that prerequisite skills are sufficiently mastered, providing models where relevant, and establishing high expectations. Other strategies involve streamlining the scoring and score recording process. These include establishing protocols to be followed when students produce products (such as including an e-mail address in each product), exploring the course management system for workarounds to inefficiencies, using software other than course management systems, and using the various hotkeys that are built into computer software.

TERMS INTRODUCED IN THIS CHAPTER

Detached feedback: related to an assignment is sent to the student separated from the student's original product. This tends to be less efficient than *integrated feedback* because the text of detached feedback often has to include information indicating what in the product is being referenced.

Integrated feedback: is written within a student's product. When students turn in physical papers, integrated feedback is written on the paper; with electronic documents, integrated feedback is written in the document, usually through editing. Integrated feedback typically is more efficiently produced than *detached feedback.*

ENHANCE YOUR UNDERSTANDING

- In a group, discuss the pros and cons of public versus private handling of students' products related to performance assessments.
- Using the Reviewing tools in Word, edit a document file. Make sure that the "Track changes" feature is activated. Also highlight text and insert a comment. Both the track changes and the comment features are available in the Reviewing toolbar. Discuss your experience with others as to whether these tools can help an instructor provide feedback to online learners.
- Working in teams, simulate what happens when online learners use a Web-based course management system to transfer products to the instructor, and then receive feedback from the instructor. Have one member of each team play the role of the instructor and collect document files. That person should insert comments in the files received and return them to their authors. Share experiences concerning potentials and problems experienced with using a Web-based system to provide students' with comments and other feedback. Try to extrapolate this experience to a full-scale application involving a class of 25 online learners.

PART V

Assessing Online Interaction and Collaboration

In order to introduce several issues related to online assessment, this book began with a historical review technology as it relates to distance education. Formal distance education began in the mid-1800s, which certainly predates the development and probably the conceptualization of digital computers. But it also predates the various electronic technologies that are or have been used to facilitate communication among individuals including the telephone, facsimile, audio recordings, and video. Learners at a distance worked in isolation. In fact learners at a distance had to be of a special breed; people who could work within a learning environment for extended periods without interactions with others. Collaboration was not a practical option if even possible.

This has changed; or more accurately, is changing dramatically. Computers and broadband access to the Internet are increasingly making interaction and collaboration among distant learners commonplace. Learners can share files or work simultaneously on common files. They can carry on asynchronous conversations using discussion boards, or face-to-face synchronous conversations with video as they work with common documents. The physical separation between learners might be measured in inches or distances that span continents.

In this last section of the book we discuss the *assessment* of online interaction and collaboration. Chapter 13 provides a prerequisite framework, addressing concepts associated with collaboration and community building. This includes a discussion of effective community building activities, an analysis of elements that impact the effectiveness of groups, and a description of procedures for building a collaborative community.

Chapter 14 is concerned with managing the assessment of interaction and collaboration. This includes how to conduct formative and summative assessments of collaborative activities using self and peer assessment tools, and how to develop the instruments used in these assessments.

13

Interaction and Collaboration Online

The benefits of collaborative interaction in a classroom-based learning environment have been discussed over the last three decades by various prominent researchers such as Johnson and Johnson (1993). Study findings indicate that collaborating learners have higher levels of participation, achievement, productivity, self-esteem, peer interaction, group cohesion, and enhanced critical thinking skills than noncollaborators do. As a result, use of collaborative activities has grown in the online environment as well as in the face-to-face classroom.

Collaborative interaction has been termed the "heart and soul of an online course." (Draves, 2002) By participating in activities such as defining and resolving problems, explaining content, and providing feedback, members of an online course become active generators of knowledge who assume mutual responsibility for constructing and managing their own learning experience and that of their peers, thus building a community of learners.

This chapter provides an overview of the concepts of online interaction, collaboration, and community building to set the stage for the discussion of assessing such work in the next chapter. Assessment of interaction and collaboration is challenging, and it cannot represent a true picture of individual knowledge and skills acquired unless the activities and teams have been planned and structured in an effective manner.

This chapter helps you achieve two skills:

- Identify characteristics of effective community-building activities

- Plan activities that promote community building

EFFECTIVE COMMUNITY-BUILDING ACTIVITIES

To identify the characteristics of effective **community-building** activities, we must begin by discussing the types of interaction that have been widely accepted in distance learning environments. Moore (1993) identified three basic types of interaction: 1) the learner interacting with instructional resources (learner-content interaction), 2) the exchange of ideas and feedback with the instructor (learner-instructor interaction), and 3) learners interacting with each other (learner-learner interaction). These are the same interactions that can occur in a classroom-based learning environment where a learner reads the text (learner-content), listens to the instructor's lecture (learner-instructor), participates in class discussion (learner-learner), and is assessed with feedback (instructor-learner). In an online-learning environment, these activities are mediated by interactive computer software, so they must be planned and implemented differently from traditional classroom procedures.

As networking technology developed, online learning became more of a reality. When first implemented by academic institutions, many online courses were merely digital correspondence courses. Text-based materials were put on the Web, and self-tests and feedback from the instructor were conveyed via e-mail. In these cases, only two of Moore's three types of interactions, learner-instructor and learner-resources, were being used, resulting in the same learner-isolation problem that had occurred with paper-based correspondence courses. This caused one of two results: learners either dropped out or turned to the instructor as the sole source of interaction. In the early days of online course implementation, instructors routinely reported that an online course required more time to manage than a classroom-based course. Perhaps one of the causes was the perception by learners that the only person they could interact with was the instructor. At that time, many online instructors had not incorporated collaborative learning techniques into their online courses; it was yet another new online option—and there were enough new things to deal with in the first online classrooms.

Some online instructors found an outlet for their frustrations in the work of Palloff and Pratt, whose book *Building Learning Communities in Cyberspace* (1999) went beyond the idea that only academic interactions should be incorporated into an online course. They endorsed a "virtual learning community" that consisted of individuals who established their personalities, resolved conflicts, developed shared values, and participated in the knowledge-building process. Using the concept of community, an online course becomes a holistic environment that incorporates the student's learning context with the development of peer synergy and academic knowledge. Instead of turning primarily to the instructor as the source of all information, community members get to know one another, learn to depend upon one another, and appreciate peers as active knowledge generators instead of passive knowledge recipients. This results in a richer experience for the learner who is able to express thoughts and opinions in a safe and receptive learning environment. The instructor is free to focus on knowledge aspects that require his or her expertise rather than on expending energy to calm the fears of a dependent and petulant learner.

Boettcher and Conrad (2004) suggest that interaction and community are at opposite ends of a continuum, with interaction being a brief exchange of information and ideas similar to the

"Hi—How are you? I'm fine," depth of comment we often use to greet one another. An online learner may or may not feel connected to a peer or motivated to deepen or repeat the knowledge exchange based only upon an interaction. Trust has usually not been built at this level. If such exchanges continue, they may not contain the depth of thought and analysis that is expected in the course. Moving up the continuum requires that learner connections be deepened through collaboration and cooperation in problem-solving activities. These types of activities establish the interdependence and social presence needed to form an online community, which is the highest form of interpersonal exchange. When learners operate as a community, they strive naturally to work with other participants in the course without being assigned to do so.

Online community building has been compared to the settling of the West by pioneers. Pioneer families gathered themselves and their supplies in covered wagons as they set out on the trail. They had individual reasons for moving West, but the common purpose of arriving at their destination intact. They looked to the leader of the wagon train for guidance and direction in this unknown territory. Not everyone knew the others in their group. Mutual trust was not high as the journey began. But, as the trip progressed, they met one another outside the confines of their wagons, perhaps over the campfire at the end of the day. They recognized others to whom they could entrust their lives and the lives of their family members should trouble arise. As the wagon train progressed deeper into the wilderness and problems arose, such as protecting the wagon train from attack, cooperation and collaboration were necessary to keep the group together. Pioneers learned to be supportive of one another and worked toward positive resolution of conflict to survive. At the end of the trail, pioneers who had shared life and death experiences became settlers who established towns with businesses and laws. By that time, there was an intertwining of lives that had not existed when that wagon train first pulled out. Communication and trust had developed, and a synergistic community had been born.

As cyber-pioneers, learners who venture into the online learning environment do so with individual goals as well as the initial common purpose of performing well academically. Depending on the level and type of interaction in the course, learners may get to know one another through discussion of the content. If teams are formed, learners might collaborate to solve problems and to support one another. However, a synergistic community will only be formed when learners have had the opportunity to incorporate life experiences into the course and to develop the perception that their individual success is intertwined with the success of others. Communication must progress beyond "How are you? I'm fine" exchanges.

The competitive learning, "I win if you lose," paradigm that developed during the Industrial Age, created several hurdles that had to be conquered before a learner could move beyond merely interacting in collaborative and community-building exchanges. In the next chapter, we establish the implications that collaboration has for the role of assessment in learning. For instance, in a collaborative setting, the dominant role of assessment is not to determine who scored the highest, or necessarily to certify what students have learned. Rather, it is on trying to answer the question, "Where are we now and where shall we go next?" In other words, assessments play a formative more than a summative role. A major challenge to overcome is that most learners do not know how to collaborate in a learning environment, and instructors often do not know how to build assessments into collaborative settings. As a result, some learners will opt out of the collaborative process and let one person or some subset of the group do all the work. This creates a chain reaction of emotions such as frustration and lack of motivation among remaining team members, particularly if all members of the group receive the same grade based on the quality of the final product. Adult learners, who are already accustomed to working individually, will be reluctant to collaborate if the process is not perceived to be a valuable and effective part of the learning experience.

While students are learning to collaborate, they must deal with the issue of interacting with others they cannot see and using technology they may not be familiar with. If left to their own devices without a framework to begin community building, learners will flounder helplessly. The first major challenge facing the instructor is how to structure interactions to promote the development of community and to deter lurking nonparticipants who can intimidate and frustrate the community with their silence. The following sections present two frameworks to consider when designing a course that encourages online community.

Phases of Engagement Design Framework

Conrad and Donaldson (2004) suggest that specific planning by instructors is needed to encourage learners to interact, collaborate, and form a community. Their framework focuses on the defined roles of learner and instructor in each phase of engagement and describes the types of activities that will encourage moving the learner from one phase to another. This framework involves the four phases summarized in Table 13.1.

In Phase 1, learners are treated as newcomers to an online-learning community. The instructor is not only the content expert at this point, but the Social Negotiator of the budding community. The instructor's goal is to provide a brief overview of the environment and to assist learners in becoming comfortable with technology-mediated interaction through initial communication with one another. For example, learners could be asked to complete a discussion activity in which they describe themselves in one word and then respond to others who have similar descriptive words.

After learners have "broken the ice" with one another, they are ready to move into Phase 2, in which their role is that of Cooperator. Learners work together in pairs on academic content with the instructor serving as the Structural Engineer

Table 13.1
Phases of engagement

Phase	Learner Role	Instructor Role
1	**Newcomer** to online learning, uncertain of communication and online learning strategies	**Social Negotiator** who helps learners become acquainted. Expresses expectations for engagement in the course. Provides orientation to course and keeps learners on track
2	**Cooperator** who works with at least one other learner to reflect upon issues and share ideas	**Structural Engineer** who begins promoting peer interaction by forming peer dyads
3	**Collaborator** who works in a small group to problem solve and generate knowledge	**Facilitator** who provides team activities and consults with the learning team as needed
4	**Initiator/Partner** who generates or leads activities such as group presentations and discussions	**Community Member/Challenger** who participates in the learning community like any other member and challenges higher-order thinking from the community, as needed

who establishes and guides the dyads based upon the introductory peer interactions at that point. The goal in this phase is for the learner to build trust and substantive academic communication skills with at least one other learner in the community in preparation for the formation of larger teams. An example of this would be an activity in which two learners collectively develop a definition for others in the course to review.

In Phase 3, the learners form small groups to solve problems and generate additional knowledge for the learning community. The instructor now begins to step into the background as a Facilitator and consultant for each group on an as-needed basis. Activities are very similar to those in the prior phase but are larger in scope and require more consensus-building due to an increase in the group size. An example of a Phase 3 activity would be a project in which the team develops a solution to a case study.

Learners in the final phase become learning partners in the community by creating and leading learning activities. The instructor is now engaged as a partner in new knowledge generation. All community members are involved in providing feedback to one another. The instructor

becomes the Challenger of ideas and new knowledge. An example of an activity in this phase is a learner-led discussion.

In each phase of engagement, various types of activities should be incorporated into the instructional plan to provide motivation to increasingly participate in and contribute to the online learning community. For instance, an activity that is often omitted from online courses but is crucial for setting the stage for community development, is an initial icebreaker activity in which learners engage in an entertaining communication activity that introduces them to one another on a personal basis rather than an academic exchange basis. It is at this point that the trust-building process begins. This type of activity also provides the instructor with individual insights that will assist in the formation of groups in later phases. The activities in each phase build on one another and provide the foundation for the next phase.

Table 13.2 outlines typical activities in each phase and the suggested time frame for such activities in a semester-long course.

In this framework, both instructor and peer assessment are incorporated. Feedback is provided by both in Phase 2 with the instructor assigning

Table 13.2
Phases of engagement time frame

Phase	Weeks	Process
1	1–2	Instructor provides activities that are interactive and that help the learners get to know one another. Expresses expectations and criteria for evaluation of engagement in the course. Provides orientation to course and keeps learners on track. Examples: icebreakers, individual introductions, discussions concerning community issues such as netiquette rules in a Virtual Lounge.
2	3–4	Instructor forms dyads of learners and provides activities that require critical thinking, reflection, and sharing of ideas. Examples: peer reviews, activity critiques.
3	5–6	Instructor provides activities that require small groups to collaborate, problem solve, reflect upon experiences. Examples: content discussions, role-plays, debates, jigsaws.
4	7–16	Activities are learner-designed and/or learner-led. Group presentations and projects. Discussions begin to go not only where the instructor intends but also where the learner directs them to go. Examples: group presentations and projects, learner-facilitated discussions.

a grade for the activities. In Phases 3 and 4, feedback and grades are determined by both instructor and peer input.

Stages of Collaboration Framework

The Phases of Engagement framework describes the roles of both the instructor and the learners in building an interactive learning community. Palloff and Pratt (2005) examine in more depth the instructor activities that promote collaboration in their Stages of Collaboration framework. They define four stages: Set the Stage, Model the Process, Guide the Process, Evaluate the Process.

In the first stage, the instructor explains the collaborative process and provides guidelines as well as "places" in the online learning environment for learner collaboration. The instructor then moves into the next two stages in which he or she first demonstrates how collaboration works and then guides the collaborative process.

The final stage is often missed by instructors. It is the evaluation of the process, which allows learners to share their insights on the collaborative experience with the instructor and for the instructor to assess whether the learning objectives have been achieved.

As in the Phases of Engagement framework, both the instructor and the learners are involved in the assessment process—not the instructor alone. The Stages of Collaboration Framework also emphasizes that both the collaborative process and the learning objectives must be evaluated.

Activity-Practice Design Framework

Another perspective to consider when building an online community is presented in the Activity-Practice Design Framework by Brooks (2001). It concentrates on a step-by-step sequencing of activities and assignments in each of the instructional phases. In this model, the learner alternates between individual learner-resource interaction and cooperative-collaborative activities. In contrast to the Phases of Engagement Design Framework, the learner begins by working on individual knowledge building through text readings and/or recorded lectures, and then moves directly to interaction with the large class group. After large group interaction, the learner uses self-tests to determine his or her knowledge acquisition and then works collaboratively in a small group to refine knowledge and skills through practical application.

Table 13.3
Activity-practice framework for course design

Phase 1	Phase 2	Phase 3	Phase 4
Individual study	Large group activity sets	Individual self-quiz	Small group practice set
Basic skills and knowledge are acquired prior to interacting with others online.	Learners share content understanding and generate knowledge collectively through online discussion.	An opportunity is provided to self-assess mastery of skills and knowledge acquired Individually and through peer interaction.	Knowledge and skills are applied to authentic tasks within a collaborative team project.

Table 13.3 summarizes activities associated with each phase of the framework developed by Brooks.

Assessment under the Activity-Practice Design framework is instructor-generated and occurs in Phases 2 through 4. In Phase 2, as learners work through large group activities, the instructor evaluates the quality of the discussion comments and includes this evaluation as part of the learner's participation grade. In Phase 3, self-assessment is used to provide individual feedback to the individual on a self-administered quiz. In Phase 4, both peers and instructor can provide feedback for individual team members.

The prior three frameworks demonstrate that there are a variety of ways to foster interaction and build online community. The Phases of Engagement and Stages of Collaboration frameworks focus on the long-term processes involved in developing community over the length of a course. Brooks' emphasis is on a short-term process that can be used in Phases 2 through 4 of the Phases of Engagement framework or in conjunction with the Stages of Collaboration.

ELEMENTS THAT IMPACT EFFECTIVENESS OF GROUPS

In planning activities that promote community building, it is imperative that group structure be considered. Learning in a community requires that students work together in groups, both large and small, with minimal guidance from the instructor to achieve an outcome or goal that requires collective and interdependent effort. Reaching the outcome or goal will probably require resolving a series of problems, such as providing peer tutoring or developing a final report or presentation.

Inadequate management of group processes, lack of individual reward, and unequal distribution of workload can all undermine the effectiveness of teams. Learners who are not accustomed to learning collaboratively will need guidance concerning key elements required to operate effectively as a team. Assessment of knowledge and skills acquired via collaborative interaction depends on the quality of the alliance that occurs. It is imperative, therefore, that certain contributors to the quality and depth of collaboration be considered both by the instructor and by the learners when planning community-building activities. For example, activities that require consensus-building might be more efficiently conducted in smaller groups. Complex group projects might be completed more effectively using team contracts and team member roles that provide adequate support for the required group tasks. These elements and others are examined in the following sections.

Group Size

Groups that are too large impede the quality of communication and collaboration. They contribute to the feelings of isolation that online learners sometimes experience. Groups that are too small can die from lack of multiple perspectives and limited knowledge generation.

Size varies according to the purpose of the group and the nature of the course content. Groups of 10 to 15 work well for large group discussions in which learners are building upon each others' views. Groups or teams who are expected to produce an end product or to negotiate and come to consensus quickly should be no smaller than three and no larger than five.

A learner might be a member of two different groups within a class. They might consist of a small group either for discussion in which a quick consensus must be reached or for a specific project that will be completed as a large group. The large group might be two small groups combined into one for expanded group discussion or role-plays.

The responsibility for analyzing the purpose of a group and establishing the appropriate size falls to the instructor, although seasoned collaborative learners often know the most effective size based upon past experiences.

Communication Standards

Learners who are new to the online environment or who are working with a new instructor need guidelines regarding the expectations for interaction. Guidelines for postings might include the number expected per week, their length, the level of response, and so forth. Initial guidelines could be provided by the instructor much like they are in a face-to-face classroom setting.

Additional rules can also be provided by the learners themselves through a discussion on the topic of "netiquette," which is a set of guidelines for acceptable online behavior that the community agrees to follow when dealing with each other. The purpose of these rules is to build respect and trust among the members. For example, a rule of netiquette that a community may choose to adopt is "Tactfully disagree with the issues expressed in a peer's posting. Don't attack the person raising the issue." Another one might be "Never use capital letters for more than three words in a posting, because capital letters denote that you are shouting. An entire posting in capital letters would indicate you are yelling at the community."

Establishing communication standards may seem trivial and unnecessary among adult learners. However, setting the code of conduct for the community is another activity that helps learners understand each other's values and moves them toward community formation.

Team Roles

In online settings, collaboration can be facilitated by establishing roles that must be played by one or more team members. Team roles may be defined and assigned by the instructor or may be collectively established within the group based on a discussion of their desired group process and organizational decisions. Here are examples of such roles:

- *Team facilitator* who organizes and leads the team meetings.

- *Project manager* who leads the team in planning the project and keeps it on track.

- *Technical mentor* who is responsible for acquiring and assisting others in the use of the technology required for effective group functioning. For example, if a group chooses to use a tool outside of those provided in the course environment, such as instant messaging, the Technical Advisor would help other team members get the tool and learn how to use it.

- *Reporter* who informs the team, the instructor, and the learning community, as needed, about the team's major decisions, activities, and progress.

- *Team liaison* who interfaces with other teams in the learning community to coordinate similar activities. This role is particularly necessary when two or more teams are working on the same problem or topic. The Team Liaison would share the view of his or her team with others and obtain their viewpoint to take back to the team for consideration.

- *Resource consultant* who researches and recommends online resources that will help the team generate additional knowledge.
- *Participant* who is responsible for identifying issues, providing appropriate recommendations for those issues, and generating ideas that promote the success of the group in achieving its goals.
- *Process analyst* who observes the team and identifies potential process issues for the team before group cohesion is undermined. For example, if team members are repeatedly ignoring the comments of another team member, the Process Analyst will bring it to the team's attention for further discussion.
- *Mediator* to whom other team members can turn for resolution of issues that are undermining the team, such as one team member being disrespectful to another.
- *Critical thinking advisor* who challenges the ideas put forth in the group with the goal of encouraging critical thinking.

The roles listed here offer a menu of possibilities for team assignments. Some of the roles may not be needed for a particular project. Some functions may be combined. For example, a team with five members might decide that they want to establish a team leader, a reporter, and a resource consultant, with the latter roles being rotated among four of the team members.

A team that is simulating a specific organizational type, such as a business management team, might use roles that have meaning within that context, such as Chief Executive Officer, President, Financial Officer, and so on. The reason for the roles is to facilitate operation of the group. Therefore, they should be tailored to best fit each collaborative activity.

Team Contracts

The purpose of a team contract is to promote group cohesion. Much like the establishment of netiquette rules that set the communication standards for the community at large, the team contract clarifies the expectations of individual conduct that will be necessary to meet the goals of the team. The introduction of the concept in the learning environment generates discussion concerning the process to be used by the team for such things as conflict resolution, which is often ignored by a group until it occurs.

Effective contracts contain clear statements of acceptable behavior such as "Each member will meet with the team weekly. Any absence must be discussed with the team and a current status report must be sent to the team before the absence occurs. In the case of an emergency, the team member should call the project leader and briefly discuss activity status."

Areas that should be considered for inclusion in the contract are

- Goals and objectives
- Definition and assignment of team roles and tasks
- Established deliverables and deadlines
- Problem-solving techniques
- Meeting guidelines, including attendance
- Tools to be used for shared work
- Communication standards, if they differ from the community netiquette
- Review of the team contract

Process Reflection and Evaluation

At specific intervals in the course, team members should be asked to reflect individually and collectively on the team process, the fulfillment of their assigned role, communication effectiveness, and conflict resolution to date. The purpose of this reflection is to detect aspects of the team's organization and processes that need adjustment.

At the very minimum, this reflection should occur at the midpoint in the team process. Ideally, reflection should occur two to three times during the course—once shortly after the team convenes, again at the midpoint of the team activity, and finally at the end of the team's activity. This reflection should be shared with the instructor who serves as an independent observer of the group and the ultimate mediator when problems arise.

DEVELOPING A PLAN FOR COMMUNITY BUILDING

The guidelines provided in this chapter are helpful when thinking about the various components needed to incorporate community-building activities. Now it is time to consider how to write an instructional plan that uses these guidelines. Table 13.4 discusses the interaction goals and provides examples of the types of activities that would occur in each week of a 16-week semester course.

From the beginning of the course, a collaborative tone is established through an introductory icebreaker activity, the expectations for interaction outlined in the syllabus or a Welcome note from the instructor, and the presence of a discussion area such as The Oasis (see Figure 13.1) in which learners communicate on a more social level about topics that are not directly related to the course content.

During the second and third weeks, at least one activity that requires learners to discuss or review a content topic with a peer would help strengthen interaction in the course. This can be accomplished quite simply through a discussion activity in which learners are required to respond to at least one colleague's post, and that colleague is required to respond back.

In preparation for the small group collaborations that will occur in the remainder of the course, an announcement or an e-mail such as the one

Table 13.4
Instructional plan for online collaborative interaction

Week(s)	Goal	Description
1	To interact with other learners on a social rather than content-driven level.	Learners enter the course site, are welcomed by the instructor who outlines the basic expectations of the course, and then directs learners to participate in an icebreaking activity.
2–3	To interact with one other learner on a cooperative, knowledge-sharing level.	Learners read the assigned content, reflect on it based on specific questions, or complete an activity based upon the content for the week. Learners are then paired with a peer and asked to share their knowledge.
4–6	To collaborate with a small group on a knowledge-sharing activity.	Learners work within their teams to introduce themselves, establish group expectations, and determine team operating procedures. The team discusses the content-based project and plans its completion.
7–16	To generate knowledge as a team and promote knowledge generation by others.	The team determines how the topics for the course might be enhanced and plans an activity for the community that expands the content of the course, such as team members leading a discussion with the community or bringing in an outside expert as a guest speaker.

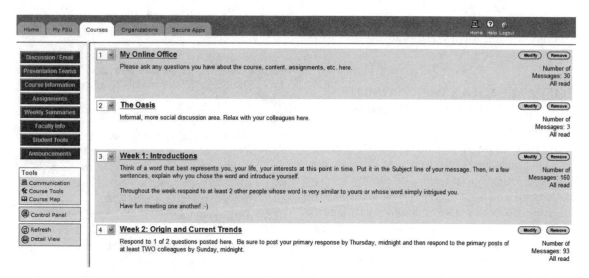

Figure 13.1
Example of course discussion areas

From: The Instructor

To: The Learning Community

In three weeks you'll post your team presentations and lead the discussion! If you have not yet had an opportunity to "meet" please do so this week and discuss how you will operate as a team. Define what tasks need to be completed, who will do them, and how often you will meet and when. Review the Team Member Evaluation form and use it to guide your performance as a team member and the operation of your team.

After each presentation is complete, participants should e-mail to me a Presentation Evaluation form for EACH presentation. I have incorporated the recommendations from your evaluation of the form in the Week 2 discussion. If you are presenting, please email to me a Team Member Evaluation form for each member of your team AND yourself after your presentation week has concluded.

The Presentation Evaluation form and the Team Member Evaluation form are available under the Course Information menu selection.

Figure 13.2
E-mail example

illustrated in Figure 13.2 reminds learners of the upcoming team activity and urges them to begin introducing themselves to one another, and discussing expectations and operating procedures.

In the last half of the course, the activities should consist of activities such as learners leading discussions, generating exam questions, or providing feedback to one another on final projects.

Through the Instructional Plan framework, the learners become increasingly involved with one another—first as knowledge sharers and then as knowledge generators. This process provides time for trust to develop within the community and for a collaborative bond to be established.

SOFTWARE TOOLS THAT PROMOTE COLLABORATION AND COMMUNITY BUILDING

Many tools to promote community are available in course management systems. At the very minimum, a course should use a discussion area for both large and small groups. An asynchronous discussion tool that allows community members to communicate at a convenient time is helpful for group discussions, individual introductions, icebreaking activities, and group presentations. A synchronous discussion tool, such as online chat, that provides an opportunity for community members to meet at the same time, is useful when conducting team meetings, obtaining consensus, and brainstorming.

Another useful tool is a communal workspace in which documents can be displayed and edited by all team members. This promotes a shared repository of community projects, documents, and presentations. One example of a communal workspace is known as a **wiki,** which is a website that allows anyone accessing it to modify the content. "Wiki" means "fast" in Hawaiian and the developer of the first wiki, known as WikiWikiWeb, developed it to support quick idea exchanges between computer programmers. This concept then expanded into other wikis such as the Wikipedia, a collaboratively developed online encyclopedia. Consider using a wiki for any type of project that requires group editing.

In some disciplines, such as mathematics, a visual tool such as an electronic whiteboard that can be used to draw spontaneous diagrams to highlight a particular content point, is a vital tool for team discussions and presentations.

As bandwidth increases and learners acquire more powerful computers, additional tools that assist in the collaborative process, such as desktop conferencing, are becoming available.

13.1 Apply What You are Learning

An online course environment must be structured in such a way as to be conducive to online interaction and collaboration. For each of the following pairs of statements, indicate which (A or B) is more conducive to building a collaborative community spirit.

1. A. Groups are assigned on the first day of class.
   B. Before groups are assigned, an initial icebreaking activity is planned for the first week through which everyone gets to know one another on a social level.
2. A. During the third week of class, students share their work with an assigned peer and discuss recommendations for change in each other's work.
   B. During the third week of class, students are asked to post their work to a large discussion board to be critiqued by the class of 30.
3. A. After teams are assigned, the members discuss how they will operate as a team.
   B. After teams are assigned, members begin discussing the assigned activity.
4. A. Team roles should be assigned only as needed.
   B. Every team member should have a defined role.

Answers can be found at the end of the chapter.

Websites listed at the end of this chapter provide insights into the possibilities of tools for online collaboration.

ACCOUNTABILITY IN COLLABORATIVE ACTIVITIES

Collaborative activities require two types of individual accountability: within-group accountability and outside-group accountability. As defined by Daniels and Gatto (1997), within-group accountability is accomplished through the fulfillment of roles and tasks by each team member to achieve common goals. Outside-group accountability refers to each team member's ability to demonstrate knowledge that should have been acquired as a result of the cooperative activity. This evaluation is usually accomplished through various assessment devices such as tests or individual papers. Effective teams require both individual accountability of member contributions and mutual accountability for the overall result of the team's effort.

While overall reports of cooperative learning have been positive, one of the most negative aspects reported by students is the unequal responsibility and workload among group members, which results from an inadequate within-group accountability of team members. Salomon (1995) defined various effects of insufficient within-group accountability:

> The "free rider" effect where one team member just leaves it to the others to complete the task; the "sucker effect" whereby a more active or able member of a team discovers that he or she is taken for a free ride by other team members; the "status sensitivity" effect whereby high ability or very active members take charge and thus have an increasing impact on the team's activity and products. (p. 1)

When learners think they are being held individually accountable, "lurking" disappears. Unless there is an equal distribution of workload, a sense of commitment to the team by individual team members, and a belief that the group product is more than a personal reflection of a select few, students will instinctively avoid collaboration.

The following chapter will explore how to develop appropriate assessments that measure knowledge acquisition and promote the necessary levels of individual accountability in a collaborative activity.

SUMMARY

The concept of online interaction and collaboration is one key to an effective online course. Interaction occurs not only between the student and course resources but also between student and instructor, and collaboratively among peers. Activities must go beyond mere interaction to promote learner collaboration with the goal of establishing an interdependent learning community.

Aspects such as group size, communication standards, team roles, and space for reflection are needed to provide an environment conducive to collaboration. Assessment of collaborative activities should consider the appropriate level of individual accountability needed for collaborative activities to be successful.

ANSWERS: APPLY WHAT YOU ARE LEARNING

13.1 1. B. To help ease learners through the initial technology-mediated communication bumps of an online course, it is recommended that learners first have a nonthreatening introductory activity that provides the instructor with a clue as to what learners have in common and how small groups might be most effectively structured.

2. A. Sharing work with and receiving feedback from one peer creates a feeling of safety that posting work for all to see and critique does not. It takes at least four weeks for most learners to become comfortable communicating in an online class. Since this activity is still within the four-week adjustment time frame, it is recommended that sharing and critiquing be done by only one or two peers.

3. A. Before a team begins any academic activity, members should first discuss how they will operate as a team, particularly as concerns resolving conflicts. This will minimize disruption of knowledge generation due to team malfunction.

4. B. While it is true that team roles could be assigned only as needed, it is recommended that each team member be assigned a defined role, even if the role is participant.

A specifically defined assigned role clarifies that everyone is expected to participate and that a learner may not opt out of collaboration or lurk in the group.

TERMS INTRODUCED IN THIS CHAPTER

Community building: is the process by which learners in an online course become active generators of knowledge who assume mutual responsibility for constructing and managing their own learning experience and that of their peers. This can be accomplished through collaboration in such activities as defining and resolving problems, explaining content, and providing feedback to colleagues.

Wiki: is a collaboration tool that allows users to collectively add, remove, or edit most content on a website. *Wikipedia*, the popular online encyclopedia, is developed through online collaboration and makes extensive use of this tool. An article about wiki in *Wikipedia* is located at *en.wikipedia.org/wiki/WIKI*.

ENHANCE YOUR UNDERSTANDING

- Using Moore's three types of interaction (resource-learner, instructor-learner, learner-learner), categorize each of the activities in your weekly course syllabus. Are all three types of interaction represented in a balanced manner? If not, determine how you might incorporate them. Using the Phases of Engagement, analyze your current course.

- Examine your course plan to determine whether activities have been incorporated to move the learners through each of the Phases of Engagement.

- Using software tools currently available to you, describe specific ways you can promote collaboration and community-building activities.

ADDITIONAL READING

Collison, G., Elbaum, B., Haavind, S., and Tinker, R. (2000). *Facilitating online learning: effective strategies for moderators.* Madison, WI: Atwood Publishing. The authors detail team roles and formation strategies that can help in the planning and implementation of community-building activities.

Conrad, R., and Donaldson, J. A. (2004). *Engaging the online learner: Activities and resources for creative instruction.* San Francisco, CA: Jossey-Bass Publishers. The Phases of Engagement are further described and actual activities for each of the phases are provided for incorporation into an instructional plan.

Horton, W., and Horton, K. (2003). *E-learning tools and technologies.* Indianapolis, IN: Wiley Publishing. The range of hardware, software, and services needed for e-learning are discussed and specific examples are provided.

Palloff, R., and Pratt, K. (2005). *Collaborating online: Learning together in community.* San Francisco, CA: Jossey-Bass Publishers. This book discusses the theory behind collaboration, the process and issues surrounding it, as well as the evaluation of collaboration and ideas for collaborative ideas.

Palloff, R., and Pratt, K. (1999). *Building learning communities in cyberspace.* San Francisco, CA: Jossey-Bass Publishers. The concept of online community is introduced and guidance is provided in designing courses that promote the formation of online communities.

Useful sites for collaborative tools and software:

E-learning Centre—a comprehensive index of collaboration tools and related articles: www.e-learningcentre.co.uk/eclipse/vendors/collaboration.htm

Electronic Collaboration: A Practical Guide for Educators—provides basic information concerning the planning and implementation of electronic collaboration. Can be downloaded from: www.alliance.brown.edu/topics/technology

14

Managing Assessment of Interaction and Collaboration

Once the community-building infrastructure is in place, the next challenge is to assess the knowledge and skills acquired as a result of the collaborative activity. A common assessment strategy used for collaborative work is to evaluate the team project or product without regard for individual contributions to the end result. This approach assumes that all participants have learned to the degree demonstrated by the final product. In many cases this is not true. A thorough assessment should also include an evaluation of the learner's individual contributions to the generation of knowledge and skills acquired from the group's interaction.

Assessment of knowledge that has been created through community activities is not usually straightforward. Input is desirable from the instructor's perspective, and also from fellow community members who might have more in-depth knowledge of a peer's contribution to a project. In addition, self-assessment by the learner can also clarify the level of knowledge and skills that he or she has mastered.

Managing multiple assessment perspectives and ensuring that the input is valid can be challenging. As collaborative interaction is increasingly recognized as a necessary pedagogical tool in the online learning environment, methods for effectively assessing its results become vital.

This chapter helps you achieve two skills:

- Conducting formative and summative assessments of collaborative activities that include self- and peer-assessment tools

- Developing effective self- and peer-assessment tools

FORMATIVE ASSESSMENT OF COLLABORATIVE ACTIVITIES

After structuring the collaborative activities and forming the teams, the instructor usually becomes less involved in the day-to-day learning events that take place among team members. In a classroom, an instructor can roam from group to group while the teams are meeting, but he or she is not usually privy to team communication that occurs outside of class. Likewise, in an online-learning environment, an instructor can read the various discussion postings of team members, but there may be other communications such as synchronous chats or e-mails that an instructor does not usually see.

As illustrated in Figure 14.1, the assessment of collaborative activities requires multiple perspectives. Instructors can assess activity that occurs within the course site, but the individual learner and peers must also assess the ongoing process and knowledge acquired offscreen and outside of the course environment as a result of the collaborations.

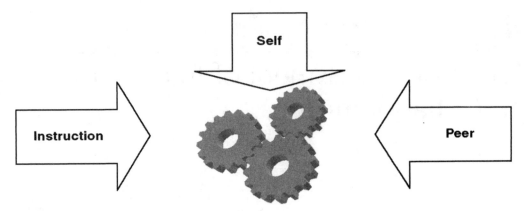

Figure 14.1
Multiple perspectives of assessing collaborative activities

With these multiple perspectives in mind, how does an instructor structure the needed assessment? How can an instructor effectively analyze the community knowledge building that is developed within the course site? How can formative assessment be effectively conducted by an instructor if only part of the picture is seen? The answers lie in the use of emerging software tools that can be used by the instructor and peers, and for self-assessment.

Instructor Assessment of Collaborative Activities

In the formative process, the instructor is most concerned with how well learners are processing and mastering new concepts and skills. This assessment is currently done mainly through discussion. A major drawback of assessing the discussion area is the amount of information an instructor must read and analyze to determine the extent to which learners are adding comments of quality and appropriate quantity.

One of the new software tools emerging is the Discussion Analysis Tool (DAT), also known as ForumManager, which can be used to analyze patterns of interactions to encourage deeper critical thinking (Jeong, 2006). Available at *bbproject. tripod.com/ForumManager,* this tool is a Microsoft Excel program that downloads threaded discussions and provides statistics that assess student participation and interactivity through content analysis and sequence analysis (Jeong, 2001).

Figure 14.2 illustrates the analysis results produced by ForumManager. It includes the average number of discussion entries per participant, the level of interactivity, and the richness and depth of the discussion.

With such information, an instructor can quickly pinpoint where formative feedback might need to be provided to the community as a whole or to a specific learner. Software tools such as ForumManager can analyze activity and help an instructor provide feedback to written communication that is visible on the course site. The communication that goes on among community members outside of the course site requires other methods of assessment, such as those discussed in the following sections.

Self-Assessment of Collaborative Activities

Self-assessment allows learners to reflect on their own performance and to make corrective steps before the summative assessment occurs. It can be used to assess both understanding of content and participation in the collaborative process. Learners can use self-quizzes, reflective journals, and checklists to determine whether they are mastering the content and whether they are performing well as a collaborative community member. For example,

	A	B	C	D	E	F	G	H	I	J	K	L	M	N	O	P	Q	R
1	Instructor	119	11	9	9	1	6	25	12	8	8	8	6	9	7			14.02
2	Student01	111	17	4	7	8	14	6	4	11	10	9	6	6	9			15.00
3	Student02	104	15	2	5	3	10	10	11	11	7	6	11	7	6			14.67
4	Student03	81	8	5	3	3	10	13	4	5	10	6	4	5	5			14.35
5	Student04	74	10	2	3	4	8	6	7	6	6	5	8	4	5			14.67
6	Student05	72	10	7	5	5	8	6	7	5	6	3	1	5	4			13.70
7	Student06	82	9	7	8	4	7	6	6	7	4	4	8	7	5			15.00
8	Student07	69	7	6	3	3	7	8	4	5	7	5	4	5	5			14.35
9	Student08	70	4	8	6	5	4	8	5	8	4	5	5	4	4			15.00
10	Student09	61	7	5	6	1	5	5	8	8	6	0	5	0	5			11.41
11	Student10	58	9	6	3	2	8	8	4	7	4	0	0	0	7			10.11
12	Student11	70	9	4	12	1	7	5	4	4	4	6	5	5	4			14.02
13	Student12	73	6	6	9	4	7	4	4	4	4	5	10	5	5			15.00
14	Student13	52	4	5	8	1	2	1	0	5	7	4	4	5	6			11.09
15	Student14	61	4	3	4	6	6	5	5	5	4	5	5	5	4			15.00
16	Student15	56	5	3	1	2	5	10	1	5	5	4	6	4	5			12.39
17	Student16	41	3	3	3	1	2	3	1	4	4	5	4	4	4			11.41
18	Student17	51	3	3	0	4	7	1	4	5	4	4	5	6	5			12.39
19	Student18	27	7	1	0	3	4	0	0	0	0	4	4	4	0			7.83
20		36	9	0	3	1	1	1	1	1	1	4	4	5	5			8.15
21																		
22																		
23																		
24																		
25																		
26	Forum	All	1.2	1.4	1.7	2.3	2.6	2.1	3.3	3.6	3.9	3.1	3.2	3.2	3.2			
27	Total Messages	1368	157	89	98	62	128	131	92	114	105	105	92	105	100			
28	Average per participant	65.14	7.85	4.45	4.90	3.10	6.40	6.55	4.60	5.70	5.25	5.25	4.60	5.25	5.00			
29	Standard deviation	27.36	3.73	2.37	3.21	1.94	3.05	5.50	3.28	2.74	2.53	2.53	2.11	2.59	1.72			
30	Messages with replies	55.77	87	29	45	37	70	86	54	71	62	46	45	46	47			
31	Interactivity (%msgs with replies)	.52	.55	.33	.46	.60	.55	.66	.59	.62	.59	.44	.49	.44	.47			
32	Richness (number of threads)	20.77	38	54	35	6	17	19	18	17	21	3	10	16	16			
33	Depth (average thread level)	3.3	4.3	2.7	3.2	3.0	4.0	3.2	3.1	3.8	3.4	4.0	2.6	2.6	2.6			
34	Minimum messages required	48	4	2	4	4	4	4	4	4	4	4	4	4				
35																		

Buttons (right panel): Main Menu · Get Student Names · Download forum · Compute Statistics · Content Analysis · Delete a Column · Sort by Names · Sort by Scores · Compute Point Totals · More Info

Total Possible Participation P: 25

Figure 14.2
ForumManager analysis results
Source: http://bbproject.tripod.com/ForumManager/screenshot1.gif

self-quizzes with automatic feedback can be used to assess how well content is being learned. The team member evaluation form that will be used for summative assessment such as that shown in Figure 14.3 can also be used as a self-check of learners' perceptions of their performance as collaborators or team members.

Self-assessment can be decidedly subjective. However, if used in combination with other assessments it might provide learners and the instructor with additional performance information. For example, if a learner has self-assessed himself or herself as "above the group" and other members of the team have assessed the learner as "below the group," this would signal that additional discussion is needed within the team and perhaps additional guidance is needed from the instructor.

Peer Assessment of Collaborative Activities

The primary focus of peer assessment is the evaluation of the collaborative process and of how much an individual has contributed to the end result of the collaboration. The conclusion inferred from peer assessment is that the higher the participation and contribution in the team process, the greater the probability that the team product reflects the individual learner's level of knowledge acquisition. Learners can provide self-assessments of their involvement, but the

Team Member Evaluation Form

Using your best, objective and fair professional analysis, complete the following evaluation form concerning your team member's performance on your team project.

1. The LEVEL of effort this team member gave toward the project was...	Below Standard	Met Standard	Above Standard
2. The QUALITY of that effort was...	Below Standard	Met Standard	Above Standard
3. The INPUT this team member contributed was . . .	Below Standard	Met Standard	Above Standard
4. How would you rate this team member's level of cooperation?	Below Standard	Met Standard	Above Standard
5. How would you rate this team member's level of time on the project?	Below Standard	Met Standard	Above Standard
6. The level of quality of the resources this team member contributed was . . .	Below Standard	Met Standard	Above Standard
7. The level of quality of products this team member contributed was . . .	Below Standard	Met Standard	Above Standard
8. This team member attended team meetings . . .	Inconsistently	Consistently	
9. This team member met team deadlines . . .	Ineffectively	Effectively	
10. How would you rate this team member's OVERALL work and contribution to this project?	BELOW Group Grade	SAME AS Group Grade	ABOVE Group Grade

Additional comments regarding this team member's work on this project:

Figure 14.3
Peer assessment of project participation

perspective of fellow team members who have worked closely with the individual throughout the collaboration is also very useful.

Peer assessment is one method of evaluation in which all team members assess the contributions, skills, and behaviors of each individual team member as they relate to group work and project completion. Peers have a unique view of significant aspects of each other's behavior that occur outside the purview of the instructor, and they can more accurately assess each team member's contributions. This is particularly true in online learning where the instructor is not able to observe group interaction outside the classroom.

Involving peers in the assessment process increases the individual and collective ownership of learning and assessment, and grants more autonomy and control of governance to the learning community. Peer assessment can also improve critical thinking and self-learning. If a student is able to evaluate another individual's performance, this might improve his or her own self-evaluation. Qualitative feedback in particular can help learners improve their performance as collaborators by affirming their contributions or providing helpful hints in cases where they are uncertain about the correctness of their actions.

Receiving feedback from peers is an emotionally charged process that must be handled carefully. Learners should be prepared for the process in a variety of ways. It should be clear from the first day of the course that peer assessment will be part of the learning experience. For example, the syllabus could provide an overview of the peer assessment process, which would be iterated as the peer assessment draws near. In addition, learners must develop their feedback skills. Palloff and Pratt (2005) stress that this is vital if peer feedback is to be effective. Providing a set of guidelines for learners to analyze their feedback before sending it is one way to accomplish this. For example, "If you are tired or angry, don't send feedback as you may be too terse or not as clear as you would like." Providing questions that the feedback should answer is another strategy that can help learners impart quality feedback to one another. Figure 14.4 is an example of directions for a peer feedback activity.

Confidentiality of the evaluator should be maintained. In a small team, this can be difficult to do if qualitative assessment is used. Learners can sometimes identify the peer assessor from the phrases and expressions used in the assessment. If qualitative feedback is a part of the peer assessment form,

---

Peer Evaluators, base your comments upon these questions:

- Are the objectives clearly stated?
- Do all activities match the objectives?
- Do assessments effectively evaluate the objectives?
- Is there appropriate interaction?
- Are the instructions clearly stated?
- Could you, as an instructor, pick up this lesson and teach it?

In addition, discuss at least three things that worked well. Discuss at least three suggestions for improvement—and if there is no need for improvement, explain how this lesson fits the best practices you discussed in a prior unit.

Figure 14.4
Example of peer feedback directions

that feedback should be reviewed by the instructor before the assessment is forwarded to the individual to ensure that it is constructive and not inflammatory, and that it does not personally attack the learner.

Learners believe that peer assessment does not always provide reliable information. Multiple peer assessments throughout the course of the project might increase their accuracy and fairness. Providing multiple opportunities for peer feedback increases the likelihood that an accurate picture will emerge and that an individual will have the opportunity to modify his or her behavior before the final peer assessment. Weekly feedback may decrease the shock of peer assessment as well. It should occur at all the critical periods throughout the project and not just the midpoint.

If multiple opportunities for peer assessment are provided, it is recommended that some of the assessments contribute to the course grade and that others do not. For example, if three formative assessments are provided by peers, consider dropping the lowest of the assessments. Or, consider weighting the grade of the assessments with the final formative assessment. This affords learners the opportunity to modify behavior during the collaboration without being punished for mistakes or intergroup flare-ups that have to be rectified over the course of the activity.

Ideally an instructor should not have to be involved in the peer assessment process. However, it is recommended that the instructor phase out his or her involvement as the group becomes more comfortable assessing one another. Initially, all peer assessments should be forwarded to the instructor for review. After the process is well underway, only peer reviews that are below an average score should be forwarded to the instructor. These reviews may require an intervention by the instructor in the group process.

After all peer assessments have been submitted to the instructor, a general review or summary of the peer reviews may be helpful for a team to develop their collaborative process further. This review should be led by the instructor on a group-by-group basis. Participants who are left to interpret the results on their own may read the comments incorrectly and unnecessarily introduce negativity into the peer assessment. This can hinder a group's effectiveness or destroy it altogether; therefore, it should be minimized whenever possible. By providing a detailed process and opportunities for trial and error, the reception of peer assessment comments could improve.

Peer assessment can have a positive effect on accountability and responsibility within groups. However, there still may be individuals who do not participate in an online project. Peer assessment cannot remedy the obstinate lurker. It is only a deterrent. But it can ensure that the lurker is not rewarded by receiving the same grade as team members who actually produced the end result.

SUMMATIVE ASSESSMENT OF COLLABORATIVE ACTIVITIES

The manner in which individual achievement in a collaborative activity is assessed is a point of contention that has been explored in past research studies. When a team produces a collective product, it is difficult for the instructor to assess individual contributions. The most common approach is to base final grades for each member of the team on the overall quality of the final product.

However, group grades can be perceived as unfair, less meaningful than individual grades, and de-motivating, and they might actually violate the principle of individual accountability. When all individuals must depend on the group effort for a grade, those who have not participated fully in the process are rewarded and the other team members, who had to go above and beyond their individual workload to compensate for the slackers, are punished. It is clear why this strategy has sometimes resulted in student dissatisfaction, usually due to unequal participation by some team members. Individual accountability is lost if the same grade is given to all group members based on the quality of the collective product. The group does not have a mechanism to correct the quality or quantity of individual team member's contributions. It also has no means to provide feedback to the instructor concerning the contributions of each team member.

Strategies that are discussed throughout this book can be used for a single group grade when assessing the team's final product, project, or presentation. However, if group assessment is used, it should be understood that it is only one indicator of an individual's success.

Summative Self-Assessment

Self-assessment can be conducted summatively the same way it was done formatively. The instrument changes because a summative evaluation of the content is needed, but the process remains the same. If other summative assessment instruments are used, they should focus solely on the individual's involvement in the collaborative process rather than on the knowledge acquired. Providing a cumulative or final self-assessment can assist learners in developing a deeper level of reflection about their participation in the collaborative process. The peer assessment form in Figure 14.3 can be used to submit a self-assessment when all peers submit assessments of one another. The form can be modified by substituting "I" for "this team member" and be used as a stand-alone self-assessment instrument.

Summative Peer Assessment

Peer assessment is often a difficult and emotional process and, as a result, is often used only for summative assessments. If learners have not been effectively coached to assess their peers, the input provided will be less useful. Learners need time to develop their evaluation techniques. Therefore, peer assessment should be used first on a formative basis and then as a summative device. The same form can be used for both formative and summative evaluations because the assessment is used to determine how well each individual performed within the team up to that point.

DEVELOPING PEER- AND SELF-ASSESSMENT INSTRUMENTS

A potential drawback in using peer assessment is that learners may not feel comfortable assessing their peers, because they do not think they have the skills to do so or, in some cases, because they perceive grading to be the instructor's responsibility. In some cases, learners might not need instructor intervention to determine their evaluation criteria. An instructor may have a peer assessment instrument developed, but it should be open to modification after the learners have reviewed it. Acquiring "buy-in" on the instrument strengthens the peer assessment process and minimizes the learner perception that peer assessment is being imposed upon them by the instructor.

The following scenarios illustrate how peer and self-assessment might be developed and implemented, based on the comfort level of the learning community. How the instrument is developed is affected by the implementation scenario chosen. In the first scenario, the instructor is in control of the peer assessment process. However, in each of the later scenarios, team members determine more of the critical components of the assessment, such as the criteria and timing, and are empowered to direct the assessment process itself.

Instructor-led Scenario.   The instructor determines the assessment criteria and leads the process. The instructor introduces the peer assessment process to the class, reviews a summary of assessment results with each team, and provides suggestions for individual improvement strategies.

Involved Scenario.   Teams negotiate assessment criteria with the instructor who determines timing, administers the peer assessment, summarizes results, and sends results to individual team members. The instructor encourages teams to discuss results at the next team meeting and to consider problems that individual team members want to discuss and improve. The instructor will meet with teams or individual team members to provide additional guidance as needed.

Self-directed Scenario.   Teams determine the assessment criteria, negotiate timing and form consensus with the rest of the learning community, administer peer assessment, and discuss results with the instructor as mediator, if needed. Each team member reports his or her strategies for improvement to their team members.

Independent Scenario. Teams create the assessment criteria using the team contract. They determine the timing of the evaluation with the rest of the learning community, administer the peer assessment and self-assessment instruments, and discuss results among themselves. Each team member determines strategies for his or her improvement.

Criteria

Figures 14.3, 14.5, and 14.6 provide examples of peer assessment forms. The criteria in each of the forms are based on the perceived quality and level of effort in various key areas, depending on the type of collaborative activity. Figures 14.3 and 14.6 both focus on the same specific statements of quality of team member interaction. The difference between the two forms lies in a qualitative versus quantitative assessment. Figure 14.3 relies on a team member's judgment concerning how a colleague met team expectations; Figure 14.6 uses a Likert-type scale to assess each statement. Figure 14.5 provides general categories for assessment and requires team members to describe behaviors that a team member should Start, Stop, or Continue. If teams have chosen to use team contracts, the criteria come directly from the wording of the contract.

Qualitative Versus Quantitative Data

A single quantitative grade may not adequately explain an individual's contribution to the community. Therefore, allowing a qualitative explanation of a number on a line-by-line basis or at the end of the assessment form can be more helpful than relying on a single averaged score for each item.

If qualitative descriptors are used on each item instead of a Likert scale response, this approach

can serve the same purpose. However, it might be more difficult to determine a quantitative score from such a form, if that is desired. Figures 14.2 and 14.3 illustrate how primarily qualitative information might be gathered. Figure 14.4 gathers quantitative information.

All peer assessments that will be included in the grade should be forwarded to the instructor. Each team member should rate themselves and

---

14.1   Apply What You Are Learning

For each of the following pairs of statements, indicate which (A or B) is a more accurate description of self- and peer-assessments.

1. A. Self-assessment alone provides an accurate picture of the involvement of the individual team member in the collaborative activity.
   B. Both peer assessment and self-assessment tools should be used to determine the quality of the involvement of the individual team member in the collaborative activity.
2. A. An instructor can determine whether or not an individual learned by the quality of the collaborative final project.
   B. An instructor needs peer assessment to infer whether or not an individual learned to the level indicated by the collaborative final project.
3. A. Peer assessment should be submitted to the instructor for review.
   B. Self-assessment should be submitted to the instructor for review.
4. A. The same peer assessment instrument can be used for both formative and summative evaluations.
   B. The same peer assessment instrument cannot be used for both formative and summative evaluations.
5. A. The same self-assessment instrument can be used for formative and summative evaluation.
   B. The same self-assessment instrument cannot be used for formative and summative evaluation.

Answers can be found at the end of the chapter.

Team Member Evaluation Form

Using your best objective and fair professional analysis, evaluate your team member's performance on your team project. For each of the elements listed, describe what the team member should CONTINUE to do when working in a team, START doing as a team member, and STOP doing when working as part of a team.

	Should CONTINUE	Should START	Should STOP
Communication			
Time Management			
Meeting Participation			
Assignments and Assessment			
Peer Interaction and Support			

Recommendations on other aspects of the team member's work not listed above:

Circle one of the responses for each statement below:

1. This team member met my expectations	Strongly Agree	Agree	Disagree	Strongly Disagree
2. I would work with this team member again	Strongly Agree	Agree	Disagree	Strongly Disagree

Figure 14.5
Qualitative peer assessment of project participation

Team Member Evaluation Form

Using your best objective and fair professional analysis, complete the following evaluation form concerning your team members' performance on your team project. For questions 1 through 10, use the following meanings for the numbers:

1 = poor (did practically nothing)

2 = fair (did as little as possible)

3 = about right (about the right amount)

4 = good (performance was better than average)

5 = excellent (performance was super! beyond the call of duty!)

1. The LEVEL of effort this team member gave toward the conference was...	1	2	3	4	5
2. The QUALITY of that effort was . . .	1	2	3	4	5
3. The amount of input this team member contributed to the TEAM DISCUSSIONS was . . .	1	2	3	4	5
4. The amount of input this team member contributed to the TEAM'S PLAN was . . .	1	2	3	4	5
5. The amount of input this team member contributed to the TEAM'S PRESENTATION was . . .	1	2	3	4	5
6. This team member's LEVEL OF COOPERATION was	1	2	3	4	5
7. This team member's LEVEL OF TIME on the project was . . .	1	2	3	4	5
8. The level of POSITIVE IMPACT this team member's work had on the total project was . . .	1	2	3	4	5
9. The level of QUALITY OF THE RESOURCES this team member contributed was . . .	1	2	3	4	5
10. This team member's COMPLETION OF ROLE RESPONSIBILITIES was . . .	1	2	3	4	5

11. This team member met team deadlines	Rarely	Sometimes	Mostly	Always
12. Relative to what they were supposed to do, HOW would you rate this team member's OVERALL work and contribution to this (project, conference, discussion, presentation)?	Well Below	Somewhat Below	Somewhat Above	Well Above

Figure 14.6

Quantitative peer assessment of project participation

every other team member. The mean of each of the responses should be calculated. The data are used to either raise or lower the group grade for the individual team member. For example, if the end project quality was a "B" but peer assessments revealed that one individual had performed above the group mean in various areas, that individual's grade would be raised appropriately.

SUMMARY

Assessment of collaborative work is complicated. The traditional method of providing one summative grade based on the quality of the demonstrable end-product of a collaborative group ignores the multiple aspects of a community-led activity. Relying solely on a group grade for assessment often contributes to the dissatisfaction of some learners participating in the collaborative process. Some participants believe that it can reward those who have not fully participated and punish the learners who actually developed the end-product. By adding self-assessment and/or peer assessment components, a better picture of the participation of an individual can be determined.

ANSWERS:
APPLY WHAT YOU ARE LEARNING

14.1 1. B. Self-assessment has its biases and therefore should be paired with peer assessment to build the most accurate picture of involvement in the collaborative process.

2. B. Multiple perspectives are needed before an instructor can infer that an individual team member learned to the level represented by the end-product. Peers can evaluate whether a learner participated fully in the project and therefore may have learned to the degree exhibited by the final team product.

3. A. An instructor should check the peer assessment before it is sent to the individual evaluated to ensure that constructive criticism is being provided. In addition, the instructor can then be aware of situations that may need mediation.

4. A. Peer assessment is concerned primarily with the collaborative process, which remains consistent throughout the life of the collaboration. Therefore, the same instrument can be used for both formative and summative evaluation.

5. A. Self-assessment measures both content development and the collaborative process. Because content varies from the formative to the summative evaluation stages, the same instrument should not be used for both formative and summative evaluation. However, the section relating to how well an individual is contributing can remain the same in the formative and summative evaluations.

ENHANCE YOUR UNDERSTANDING

- Examine your course plan to determine when peer assessment should be used in the course of collaborative activities.
- Choose one of the team member evaluations in this chapter or develop one of your own to assess individual contributions to collaborative activities.

GLOSSARY

Ability-referenced interpretation involves interpreting a learner's performance in the context of that person's maximum possible performance. Statements such as, "That's about all this person can do" are usually ability-referenced. (Statements such as "That's not typical of what this person does" is actually a norm-referenced interpretation.) Significant problems with ability-referenced interpretations include not having a good estimate of the person's maximum possible performance, and not knowing precisely which abilities are prerequisite to learning the skills being assessed.

Analytical scoring is assigning points for each of multiple qualities, with a student's score on the test question being the total number of points received on the respective qualities. Analytical scoring tends to be more reliable than holistic scoring.

Authentic assessment involves students demonstrating proficiency with a skill by performing a task similar to how that skill is used in real-world settings. For instance, an authentic assessment of using algebra to solve for one unknown would involve completing tasks similar to those encountered by surveyors or engineers.

Checklists are used for scoring performance assessments when the correctness of a process or product can be judged in terms of the presence or absence of a series of conditions. Figure 10.2 illustrates a checklist used for scoring an assessment. The use of a checklist is an example of analytical scoring.

Community building is the process by which learners in an online course become active generators of knowledge who assume mutual responsibility for constructing and managing their own learning experience and that of their peers. This can be accomplished through collaboration in such activities as defining and resolving problems, explaining content, and providing feedback to colleagues.

Comparison with a model involves holistic scoring. It is a scoring strategy in which each student's performance or product is compared with a previously produced model that would receive full credit when scored. These models often are the products of prior students' performances on the same assessment. Scores are assigned by comparing each student's performance with the model using a scale such as the one in Figure 10.1.

Completion items, a type of *constructed-response item,* require the learner to write words in one or more blanks embedded in the item. A computer can automatically score answers if it is given the correct responses.

Complex-task performance assessment involves problem solving, in which the learner is asked to apply a complex of information, concepts, and rules to solve a problem. Complex-task performance assessments tend to be more difficult to create. Written tests cannot measure skills assessed with a complex-task performance assessment. (See also *single-task performance assessment,* and *problem solving.*)

Confidence is the certainty with which one judges a student's level of proficiency with a particular skill. High confidence should be established for critical skills, with lower confidence tolerated for noncritical skills. More test items, more products, or other observations are required to obtain high confidence in an assessment.

Constructed-response items represent one of the two categories of items used in written tests, and include the completion and essay formats. With constructed-response items, the learner enters or writes out the answer rather than choosing among options provided by the item. (See also *fixed-response items.*)

Construct-related evidence involves establishing a link between the underlying construct being measured (knowledge to be learned) and the student performances that will provide visible indicators of what they have learned. Establishing this linkage involves understanding the knowledge to be assessed, identifying the types of capabilities embedded within this knowledge, and (given the types of capabilities involved) determining specific examples of student performance that can legitimately serve as indicators of that knowledge.

Content-related evidence involves controlling the content of an assessment, usually by outlining its content. Performance objectives, a table of specifications, and performance assessment specifications are three common techniques used to outline the content. After identifying the appropriate performances to be observed through the assessment (see *construct-related evidence*), outlining the content of an assessment helps ensure that the appropriate knowledge and skills will be assessed.

Criterion-referenced interpretation involves comparing a learner's performance to a well-defined content domain to establish what the person can or cannot do. A statements such as "This person can create performace objectives" involves a well-defined content domain and is criterion-referenced. However, a statement such as "This person can design an online course" does not involve a well-defined domain, therefore it is not criterion-referenced and does not establish what specifically the person can do.

Criterion-related evidence involves establishing how well performance on the test correlates with performance on a relevant criterion outside the test. With standardized tests, statistical correlations are often used. With an instructor's test, qualitative judgments are more common. Performance on the test is correlated with what is observed outside the test, often through informal observations that occur from e-mails, from performance on other projects and other assignments, and through discussions.

Declarative knowledge is knowing that something is the case. It is information that can be conveyed in words; that is, knowledge that can be declared. Declarative knowledge varies considerably in complexity, ranging from very simple, such as dates of events, to very complex, such as trends in global climate change. Declarative knowledge can be assessed by having learners state or talk about what they know. (See also *procedural knowledge* and *problem solving*.)

Detached feedback related to an assignment is sent to the student separated from the student's original product. This tends to be less efficient than *integrated feedback* because the text of detached feedback often has to include information indicating what in the product is being referenced.

Education is to provide learners with a framework for further learning from which unanticipated problems can be solved. Assessments involve broader domains of knowledge, and measure only samples of specific skills within these domains.

Essay items are a type of *constructed-response item* that asks the learner to provide a narrative response to the test question. Computer programs have been developed that can automatically score essay responses; however, use of these scoring programs is generally limited to large-scale testing programs involving *standardized tests*.

Fixed-response items are one of two categories of items used in written tests. The learner chooses among or manipulates in some manner response options provided by the item. The numerous variations of the basic multiple-choice and true-false formats are examples of structured-response items. (See also *constructed-response items*.)

Formative assessments occur throughout and during the unit of instruction. Their purpose is to redirect instruction or learning to help ensure high achievement at the end of instruction. Formative assessments often are informal in nature, such as a teacher watching students' facial expressions or probing students' knowledge with casual questions. Formative assessments can involve exercises embedded within instructional materials, such as the "Apply what you are learning" exercises throughout this book.

Generalizability in educational measurement, is an approach used to evaluate *sampling error*. Within educational tests, sampling errors exist in various forms. For instance, in a sampling of items, sampling error exists because only a sample of items can be included in a test. An important question is how well students' performances on the test would generalize to their performance had they responded to all possible items associated with the content being assessed. Another form of sampling error is between scorers, such as between readers scoring responses to an essay item. Only a sample of possible readers (maybe just one reader) scores the essay responses. An important question is how well students' scores assigned by the sample of readers would generalize to their scores had all possible readers scored their essay responses. Other forms of sampling error, and therefore questions of generalizability, are also relevant to educational measurements.

Goal is a desired instructional outcome, typically stated more broadly than a performance objective. A goal may be equivalent to a group of performance objectives. In the case of highly complex skills that cannot be broken down into observable statements of performance, a goal may be used as a substitute for performance objectives.

Growth-referenced interpretation involves interpreting a learner's performance relative to the learner's earlier performance. It requires good measures of the person's earlier and present performance.

High-stakes examination is a written test or other assessment where performance on one test has significant implications for the person taking the test. Examples include professional licensure examinations or even unit tests when considerable weight is given to the exam. A great deal of planning and care is required when developing a high-stakes examination because of the considerable consequences of producing a defective assessment. Test security becomes a higher priority when high-stakes examinations are involved. The high stakes of assessments can be reduced by using a larger number of smaller assessments.

Holistic scoring is assigning a score based on the rater's overall impression of each student's response. Holistic scoring usually can be accomplished more quickly than analytical scoring.

Hotkey is a combination of keyboard strokes built into software programs to save the user time. An example of a hotkey is Ctrl>S (pressing the Ctrl key and prior to its release pressing the S key), which often saves the file being edited. Other examples are Ctrl>C to copy and Ctrl>V to then paste material from one place to another. In Windows, Alt>Tab allows the user to jump from one window to another when multiple programs are running.

Hotspot is a defined area in a graphic or picture containing a hyperlink. Clicking anywhere within the area results in the action associated with the hyperlink, such as opening another image, playing a sound, or making a record within a database. A page within a website can contain multiple hotspots. Within a test, this allows creation of test items in which students click on various parts of a graphic or picture in response to prompts provided by the test item. A person can tell that a hotspot is present because the mouse pointer changes appearance when moved over the hotspot.

HTML is the acronym for Hypertext Markup Language, which is a language in which web pages are written. Often, developers of websites use a specialized editor that generates HTML code corresponding to the text, graphics, hyperlinks, and other material entered using the editor.

Inconsistency in assessments, as the name suggests, is a change in students' performance that is unpredictable and is caused by factors unrelated to students' level of achievement. These inconsistencies are related to sampling error. Major sources of inconsistency include inconsistencies among tasks that get included in a test and inconsistencies among raters when assessments have to be subjectively scored.

Integrated feedback is written within a student's product. When students turn in physical papers, integrated feedback is written on the paper; with electronic documents, integrated feedback is written in the document, usually through editing. Integrated feedback typically is more efficiently produced than *detached feedback*.

Multiple-choice items are the most frequently used *fixed-choice* option. In its most traditional form, it consists of a statement that describes a task that learners are to complete, often referred to as the stem, and a series of response options that provide possible responses to the stem. A number of variations to the traditional multiple-choice item are available. For instance, instead of selecting the correct response among incorrect distactors, learners can be asked to rank order the options based on criteria given in the stem.

Norm-referenced interpretation involves comparing a learner's performance to a range of previously observed performances, such as those of students presently or previously enrolled in the class. Norm-referenced interpretations help establish typical and reasonable performance. Unlike *criterion-referenced* interpretations, a norm-referenced interpretation does not require a well-defined content domain to be useful, but does require a well-defined norm to which performance is compared.

Performance assessment is a measure of a learner's competence where the performance to be observed (or the product resulting from the performance) is an explicit goal of instruction. Performance assessments are uniquely able to measure problem solving. The measurement of many skills other than problem solving requires the use of performance assessments because of the motor skills involved, such as in speech and language, science labs, the performing arts, and sports.

Performance assessment specification is used to help plan and ultimately define a performance assessment. It includes three basic elements: the capability to be assessed, the performance to be observed, and the scoring plan. Performance assessment specifications are illustrated in Figures 11.2 through 11.6.

Performance objective is a description of an observable event that can indicate whether a student has learned a particular knowledge. A performance objective is not a description of the knowledge, but rather a description of a performance that shows whether the targeted knowledge has been learned. (See also *goal*.)

Problem solving is involved when one has a goal but has not yet identified a means for reaching that goal. Problem solving requires the use of previously learned declarative and procedural knowledge. It may involve domain-specific strategies, suggesting that different strategies are employed when solving problems in different content areas, such as math and writing. Problem solving may involve a very simple or a very complex task. Complexity is not the distinction between procedural knowledge of a rule and problem solving. With a rule, the procedure, once learned, is established. With problem solving, the procedure for solving the problem is unknown and must be established. However, existing declarative and procedural knowledge helps establish an appropriate solution to the problem. (See also *declarative knowledge* and *procedural knowledge*.)

Procedural knowledge is knowing how to do something. Procedural knowledge involves making discriminations, understanding concepts, and applying rules that govern relationships. Concepts, rules, and even discriminations can be very complex or very simple. Procedural knowledge is assessed by giving learners a task to complete that requires application of the procedural knowledge. The specific application must be one that the student has not applied earlier, and must be provided to the student rather than allowing the student to choose the application. Asking learners to explain a concept or rule provides a good indication of their declarative knowledge of the concept or rule, but not their procedural knowledge. (See also *declarative knowledge* and *problem solving*.)

Rating scales are similar to a checklist in that performance is judged in terms of a series of separate qualities. As illustrated in Figure 10.3, unlike a checklist, rating scales associate a range of values with each item. They are used when judgments need to be made as to the degree to which each characteristic is present, rather than simply the presence or absence of each quality. The use of rating scales is an example of analytical scoring.

Response options are the list of choices a learner has to work with when responding to fixed-response items. With *true-false* items, the options are simply true and false, but the options are more involved with other variations of fixed-choice items. With traditional *multiple-choice* items, the response options include one correct response, and one or more incorrect answers that are often referred to as the distractors. With *option ranking* items, the learner re-orders or ranks the options according to criteria specified in the item.

Sample refers to a subset from a larger population, usually with the intent of making inferences from the smaller sample to the larger population. A sample of respondents is typically involved in survey research; samples of approximately 1,000 respondents are common. When carefully selected, samples of this size allow accurate inferences to the population being sampled. With assessments, the content being assessed is sampled rather than people. For instance, all students (rather than a sample of students) will complete a written test, but the test will include only a sample of items that could be drawn from the content area being assessed. The number of test items sampled from a particular content area is typically very small—far smaller than the sample of approximately 1,000 people often used in survey research. The consequence is that scores on tests and other assessments often do not generalize very well to the scores that would have been obtained had a larger sample of items been included in the assessment.

Sampling error occurs when a sample is used, for instance the people who complete an opinion survey make up a sample of the population. Sampling error is the difference between responses provided by the sample and responses that would have been obtained had everyone in the population participated in the survey. Sampling is also involved in assessments. For instance, when a test is used to assess knowledge of a particular content area, only a sample of possible test items can be included in the test. Sampling error would be the difference between the students' scores (e.g., percentage scores) on the sample of items included in the test and the scores these students would have obtained had they answered all possible test items associated with this content domain.

Scoring plan is a detailed description of how responses to an open-ended test item will be scored, whether it be an essay item, a performance assessment, or a portfolio assessment. A scoring plan is vital to ensuring that one rater's response will generalize fairly well to scores assigned by other raters.

Scoring rubric is a type of scoring plan used when holistic judgments are to be made simultaneously on a series of interrelated qualities. As illustrated in Figure 10.6, a scoring rubric typically involves the same set of qualities described at different levels of proficiency.

Single-task performance assessment is a performance assessment used to measure knowledge of a concept or a rule. Single-task performance assessments are usually easy to produce, although they require more time to administer and score than do their written-test counterparts. The *specification* for a single-task performance assessment often can be developed in one's mind, without writing it down. However, addressing each of the components of a performance assessment specification remains an important procedure. (See also *complex-task performance assessment.*)

Standardized test is typically administered to a large number of individuals and includes college admission tests and tests that are used in primary and secondary schools as part of a statewide assessment program. The term *standardized* refers to the fact that these tests are designed to be administered the same way or in a *standardized* way, even though they are administered to students at different times and locations.

Style is a software tool available in word processors and other editors that helps the user format a document. For instance, styles can be created for titles, headings, and various paragraphs within a document. For example, once a style is created for a heading, a single action by the user changes the font and paragraph formats of text to those preset for that particular type of heading. Many styles usually come preprogrammed with editors, however users and programmers can create their own additional sets of styles. For instance, with multiple-choice items, a style can be created for

an item's options that sequences letters at the front of each option, establishes a hanging or negative indentation for the first line of every option, and controls paragraph spacing. Online course management systems should use styles to expedite importing text from widely used editors such as Word.

Summative assessments occur at the end of instruction. Unit tests and projects are often given at or near the end of a unit of instruction to help establish how well the learner has achieved the knowledge and skills associated with that unit. The purpose of summative assessments is to certify achievement, and often provide a basis for assigning course grades.

Survey research encompasses a broad area in which questionnaires are used to determine attitudes or opinions of people concerning a particular topic. For instance, survey research is used by manufacturers to evaluate consumers' awareness and opinions of their products, by politicians to determine constituents' attitudes toward various policies, and by the news media to examine the public's attitudes toward particular politicians and their actions. Surveys typically involve carefully selected samples of people.

Table of specifications is an efficient way to outline and thereby control the content of a written test. The table consists of columns that list the content areas that are to be assessed by the test and rows that list the types of capabilities. Cells within the table identify the number of items within each content area associated with the respective types of capabilities.

Training aims to teach learners to perform a particular task, often with a high degree of proficiency and consistency. Skills to be assessed are more narrowly defined and proficiency with every skill is usually assessed.

True-false items typically consist of a statement or proposition that learners are asked to classify as a true or false statement. Considerable variation from this basic format is possible. For instance, learners can be asked to determine whether each highlighted word in a paragraph is a true or false instance of some quality, such as being correctly versus incorrectly spelled, or being an example or nonexample of a verb or another part of speech.

Validity is the degree to which a test measures what it is supposed to measure or is expected to measure. Alternately, the degree to which a test is interpreted or used in a manner consistent with interpretations and uses that the test can reasonably support. Validity is established through evidence; common types include *construct-content-* and *criterion-related evidence.*

Wiki is a collaboration tool that allows users to collectively add, remove, or edit most content on a website. *Wikipedia,* the popular online encyclopedia, is developed through online collaboration and makes extensive use of this tool. An article about wiki in *Wikipedia* is located at *en.wikipedia.org/ wiki/WIKI.*

REFERENCES

Allen, I. E., & Seaman, J. (2005). *Growing by degrees: Online education in the United States, 2005*. Needham, MA: Sloan Consortium. (Available online at *http://www.sloan-c.org/resources/survey.asp*).

American Psychological Association, Educational Research Association, & National Council on Measurement in Education. (1999). *Standards for educational and psychological testing*. Washington, DC: American Psychological Association.

Bates, A. W. (1995). *Open learning and distance education*. London: Routledge Publishing.

Bloom, B. S. (Ed.). (1956). *Taxonomy of educational objectives: Handbook 1. Cognitive domain*. New York: McKay.

Bloom, B. S., Hastings, J. T., & Madaus, G. F. (Eds.). (1971). *Handbook on formative and summative evaluation of student learning*. New York: McGraw-Hill.

Boettcher, J. V., & Conrad, R. M. (2004). *Moving teaching and learning to the Web* (2nd ed.). League for Innovation in the Community College, Miami, Florida.

Brooks, R. F. (2001). *Humanizing online learning: An activity-practice model of course design*. Paper presented at the 12th International Conference on College Teaching and Learning, Jacksonville, FL.

Budescu, D., & Nevo, B. (1985). Optimal number of options: An investigation of the assumption of proportionality. *Journal of Educational Measurement, 22*, 183–196.

Chase, C. I. (1979). Impact of achievement expectations and handwriting quality on scoring essay tests. *Journal of Educational Measurement, 16*, 39–42.

Chase, C. I. (1986). Essay test scoring: Interaction of relevant variables. *Journal of Educational Measurement, 23*, 33–41.

Clark, R. (1983). Reconsidering research on learning from media. *Review of Educational Research, 53*(4), 445–459.

Confrey, J. (1990). A review of the research on student conceptions in mathematics, science, and programming. In C. B. Cazden (Ed.), *Review of Research in Education: Vol. 16* (pp. 3–56). Washington, DC: American Educational Research Association.

Conrad, R. M., & Donaldson, J. A. (2004). *Engaging the online learner: Activities and resources for creative instruction*. San Francisco, CA: Jossey-Bass Publishers.

Daly, J. A., & Dickson-Markman, F. (1982). Contrast effects in evaluating essays. *Journal of Educational Measurement, 19*, 309–316.

Daniels, E., & Gatto, M. (1997). Thinking about the nature and power of cooperative learning. *The Cooperative Companion Digest, 3*. *http://sbnews.sunysb.edu/sbnews/ceinews.node*.

Draves, W. (2002). *Teaching online* (2nd. ed.). River Falls, WI: LERN Books.

Duchastel, P. C., & Merrill, P. F. (1973). The effects of behavioral objectives on learning: A review of empirical studies. *Review of Educational Research, 43*, 53–70.

Ebel, R. L. (1982). Proposed solutions to two problems of test construction. *Journal of Educational Measurement, 19*, 267–278.

Frisbie, D. A. (1973). Multiple-choice vs. true-false: A comparison of reliabilities and concurrent validities. *Journal of Educational Measurement, 10*, 297–304.

Frisbie, D. A. (1988). An NCME instructional module on reliability of scores on teacher-made tests. *Educational Measurement: Issues and Practice, 7*(1), 25–33.

Gagné, E. D., Yekovich, C. W., & Yekovich, F. R. (1997). *The cognitive psychology of school learning* (2nd ed.). Boston: Allyn & Bacon.

Gagné, R. M. (1985). *The conditions of learning and theory of instruction*. New York: Holt, Rinehart & Winston.

Gagné, R. M., Briggs, L. J., & Wager, W. W. (1992). *Principles of instructional design* (4th ed.). Chicago: Holt, Rinehart & Winston.

Gierl, M. J. (1997). Comparing cognitive representations of test developers and students on a mathematics test with Bloom's taxonomy. *Journal of Educational Research, 91*, 26–32.

Holmberg, B. (1986). *Growth and structure of distance education*. London: Croom Helm.

Hughes, D. C., & Keeling, B. (1984). The use of essays to reduce context effects in essay scoring. *Journal of Educational Measurement, 21*, 277–281.

Hughes, D. C., Keeling, B., & Tuck, B. F. (1980). The influence of context position and scoring method on essay scoring. *Journal of Educational Measurement, 17,* 131–135.

Jeong, A. (2001). *The forum manager.* Available online at: *http://bbproject.tripod.com/ForumManager/index.htm.*

Jeong, A. (2006). *The forum manager.* Available at: *http://bbproject.tripod.com/ForumManager/index.htm.*

Johnson, D. W., & Johnson, R. T. (1993). Cooperative learning and feedback in technology-based instruction. In J. V. Dempsey and G. C. Sales (Eds.), *Interactive instruction and feedback* (pp. 133–157). Englewood Cliffs, NJ: Educational Technology Publications.

Linn, R. L., Baker, E. L., & Dunbar, B. D. (1991). Complex, performance-based assessment: Expectations and validation criteria. *Educational Researcher, 20*(8), 15–21.

Lord, F. M. (1977). Optimal number of choices per item: A comparison of four approaches. *Journal of Educational Measurement, 14,* 33–38.

Mager, R. (1984). *Preparing instructional objectives* (2nd ed.). Belmont, CA: David S. Lake.

Mathieson, D. E. (1971). *Correspondence study: A summary review of the research and development literature.* Syracuse, NY: ERIC Clearinghouse on Adult Education.

Melton, R. F. (1978). Resolution of conflicting claims concerning the effect of behavioral objectives on student learning. *Review of Educational Research, 48,* 291–302.

Messick, S. (1989a). Meaning and values in test validation: The science and ethics of assessment. *Educational Researcher, 18*(2), 5–11.

Messick, S. (1989b). Validity. In R. L. Linn (Ed.), *Educational measurement* (3rd ed., pp. 13–103). New York: American Council on Education.

Moore, M. G. (1993). Is teaching like flying? A total systems view of distance education. *American Journal of Distance Education, 7,* 1–10.

Moore, M. G., & Kearsley, G. (1996). *Distance education: A systems view.* Belmont, CA: Wadsworth Publishing Company.

Nasseh, B. *A brief history of distance education.* Available online at *http://www.seniornet.org/edu/art/history.html.*

Nava, F. J. G., & Loyd, B. H. (1991). *The effect of student characteristics on the grading process.* Paper presented at the annual meeting of the National Council on Measurement in Education, San Francisco.

Nitko, A. J. (1984). Defining "criterion-referenced test." In R. A. Berk (Ed.), *A guide to criterion-referenced test construction* (pp. 8–23). Baltimore, MD: Johns Hopkins University Press.

Nitko, A. J., & Brookhart, S. M. (2007). *Educational assessment of students* (5th ed.). Upper Saddle River, NJ: Merrill/Prentice Hall.

Oosterhof, A. (2000). Creating individualized e-mail to students. *Journal of Computing in Higher Education, 11*(2), 75–90.

Oosterhof, A. (2001). *Classroom applications of educational measurement* (3rd ed.). Upper Saddle River, NJ: Merrill/Prentice Hall.

Oosterhof, A. (2003). *Developing and using classroom assessments* (3rd ed.). Upper Saddle River, NJ: Merrill/Prentice Hall.

Oosterhof, A. (2006). *Strategies for increasing the efficiency of reviewing online learners' written products.* Paper presented at the annual meeting of the American Educational Research Association, San Francisco.

Oosterhof, A., & Coats, P. K. (1984). Comparison of difficulties and reliabilities of quantitative word problems in completion and multiple-choice item formats. *Applied Psychological Measurement, 8,* 287–294.

Oosterhof, A., & Glasnapp, D. R. (1974). Comparative reliabilities and difficulties of the multiple-choice and true-false formats. *Journal of Experimental Education, 42,* 62–64.

Page, E. (1968). *The analysis of essays by computer: Final report.* Office of Education (DHEW), Washington, DC. Available from ERIC: ED028633.

Palloff, R., & Pratt, K. (1999). *Building learning communities in cyberspace.* San Francisco, CA: Jossey-Bass Publishers.

Palloff, R., & Pratt, K. (2005). *Collaborating online: Learning together in community.* San Francisco, CA: Jossey-Bass Publishers.

Posey, C. (1932). Luck and examination grades. *Journal of Engineering Education, 23,* 292–296.

Rumble, G. (1986). *The planning and management of distance education.* New York: St. Martin's Press.

Salomon, G. (1995). *What does the design of effective CSCL require and how do we study its effects?* Available online at *http://www.cscl95.indiana.edu/csc195/outlook/62_Salomon.html.*

Shavelson, R. J., Baxter, G. P., & Pine, J. (1992). Performance assessments: Political rhetoric and measurement reality. *Educational Researcher, 21*(4),

22–27. Los Angeles: University of California, National Center for Research on Evaluation, Standards, and Student Testing/Center for the Study of Evaluation.

Shavelson, R. J., Ruiz-Primo, M. A., Schultz, S. E., & Wiley, E. W. (1998). *On the development and scoring of classification and observation science performance assessments* (CSE Report 458). Los Angeles: University of California, National Center for Research on Evaluation, Standards, and Student Testing/Center for the Study of Evaluation.

Shepard, L. A. (2000). *The role of classroom assessment in teaching and learning.* (CSE Technical Report 517). Los Angeles: University of California, Center for Research on Evaluation, Standards, and Student Testing. Also available online at *http://www.cse.ucla.edu/CRESST/Reports/TECH517.pdf.*

Sherron, G. T., & Boettcher, J. V. (1997). Distance learning: The shift to interactivity. *CAUSE Professional Papers Series, #17.* Boulder, CO: CAUSE.

Simonson, M., Smaldino, S., Albright, M., & Zvacek, S. (2003). *Teaching and learning at a distance: Foundations of distance education* (2nd ed.). Upper Saddle River, NJ: Merrill/Prentice Hall.

Snow, R. E. (1989). Toward assessment of cognitive and conative structure in learning. *Educational Research, 18*(9), 8–14.

Solano-Flores, G., Shavelson, R. J., Ruiz-Primo, M. A., Schultz, S. E., & Wiley, E. W. (1997). *On the development and scoring of classification and observation science performance assessments* (CSE Technical Report 458). Los Angeles: University of California, National Center for Research on Evaluation, Standards, and Student Testing. Also available online at *http://www.cse.ucla.edu/CRESST/Reports/TECH458.pdf.*

Taylor, W. L. (1953). Cloze procedure: A new tool for measuring readability. *Journalism Quarterly, 30,* 415–433.

Tittle, C. K., Hecht, D., & Moore, P. (1993). Assessment theory and research for classrooms: From taxonomies to constructing meaning in context. *Educational Measurement: Issues and Practice, 12*(4), 13–19.

Um, K. R. (1995). *Sampling effects of writing topics and discourse modes on generalizability of individual student and school writing performance on a standardized fourth grade writing assessment.* Unpublished doctoral dissertation, Florida State University, Tallahassee.

Verduin, J. R. Jr., & Clark, T. A. (1991). *Distance education: The foundations of effective practice.* San Francisco: Jossey-Bass.

Yen, W. M. (1997). The technical quality of performance assessments: Standard errors of percents of pupils reaching standards. *Educational Measurement: Issues and Practice, 16*(3), 5–15.

INDEX